GENETIC PROGRAMMING – NEW APPROACHES AND SUCCESSFUL APPLICATIONS

Edited by **Sebastián Ventura**

Genetic Programming – New Approaches and Successful Applications
http://dx.doi.org/10.5772/3102
Edited by Sebastián Ventura

Contributors

Uday Kamath, Jeffrey K. Bassett, Kenneth A. De Jong, Cyril Fonlupt, Denis Robilliard, Virginie Marion-Poty, Yoshihiko Hasegawa, Guilherme Esmeraldo, Robson Feitosa, Dilza Esmeraldo, Edna Barros, Douglas A. Augusto, Heder S. Bernardino, Helio J.C. Barbosa, Giovanni Andrea Casula, Giuseppe Mazzarella, Fathi Abid, Wafa Abdelmalek, Sana Ben Hamida, Polona Dobnik Dubrovski, Miran Brezočnik, Shreenivas N. Londhe, Pradnya R. Dixit, J. Sreekanth, Bithin Datta, M.L. Arganis, R. Val, R. Domínguez, K. Rodríguez, J. Dolz, J.M. Eaton, M. A. Ghorbani, R. Khatibi, H. Asadi and P. Yousefi

Published by InTech

Janeza Trdine 9, 51000 Rijeka, Croatia

Publishing Process Manager Marijan Polic
Technical Editor InTech DTP team
Cover InTech Design team

Additional hard copies can be obtained from orders@intechopen.com

Genetic Programming – New Approaches and Successful Applications, Edited by Sebastián Ventura
p. cm.
ISBN 978-953-51-0809-2

For EU product safety concerns:
IN TECH d.o.o., Prolaz Marije Krucifikse Kozulić 3, 51000 Rijeka, Croatia,
info@intechopen.com or visit our website at intechopen.com.

Meet the editor

Sebastian Ventura was born in Cordoba (Spain) in 1966. He received the B.Sc. and Ph.D. degrees in sciences from the University of Cordoba in 1989 and 1996, respectively. He is currently an Associate Professor in the Department of Computer Science and Numerical Analysis, University of Cordoba, where he is the Head of the Knowledge Discovery and Intelligent Systems Research Laboratory. He has authored or coauthored more than 150 international publications. He has also edited several special issues in scientific journals and two scientific books in his areas of expertise. He has also worked on eleven research projects (being the Coordinator of three of them) that were supported by the Spanish and Andalusian governments and the European Union. His research interests include soft computing (mostly evolutionary computing and genetic programming), machine learning, data mining, and their applications.

Contents

Preface

Genetic programming (GP) is a branch of Evolutionary Computing that aims the automatic discovery of programs to solve a given problem. Since its appearance, in the earliest nineties, GP has become one of the most promising paradigms for solving problems in the artificial intelligence field, producing a number of human-competitive results and even patentable new inventions. And, as other areas in Computer Science, GP continues evolving quickly, with new ideas, techniques and applications being constantly proposed.

The purpose of this book is to show recent advances in the field of GP, both the development of new theoretical approaches and the emergence of applications that have successfully solved different real world problems. It consists of twelve openly solicited chapters, written by international researchers and leading experts in the field of GP.

The book is organized in two sections. The first section (*chapters 1 to 5*) introduces a new theoretical framework (the use of quantitative genetics and phenotypic traits – *chapter 1*) to analyse the behaviour of GP algorithms. Furthermore, the section contains three new GP proposals: the first one is based on the use of continuous values for the representation of programs (*chapter 2*), the second is based on the use of estimation of distribution algorithms (*chapter 3*), and the third hybridizes the use of GP with statistical models in order to obtain and formally validate linear regression models (*chapter 4*). The section ends with a nice introduction about the implementation of GP algorithms on graphics processing units (*chapter 5*).

The second section of the book (*chapters 6 to 12*) shows several successful examples of the application of GP to several complex real-world problems. First of these applications is the use of GP in the automatic design of wireless antennas (*chapter 6*). The two following chapters show two interesting examples of industrial applications: the forecasting of the volatility of materials (*chapter 7*) and the prediction of fabric porosity (*chapter 8*). In both chapters GP models outperformed the results yield by the state-of-the art methods. The next three chapters are related to the application of GP to modelling water flows, being the first of them a gentle introduction to the topic (*chapter 9*) and the following two remarkable case studies (*chapters 10 and 11*). The last chapter of the book (*chapter 12*) shows the application of GP to an interesting time series modelling problem: the estimation of suspended sediment loads in the Mississippi river.

The volume is primarily aimed at postgraduates, researchers and academics. Nevertheless, it is hoped that it may be useful to undergraduates who wish to learn about the leading techniques in GP.

Sebastián Ventura
Department of Computers Science and Numerical Analysis,
University of Cordoba,
Spain

Section 1

New Approaches

Chapter 1

Using Quantitative Genetics and Phenotypic Traits in Genetic Programming

Uday Kamath, Jeffrey K. Bassett and Kenneth A. De Jong

Additional information is available at the end of the chapter

http://dx.doi.org/10.5772/50143

1. Introduction

When evolving executable objects, the primary focus is on the behavioral repertoire that objects exhibit. For an evolutionary algorithm (EA) approach to be effective, a fitness function must be devised that provides differential feedback across evolving objects and provides some sort of fitness gradient to guide an EA in useful directions. It is fairly well understood that needle-in-a-haystack fitness landscapes should be avoided (e.g., was the tasked accomplished or not), but much less well understood as to the alternatives.

One approach takes its cue from animal trainers who achieve complex behaviors via some sort of "shaping" methodology in which simpler behaviors are learned first, and then more complex behaviors are built up from these behavior "building blocks". Similar ideas and approaches show up in the educational literature in the form of "scaffolding" techniques. The main concern with such an approach in EC in general and GP in particular is the heavy dependence on a trainer within the evolutionary loop.

As a consequence most EA/GP approaches attempt to capture this kind of information in a single fitness function with the hope of providing the necessary bias to achieve the desired behavior without any explicit intervention along the way. One attempt to achieve this involves identifying important quantifiable behavior traits and including them in the EA/GP fitness function. If one then proceeds with a standard "blackbox" optimization approach in which behavioral fitness feedback is just a single scalar, there are in general a large number of genotypes (executable objects) that can produce identical fitness values and small changes in executable structures can lead to large changes in behavioral fitness. In general, what is needed is a notion of behavioral inheritance.

We believe that there are existing tools and techniques that have been developed in the field of quantitative genetics that can be used to get at this notion of behavioral inheritability. In this chapter we first give a basic tutorial on the quantitative genetics approach and metrics required to analyze evolutionary dynamics, as the first step in understanding how this can be used for GP analysis. We then discuss some higher level issues for obtaining useful behavioral phenotypic traits to be used by the quantitative genetics tools. We give some background of other tools used like the diversity measurements and bloat metrics to analyze and correlate the behavior of a GP problem. Three GP benchmark problems are explained in detail exemplifying how to design the phenotypic traits, the quantitative genetics analyses when using these traits in various configurations and evolutionary behaviors deduced from these analyses.

2. Related work

Prior to the introduction of quantitative genetics to the EC community, research along similar lines was already being conducted. Most notable among these was the discovery that parent-offspring fitness correlation is a good predictor of an algorithm's ability to converge on highly fit solutions [18].

Mühlenbein and Altenberg began to introduce elements of biology theory to EC at roughly the same time. Mühlenbein's work has focused mainly on adapting the equation for the response to selection (also known as the breeder's equation) for use with evolutionary algorithms [19] Initial work involved the development several improved EAs and reproductive operators [21, 23, 24], and progressed to the development of Estimation of Distribution Algorithms (EDAs) [20, 22].

Altenberg's work used Price's Theorem [27] as a foundation for his EC theory. One of his goals was to measure the ability of certain EA reproductive operators to produce high quality individuals, and identify what qualities were important in achieving this [1]. He referred to this as evolvability, and the equations he developed looked similar in some regards to the response to selection equation. In particular he provided a theoretics foundation for why the relationship between parent and offspring fitness (i.e. heritability of fitness) was important.

Another aspect of Altenberg's work involved going beyond a simple aggregation of the relationships between parent and offspring fitness. He focused on the idea that the upper-tail of the distribution was a key element. After all, creating a few offspring that are more fit than their parents can be much more important than creating all offspring with the same fitness as their parents. This is why his equation really became a measure of variance instead of mean, which is what Price's Theorem typically measures. As an indication that his theories were in some sense fundamental to how EAs work, he was able to use them to re-derive the schema theorem [2].

Langdon [14] developed tools based on quantitative genetics for analyzing EA performance. He used both Price's Theorem and Fisher's Fundamental Theorem [26] to model GP gene frequencies, and how they change in the population over time.

Work by Potter et al. [25] also used Price's Theorem as a basis for EA analysis. They also recognized the importance of variance, and developed some approaches to visualizing the distributions during the evolutionary process [5, 6].

The work of Prügel-Bennett & Shapiro [29] [28] is based on statistical mechanics, but it has some important similarities to the methods used in quantitative genetics. Here, populations are also modeled as probability distributions, but the approach taken is more predictive than diagnostic. This means that detailed information about the fitness landscape and reproductive operators is needed in order to analyze an EA. Still, this approach has some interesting capabilities. For example, up to six higher-order cumulants are used to describe the distributions, allowing it to move beyond assumptions of normality, and thus providing much more accurate descriptions of the actual distributions.

Radcliffe [30] developed a theoretical framework that, while not directly related to quantitative genetics, has certain similarities. His formae theory is a more general extension of the schema theorem, and can be applicable at a phenotypic level.

3. Methodology

3.1. Quantitative genetics basics

Quantitative Genetics theory [9, 31]is concerned with tracking quantitative phenotypic traits within an evolving population in order to analyze the evolutionary process. One group that commonly uses the approach are animal breeders for the purpose of estimating what would be involved in accentuating certain traits (such as size, milk production or pelt color) within their populations.

A quantitative trait is essentially any aspect of an individual that can be measured. Since much of the theory was developed before the structure of DNA was known, traits have tended to measure phenotypic qualities like the ones listed in the paragraph above. Traits can measure real values, integer or boolean (threshold) properties, although real valued properties are generally preferred [9].

This approach offers a potential advantage to EC practitioners. Most EC theory is defined in terms of the underlying representation. As a consequence, it becomes difficult to adapt these theories to new types of problems and representations when they are developed. This generally means that the practitioner must modify or re-derive the theoretical equations before they can apply these theories to a new EA that has been customized for a new problem. For the few theories where this is not the case, a detailed understanding of the problem landscape is typically needed instead. Again this presents problems for the practitioner. After all, if they knew this much about their problem, they would not need an EA to solve it in the first place. Quantitative genetics is one of the few theories that does not suffer from these problems.

Populations are modeled as probability distributions of traits by using simple statistical measures like mean, variance and covariance. A set of equations then describe how the distributions change from one generation to the next as a result of certain evolutionary forces like selection and heritability.

An extended version of the theory called multivariate quantitative genetics [13] aims to model the behaviors and interactions of multiple traits within the population simultaneously. This approach represents multiple traits as a vector. As a result, means are also represented as a vector, and variance calculations produce covariance matrices, as do cross-covariance calculations. In other words, a vector and a covariance matrix are needed to describe a joint probability distribution. Other than this change, the equations remain largely the same.

It is difficult to do any long term prediction with this theory [11]. Instead, its value lies in its ability to perform analysis after the fact [11]. In other words, for our purposes the theory is most useful for understanding the forces at work inside an existing algorithm during or after it has been run, rather than predicting how an proposed algorithm might work.

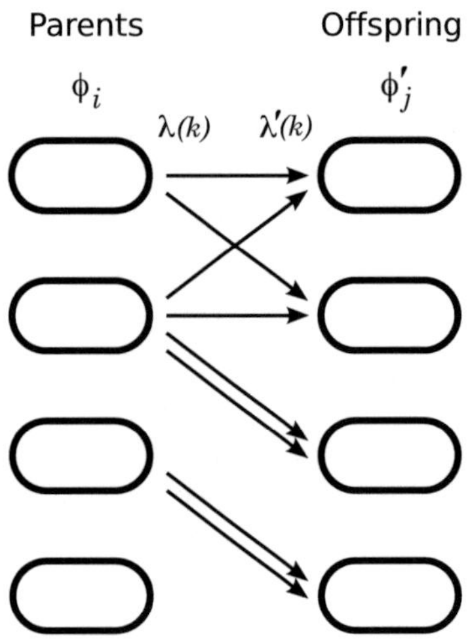

Figure 1. A sample generation showing offspring and parents [3]

In previous work [3], we adapted multivariate quantitative genetics for use with evolutionary algorithms. The goal of that work was to demonstrate how these theories can be used to aid in customizing EA operators for new and unusual problems. Here we will review some important aspects of that model.

To describe the equations, we will refer to Figure 1, which shows a directed graph illustrating two successive generations during an EA run. A subset of parents (left) are selected and produce offspring, either through crossover, mutation or cloning. Directed edges are draw from each selected parent to all the offspring (right) that it produces. Because the quantitative genetics models are built on the idea of a generational evolutionary process, they are most easily applied to to generational EAs like GAs and GP.

It is important that each directed edge represent the same amount of "influence" that a parent has on its offspring. In the figure, each edge represents an influence of $1/2$. That is why two edges are drawn between parent and offspring in instances where only cloning or mutation are performed. A vector of quantitative traits ϕ_i is associated with each parent i and another vector of traits ϕ'_j is associated with each offspring j. The two functions $\lambda(k)$ and $\lambda'(k)$ are defined such that they return the index of corresponding parent and offspring, for a given edge k.

We also use the abbreviations ϕ and ϕ' to describe all the traits in the different populations. The symbol ϕ describes all the parent traits, while ϕ' describes all offspring traits. Similarly ϕ_λ refers to all traits of the *selected* parents, and $\phi'_{\lambda'}$ again refers to all the traits of the offspring, although in the case of figure 1 there are two copies of each child.

Several covariance matrices are defined to describe the populations distributions and the forces that cause them to change. **P** and **O** are covariance matrices that describe the distributions of the *selected* parent and offspring populations respectively. **D** describes the amount of trait variation that the operators are adding to the offspring, and $\mathbf{G}'$ can be thought of as quantifying the amount of variation from **P** that is retained in **O**.

$\mathbf{P}$, $\mathbf{O}$, $\mathbf{D}$ are all covariance matrices of the traits defined as $\mathbf{P} = \text{Var}(\phi_\lambda)$, $\mathbf{O} = \text{Var}(\phi')$, and $\mathbf{D} = \text{Var}(\phi'_{\lambda'} - \phi_\lambda)$. $\mathbf{G}'$ is a cross-covariance matrix defined as $\mathbf{G}' = \text{Cov}(\phi'_{\lambda'}, \phi_\lambda)$.

Given these matrices, we can now describe how the population distributions change from one generation to the next using the following equation:

$$\mathbf{O} = 2\mathbf{G}' + \mathbf{D} - \mathbf{P}, \tag{1}$$

which can be rewritten as

$$\mathbf{O} = \mathbf{P}[2\mathbf{G}'\mathbf{P}^{-1} + \mathbf{D}\mathbf{P}^{-1} - \mathbf{I}], \tag{2}$$

where $\mathbf{I}$ is the identity matrix. In this case, we can view everything within the brackets as defining a transformation matrix that describes how the trait distribution of the selected parents ($\mathbf{P}$) is transformed by the operators into the distribution of the offspring population traits ($\mathbf{O}$).

The factor $\mathbf{G}'\mathbf{P}^{-1}$ is a regression coefficient matrix, and it is very similar to the quantitative genetics notion of narrow-sense heritability (commonly just called heritability). It describes the average similarity between an offspring and *one* of it's parents. The term $\mathbf{D}\mathbf{P}^{-1}$, which we refer to as perturbation, describes the amount of new phenotypic variation that the operators are introducing into the population relative to what already exists. Perturbation can be thought of as measuring an operator's capacity for exploration, while heritability provides an indication of it's ability to exploit existing information in the population. If heritability is low, that indicates that there is an unexpected bias in the search.

Another relationship that can be drawn from equation 2 is $\mathbf{O}\mathbf{P}^{-1}$. This does not have a corresponding concept in biology, although it is similar in some ways to broad-sense heritability and repeatability. This term describes the similarity of the parent and offspring *populations*, and so we refer to it as population heritability. This is another measure of exploitation, in addition to narrow-sense heritability. We think it is the better choice because it is measuring the larger scale behavior of the EA.

3.1.1. Scalar metric for matrices and vector operations

Biologists consider the multivariate notion of heritability as the degree of similarity between the two probability distributions that $\mathbf{P}$ and $\mathbf{G}$ describe. These comparisons are often performed using statistical techniques like Common Principle Component Analysis [10, 12].

For simplicity and ease of understanding, it would be ideal to find a metric that expresses terms like heritability and perturbation as a single scalar value. We have chosen to use the following metric,

$$\text{m}(\mathbf{G}', P) = \text{tr}(\mathbf{G}')/\text{tr}(\mathbf{P}) \tag{3}$$

where m is the metric function, and $\mathbf{G}'$ and $\mathbf{P}$ are M by M covariance matrices as described in the previous section.

The result of equation 3 is, of course, our scalar version of heritability from a single parent. Similarly, $\text{tr}(\mathbf{D})/\text{tr}(\mathbf{P})$ would measure perturbation, and $\text{tr}(\mathbf{O})/\text{tr}(\mathbf{P})$ gives us a measure of the overall similarity between the selected parent population and the resulting offspring population.

We chose to use trace because they have an intuitive geometric interpretation. The trace functions is equal to the sum of the diagonal elements in the matrix. It's also equal to the sum of the eigenvalues of the matrix. In geometric representation it shows the sum total of all the variation in the distribution. Determinants are normally used as single measure for matrix operation. It was observed that determinants couldn't be computed for representation like GP, due to generation of individuals that can lead to non-positive semidefinite matrices.

3.2. Phenotypic trait design

Understanding the problem phenotypic landscape along with the search characteristics of the individual (GP program) will be an important step in designing the quantitative phenotypic traits. The key element is that the trait measure defines some search aspect of the individual in the phenotypic landscape. The design of phenotypic trait measures is similar to designing a fitness function for EA - they are problem-specific, and it is more an art and an iterative process to come up with one or more functions that capture the behavior. We have given some broad high level ideas below that can help the designer in more concrete way in coming up with the phenotypic traits for a given problem. Broadly speaking, we can devise the traits thus:

1. At the application domain specific level to see the search behavior measured as quantitative traits.
2. By decomposing an already aggregated fitness function into individual quantitative traits.

1. Application domain specific traits:
   Since most GP programs are used in agent based environments, we will generalize application domain traits to be more for agent based individuals.
   - Agent Based Individuals
     Agent based individuals, can be considered to have some sensors and to execute series of tasks in an environment. One may use several interesting properties as traits such as recognizing the sensors available for the agents , constraints in motion, number of tasks allowed, traps in the environment and way to avoid the traps etc can be interesting set of properties that user might want to use as traits. These properties will vary amongst the individuals and using them as phenotypic traits can give interesting multivariate analyses like the correlation between properties, correlation of these properties with fitness, etc. We can come up with more traits based on exact nature of the agents and tasks they are performing. Some of these may be orthogonal while some may have an overlap with each other. Having an overlap should be avoided as correlated traits can lead to problems likenon-positive semi-definite matrices.
     - Task Oriented Individuals
       In many GP applications, the agent is meant to be working on various sub-tasks. These tasks can be considered decomposable into smaller units. Normally the fitness measures only the end goal or just the higher level tasks performed, sometimes for example the amount of food eaten by the ant agent as the fitness in the ant trail problem. Various behaviors that lead to (or do not lead to) the tasks when quantified, might give good phenotypic behavior of the individuals. Some of the tasks or units can be very important and can be weighted higher as compared to others.

- Competitive and Co-Competitive Individuals
  Many agent-based systems are competitive in nature, like the predator and prey class of the problems. Effective traits that determine metrics leading to success and failure of competing individuals may be more useful than agent-based traits. For instance, in a predator-prey based agents the fitness is basically how well you are doing against the other. If lower level details like "closeness"ï£¡ to the others, number of moves till attacked, number of changes in directions while moving, etc. can provide interesting metrics that can be used as traits in these domains.
- Cooperative Individuals
  Another subclass of the agent based problems is the cooperative based agents. These individuals have to be in some kind of team to accomplish the goal. The individual behaviors can be specific decomposable ones or can be evolved during the execution. The performance evaluation of most fitness functions in these domains is measured by weighting individual and team performances. Various cooperative metrics can be measured again at different levels like attempts of cooperative moves, success and failures in the moves, ratio of total attempts to the success or failures, etc.

- Design based Individuals
  Many GP applications are used mostly in design sub class of problems like circuit design, layout and network design and plan generation problems. Each of these use very high level measures combined in weights like the cost saved, components used, power distribution, etc. Again, using individualized measures and adding as many metrics that are circuit or layout specifics may give more clarity to the search behavior.
- Regression based Individuals
  Many GP applications are used in curve fitting- finding equations hidden in the data as a category of problems. Various mathematical values ranging from values at different interesting points on the landscape, distances from each point projected to that on the curve, relative errors, etc can form good traits for such individuals to show the phenotypic search behaviors.

2. Aggregated Fitness Functions
   In general there is a certain class of problems where you can use a general notion of decomposing the aggregated fitness function to individualized metrics as traits. In bioinformatics, GP is used in wide range of protein conformation, motif search, feature generations, etc. Most fitness functions are complex aggregated values combining many search metrics. For example, in sequence /structure classification programs many aspects of classification into one value, like true positives, false positives, true negatives, weighted distance and angles etc are combined to give a single score to the individuals. Instead of having such a single aggregated function value, we can use each of them as phenotypic traits.

3.2.1. Issues

After discussing some design principles and methodology, issues related to choice of the traits are discussed in this section.

- Coverage/Completeness
  Ideally we would like to develop as complete a set of traits as possible. By "complete"

we mean that we would like to have a set of traits that describe the whole phenotypic search space as well as possible. Another way of viewing this is to ask "Do the traits that we have uniquely define an individual?" As we mentioned earlier, previous applications of quantitative genetics to EA have used fitness alone, this provided a very limited and incomplete view of the nature of the fitness landscape, especially individuals that are very different can have the same fitness. Similarly an incomplete set of traits can fail to illuminate certain important aspects of a problem.

Domains involving executable objects (like GP), and most machine learning in general, are particularly susceptible to this problem. This is because generalization is a critical part of the learning process. We expect our systems to be able to handle new situations that they never faced during training. One way of addressing this issue is to create traits that are, in a sense, general too. Traits that measure a set of behaviors that all fall into a broad category will be able to achieve the best coverage of the search space.

It is difficult to offer advice as to how one can recognize when they face this situation. Asking the question about uniqueness seems to offer the best general approach. It may be wise to ask oneself this question throughout the design and implementation process. One advantage that quantitative genetics offer though, is that it degrades gracefully in the sense that all the equations are still completely accurate, even with an incomplete set of traits. Ultimately one may only need a subset of traits in order to observe the important behaviors their algorithms, just so long as they are the right subset.

- Unnecessary traits
  Unnecessary traits are either those that are always constant, or those that are so closely correlated with another trait that they essentially are measuring the same thing. These can be more problematic because they can result in matrices that are non-positive definite. In this particular case it would mean that the matrices have one or more eigenvalues that are zero. While this is not actually wrong, with just a small amount of measurement error, or round-off error, the matrices could have negative eigenvalues, which is more problematic. We have devised the metric equation (equation 3) to minimize computational problems related to this situation, but one should try to avoid it if possible.
- Phenotype to Genotype Linking
  If one's goal in using these tools is to identify and fix problem in an algorithm, then one will need to make a connection between the traits, and any aspects of the representation or reproductive operators that are affecting those traits. The more abstract the traits are, the more difficult this becomes, and so very low-level descriptions of behaviors may be more appropriate to achieve this.

  Unfortunately, this can creates a conflict with the issue of trait completeness described above. There we suggested that higher-level traits may be better for getting the best landscape description possible. For example, consider a problem where we are trying to teach an agent to track another agent without being detected. A high-level set of traits might measure thing like: how much distance an agent keeps between itself and the target, the length of time that it is able to maintain surveillance, and the number of times it is detected. These traits may be ideal for covering all the skills that may be necessary for describing the fitness landscape, but they may not be very helpful in identifying what aspect of a representation or reproductive operators are problematic for learn well in this domain. Such connections would be tenuous at best.

At the other end of the scale, a low-level phenotype (conceptually, at least) might be something as simple as the input-output map that exactly describes the actions the agent would take for any given set of inputs. Here we have a much better chance of relating such information to the representational structure, and the effects of the reproductive operators. Unfortunately, it becomes much more difficult to define a complete set of traits. Such a set would have to describe the entire map, and this might mean thousands of traits. The only viable option is to create sample sets of inputs, where each sample would define a single trait. If one can define enough traits to get a reasonable sampling of the input space, or identify important samples that yield particularly valuable information, then this approach could still be useful.

Exactly how to solve this trade-off remains an open issue. Some possible solutions include combining low-level and high-level traits, using different kinds of traits depending on ones goals, or trying to find traits that achieve a middle ground between these two extremes.

3.3. Genetic diversity using lineage

To correlate some important evolutionary behaviors we need to measure genotypic diversity changes in the populations. There are many ways to measure genotypic diversity measurements like tree-edit distances, genetic lineages, entropy etc for understanding the genotypic behavior and correlating it with phenotypic behaviors [7]. Genetic Lineage is the metric more commonly used as it shows significant correlation to fitness [8]. In context of GP, with individuals as trees, when an operator like crossover breeds and produces an offspring, the offspring that has the root node of parent has the lineage of that parent. This provides a way to measure distribution of lineage over generations and also the count of unique lineages in the population over generations.

3.4. Bloat measure

Another important factor that we use to correlate the evolutionary behavior changes is with bloat. Bloat, has been described in various researches but very few of them have defined it quantitatively. In our study since we have to measure bloat quantitatively we use the metrics as defined in the recent research [32].

$$bloat(g) = \frac{(\overline{\delta}(g) - \overline{\delta}(0))/\overline{\delta}(0)}{\overline{f}(0) - \overline{f}(g))/\overline{f}(0)} \tag{4}$$

where $\overline{\delta}(g)$ is the average number of nodes per individual in the population at generation g, and $\overline{f}(g)$ is the average fitness of individuals in the population at generation g.

4. GP benchmark problems and analyses

In next subsections we will walk through three different GP problems, to discuss the methodology of defining traits, performing experiments with different evolutionary operators and understanding the evolutionary behaviors in context of the given problem. We start with the ant trail problem and perform various experiments by changing the operators, selection mechanisms and pressure to investigate the evolutionary behavior with respect to quantitative genetics metrics. We then move to another agent oriented problem, lawn mower problem showing few experiments involving breeding operators and different selection mechanisms.

Finally we use the symbolic regression problem to describe how traits can be defined and the observations showing generality of our methodology.

All the experiments are performed using ECJ [17] with various standard default parameters like population size of 1024, a crossover depth limit of 17,and the ramped half and half method of generating tree (min/max of 2 and 6) for creating individuals. We will plot average $\text{tr}(\mathbf{D})/\text{tr}(\mathbf{P})$, $\text{tr}(\mathbf{G})/\text{tr}(\mathbf{P})$ and $\text{tr}(\mathbf{O})/\text{tr}(\mathbf{P})$ as quantitative genetics metrics for each generations. We will also plot the average unique ancestors as our genetic lineage diversity measure and bloat metrics from above for some correlations.

4.1. Experiment 1: Santa-Fe Ant trail

Artificial Ant is representative of an agent search problem and also it is considered to be highly deceptive and difficult for genetic programming [16]. The Santa-fe ant problem has a difficult trail and the objective is to devise a program which can successfully navigate an artificial ant to find all pieces of food located on a grid. The total amount of food consumed is used as single point measure of the fitness of the program. The program has three terminal operations forward, left and right for navigation. It has three basic actions like IfFoodAhead, progn2 and progn3 for performing single action and parameter based execution in the sequence. It has three basic actions like IfFoodAhead, progn2 and progn3 for performing single action and parameter based execution in the sequence. IfFoodAhead is a non-terminal function that takes two parameters and executes the first if there is food one step ahead and the second otherwise. Progn2 takes 2 parameters while progn3 takes 3 parameters and executes them in a sequence.

1. **Quantitative Traits for Santa-Fe Ant trail**
   As per our discussions in the phenotypic traits section, various search properties are devised to measure quantitatively behavior of an agent like ant and used for phenotypic traits in the calculations for equation above.

   For all the formulas
   m= moves, d= dimension, trail= point on trail,closest-trail= closest point on trail
   $\delta = distance$

   - **Sum of Distances from Last Trail**: This is the manhattan distance computed for all the moves from where it is to where it was last on the trail. This trait measures the "moving away effect" of the agent to the trail.

   $$\sum_{i=1}^{m} \sum_{j=1}^{d} ||\delta_{i,d} - \delta_{trail,d}|| \tag{5}$$

   - **Sum of Distances to Closest Point on Trail**:This is the manhattan distance computed for all the moves from where it is to point closest on the trail. This trait measures the "closeness" of the agent to the trail.

   $$\sum_{i=1}^{m} \sum_{j=1}^{d} ||\delta_{i,d} - \delta_{closest-trail,d}|| \tag{6}$$

- **Sum of Distances from Last Point**:This is the manhattan distance computed for all the moves from where it is to point last point. This trait measures the "geometric displacement effect" irrespective of trail for the agent.

$$\sum_{i=1}^{m}\sum_{j=1}^{d} ||\delta_{i,d} - \delta_{i-1,d}|| \tag{7}$$

- **Count of Null Movements**:This is the count of zero movements, i.e. no change in displacement for the agent over all its moves. This trait measures the effect of changing code not altering the behavior of the agent.

$$\sum_{i=1}^{m} \forall d, \{if(\delta_{i,d} - \delta_{i-1,d}) = 0, count = count + 1\} \tag{8}$$

Most of these quantitative traits show exponential distribution and hence they are transformed to the new set of derived traits by taking the *log* of the originals as insisted by various biologist [9].

2. **Santa-Fe Ant trail GP Experiments**
To understand the effects of the operator and selection, we will be performing one operator at a time with the selection mechanism mentioned to see the impact.
   - **Subtree Crossover and Tournament Selection size 7**
   Since most GP problems use subtree crossover as the main breeding operator and normally higher selection pressure with tournament size 7 are employed, we use these to plot different metrics explained in the quantitative genetics section as shown in Figure 2.
   - **Subtree Crossover and tournament Selection size 2**
   We change the tournament selection to have lower pressure by changing the tournament size to 2, and observing all the metrics are shown in Figure 3.
   - **Subtree Crossover and Fitness Proportionate Selection**
   Fitness Proportionate Selection generally has lower selection pressure as compared to tournament selection, and by changing the selection mechanism the metrics are shown in the Figure 4.
   - **Homologous Crossover and Tournament Selection size 7**
   Homologous Crossover was designed and successfully employed to control bloat and improve fitness in many GP problems [15]. The impact of using homologous crossover on tournament selection size 2 using the metrics is shown in Figure 5.
3. **Santa-Fe Ant trail Observations**
   - Tournament size 2 gives a weaker selection pressure than tournament size 7. It can be seen that with selection 7 as compared to selection 2, there is rapid convergence in genotypic diversity. This correlates to rapid convergence in the phenotypic trait measurements of O and P. It can be observed that when the genotypic diversity and corresponding phenotypic traits converge, there is rise in the perturbation $\text{tr}(\mathbf{D})/\text{tr}(\mathbf{P})$ curve. The point at which this happens and magnitude of change shifts in generations with selection pressure, i.e with tournament selection size 2 it happens later around generation 50 as compared to around generation 20 with selection 7. Also the increase is

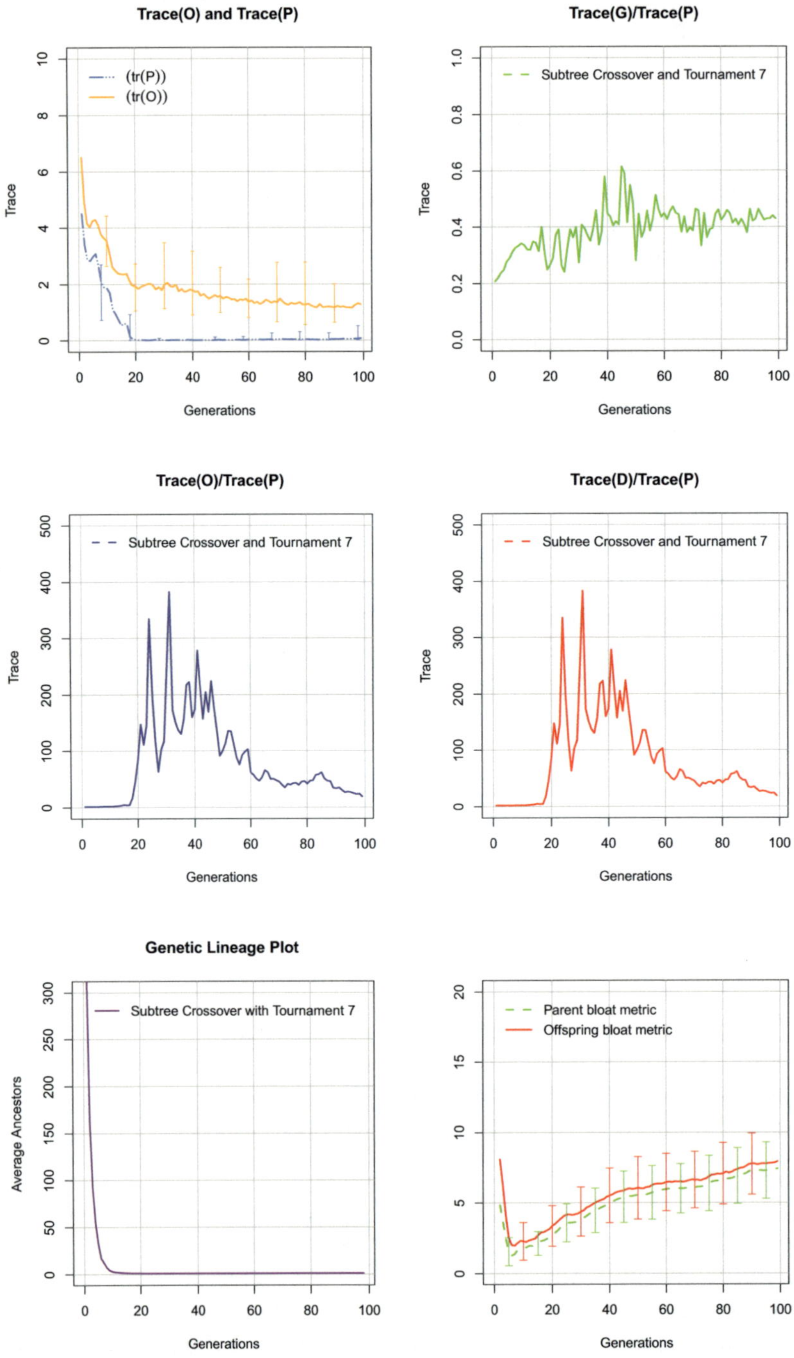

Figure 2. Ant, Subtree crossover, tournament size 7, depth limit 17

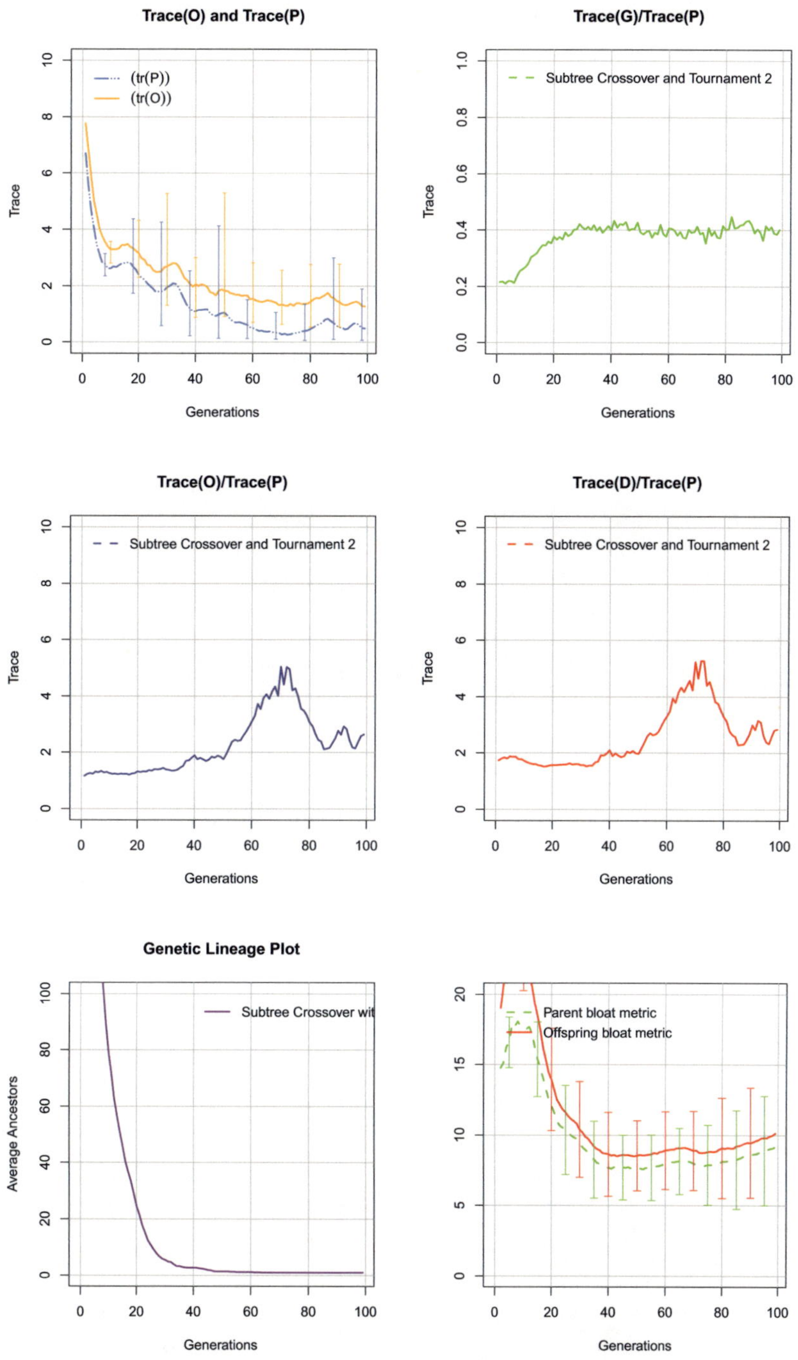

Figure 3. Ant, Subtree crossover, tournament size 2, depth limit 17

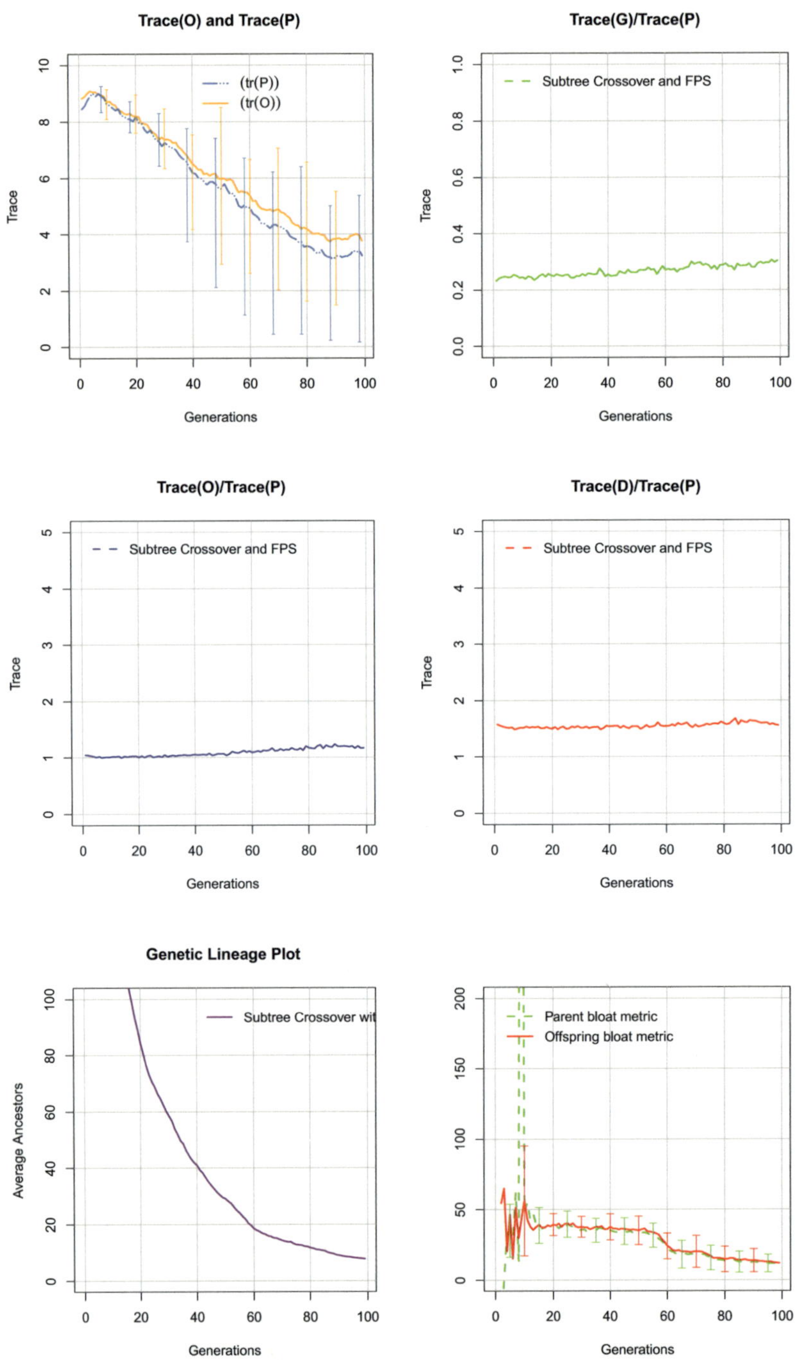

Figure 4. Ant, Subtree Crossover, Fitness Proportionate Selection (FPS), depth limit 17

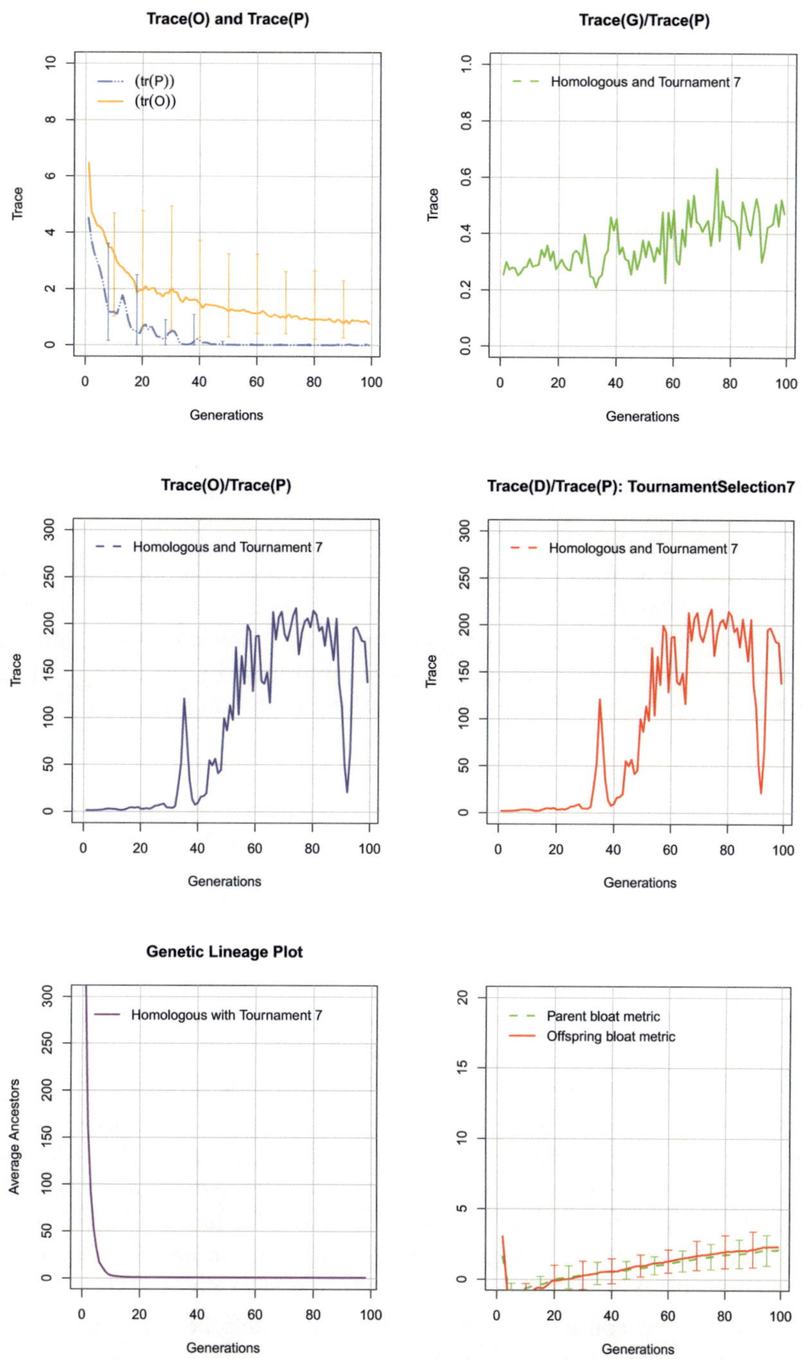

Figure 5. Ant, Homologous crossover, tournament size 7, depth limit 17

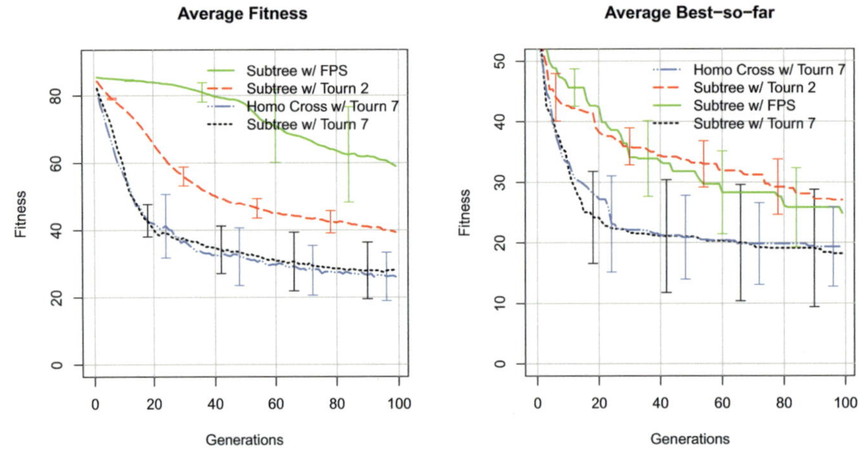

Figure 6. Average and BSF fitness for ant experiments

magnitude lesser (scale of DP, OP with selection 2 as compared to selection 7). Increased selection pressure which may result in lack of diversity may increase perturbation in the system. This increase may be useful in some difficult problems for finding area in the landscape that is not reachable otherwise and may not be effective when more of greedy local search is necessary to reach optimum. In ant trail problem, being a difficult landscape, increased perturbation is helpful to find solution faster as shown in the fitness curves in the Figure 6.

- It can be observed that the increase in perturbation with selection size 7, eventually tapers down and may be attributed to rise in the bloat. As bloat increases beyond a threshold, the effect of changes is reduced and that brings the perturbation down.
- Another important thing to note is with higher selection pressure, when there is premature convergence, it results in statistically significant (95% confidence) difference between the phenotypic behavior of offsprings and parents, while lower selection pressure reduces the difference.
- FPS results in higher genotypic diversity amongst the individuals as observed in the Figure 4, and that results in lower convergence in the population phenotypically and as a result the perturbation effect is constant across all the generations.
- Figure 5 shows that the perturbation increases with reduction in diversity exactly like in subtree crossover, but the perturbation continues to stay higher because of bloat control, however the max-value of perturbation is still lower than in normal crossover. Thus bloat which helped subtree crossover to reduce the impact of perturbation, when controlled by homologous crossover, showed constant value. This is consistent with theory that the bloat is a defensive mechanism against crossover [1].
- Figure 6 show the comparative plots of average and best so far (bsf) with 95% confidence intervals as whiskers. It can be seen that tournament selection with 7 with subtree or homologous are similar. Homologous crossover with reduced perturbations and bloat has real advantage over subtree crossover in this experiment.

4.2. Experiment 2: Lawn mower

The essence of this problem is to find a solution for controlling the movement of a robotic lawn mower so that the lawn mower visits each of the squares on two-dimensional n x m toroidal grid. The toroidal nature of the grid allows the lawnmower to wrap around to the opposite side of the grid when it moves off one of the edges. The lawnmower has state consisting of the squares on which the lawnmower is currently residing and the direction (up,down,left and right) which is facing. The lawnmower has 3 actions that change its state: turning left, moving forward and jumping to specified squares.

1. **Quantitative Traits for Lawn Mower**
   Similar to ant problem, we came up with some quantitative traits to measure the lawn mower behavior in the phenotypic landscape using the design principles. We keep a memory of visited location and have a function *visited(d)* for validating the revisit. We also keep memory of last orientation using omega in for measuring change in orientations in the movements.
   For all the formulas below
   m= moves, d= dimension, δ = *distance and* Ω = *orientation*

   - **Number of Moves**:This measures total number of moves performed by the agent in the execution, which we will refer as m.
   - **Count of Null Movements**:This is the count of zero movements, i.e. no change in displacement for the lawn mower over all its moves. This trait measures the effect of changing code not altering the behavior of the agent.

   $$\sum_{i=1}^{m} \forall d, \{if(\delta_{i,d} - \delta_{i-1,d}) = 0, count = count + 1\} \tag{9}$$

   - **Sum of Distances**:This is the manhattan distance computed for all the moves. This trait measures the "geometric displacement effect" in the movement.

   $$\sum_{i=1}^{m} \sum_{j=1}^{d} ||\delta_{i,d} - \delta_{i-1,d}|| \tag{10}$$

   - **Number of Orientation changes**:This measures number of times the orientation of the lawn mower is changed.

   $$\sum_{i=1}^{m} \forall d, \{if(\Omega_{i,d} \neq \Omega_{i-1,d}), count = count + 1\} \tag{11}$$

   - **Count of Revisits**:This measures number of times the already visited spot is visited.

   $$\sum_{i=1}^{m} \forall d, \{if(visited(d)), count = count + 1\} \tag{12}$$

2. **Lawn Mower GP Experiments**
   We performed subset of experiments from our ant problem on the lawn mower to see differences and similarity in the evolutionary behaviors.

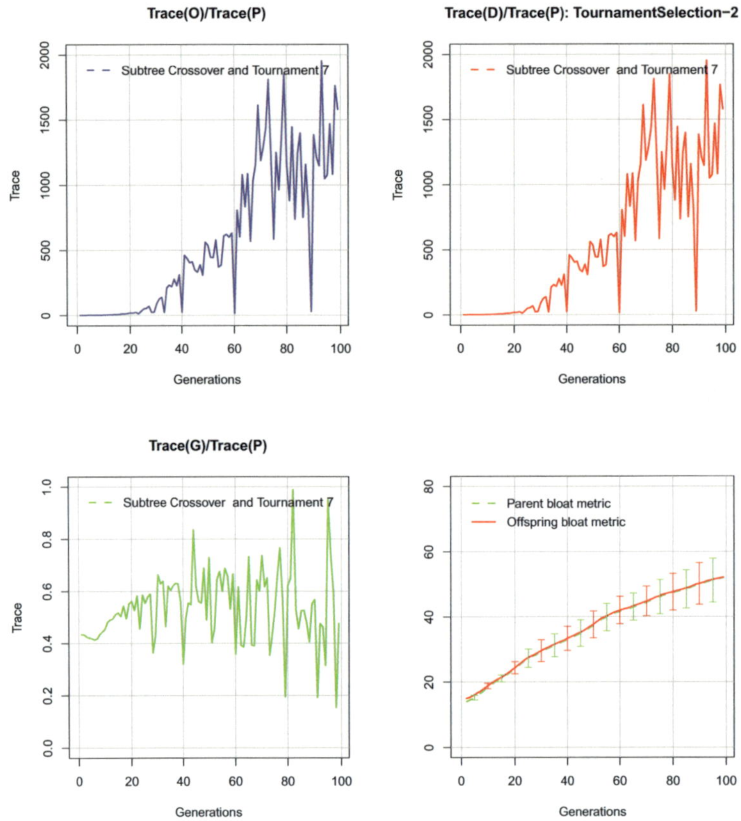

Figure 7. Lawn Mower Subtree crossover, tournament size 2, depth limit 17

- **Subtree Crossover and Tournament Selection size 2**
  We perform comparative subtree crossover with lower selection pressure on our lawn mower problem and show the quantitative genetics metrics plotted in the Figure 7.
- **Subtree Crossover and Fitness Proportionate Selection**
  We change the selection pressure totally by going for FPS instead of tournament selection and plot various metrics in the Figure 8.
- **Homologous Crossover and Tournament Selection size 2**
  Impact of bloat control by using homologous crossover with tournament selection with size 2 with various metrics are shown in the Figure 9.

3. **Lawn Mower Observations**
   - An interesting observation about the perturbation $\mathrm{tr}(\mathbf{D})/\mathrm{tr}(\mathbf{P})$ and $\mathrm{tr}(\mathbf{O})/\mathrm{tr}(\mathbf{P})$ curves can be made from Figures 8 and 9. Both curves tend to increase to a higher level with binary tournament selection as compared to FPS. This is actually a result of the fact that the GP crossover operators have a lower bound on the amount of variation they add to the population [4]. Higher selection pressures will reduce the phenotypic variation in the population more that lower selection pressures. Reproductive operators then return the variation to the operators minimum levels. When selection pressures are higher,

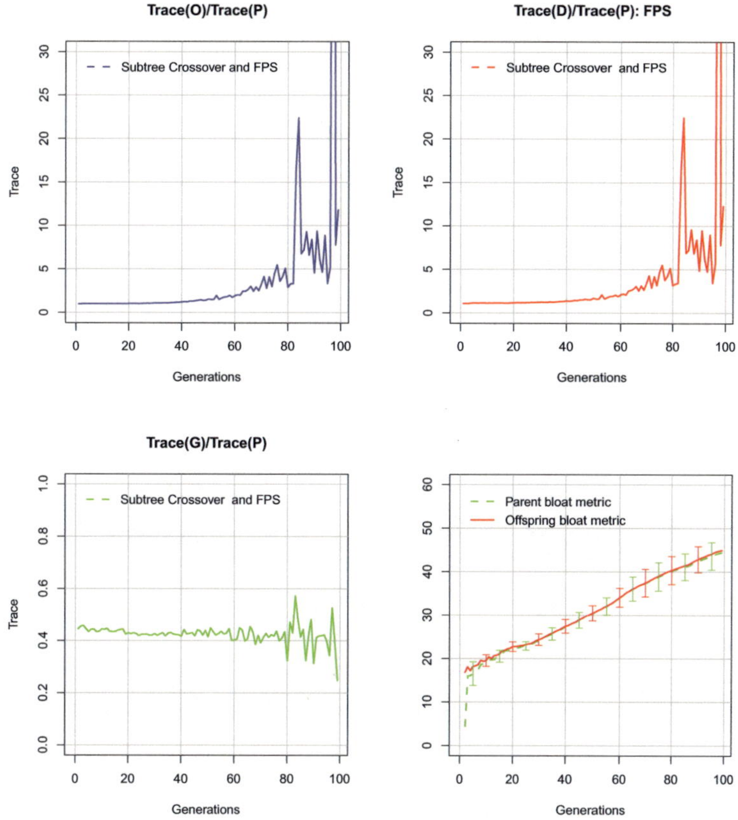

Figure 8. Lawn Mower Subtree crossover, Fitness Proportionate Selection, depth limit 17

the difference between these two amounts will be higher relative to the amount of variation in the selection parent populations. As a result, perturbation and population heritability will appear higher, but this is only because they had further to go to get back to the same place (i.e. the lower bound defined by the operators).

- Homologous crossover shows fairly stable $\mathrm{tr}(\mathbf{D})/\mathrm{tr}(\mathbf{P})$, $\mathrm{tr}(\mathbf{O})/\mathrm{tr}(\mathbf{P})$ and $\mathrm{tr}(\mathbf{G})/\mathrm{tr}(\mathbf{P})$ curves as shown in Figure 9, where the operator on this problem acts similar to the GA based crossover on a simple problem like sphere [3]. As the population converges in phenotype space, crossover is able to adapt and create offspring populations with similar distributions to those of the parent population (as can be seen by the fact that $\mathrm{tr}(\mathbf{G})/\mathrm{tr}(\mathbf{P})$ stays close to 0.5, and even more importantly that O/P stays relatively close to 1). The fact that it is able to do this even at the end of the run is important. It allows the population to truly converge on a very small part of the search space until there is (almost) no variation left. This is often considered to be a weakness of crossover, but in some ways it is really a strength. Without this ability, the algorithm cannot fully exploit the information it gains.
- Figure 10 shows again at the end of the generations there is no significant difference between subtree crossover and homologous crossover, while homologous crossover with better perturbation and heritability may be at advantage.

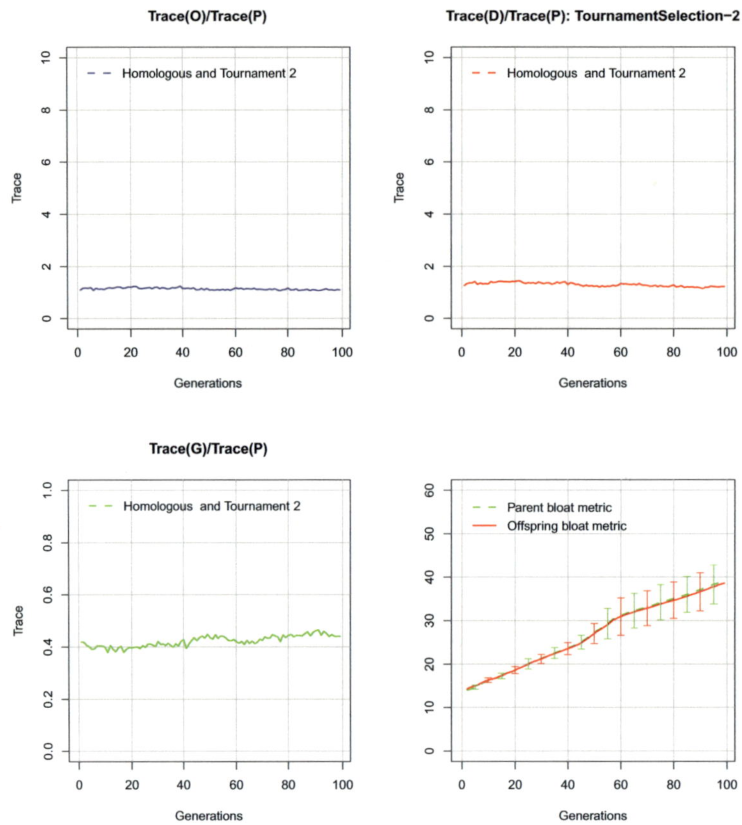

Figure 9. Lawn Mower Homologous crossover, tournament size 2, depth limit 17

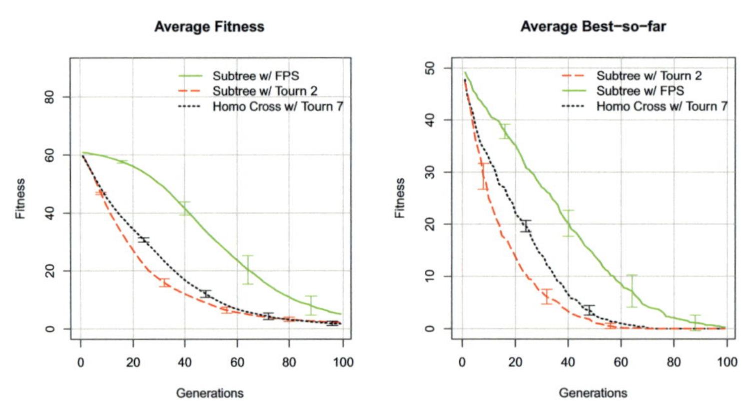

Figure 10. Average and BSF fitness for lawn mower experiments

4.3. Experiment 3: Symbolic regression

Symbolic Regression problem is about finding the equation closest to the given problem, by generating different curves and testing on the sample training points. The absolute error over the training points is used as the fitness function. Terminal would be the variable X and the non-terminals would be mathematical functions like log, sine, cosine, addition, multiplication etc. We used the quintic function for our test. Quintic is given by equation

$$y = x^5 - 2x^3 + x, \quad x = [-1,1] \tag{13}$$

1. **Quantitative Traits for Symbolic Regression** Regression being a mathematical problem in an euclidean space rather than a behavior based agent, we used the values of 10 random points equally distributed on the curve as the trait measurements like [-0.9, -0.7,-0.5...0.5,0.7,0.9]. This is similar to fitness being evaluated over fixed training point, but the difference being here we get individual values rather than aggregated measure. These individual trait values can be important in identifying how the curve changes between parent and offspring during the evolutionary process.

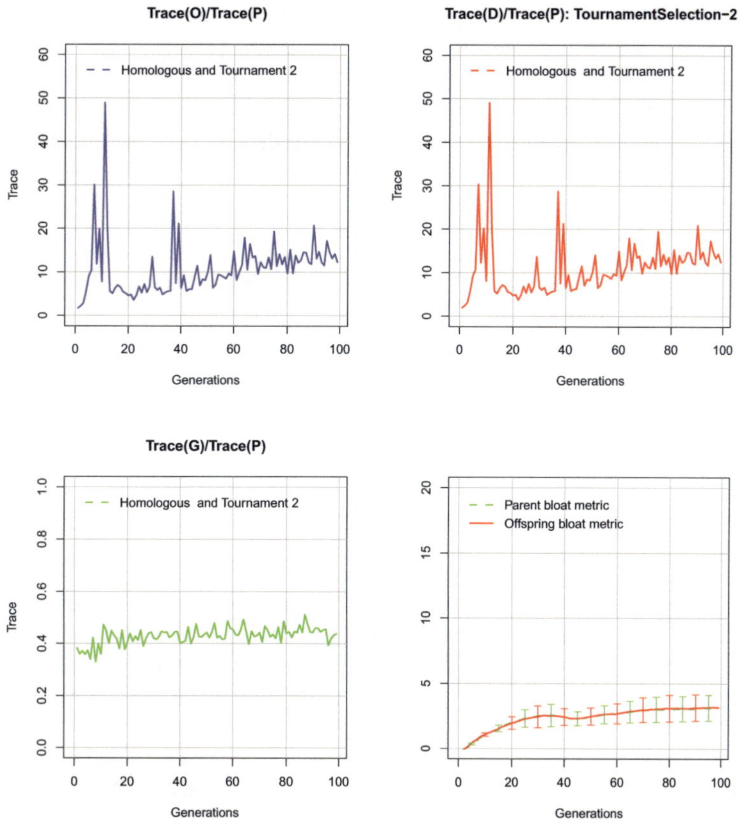

Figure 11. Symbolic Regression, Homologous crossover, tournament size 2, depth limit 17

2. **Regression GP Experiment**
   We will analyze one experiment using Homologous crossover and tournament selection to see generic behavior of GP problems given similar operators and selection pressure.
   - **Homologous Crossover with Tournament Selection size 2**
     Figure 11 shows various quantitative genetic metrics similar to previous experiments for quintic regression problem.
3. **Symbolic Regression Observations**
   - The results of the experiment as seen in Figure 11 is comparative to the results on the ant problem in figure 5. We can see several trends that we saw before, for example, the curve for **D** follows the same type of path, converging until a fixed level of variation is reached, and then staying there.
   - Also, the perturbation curve and the population heritability curve show the same trend of continual increase over generations.

5. Conclusions and future work

In this chapter we have provided a detailed tutorial on quantitative genetics and some high level design methods to define phenotypic traits needed by quantitative genetics. Using these methods we performed various experiments changing the selection and breeding operator in GP to analyze different evolutionary behaviors of the problem. Evolutionary forces like exploration and exploitation were quantified using quantitative genetics tool set and some interesting correlation with other forces like bloat, diversity, convergence and fitness were made. Many observations and correlations made were generalized across different benchmark GP problems.

In future we would like to perform more experiments to further understand the balance of bloat, selection and breeding operators, as well as designing new operators for resolving issues in a given problem domain.

Author details

Uday Kamath, Jeffrey K. Bassett and Kenneth A. De Jong
Computer Science Department, George Mason University, Fairfax, USA

6. References

[1] Altenberg, L. [1994]. The evolution of evolvability in genetic programming, *in* K. E. Kinnear (ed.), *Advances in Genetic Programming*, MIT Press, Cambridge, MA, pp. 47–74.
[2] Altenberg, L. [1995]. The schema theorem and Price's theorem, *in* L. D. Whitley & M. D. Vose (eds), *Foundations of Genetic Algorithms III*, Morgan Kaufmann, San Francisco, CA, pp. 23–49.
[3] Bassett, J. K. & De Jong, K. [2011]. Using multivariate quantitative genetics theory to assist in ea customization, *Foundations of Genetic Algorithms 7*, Morgan Kaufmann, San Francisco.
[4] Bassett, J. K., Kamath, U. & De Jong, K. A. [2012]. A new methodology for the GP theory toolbox, *Proceedings of the Genetic and Evolutionary Computation Conference (GECCO-2012)*, ACM.

[5] Bassett, J. K., Potter, M. A. & De Jong, K. A. [2004]. Looking under the EA hood with Price's equation, *in* K. Deb, R. Poli, W. Banzhaf, H.-G. Beyer, E. Burke, P. Darwen, D. Dasgupta, D. Floreano, J. Foster, M. Harman, O. Holland, P. L. Lanzi, L. Spector, A. Tettamanzi, D. Thierens & A. Tyrrell (eds), *Genetic and Evolutionary Computation – GECCO-2004, Part I*, Vol. 3102 of *Lecture Notes in Computer Science*, Springer-Verlag, Seattle, WA, USA, pp. 914–922.

[6] Bassett, J. K., Potter, M. A. & De Jong, K. A. [2005]. Applying Price's equation to survival selection, *in* H.-G. Beyer, U.-M. O'Reilly, D. V. Arnold, W. Banzhaf, C. Blum, E. W. Bonabeau, E. Cantu-Paz, D. Dasgupta, K. Deb, J. A. Foster, E. D. de Jong, H. Lipson, X. Llora, S. Mancoridis, M. Pelikan, G. R. Raidl, T. Soule, A. M. Tyrrell, J.-P. Watson & E. Zitzler (eds), *GECCO 2005: Proceedings of the 2005 Conference on Genetic and Evolutionary Computation*, Vol. 2, ACM Press, Washington DC, USA, pp. 1371–1378.
URL: *http://www.cs.bham.ac.uk/ wbl/biblio/gecco2005/docs/p1371.pdf*

[7] Burke, E., Gustafson, S. & Kendall, G. [2002]. A survey and analysis of diversity measures in genetic programming, pp. 716–723.

[8] Burke, E. K., Gustafson, S., Kendall, G. & Krasnogor, N. [2003]. Is increased diversity in genetic programming beneficial? an analysis of lineage selection, *Congress on Evolutionary Computation*, IEEE Press, pp. 1398–1405.

[9] Falconer, D. S. & Mackay, T. F. C. [1981]. *Introduction to quantitative genetics*, Longman New York.

[10] Flury, B. [1988]. *Common Principal Components and Related Multivariate Models*, Wiley series in probability and mathematical statistics, Wiley, New York.

[11] Frank, S. A. [1995]. George price's contributions to evolutionary genetics, *Journal of Theoretical Biology* 175(3): 373–388.
URL: *http://www.sciencedirect.com/science/article/B6WMD-45R8FXC-3N/2/01fea9e865de0a05 4158ee82d6237ef7*

[12] Game, E. T. & Caley, M. J. [2006]. The stability of P in coral reef fishes, *Evolution* 60(4): 814–823.
URL: *http://dx.doi.org/10.1111/j.0014-3820.2006.tb01159.x*

[13] Lande, R. & Arnold, S. J. [1983]. The measurement of selection on correlated characters, *Evolution* 37(6): 1210–1226.
URL: *http://www.jstor.org/stable/2408842*

[14] Langdon, W. B. [1998a]. *Genetic Programming and Data Structures: Genetic Programming + Data Structures = Automatic Programming!*, The Kluwer international series in engineering and computer science, Kluwer Academic Publishers, Boston.

[15] Langdon, W. B. [1998b]. Size fair and homologous tree genetic programming crossovers. genetic programming and evolvable machines.

[16] Langdon, W. B. & Poli, R. [2002]. *Foundations of Genetic Programming*, Springer-Verlag.

[17] Luke, S., Panait, L., Balan, G., Paus, S., Skolicki, Z., Popovici, E., Sullivan, K., Harrison, J., Bassett, J., Hubley, R., Chircop, A., Compton, J., Haddon, W., Donnelly, S., Jamil, B. & O'Beirne, J. [2010]. ECJ: A java-based evolutionary computation research.
URL: *http://cs.gmu.edu/ eclab/projects/ecj/*

[18] Manderick, B., de Weger, M. & Spiessens, P. [1991]. The genetic algorithm and the structure of the fitness landscape, *in* R. K. Belew & L. B. Booker (eds), *Proc. of the Fourth Int. Conf. on Genetic Algorithms*, Morgan Kaufmann, San Mateo, CA, pp. 143–150.

[19] Mühlenbein, H. [1997]. The equation for response to selection and its use for prediction, *Evolutionary Computation* 5(3): 303–346.

[20] Mühlenbein, H., Bendisch, J. & Voigt, H.-M. [1996]. From recombination of genes to the estimation of distributions: II. continuous parameters, *in* H.-M. Voigt, W. Ebeling, I. Rechenberg & H.-P. Schwefel (eds), *Parallel Problem Solving from Nature – PPSN IV*, Springer, Berlin, pp. 188–197.

[21] Mühlenbein, H. & michael Voigt, H. [1995]. Gene pool recombination in genetic algorithms, *Metaheuristics: Theory and Applications* pp. 53—62.
URL: *http://citeseerx.ist.psu.edu/viewdoc/summary?doi=10.1.1.56.3488*

[22] Mühlenbein, H. & Paaß, G. [1996]. From recombination of genes to the estimation of distributions: I. Binary parameters, *in* H.-M. Voigt, W. Ebeling, I. Rechenberg & H.-P. Schwefel (eds), *Parallel Problem Solving from Nature – PPSN IV*, Springer, Berlin, pp. 178–187.

[23] Mühlenbein, H. & Schlierkamp-Voosen, D. [1993]. Predictive models for the breeder genetic algorithm: I. continuous parameter optimization, *Evolutionary Computation* 1(1): 25–49.

[24] Mühlenbein, H. & Schlierkamp-Voosen, D. [1994]. The science of breeding and its application to the breeder genetic algorithm (BGA), *Evolutionary Computation* 1(4): 335–360.

[25] Potter, M. A., Bassett, J. K. & De Jong, K. A. [2003]. Visualizing evolvability with Price's equation, *in* R. Sarker, R. Reynolds, H. Abbass, K. C. Tan, B. McKay, D. Essam & T. Gedeon (eds), *Proceedings of the 2003 Congress on Evolutionary Computation CEC2003*, IEEE Press, Canberra, pp. 2785–2790.

[26] Price, G. [1972]. Fisher's 'fundamental theorem' made clear, *Annals of Human Genetics* 36(2): 129–140.
URL: *http://dx.doi.org/10.1111/j.1469-1809.1972.tb00764.x*

[27] Price, G. R. [1970]. Selection and covariance, *Nature* 227: 520–521.
URL: *http://adsabs.harvard.edu/abs/1970Natur.227..520P*

[28] Prügel-Bennett, A. [1997]. Modelling evolving populations, *Journal of Theoretical Biology* 185(1): 81–95.
URL: *http://www.sciencedirect.com/science/article/B6WMD-45KKVJV-7/2/3ac11d9873754b7db89bc424fc4919ad*

[29] Prügel-Bennett, A. & Shapiro, J. L. [1994]. Analysis of genetic algorithms using statistical mechanics, *Physical Review Letters* 72(9): 1305–1309.
URL: *http://link.aps.org/abstract/PRL/v72/p1305*

[30] Radcliffe, N. J. [1991]. Forma analysis and random respectful recombination, *in* R. K. Belew & L. B. Booker (eds), *Proceedings of the Fourth International Conference on Genetic Algorithms (ICGA'91)*, Morgan Kaufmann Publishers, San Mateo, California, pp. 222–229.

[31] Rice, S. H. [2004]. *Evolutionary Theory: Mathematical and Conceptual Foundations*, Sinauer Associates, Inc.

[32] Vanneschi, L., Castelli, M. & Silva, S. [2010]. Measuring bloat, overfitting and functional complexity in genetic programming, *in* B. et al.Editors (ed.), *GECCO 10 Proceedings of the 10th annual conference on Genetic and evolutionary computation*, ACM, pp. 877–884.

Chapter 2

Continuous Schemes for Program Evolution

Cyril Fonlupt, Denis Robilliard and Virginie Marion-Poty

Additional information is available at the end of the chapter

http://dx.doi.org/10.5772/50023

1. Introduction

Genetic Programming (GP) is a technique aiming at the automatic generation of programs. It was successfully used to solve a wide variety of problems, and it can be now viewed as a mature method as even patents for old and new discovery have been filled, see e.g. [1, 2]. GP is used in fields as different as bio-informatics [3], quantum computing [4] or robotics [5], among others.

The most widely used scheme in GP was proposed by Koza, where programs are represented as Lisp-like trees and evolved by a genetic algorithm. Many other paradigms were devised these last years to automatically evolve programs. For instance, linear genetic programming (LGP) [6] is based on an interesting feature: instead of creating program trees, LGP directly evolves programs represented as linear sequences of imperative computer instructions. LGP is successful enough to have given birth to a derived commercial product named *discipulus*. The representation (or genotype) of programs in LGP is a bounded-length list of integers. These integers are mapped into imperative instructions of a simple imperative language (a subset of C for instance).

While the previous schemes are mainly based on discrete optimization, a few other evolutionary schemes for automatic programming have been proposed that rely on some sort of continuous representation. These include notably Ant Colony Optimization in AntTAG [7, 8], or the use of probabilistic models like Probabilistic Incremental Program Evolution [9] or Bayesian Automatic Programming [10].

In 1997, Storn and Price proposed a new evolutionary algorithm for continuous optimization, called Differential Evolution (DE) [11]. Another popular continuous evolution scheme is the Covariance Matrix Adaptation Evolution Strategy (CMA-ES) that was proposed by Hansen and Ostermeier [12] in 1996. Differential Evolution differs from Evolution Strategies in the way it uses information from the current population to determine the perturbation brought to solutions (this can be seen as determining the direction of the search).

In this chapter, we propose to evolve programs with continuous representation, using these two continuous evolution engines, Differential Evolution and CMA Evolution Strategy. A program is represented by a float vector that is translated to a linear sequence of imperative instructions, *a la* LGP.

The chapter is organized in the following way. The first section introduces the Differential Evolution and CMA Evolution Strategy schemes, focusing on the similarities and main differences. We then present our continuous schemes, LDEP and CMA-LEP, respectively based on DE and CMA-ES. We show that these schemes are easily implementable as plug-ins for DE and CMA-ES. In Section 4, we compare the performance of these two schemes, and also traditional GP, over a range of benchmarks.

2. Continuous evolutionary schemes

In this section we present DE and CMA-ES, that form the main components of the evolutionary algorithms used in our experiments.

2.1. Previous works on evolving programs with DE

To our knowledge O'Neill and Brabazon were the firsts to use DE to evolve programs within the well known framework of Grammatical Evolution (GE) [13]. In GE, a population of variable length binary strings is decoded using a Backus Naur Form (BNF) formal grammar definition into a syntactically correct program. The genotype-to-phenotype mapping process allows to use almost any BNF grammars and so to evolve programs in many different languages. GE has been applied to various problems ranging from symbolic regression problems or robot control [14] to physical-based animal animations [15] including neural network evolution, or financial applications [16]... In [13], Grammatical Differential Evolution is defined by retaining the GE grammar decoding process for generating phenotypes, with genotypes being evolved with DE. A diverse selection of benchmarks from the GP literature were tackled with four different flavors of GE. Even if the experimental results indicated that the grammatical differential evolution approach was outperformed by standard GP on three of the four problems, the results were somewhat encouraging.

More recently, Veenhuis also introduced a successful application of DE for automatic programming in [17], mapping a continuous genotype to trees, so called Tree based Differential Evolution (TreeDE). TreeDE improved somewhat on the performance of grammatical differential evolution, but it requires an additional low-level parameter, the tree depth of solutions, that has to be set beforehand. Moreover evolved programs do not include random constants.

Another recent proposal for program evolution based on DE is called Geometric Differential Evolution, and was issued in [18]. These authors introduced a formal generalization of DE to keep the same geometric interpretation of the search dynamic across diverse representations, either for continuous or combinatorial spaces. This scheme is interesting, although it has some limitations: it is not possible to model the search space of Koza style subtree crossover for example. Anyway, experiments on four standard benchmarks against Langdon's homologous crossover GP were promising.

Our proposal differs from these previous works by being based on Banzhaf's Linear GP representation of solutions. This allows us to implement real-valued constant management inspired from the LGP literature, that are lacking in TreeDE. The tree-depth parameter from TreeDE is also replaced by the maximum length of the programs to be evolved: this is a lesser constraint on the architecture of solutions and it still has the benefit of limiting the well known bloat problem (uncontrolled increase in solution size) that plagues standard GP.

2.2. Differential evolution

This section only introduces the main Differential Evolution (DE) concepts. The interested reader might refer to [11] for a full presentation. DE is a population-based search algorithm that draws inspiration from the field of evolutionary computation, even if it is not usually viewed as a typical evolutionary algorithm.

DE is a real-valued, vector based, heuristic for minimizing possibly non-differentiable and non linear continuous space functions. As most evolutionary schemes, DE can be viewed as a stochastic directed search method. But instead of randomly mating two individuals (like crossover in Genetic Algorithms), or generating random offspring from an evolved probability distribution (like PBIL [19] or CMA-ES [20]), DE takes the difference vector of two randomly chosen population vectors to perturb an existing vector. This perturbation is made for every individual (vector) inside the population. A newly perturbated vector is kept in the population only if it has a better fitness than its previous version.

2.2.1. *Principles*

DE is a search method working on a set or population $X = (X_1, X_2, \ldots, X_N)$ of N solutions that are $d-$dimensional float vectors, trying to optimize a fitness (or objective) function $f(X_i)_{i \in [1,N]} : \mathbb{R}^d \to \mathbb{R}$.

DE can be roughly decomposed into an initialization phase and three very simple steps that are iterated on:

1- initialization
2- mutation
3- crossover
4- selection
5- end if termination criterion is fulfilled else
go to step 2

At the beginning of the algorithm, the initial population is randomly initialized and evaluated using the fitness function f. Then new potential individuals are created: a new trial solution is created for every vector X_j, in two steps called mutation and crossover. A selection process is triggered to determine whether or not the trial solution replaces the vector X_j in the population.

2.2.2. *Mutation*

Let t indicate the number of the current iteration (or generation), for each vector $X_j(t)$ of the population, a variant vector $V_j(t+1) = (v_{j1}, v_{j2}, \ldots, v_{jd})$ is generated according to Eq. 1:

$$V_j(t+1) = X_{r_1}(t) + F \times (X_{r_2}(t) - X_{r_3}(t)) \tag{1}$$

where:

- r_1, r_2 and r_3 are three mutually *different* randomly selected indices in the population that are also different from the current index j.
- the scaling factor F is a real constant which controls the amplification of differential evolution and avoids the stagnation in the search process — typical values for F are in the range $[0,2]$.
- The expression $(X_{r_2}(t) - X_{r_3}(t))$ is referred to as the difference vector.

Many variants were proposed for equation 1, including the use of more than 3 individuals. According to [17, 21], the mutation method that is the more robust over a set of experiments is the method DE/best/2/bin, defined by Eq. 2:

$$V_j(t+1) = X_{\text{best}}(t) + F \times (X_{r_1}(t) + X_{r_2}(t) - X_{r_3}(t) - X_{r_4}(t)) \tag{2}$$

where $X_{\text{best}}(t)$ is the best individual in the population at the current generation. This method DE/best/2/bin is used throughout the chapter.

2.2.3. Crossover

As explained in [11], the crossover step ensures to increase or at least to maintain the diversity. Each trial vector is partly crossed with the variant vector. The crossover scheme ensures that at least one vector component will be crossovered.

The trial vector $U_j(t+1) = (u_{j1}, u_{j2}, \ldots, u_{jd})$ is generated using Eq. 3:

$$u_{ji}(t+1) = \begin{cases} v_{ji}(t+1) & \text{if } (rand \leq CR) \text{ or } j = rnbr(i) \\ x_{ji}(t) & \text{if } (rand > CR) \text{ and } j \neq rnbr(i) \end{cases} \tag{3}$$

where:

- $x_{ji}(t)$ is the jth component of vector $X_i(t)$;
- $v_{ji}(t+1)$ is the jth component of the current variant vector $V_j(t+1)$ (see above Eq. 1 and 2);
- $rand$ is a random float drawn uniformly in the range $[0,1[$;
- CR is the crossover rate in the range $[0,1]$ which has to be determined by the user;
- $rnbr(i)$ is a randomly chosen index drawn in the range $[1,d]$ independently for each vector $X_i(t)$ which ensures that $U_j(t+1)$ gets at least one component from the variant vector $V_j(t+1)$.

2.2.4. Selection

The selection step decides whether the trial solution $U_i(t+1)$ replaces the vector $X_i(t)$ or not. The trial solution is compared to the target vector $X_i(t)$ using a greedy criterion. Here we assume a minimization framework: if $f(U_i(t+1)) < f(X_i(t))$, then $X_i(t+1) = U_i(t+1)$ otherwise the old value is kept: $X_i(t+1) = X_i(t)$.

2.2.5. Iteration and stop criterion

These three steps (mutation, crossover, selection) are looped over until a stop criterion is triggered: typically a maximum number of evaluations/iterations is allowed, or a given value of fitness is reached. Overall DE is quite simple, only needing three parameters: the population size N, the crossover rate CR, and the scaling factor F.

2.3. Covariance matrix adaptation evolution strategy

Among continuous optimization methods, DE was often compared (in e.g. [22, 23]) to the Covariance Matrix Adaptation Evolution Strategy (CMA-ES), initially proposed in [12]. The CMA Evolution Strategy is an evolutionary algorithm for difficult non-linear non-convex optimization problems in continuous domains. It is typically applied to optimization problems of search space dimensions between three and one hundred. CMA-ES was designed to exhibit several invariances: (a) invariance against order preserving (i.e. strictly monotonic) transformations of the objective function value; (b) invariance against angle preserving transformations of the search space (e.g rotation, reflection); (c) scale invariance. Invariances are highly desirable as they usually imply a good behavior of the search strategy on ill-conditioned and on non-separable problems.

In this section we only introduce the main CMA-ES concepts, and refer the interested reader to the original paper for a full presentation of this heuristic. An abundant literature has brought several refinements to this algorithm (e.g. [24] and [25]), and has shown its strong interest as a continuous optimization method.

2.3.1. Principles

The basic CMA-ES idea is sampling search points using a normal distribution that is centered on an updated model of the ideal solution. This ideal solution can be seen as a weighted mean of a best subset of current search points. The distribution is also shaped by the covariance matrix of the best solutions sampled in the current iteration. This fundamental scheme was refined mainly on two points:

- extracting more information from the history of the optimization run; this is done through the so-called accumulation path whose idea is akin to the momentum of artificial neural networks;
- allocating an increasing computational effort via an increasing population size in a classic algorithm restart scheme.

The main steps can be summed-up as:

1. sample points are drawn according to the current distribution
2. the sample points are evaluated
3. the probability distribution is updated according to a best subset of the evaluated points
4. iterate to step 1, until the stop criterion is reached

2.3.2. Sampling step

More formally, the basic equation for sampling the search points (step 1) is:

$$x_k^{(g+1)} \leftarrow m^{(g)} + \sigma^{(g)} N(0, C^{(g)}) \tag{4}$$

where:

- g is the generation number
- $k \in 1, ..., N$ is an index over the population size
- $x_k^{(g+1)}$ is the k-th offspring drawn at generation g + 1
- $m^{(g)}$ is the mean value of the search distribution at generation g
- $\sigma^{(g)}$ is the "overall" standard deviation (or step-size) at generation g
- $N(0, C^{(g)})$ is a multivariate normal distribution with zero mean and covariance matrix $C^{(g)}$ at generation g

2.3.3. Evaluation and selection step

Once the sample solutions are evaluated, we can select the current best μ solutions, where μ is the traditional parameter of Evolution Strategies. Then the new mean $m^{(g+1)}$, the new covariance matrix $C^{(g+1)}$ and the new step size control $\sigma^{(g+1)}$ can be computed in order to prepare the next iteration, as explained in the following section.

2.3.4. Update step

The probability distribution for sampling the next generation follows a normal distribution. The new mean $m^{(g+1)}$ of the search distribution is a weighted average of the μ selected best points from the sample $x_1^{(g+1)}, \ldots, x_N^{(g+1)}$, as shown in Eq. 5:

$$m^{(g+1)} = \sum_{i=1}^{\mu} w_i x_{i:N}^{(g+1)} \tag{5}$$

where:

- $\mu \leq N$, μ best points are selected in the parent population of size N.
- $x_{i:N}^{(g+1)}$, i-th best individual out of $x_1^{(g+1)}, \ldots, x_N^{(g+1)}$ from Eq. 4.
- $w_1 \geq \ldots \geq w_\mu$ are the weight coefficients with $\sum_{i=1}^{\mu} w_i = 1$

Thus the calculation of the mean can also be interpreted as a recombination step (typically by setting the weights $w_i = 1/\mu$). Notice that the best μ points are taken from the new current generation, so there is no elitism.

Adapting the covariance matrix of the distribution is a complex step, that consists of three sub-procedures: the rank-μ-update, the rank-one-update and accumulation. They are similar to a Principal Component Analysis of steps, sequentially in time and space. The goal of the adaptation mechanism is to increase the probability of successful consecutive steps.

In addition to the covariance matrix adaptation rule, a step-size control is introduced, that adapts the overall scale of the distribution based on information obtained by the evolution path. If the evolution path is long and single steps are pointing more or less to the same direction, the step-size should be increased. On the other hand, if the evolution path is short and single steps cancel each other out, then we probably oscillate around an optimum, thus the step-size should be decreased.

For the sake of simplicity, the details of the update of the covariance matrix C and step-size control are beyond the scope of this chapter.

2.4. Main differences between DE and CMA-ES

The Differential Evolution method and the CMA Evolution Strategy are often compared, since they are both population-based continuous optimization heuristics. Unlike DE, CMA-ES is based on strong theoretical aspects that allow it to exhibit several invariances that make it a robust local search strategy, see [12]. Indeed it was shown to achieve superior performance versus state-of-the art global search strategies (e.g. see [26]). On the other hand and in comparison with most search algorithms, DE is very simple and straightforward both to implement and to understand. This simplicity is a key factor in its popularity especially for practitioners from other fields.

Despite or maybe thanks to its simplicity, DE also exhibits very good performance when compared to state-of-the art search methods. Furthermore the number of control parameters in DE remains surprisingly small for an evolutionary scheme (Cr, F and N) and a large amount of work has been proposed to select the best equation for the construction of the variant vector.

As explained in [27], the space complexity of DE is low when compared to the most competitive optimizers like CMA-ES. Although CMA-ES remains very competitive over problems up to 100 variables, it is difficult to extend it to higher dimensional problems due mainly to the cost of computing and updating the covariance matrix.

Evolving programs which are typically a mix of discrete and continuous features (e.g. regression problems) is an interesting challenge for these heuristics, since they were not designed for this kind of task.

3. Linear programs with continuous representation

We propose to use Differential Evolution and CMA Evolution Strategy to evolve float vectors, which will be mapped to sequences of imperative instructions in order to form linear programs, similar to the LGP scheme from [6]. For the sake of simplicity, these schemes are respectively denoted:

- LDEP, for Linear Differential Evolutionary Programming, when DE is used as the evolutionary engine;

- CMA-LEP, for Covariance Matrix Adaption Linear Evolutionary Programming, when the evolutionary engine is CMA-ES.

First we recall the basis of linear programs encoding, and execution, and then we explain the mapping process from continuous representation to imperative instructions. We conclude with some remarks on the integration of this representation and mapping with the DE and CMA-ES engines.

3.1. Linear sequence of instructions

In LGP a program is composed of a linear sequence of imperative instructions (see [6] for more details). Each instruction is typically 3-register instruction. That means that every instruction includes an operation on two operand registers, one of them could be holding a constant value, and then assigns the result to a third register:

$$r_i = \begin{cases} r_j \text{ op } (r_k | c_k) \\ (r_j | c_j) \text{ op } r_k \end{cases}$$

where *op* is the operation symbol, r_i is the destination register, r_j, r_k are calculation registers (or operands) and c_j, c_k are constant registers (only one constant register is allowed per instruction).

On the implementation level of standard LGP, each imperative instruction is represented by a list of four integer values where the first value gives the operator and the three next values represent the three register indices. For instance, an instruction like $r_i = r_j \times r_k$ is stored as a quadruple $< \times, i, j, k >$, which in turn is coded as four indices indicating respectively the operation number in the set of possible operations, and 3 indices in the set of possible registers (and/or constant registers). Of course, even if the programming language is basically a 3-register instruction language, it is possible to ignore the last index in order to include 2-register instructions like $r_i = \sin(r_k)$.

Instructions are executed by a virtual machine using floating-point value registers to perform the computations required by the program. The problem inputs are stored in a set of registers. Typically the program output is read in a dedicated register (usually named r_0) at the end of the program execution. These input and output registers are read-write and can serve for intermediate calculations. Usually, additional read-only registers store user defined constants, and extra read-write registers can be added to allow for complex calculations. The use of several calculation registers makes possible a number of different program paths, as explained in [6] and in [28].

3.2. Mapping a float vector to a linear program

Here we explain how a float vector (i.e. an individual of the population), evolved by either DE or CMA-ES, is translated to a linear program in the LGP form.

As explained in the previous section, we need 4 indices to code for the operation number and 3 registers involved. Thus we split the float vector individual into consecutive sequences of 4 floats $< v_1, v_2, v_3, v_4 >$, where v_1 encodes the operator number, and v_2, v_3, v_4 encode the destination and operand registers. In order to convert a float v_i into an integer index, we apply one of the following computations:

- Conversion of the operator index:

$$\#\text{operator} = \lfloor (v_i - \lfloor v_i \rfloor) \times n_{\text{operators}} \rfloor \tag{6}$$

  where $n_{\text{operators}}$ denotes the number of possible operators.

- Conversion of the destination register index:

$$\#\text{register} = \lfloor (v_i - \lfloor v_i \rfloor) \times n_{\text{registers}} \rfloor \tag{7}$$

  where $n_{\text{registers}}$ denotes the number of possible read-write registers.

- The conversion of an operand register depends whether it is a constant or a read-write register. This is controlled by a user defined probability of selecting constant registers, denoted P_C in the following equation:

$$\begin{cases} \#\text{ read-write register} = \lfloor (\frac{v_i - \lfloor v_i \rfloor - P_c}{1 - P_c}) \times n_{\text{registers}} \rfloor & \text{if } (v_i - \lfloor v_i \rfloor) > P_C \\ \#\text{ constant register} \quad = \lfloor v_i \rfloor \text{mod } n_{\text{constants}} & \text{otherwise} \end{cases} \tag{8}$$

  where $n_{\text{registers}}$ denotes the number of possible read-write registers, and $n_{\text{constants}}$ denotes the number of possible constant registers.

Example of a mapping process

Let us suppose we work with 6 read-write registers (r_0 to r_5), 50 constant registers, and the 4 following operators:

$$0:+ \quad 1:- \quad 2:\times \quad 3:\div$$

We set up the constant register probability to $P_C = 0.1$ and we consider the following vector composed of 8 floats, to be translated into 2 imperative instructions ($< v_1, v_2, v_3, v_4 >$ and $< v_5, v_6, v_7, v_8 >$):

v_1	v_2	v_3	v_4	v_5	v_6	v_7	v_8
0.17	2.41	1.86	3.07	0.65	1.15	1.25	4.28

Value v_1 denotes one operator among the four to choose from. Applying Eq. 6, we get $\#\text{operator} = \lfloor (0.17 - \lfloor 0.17 \rfloor) \times 4 \rfloor = 0$, meaning that the first operator is $+$.

The second value $v_2 = 2.41$ is turned into a destination register. According to Eq. 7, we obtain $\#\text{register} = \lfloor (2.41 - \lfloor 2.41 \rfloor) \times 6 \rfloor = \lfloor 2.46 \rfloor = 2$, meaning that the destination register is r_2.

The next value $v_3 = 1.86$ gives an operand register. According to Eq. 8, it is a read-write register since $(1.86 - \lfloor 1.86 \rfloor) = 0.86 > P_C$. Thus the first operand register is: $\#\text{register} = \lfloor ((1.86 - \lfloor 1.86 \rfloor - 0.1)/0.9) \times 6 \rfloor = \lfloor 5.07 \rfloor = 5$, meaning read-write register r_5.

The last of the four first operands is decoded as a constant register since $(3.07 - \lfloor 3.07 \rfloor) = 0.07 \leq P_C$. The index is $\lfloor 3.07 \rfloor$ mod $50 = 3$, meaning constant register c_3.

So the 4 first values of the genotype are translated as:

$$r_2 = r_5 + c_3$$

The mapping process continues with the four next values, until we are left with the following program:

$$r_2 = r_5 + c_3$$

$$r_0 = r_1 \times r_1$$

3.3. Algorithm

To finalize the LDEP and CMA-LEP algorithms, the basic idea is to simply plug the float vector to program translation and the virtual machine program evaluation into the DE and CMA-ES schemes. However some technical points need to be taken into account to allow this integration and they are detailed below.

Initialization

We have to decide about the length of the individuals (float vectors) since we usually cannot extract this feature from the problem. This length will determine the maximum number of instructions allowed in the evolved programs.

Moreover we need to fix a range of possible initial values to randomly generate the components of the initial population $\{X_i\}_{1 \leq i \leq N}$, as typical in DE.

Constant registers are initialized at the beginning of the run, and then are only accessed in read-only mode. This means that our set of constants remains fixed and does not evolve during the run. The number and value range of constant registers are user defined, and the additional parameter P_C must be set to determine the probability of using a constant register in an expression, as explained above in Eq. 8.

Main algorithm iteration

For LDEP, we tried two variants of the iteration loop described in Section 2.2: either generational replacement of individuals as in the original Storn and Price paper [11], or steady state replacement, which seems to be used in [17]. In the generational case, newly created individuals are stored in a temporary set, and once the generation is completed, they replace their respective parent if their fitness is better. In the steady state scheme, each new individual is immediately compared with its parent and replaces it if its fitness is better, and thus it can be used in remaining crossovers for the current generation. Using the steady state variant seems to accelerate convergence, see Section 4.

During the iteration loop of either LDEP or CMA-LEP, the vector solutions are decoded using equations 6, 7 and 8. The resulting linear programs are then evaluated on a set of fitness cases (training examples). The fitness value is then returned to the evolution engine that continues the evolution process.

Heuristic	Problem	Pop.	Ind. size	# eval.	extra params
LDEP	Regressions	20	128	5E4	$F = 0.5$, $CR = 0.1$
	Ant	30	50	2E5	$F = 0.5$, $CR = 0.1$
CMA-LEP	Regressions	20	128	5E4	$\sigma \in \{1, 10\}$, $\lambda \in \{10, 100\}$,
	Ant	30	50	2E5	$\sigma \in \{1, 10\}$, $\lambda \in \{10, 100\}$
GP	Regressions	1000	N.A.	5E4	Elitism, max Depth=11, 80% Xover, 10% Mut, 10% Copy
	Ant	4000	N.A.	2E5	Elitism, max Depth=11, 80% Xover, 10% Mut, 10% Copy

Table 1. Main experimental parameters

4. Experiments

We use the same benchmark problems as in [17] (4 symbolic regressions and the Santa Fe artificial ant), and we also add two regression problems that include float constants.

Before listing our experimental parameters in Table 1, we explain some of our implementation choices:

- We run all standard GP experiments using the well-known ECJ library[1].
- For GP we use a maximum generation number of 50 and set the population size in accordance with the maximum number of evaluations. We keep the best (elite) individual from one generation to the next.
- We use the publicly available C language version of CMA-ES[2], with overall default parameters.
- For TreeDE we take the results as they are reported in [17]:
    - For regression, 1500 iterations on a population of 20 vectors were allowed, and runs were done for every tree depth in the range $\{1, \ldots, 10\}$. It thus amounts to a total of 300,000 evaluations. Among these runs, reference [17] reported only those associated to the tree depth that obtained the best result (which may well imply a favorable bias, in our opinion). As we could not apply this notion of best tree depth in our heuristic, we decided as a trade-off to allow 50,000 evaluations for regression with both LDEP, CMA-LEP and GP.
    - For the Santa Fe Trail artificial ant problem, the same calculation gives a total of 450,000 evaluations for TreeDE. We decided for a trade-off of 200,000 evaluations for LDEP, CMA-LEP and GP.

4.1. Symbolic regression problems

The aim of these 1-dimensional symbolic regression problems is to find some symbolic mathematical expression (or program) that best approximates a target function that is known only by a set of examples, or fitness cases, $(x_k, f(x_k))$. In our case, 20 values x_k are chosen evenly distributed in the range $[-1.0, +1.0]$. The evaluation of programs (or *fitness*

[1] http://cs.gmu.edu/~eclab/projects/ecj/

[2] http://www.lri.fr/~hansen/cmaes_inmatlab.html

computation) is done according to the classic Koza's book [1], that is computing the sum of deviations by looping over all fitness cases:

$$fitness = \sum_{1 \leq k \leq N} |f(x_k) - P(x_k)|$$

where $P(x_k)$ is the value computed by the evolved program P on input x_k, f is the benchmark function and $N = 20$ is the number of (input, output) fitness cases. A *hit solution* means that the deviation is less than 10^{-4} on each fitness case.

The first 4 test functions are from [17]:

$$f_1(x) = x^3 + x^2 + x$$
$$f_2(x) = x^4 + x^3 + x^2 + x$$
$$f_3(x) = x^5 + x^4 + x^3 + x^2 + x$$
$$f_4(x) = x^5 - 2x^3 + x$$

While TreeDE benchmarks were run without constants in [17], we strongly believe that it is interesting to use benchmark problems that are expressed as functions both with and without float constants, in order to assess the impact of constant management by the heuristics. Moreover in the general case, especially on real world problems, one cannot know in advance whether or not float constants may be useful. For this reason we add two benchmarks:

$$f_5(x) = \pi \quad \text{(a constant function)}$$
$$f_6(x) = \frac{x}{\pi} + \frac{x^2}{\pi^2} + 2x\pi$$

The set of operators is $\{+, -, \times, \div\}$ with $\div$ being the protected division (*i.e.* $a \div b = a/b$ if $b \neq 0$ else $a \div b = 0$ if $b = 0$).

For LDEP and CMA-LEP, 6 read-write registers are used for calculation (from r_0 to r_5), with r_0 being the output register. For each fitness case $(x_k, f(x_k))$ that is submitted to the evolved program inside the evaluation loop, all 6 calculation registers are initialized with the same input value x_k. This standard LGP practice provides redundancy of the input value and thus more robustness to the run.

Runs without constants

In the first set of experiments, programs are evolved without constants. This unrealistic setting is proposed here only to allow a comparison of DE-based scheme, confronting LDEP versus Veenhuis's TreeDE, and excluding CMA-LEP. Results are reported in table 2, all three heuristics exhibit close results on the f_1, f_2, f_3, f_4 problems, with GP providing the overall most precise approximation, and LDEP needing the largest number of evaluations (notwithstanding the possible bias in the TreeDE figures, as mentioned at the beginning of Section 4). Note that the steady state variant of LDEP converges faster than the generational, as shown by the average number of evaluations for perfect solutions. It seems safe to conclude that this increased speed of convergence is the explanation for the better result of the steady

	generational LDEP			steady state LDEP			TreeDE		
Problem	Fit.	% hits	Eval.	Fit.	% hits	Eval.	Fit.	% hits	Eval.
f_1	0.0	100%	4297	0.0	100%	2632	0.0	100%	1040
f_2	0.0	100%	12033	0.0	100%	7672	0.0	100%	3000
f_3	0.28	72.5%	21268	0.08	85%	21826	0.027	98%	8440
f_4	0.20	62.5%	33233	0.13	75%	26998	0.165	68%	14600

	standard GP		
Problem	Fit.	% hits	Eval.
f_1	0.0	100%	1815
f_2	0.0	100%	2865
f_3	0.03	97%	6390
f_4	0.01	80%	10845

For each heuristic, over 40 independent runs, the column Fit. gives the average of the best fitness (taken from [17] for TreeDE), then we have the percentage of run reaching a hit solution, then the average number of evaluations to produce the first hit solution (if ever produced).

Table 2. Results for symbolic regression problems without constants.

state variant versus generational, in a limited number of evaluations. This steady state faster convergence may also benefit to TreeDE.

Runs with constants

In the second set of experiments, presented in Table 3, heuristics are allowed to evolve programs with constants, thus ruling out TreeDE from the comparison. All problems from f_1 to f_6 are tested, which means that heuristics manage float constants even on the first 4 problems when they are not needed. This simulates the frequent absence of background knowledge on a new problem and this also tests the robustness of heuristics.

- For LDEP and CMA-LEP, we add 50 constant registers, with a probability of occurrence $P_C = 0.05$, and initial values in the range $[-1.0, +1.0]$.
- For GP, we define 4 redundant input terminals reading the same input value x_k for each fitness case (x_k, y_k), against only one ephemeral random constant (ERC) terminal, that draws new random value instances when needed, in the range $[-1.0, +1.0]$. Thus the probability to generate a constant, e.g. during program initialization or in a subtree mutation, is much lower than the usual 50% when having only one x terminal. This is closer to the LDEP setting and it significantly improves the GP results.

In Table 3, we again observe that the steady state variant of LDEP is better than the generational. For its best version LDEP is comparable to GP, with a slightly higher hit ratio and better average fitness (except on f_6), with more evaluations on average. For CMA-LEP, two values for $\sigma \in \{1, 10\}$ and two values for $\lambda \in \{10, 100\}$ were tried with no significant differences. In contrast with the other methods, CMA-LEP results are an order of magnitude worse. Tuning the CMA-ES engine to tackle the problem as separable did not improve the results. We think this behavior may result from the high dimensionality of the problem (N=128), that certainly disrupts the process of modeling an ideal mean solution from a comparatively tiny set of search points. This is combined to the lack of elitism, inherent to the CMA-ES method, thus when it comes to generate new test points, the heuristic is left solely with a probably imperfect model.

	generational LDEP			steady state LDEP		
Problem	Fit.	%hits	Eval.	Fit.	%hits	Eval.
f_1	0.0	100%	7957	0.0	100%	7355
f_2	0.02	95%	16282	0.0	100%	14815
f_3	0.4	52.5%	24767	0.0	100%	10527
f_4	0.36	42.5%	21941	0.278	45%	26501
f_5	0.13	2.5%	34820	0.06	15%	29200
f_6	0.59	0%	NA	0.63	0%	NA

	standard GP			CMA-LEP		
Problem	Fit.	%hits	Eval.	Fit.	%hits	Eval.
f_1	0.002	98%	3435	0.03	20%	6500
f_2	0.0	100%	4005	2.76	0%	NA
f_3	0.02	93%	7695	5.33	0%	NA
f_4	0.33	23%	24465	2.06	6%	10900
f_5	0.07	0%	NA	13.35	0%	NA
f_6	0.21	0%	NA	5.12	0%	NA

For each heuristic, over 40 independent runs, the column Fit. gives the average of the best fitness, then we have the percentage of run reaching a hit solution, then the average number of evaluations to produce the first hit solution (if ever produced or else NA if no run produced a hit solution).

Table 3. Results for symbolic regression problems with constants.

Overall, these results confirm that DE is an interesting heuristic, even when the continuous representation hides a combinatorial type problem, and thus the heuristic is used outside its original field. The LDEP mix of linear programs and constant management appears competitive with the standard GP approach.

4.2. Santa Fe ant trail

The Santa Fe ant trail is a famous problem in the GP field. The objective is to find a computer program that is able to control an artificial ant so that it can find all 89 pieces of food located on a discontinuous trail within a specified number of time steps. The trail is drawn on a discrete 32×32 toroidal grid illustrated in Figure 1. The problem is known to be rather hard, at least for standard GP (see [29]), with many local and global optima, which may explain why the size of the TreeDE population was increased to $N = 30$ in [17].

Only a few actions are allowed to the ant. It can turn left, right, move one square forward and it may also look into the next square in the direction it is facing, in order to determine if

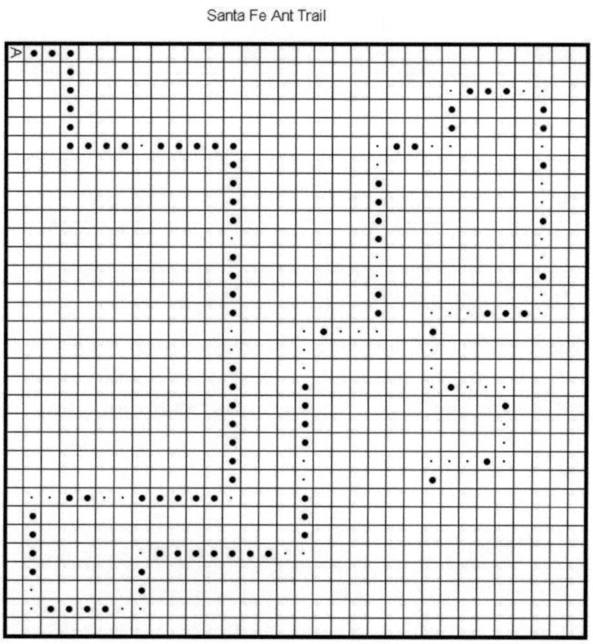

Figure 1. Illustration of the Santa Fe Trail (the ant starts in the upper left corner, heading to the east, large dots are food pellets, and small dots are empty cells on the ideal path).

it contains a piece of food or not. Turns and moves cost one time step, and a maximum time steps threshold is set at start (typical values are either 400 or 600 time steps). If the program finishes before the exhaustion of the time steps, it is restarted (which amounts to iterating the whole program).

We do not need mathematical operators nor registers, only the following instructions are available:

- `MOVE`: moves the ant forward one step (grid cell) in the direction the ant is facing, retrieving an eventual food pellet in the cell of arrival;
- `LEFT`: turns on place 45 degrees anti-clockwise;
- `RIGHT`: turns on place 45 degrees clockwise;
- `IF-FOOD-AHEAD`: conditional statement that executes the next instruction or group of instructions if a food pellet is located on the neighboring cell in front of the ant, else the next instruction or group is skipped;
- `PROGN2`: groups the two instructions that follow in the program vector, notably allowing `IF-FOOD-AHEAD` to perform several instructions if the condition is true (the `PROGN2` operator does not affect *per se* the ant position and direction);
- `PROGN3`: same as the previous operator, but groups the three following instructions.
- Each `MOVE`, `RIGHT` and `LEFT` instruction requires one time step.

	generational LDEP			steady state LDEP			standard GP		
# steps	Fit.	% hits	Eval.	Fit.	% hits	Eval.	Fit.	% hits	Eval.
400	11.55	12.5%	101008	14.65	7.5%	46320	8.87	37%	126100
600	0.3	82.5%	88483	1.275	70%	44260	1.175	87%	63300

	CMA-LEP			TreeDE		
# steps	Fit.	% hits	Eval.	Fit.	% hits	Eval.
400	37.45	0%	NA	17.3	3%	24450
600	27.05	0%	NA	1.14	66%	22530

The 1st column is the number of allowed time steps, then for each heuristic, over 40 independent runs, we give the average of the best fitness (taken from [17] for TreeDE), then the percentage of run reaching a hit solution (solution that found all 89 food pellets), then the average number of evaluations to produce the first hit solution (if ever produced or else NA if no run produced a hit solution).

Table 4. Santa Fe Trail artificial ant problem.

Programs are again vectors of floating point values. Each instruction is represented as a single value which is decoded in the same way as operators are in the regression problems, that is using Eq. 6. Instruction are decoded sequentially, and the virtual machine is refined to handle jumps over an instruction or group of instructions, so that it can deal with `IF-FOOD-AHEAD` instructions. Incomplete programs may be encountered, for example if a `PROGN2` is decoded for the last value of a program vector. In this case the incomplete instruction is simply dropped and we consider that the program has reached normal termination (and the program is iterated if there are remaining time steps).

The Santa Fe trail being composed of 89 pieces of food, the fitness function is the remaining food (89 minus the number of food pellets taken by the ant before it runs out of time). So, the lower the fitness, the better the program, a hit solution being a program with fitness 0, i.e. a program able to pick up all the food on the grid.

Results are summed-up in Table 4. Contrary to the regression experiment, the generational variant of LDEP is now better than the steady state. We think this behavior is explained by the hardness of the problem: more exploration is needed, and it pays no more to accelerate convergence.

GP gives the best results for 400 time steps, but it is LDEP that provides the best average fitness for 600 steps, at the cost of a greater number of evaluations, meaning LDEP is better at exploiting the available amount of computing time. LDEP is also better than TreeDE on both steps limits. For CMA-LEP, two values for $\sigma \in \{1, 10\}$ and two values for $\lambda \in \{10, 100\}$ were again tried, the best setting being $\sigma = 10$ and $\lambda = 100$ (whose results are reported here). CMA-LEP performed really poorly, and its first results were so bad that it motivated us to try this rather high initial variance level ($\sigma = 10$), which brought a sensible but insufficient improvement. We think that the lack of elitism is, here again, a probable cause of CMA-ES bad behavior, on a very chaotic fitness landscape with many neutral zones (many programs exhibit the same fitness).

```
If food{ Move } else {
  Progn3{
    Progn3{
      Progn3{ Right ;
        If food{ Right } else { Left } ;
        Progn2{ Left ;
          If food{ Progn2{ Move ; Move } }
              else { Right } } } ; // end Progn3
      Move ;
      Right } ; // end Progn3
    If food{ Move } else { Left } ; //end Progn3
  Move } }
```

Table 5. Example of a perfect solution for the Ant Problem found by LDEP in 400 time steps

Here again LDEP appears as a possible competitor to GP. Table 5 shows an example of a perfect solution found by LDEP for 400 time steps.

4.3. Evolving a stack

As the LDEP continuous approach for evolving programs achieved interesting results on the previous GP benchmarks, we decided to move forward and to test whether or not we were able to evolve a more complex data structure: a stack. Langdon successfully showed in [30] that GP was able to evolve not only a stack with its minimal set of operations (`push`, `pop`, `makenull`), but also two other optional operations (`top`, `empty`), which are considered to be inessential. We followed this setting, and the five operations to evolve are described in Table 6.

Operation	Comment
makenull	initialize stack
empty	is stack empty?
top	return top of stack
pop	return top of stack and remove it
push(x)	store x on top of stack

Table 6. The five operations to evolve

This is in our opinion a more complex problem than the previous ones, since the correctness of each trial solution is established using only the values returned by the stack operations and only `pop`, `top` and `empty` return values.

Choice of primitives

As explained in [30], the set of primitives that was chosen to solve this problem is a set that a human programmer might use. The set basically consists in functions that are able to read and write in an indexed memory, functions that can modify the stack pointer and functions that can perform simple arithmetic operations. The terminal set consists in zero-arity functions (stack pointer increment and decrement) and some constants.

The following set was available for LDEP:

- arg1, the value to be pushed on to the stack (read-only argument)
- aux, the current value of the stack pointer
- arithmetic operators + and −
- constants 0, 1 and MAX (maximum depth of the stack, set to 10)
- indexed memory functions read and write. The write function is a two argument function arg1 and arg2. It evaluates the two arguments and sets the indexed memory pointed by arg1 to arg2 (i.e. stack[arg1] = arg2). It returns the original value of aux.
- functions to modify the stack pointer: inc_aux to increment the stack pointer, dec_aux to decrement it, write_aux to set the stack pointer to its argument and returns the original value of aux.

Algorithm and fitness function

We used a slightly modified version of our continuous scheme as the stack problem requires the simultaneous evolution of the five operations (`push`, `pop`, `makenull`, `top`, `empty`). An individual is composed of 5 vectors, one for each operation. Mutation and crossover are only performed with vectors of the same type (i.e. vectors evolving the `push` operation for example).

Programs are coded in prefix notation, that means that an operation like `(arg1 + MAX)` was coded as `+ arg1 MAX`. We did not impose any restrictions on each program's size except that each vector has a maximum length of 100 (this is several times more than sufficient to code any of the five operations needed to manipulate the stack).

In his original work, Langdon chose to use a population of size 1,000 individuals with 101 generations. In the DE case, it is known from experience that using large populations is usually inadequate. So, we fixed a population of 10 individuals with 10,000 generations for LDEP, amounting to about the same number of evaluations.

We used the same fitness function that was defined by Langdon. It consists in 4 test sequences, each one being composed of 40 stack operations. As explained in the previous section, the `makenull` and `push` operations do not return any value, they can only be tested indirectly by seeing if the other operations perform correctly.

Results

In Langdon's experiments, 4 runs out of 60 produced successful individuals (i.e. a fully operational stack). We obtained the same success ratio with LDEP: 4 out of the first 60 runs yielded perfect solutions. Extending the number of runs, LDEP evolved 6 perfect solutions out of 100 runs, providing a convincing proof of feasibility. Regarding CMA-LEP, results are less convincing, since only one run out of 100 was able to successfully evolve a stack.

An example of successful solution is given in table 7 with the raw evolved code and a simplified version where redundant code is removed.

Operation	Evolved operation	Simplified operation
push	write(1 ,write(dec_aux ,arg1))	stack[aux] = arg1 aux = aux - 1

pop	write(aux ,((aux + (dec_aux + inc_aux)) + read(inc_aux)))	aux = aux + 1
		tmp = stack[aux];
		stack[aux] = tmp + aux;
		return tmp

top	read(aux)	return sp[aux]
empty	aux	if (aux > 0) return true else return false
makenull	write((MAX - (0 + write_aux(1))),MAX)	aux = 1

Table 7. Example of an evolved push-down stack

5. Conclusions

This chapter explores evolutionary continuous optimization engines applied to automatic programming. We work with Differential Evolution (LDEP) and CMA-Evolution Strategy (CMA-LEP), and we translate the continuous representation of individuals into linear imperative programs. Unlike the TreeDE heuristic, our schemes include the use of float constants (e.g. in symbolic regression problems).

Comparisons with GP confirm that LDEP is a promising optimization engine for automatic programming. In the most realistic case of regression problems, when using constants, steady state LDEP slightly outperforms standard GP on 5 over 6 problems. On the artificial ant problem, the leading heuristic depends on the number of steps: for the 400 steps version GP is the clear winner, while for 600 steps generational LDEP yields the best average fitness. LDEP improves on the TreeDE results for both versions of the ant problem, without needing a fine-tuning of the solutions tree-depth.

For both regression and artificial ant, CMA-LEP performs poorly with the same representation of solutions than LDEP. This can be deemed not really surprising since the problems we tackle are clearly outside the domain targeted by the CMA-ES heuristic that drives evolution. Nonetheless it is also the case for DE, which still produces interesting solutions, thus this points to a fundamental difference in behavior between these two heuristics. We suspect that CMA-ES lack of elitism may be an explanation. It also points to a possible inherent robustness of the DE method, on fitness landscapes that are possibly more chaotic than the usual continuous benchmarks.

The promising results of LDEP on the artificial ant and on the stack problems are a great incentive to deepen the exploration of this heuristic. Many interesting questions remain open. In the beginnings of GP, experiments showed that the probability of crossover had to be set differently for internal and terminal nodes: is it possible to improve LDEP in similar ways? It is to be noticed that in our experiments the individual vector components take their values in the range $(-\infty, +\infty)$, since it is required by the standard CMA-ES algorithm. It could be interesting to experiment DE-based algorithms with a reduced range of vector component values, for example $[-1.0, 1.0]$, that would require to modify the mapping of constant indices.

Author details

Cyril Fonlupt, Denis Robilliard, Virginie Marion-Poty
LISIC, ULCO, Univ Lille Nord de France, France

6. References

[1] John R. Koza, Martin A. Keane, Matthew J. Streeter, William Mydlowec, Jessen Yu, and Guido Lanza. *Genetic Programming IV Routine Human-Competitive Machine Intelligence*. Kluwer Academic Publishers, 2003.

[2] Sameer H. Al-Sakram, John R. Koza, and Lee W. Jones. Automated re-invention of a previously patented optical lens system using genetic programming. In *[31]*, pages 25–37, 2005.

[3] Kun-Hong Liu and Chun-Gui Xu. A genetic programming-based approach to the classification of multiclass microarray datasets. *Bioinformatics*, 25(3):331–337, 2009.

[4] Adrian Gepp and Phil Stocks. A review of procedures to evolve quantum algorithms. *Genetic Programming and Evolvable Machines*, 10(2):181–228, 2009.

[5] M. Szymanski, H. Worn, and J. Fischer. Investigating the effect of pruning on the diversity and fitness of robot controllers based on MDL2E during genetic programming. In *[33]*, pages 2780–2787, 2009.

[6] Markus Brameier and Wolfgang Banzhaf. *Linear Genetic Programming*. Genetic and Evolutionary Computation. Springer, 2007.

[7] H.A. Abbass, NX Hoai, and R.I. Mckay. AntTAG: A new method to compose computer programs using colonies of ants. In *The IEEE Congress on Evolutionary Computation*, pages 1654–1659, 2002.

[8] Y. Shan, H. Abbass, RI McKay, and D. Essam. AntTAG: a further study. In *Proceedings of the Sixth Australia-Japan Joint Workshop on Intelligent and Evolutionary Systems, Australian National University, Canberra, Australia*, volume 30, 2002.

[9] R. P. Salustowicz and J. Schmidhuber. Probabilistic incremental program evolution. *Evolutionary Computation*, 5(2):123–141, 1997.

[10] Evandro Nunes Regolin and Aurora Trindad Ramirez Pozo. Bayesian automatic programming. In *[31]*, pages 38–49, 2005.

[11] Rainer Storn and Kenneth Price. Differential evolution – a simple and efficient heuristic for global optimization over continuous spaces. *Journal of Global Optimization*, 11(4):341–359, 1997.

[12] Nikolaus Hansen and Andreas Ostermeier. Adapting arbitrary normal mutation distributions in evolution strategies: The covariance matrix adaptation. In *International Conference on Evolutionary Computation*, pages 312–317, 1996.

[13] Michael O'Neill and Anthony Brabazon. Grammatical differential evolution. In *International Conference on Artificial Intelligence (ICAI'06)*, pages 231–236, Las Vegas, Nevada, USA, 2006.

[14] Michael O'Neill and Conor Ryan. Grammatical evolution. *ieeetec*, 5(4):349–357, aug 2001.

[15] James E. Murphy, Michael O'Neill, and Hamish Carr. Exploring grammatical evolution for horse gait optimisation. In *[32]*, pages 183–194, 2009.

[16] Michael O'Neill and Conor Ryan. *Grammatical Evolution: Evolutionary Automatic Programming in an Arbitrary Language*. Kluwer Academic Press, 2003.

[17] Christian B. Veenhuis. Tree based differential evolution. In *[32]*, pages 208–219, 2009.

[18] Alberto Moraglio and Sara Silva. Geometric differential evolution on the space of genetic programs. In Anna Isabel Esparcia-Alcázar, Aniko Ekart, Sara Silva, Stephen Dignum, and A. Sima Uyar, editors, *Proceedings of the 13th European Conference on Genetic Programming, EuroGP 2010*, volume 6021 of *LNCS*, pages 171–183, Istanbul, 7-9 April 2010. Springer. Best paper.

[19] Shumeet Baluja and Rich Caruana. Removing the genetics from the standard genetic algorithm. In *Proceedings of the 12th International Conference on Machine Learning*, pages 38–46, Morgan Kaufmann Publishers, 1995.

[20] A. Auger and N. Hansen. A restart CMA evolution strategy with increasing population size. In *Evolutionary Computation, 2005. The 2005 IEEE Congress on*, volume 2, pages 1769 – 1776 Vol. 2, September 2005.

[21] K. Price. Differential evolution: a fast and simple numerical optimizer. In *Biennial conference of the North American Fuzzy Information Processing Society*, pages 524–527, 1996.

[22] S. Rahnamayan and P. Dieras. Efficiency competition on n-queen problem: DE vs. CMA-ES. In *Electrical and Computer Engineering, 2008. CCECE 2008. Canadian Conference on*, pages 000033 –000036, May 2008.

[23] Carmen G. Moles, Pedro Mendes, and Julio R. Banga. Parameter Estimation in Biochemical Pathways: A Comparison of Global Optimization Methods. *Genome Research*, 13(11):2467–2474, 2003.

[24] N. Hansen and S. Kern. Evaluating the CMA evolution strategy on multimodal test functions. In X. Yao et al., editors, *Parallel Problem Solving from Nature PPSN VIII*, volume 3242 of *LNCS*, pages 282–291. Springer, 2004.

[25] A. Auger and N. Hansen. A restart CMA evolution strategy with increasing population size. In *Evolutionary Computation, 2005. The 2005 IEEE Congress on*, volume 2, pages 1769 – 1776 Vol. 2, September 2005.

[26] Nikolaus Hansen and Stefan Kern. Evaluating the CMA evolution strategy on multimodal functions. In Springer-Verlag, editor, *Parallel Problem Solving from Nature, PPSN VIII*, volume 3242 of *lncs*, pages 282–291, 2004.

[27] Swagatam Das and Ponnuthurai Nagaratnam. Differential evolution: A survey of the state-of-the-art. *IEEE Transactions on Computers*, pages 4–31, feb 2011.

[28] Garnett Wilson and Wolfgang Banzhaf. A comparison of cartesian genetic programming and linear genetic programming. In Michael O'Neill, Leonardo Vanneschi, Steven Gustafson, Anna Esparcia Alcázar, Ivanoe De Falco, Antonio Della Cioppa, and Ernesto Tarantino, editors, *Genetic Programming*, volume 4971 of *Lecture Notes in Computer Science*, pages 182–193. Springer Berlin / Heidelberg, 2008.

[29] W. B. Langdon and R. Poli. Why ants are hard. Technical Report CSRP-98-4, University of Birmingham, School of Computer Science, January 1998. Presented at GP-98.

[30] William B. Langdon. *Genetic Programming and Data Structures = Automatic Programming !* Kluwer Academic Publishers, 1998.

[31] Maarten Keijzer, Andrea Tettamanzi, Pierre Collet, Jano van Hemert, and Marco Tomassini, editors. *8th European Conference, EuroGP 2005*, volume 3447 of *LNCS*, Lausanne, Switzerland, mar 2005.

[32] Leonardo Vanneschi, Steven Gustafson, Alberto Moraglio, Ivanoe De Falco, and Marc Ebner, editors. *12th European Conference, EuroGP 2009*, volume 5481 of *LNCS*, Tubingen, Germany, apr 2009.

[33] *Congress on Evolutionary Computation*, Trondheim, Norway, may 2009.

Chapter 3

Programming with Annotated Grammar Estimation

Yoshihiko Hasegawa

Additional information is available at the end of the chapter

http://dx.doi.org/10.5772/51662

1. Introduction

Evolutionary algorithms (EAs) mimic natural evolution to solve optimization problems. Because EAs do not require detailed assumptions, they can be applied to many real-world problems. In EAs, solution candidates are evolved using genetic operators such as crossover and mutation which are analogs to natural evolution. In recent years, EAs have been considered from the viewpoint of distribution estimation, with estimation of distribution algorithms (EDAs) attracting much attention ([14]). Although genetic operators in EAs are inspired by natural evolution, EAs can also be considered as algorithms that sample solution candidates from distributions of promising solutions. Since these distributions are generally unknown, approximation schemes are applied to perform the sampling. Genetic algorithms (GAs) and genetic programmings (GPs) approximate the sampling by randomly changing the promising solutions via genetic operators (mutation and crossover). In contrast, EDAs assume that the distributions of promising solutions can be expressed by parametric models, and they perform model learning and sampling from the learnt models repeatedly. Although GA-type sampling (mutation or crossover) is easy to perform, it has the disadvantage that GA-type sampling is valid only for the case where two structurally similar individuals have similar fitness values (e.g. the one-max problem). GA and GP have shown poor search performance in deceptive problems ([6]) where the condition above is not satisfied. However, EDAs have been reported to show much better search performance for some problems that GA and GP do not handle well. As in GAs, EDAs usually employ fixed length linear arrays to represent solution candidates (these EDAs are referred to as GA-EDAs in the present chapter). This decade, EDAs have been extended so as to handle programs and functions having tree structures (we refer to these as GP-EDAs in the present chapter). Since tree structures have different node number, the model learning is much more difficult than that of GA-EDAs. From the viewpoint of modeling types, GP-EDAs can be broadly classified into two groups: probabilistic proto-type tree (PPT) based methods and probabilistic context-free grammar (PCFG) based methods. PPT-based methods employ techniques devised in GA-EDAs by transforming variable length tree structures into fixed length linear arrays. PCFG-based methods employ

PCFG to model tree structures. PCFG-based methods are more advantageous than PPT-based methods in the sense that PCFG-based methods can estimate position-independent building blocks.

The conventional PCFG adopts the context freedom assumption that the probabilities of production rules do not depend on their contexts, namely parent or sibling nodes. Although the context freedom assumption makes parameter estimation easier, it cannot in principle consider interaction among nodes. In general, programs and functions have dependencies among nodes, and as a consequence, the conventional PCFG is not suitable as a baseline model of GP-EDAs. In the field of natural language processing (NLP), many approaches have been proposed in order to weaken the content freedom assumption of PCFG. For instance, the vertical Markovization annotates symbols with their ancestor symbols and has been adopted as a baseline grammar of vectorial stochastic grammar based GP (vectorial SG-GP) or grammar transformation in an EDA (GT-EDA) ([4]) (see Section 2). Matsuzaki *et al.* ([17]) proposed the PCFG with latent annotations (PCFG-LA), which assumes that all annotations are latent and the annotations are estimated from learning data. Because the latent annotation models are much richer than fixed annotation models, it is expected that GP-EDAs using PCFG-LA may more precisely grasp the interactions among nodes than other fixed annotation based GP-EDAs. In GA-EDAs, EDAs with Bayesian networks or Markov networks exhibited better search performance than simpler models such as a univariate model. In a similar way, it is generally expected that GP-EDAs using PCFG-LA are more powerful than GP-EDAs with PCFG with heuristics-based annotations because the model flexibility of PCFG-LA is much richer. We have proposed a GP-EDA named programming with annotated grammar estimation (PAGE) which adopts PCFG-LA as a baseline grammar ([9, 12]). In Section 4 of the present chapter, we explain the details of PAGE, including the parameter update formula.

As explained above, EDAs model promising solutions with parametric distributions. For the case in multimodal problems, it is not sufficient to express promising solutions with only one model, because dependencies for each optimal solution are different in general. When considering tree structures, this problem arises even in unimodal optimization problems due to diversity of tree expression. These problems can be tackled by considering global contexts in each individual, which represents which optima (e.g. multiple solutions in multimodal problems) it derives from. Consequently, we have proposed the PCFG-LA mixture model (PCFG-LAMM) which extends PCFG-LA into a mixture model, and have also proposed a new GP-EDA named unsupervised PAGE (UPAGE) which employs PCFG-LAMM as a baseline grammar ([11]). By using PCFG-LAMM, not only local dependencies but also global contexts behind individuals can be taken into account.

The main objectives of proposed algorithms may be summarized as follows:

1. PAGE employs PCFG-LA to consider local dependencies among nodes.
2. UPAGE employs PCFG-LAMM to take into account global contexts behind individuals in addition to the local dependencies.

This chapter is structured as follows: Following a section on related work, we briefly introduce the basics of PCFG. We explain PAGE in Section. 4, where details of PCFG-LA, forward–backward probabilities and a parameter update formula are provided. In Section 5, we propose UPAGE, which is a mixture model extension of PAGE. We describe PCFG-LAMM and also derive a parameter update formula for UPAGE. We compare the performance of

UPAGE and PAGE using three benchmark tests selected for experiments. We discuss the results obtained in these experiments in Section 6. Finally, we conclude the present chapter in Section 7.

2. Related work

Many GP-EDAs have been proposed, and these methods can be broadly classified into two groups: (i) PPT based methods and (ii) grammar model based methods.

Methods of type (i) employ techniques developed in GA-EDAs. This type of algorithm converts tree structures into the fixed-length chromosomes used in GA and applies probabilistic models of GA-EDAs. Probabilistic incremental program evolution (PIPE) ([25]) is a univariate model, which can be considered to be a combination of population-based incremental learning (PBIL) ([3]) and GP. Because tree structures have explicit edges between parent and children nodes, estimation of distribution programming (EDP) ([37, 38]) considers the parent–children relationships in the tree structures. Extended compact GP (ECGP) ([26]) is an extension of the extended compact GA (ECGA) ([7]) to GP and ECGP can take into account the interactions among nodes. ECGP infers the group of marginal distribution using the minimum description length (MDL) principle. BOA programming (BOAP) ([15]) uses Bayesian networks for grasping dependencies among nodes and is a GP extension of the Bayesian optimization algorithm (BOA) ([20]). Program optimization with linkage estimation (POLE) ([8, 10]) estimates the interactions among nodes by estimating the Bayesian network. POLE uses a special chromosome called an *expanded parse tree* ([36]) to convert GP programs into linear arrays, and several extended algorithms of POLE have been proposed ([27, 39]). Meta-optimizing semantic evolutionary search (MOSES) ([16]) extends the hierarchical Bayesian optimization algorithm (hBOA) ([19]) to program evolution.

Methods of type (ii) are based on Whigham's grammar-guided genetic programming (GGGP) ([33]). GGGP expresses individuals using derivation trees (see Section 3), which is in contrast with the conventional GP. Whigham indicated the connection between PCFG and GP ([35]), and actually, the probability table learning in GGGP can be viewed as an EDA with local search. Stochastic grammar based GP (SG-GP) ([23]) applied the concept of PBIL to GGGP. The authors of SG-GP also proposed vectorial SG-GP, which considers depth in its grammar (simple SG-GP is then called scalar SG-GP). Program evolution with explicit learning (PEEL) ([28]) takes into account the positions (arguments) and depths of symbols. Unlike SG-GP and PEEL, which employ predefined grammars, grammar model based program evolution (GMPE) ([29]) learns not only parameters but also the grammar itself from promising solutions. GMPE starts from specialized production rules which exclusively generate learning data and merges non-terminals to yield more general production rules using the MDL principle. Grammar transformation in an EDA (GT-EDA) ([4]) extracts good subroutines using the MDL principle. GT-EDA starts from general rules and expands non-terminals to yield more specialized production rules. Although the concept of GT-EDA is similar to that of GMPE, the learning procedure is opposite to GMPE [specialized to general (GMPE) versus general to specialized (GT-EDA)]. Tanev proposed GP based on a probabilistic context sensitive grammar ([31, 32]). He used sibling nodes and a parent node as context information, and production rule probabilities are expressed by conditional probabilities of these context information. Bayesian automatic programming (BAP) ([24]) uses a Bayesian network to consider relations among production rules in PCFG.

There are other GP-EDAs not belonging to either of the groups presented above. N-gram GP ([21]) is based on the linear GP ([18]), which is the assembly language of a register-based CPU, and learns the sub-sequences using an N-gram model. The N-gram model is very popular in NLP which considers N consecutive sub-sequences for calculating the probabilities of symbols. AntTAG ([1]) also shares similar concepts with GP-EDAs, although AntTAG does not employ a statistical inference method for probability learning; instead, AntTAG employs the ant colony optimization method (ACO), where the pheromone matrix in ACO can be interpreted as a probability distribution.

3. Basics of PCFG

In this section, we explain basic concepts of PCFG.

The context-free grammar (CFG) G is defined by four variables $G = \{\mathcal{N}, \mathcal{T}, \mathcal{R}, \mathcal{B}\}$, where the meanings of these variables are listed below.

- $\mathcal{N}$: Finite set of non-terminal symbols
- $\mathcal{T}$: Finite set of terminal symbols
- $\mathcal{R}$: Finite set of production rules
- $\mathcal{B}$: Start symbol

It is important to note that the terms "non-terminal" and "terminal" in CFG are different from those in GP (for example in symbolic regression problems, not only variables x, y but also $\sin, +$ are treated as terminals in CFG). In CFG, sentences are generated by applying production rules to non-terminal symbols, which are generally given by

$$A \to \alpha \quad (A \in \mathcal{N}, \alpha \in (\mathcal{N} \cup \mathcal{T})^*). \tag{1}$$

In Equation 1, $(\mathcal{N} \cup \mathcal{T})^*$ represents a set of possible elements composed of $(\mathcal{N} \cup \mathcal{T})$. By applying production rules to the start symbol $\mathcal{B}$, grammar G generates sentences. A language generated by grammar G is represented by $L(G)$. If $W \in L(G)$, then $W \in \mathcal{T}^*$.

By applying production rules, non-terminal A is replaced by another symbol. For instance, application of the production rule represented by Equation 1 to $\alpha_1 A \alpha_2 (\alpha_1, \alpha_2 \in (\mathcal{N} \cup \mathcal{T})^*, A \in \mathcal{N})$ yields $\alpha_1 \alpha \alpha_2$. In this case, it is said that "$\alpha_1 A \alpha_2$ derived $\alpha_1 \alpha \alpha_2$", and this process is represented as follows:

$$\alpha_1 A \alpha_2 \underset{G}{\Rightarrow} \alpha_1 \alpha \alpha_2.$$

Furthermore, if we have the following consecutive applications

$$\alpha_1 \underset{G}{\Rightarrow} \alpha_2 \cdots \underset{G}{\Rightarrow} \alpha_n (\alpha_i \in (\mathcal{N} \cup \mathcal{T})^*),$$

α_n is derived from α_1 and is described by $\alpha_1 \overset{*}{\underset{G}{\Rightarrow}} \alpha_n$. This derivation process can be represented by a tree structure, which is known as a *derivation tree*. Derivation trees of grammar G are defined as follows.

1. Node is an element of $(\mathcal{N} \cup \mathcal{T})$
2. Root is $\mathcal{B}$

3. Branch node is an element of $\mathcal{N}$
4. If children of $A \in \mathcal{N}$ are $\alpha_1\alpha_2 \cdots \alpha_k$ ($\alpha_i \in (\mathcal{N} \cup \mathcal{T})$) from left, production rule $A \to \alpha_1\alpha_2 \cdots \alpha_k$ is an element of $\mathcal{R}$

We next explain CFG with an example. We now consider a univariate function $f(x)$ composed of sin, cos, exp, log and arithmetic operators ($+$, $-$, $\times$ and $\div$). A grammar G_{reg} can be

$$\mathcal{B} = \{\langle expr \rangle\},$$
$$\mathcal{N} = \{\langle expr \rangle, \langle op2 \rangle, \langle op1 \rangle, \langle var \rangle, \langle const \rangle\},$$
$$\mathcal{T} = \{+, -, \times, \div, \sin, \cos, \exp, \log, x, C\}.$$

We define the following production rules.

#	Production rule
0	$\langle expr \rangle \to \langle op2 \rangle \; \langle expr \rangle \; \langle expr \rangle$
1	$\langle expr \rangle \to \langle op1 \rangle \; \langle expr \rangle$
2	$\langle expr \rangle \to \langle var \rangle$
3	$\langle expr \rangle \to \langle const \rangle$
4	$\langle op2 \rangle \to +$
5	$\langle op2 \rangle \to -$
6	$\langle op2 \rangle \to \times$
7	$\langle op2 \rangle \to \div$
8	$\langle op1 \rangle \to \sin$
9	$\langle op1 \rangle \to \cos$
10	$\langle op1 \rangle \to \exp$
11	$\langle op1 \rangle \to \log$
12	$\langle var \rangle \to x$
13	$\langle const \rangle \to C$ (constant)

G_{reg} derives univariate functions by applying the production rules. Suppose we have the following derivation:

$$\begin{aligned}
\langle expr \rangle &\to \langle op2 \rangle \; \langle expr \rangle \; \langle expr \rangle \\
&\to + \langle expr \rangle \; \langle expr \rangle \\
&\to + \langle op2 \rangle \; \langle expr \rangle \; \langle expr \rangle \; \langle expr \rangle \\
&\to + + \langle expr \rangle \; \langle expr \rangle \; \langle expr \rangle \\
&\to + + \langle op1 \rangle \; \langle expr \rangle \; \langle expr \rangle \; \langle expr \rangle \\
&\to + + \log \langle expr \rangle \; \langle expr \rangle \; \langle expr \rangle \\
&\to + + \log \langle var \rangle \; \langle expr \rangle \; \langle expr \rangle \\
&\to + + \log x \; \langle expr \rangle \; \langle expr \rangle \\
&\to + + \log x \; \langle var \rangle \; \langle expr \rangle \\
&\to + + \log x \, x \; \langle expr \rangle \\
&\to + + \log x \, x \; \langle const \rangle \\
&\to + + \log x \, x \, C.
\end{aligned}$$

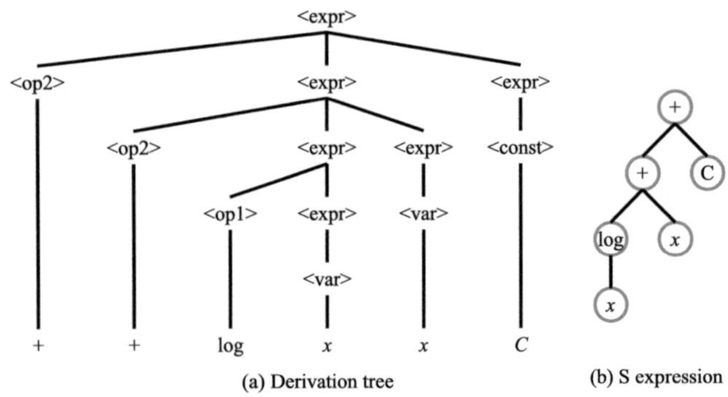

Figure 1. (a) Derivation tree for $\log x + x + C$ and (b) its corresponding S-expression in GP.

In this case, the derived function is

$$f(x) = \log x + x + C,$$

and its derivation process is represented by the derivation tree in Figure 1(a).

Although functions and programs are represented with standard tree representations (S-expression) in the conventional GP (Figure 1(b)), derivation trees can express the same functions and programs. Consequently, derivation trees can be used in program evolution, and GGGP ([33, 34]) adopted derivation trees for its chromosome.

We next proceed to PCFG, which extends CFG by adding probabilities to each production rule. For example, the likelihood (probability) of the derivation tree in Fig. 1(a) is

$$\begin{aligned} P(W,T) &= \pi(\langle expr \rangle)\beta(\langle expr \rangle \to \langle op2 \rangle \langle expr \rangle \langle expr \rangle)^2 \beta(\langle op2 \rangle \to +)^2 \\ &\times \beta(\langle expr \rangle \to \langle op1 \rangle \langle expr \rangle)\beta(\langle op1 \rangle \to \log) \\ &\times \beta(\langle expr \rangle \to \langle const \rangle)\beta(\langle expr \rangle \to \langle var \rangle)^2 \beta(\langle const \rangle \to C)\beta(\langle var \rangle \to x)^2, \end{aligned}$$

where $W \in \mathcal{T}^*$ is a sentence (i.e. W corresponds to $\log x + x + C$ in G_{reg}), T is a derivation tree, $\pi(\langle expr \rangle)$ is the probability of $\langle expr \rangle$ and $\beta(A \to \alpha)$ is the probability of a production rule $A \to \alpha$. Furthermore, the probability $P(W)$ of sentence W is given by calculating the marginal probability in terms of $T \in \Phi(W)$:

$$P(W) = \sum_{T \in \Phi(W)} P(W,T), \qquad (2)$$

where $\Phi(W)$ is the set of all possible derivation trees which derive W. In NLP, inference of the production rule parameters $\beta(A \to \alpha)$ is carried out with learning data $\mathbf{W} = \{W_1, W_2, \cdots\}$, which is a set of sentences. The learning data does not have information about derivation processes. Because there are many possible derivations $\Phi(W)$ for large sentences, directly calculating $P(W)$ with marginalization in terms of $\Phi(W)$ (Equation 2) is computationally intractable. Consequently, a computationally efficient method called the *inside–outside algorithm* is used to estimate the parameters. The inside–outside algorithm takes advantage of dynamic programming to reduce the computational cost. However, in contrast to the case of NLP, the derivation trees are observed in GP-EDAs, and the parameter estimation of production rules in GP-EDAs with PCFG is very easy. However, when using

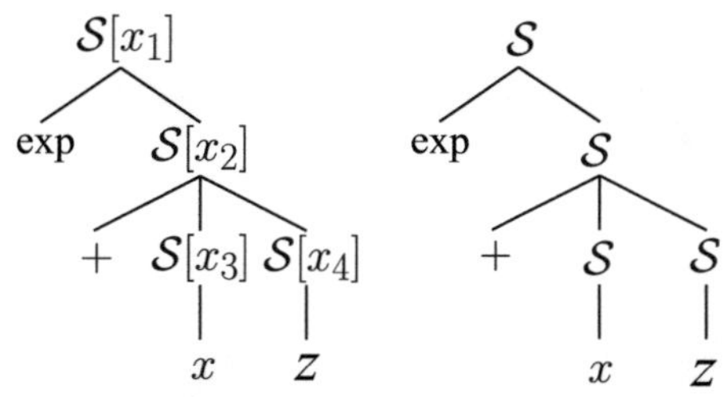

(a) Complete tree (b) Observed tree

Figure 2. (a) Complete tree with annotations and (b) its observed tree.

more complicated grammars such as PCFG-LA, more advanced estimation methods (i.e. the expectation maximization (EM) algorithm ([5])) have to be used even when derivation trees are given.

4. PAGE

Our proposed algorithm PAGE is based on PCFG-LA. In PCFG-LA, latent annotations are estimated from promising solutions using the EM algorithm, and PCFG-LA takes advantage of forward–backward probabilities for computationally efficient estimation. In this section, we describe the details of PCFG-LA, forward-backward probabilities and a parameter update formula derived from the EM algorithm.

4.1. PCFG-LA

Although the PCFG-LA used in PAGE has been developed specifically for the present application, it is essentially identical to the conventional PCFG-LA. In this section, we describe the specialized version of PCFG-LA. For further details on PCFG-LA, the reader may refer to Ref. ([17]).

PCFG-LA assumes that every non-terminal is labeled with annotations. In the complete form, non-terminals are represented by $A[x]$, where A is the non-terminal symbol, $x(\in H)$ is an annotation (which is latent), and H is a set of annotations (in this paper, we take $H = \{0, 1, 2, 3, \cdots, h-1\}$, where h is the annotation size). Fig. 2 shows an example of a tree with annotations (a), and the corresponding observed tree (b). The likelihood of an annotated tree (complete data) is given by

$$P(T_i, X_i; \boldsymbol{\beta}, \boldsymbol{\pi}) = \prod_{x \in H} \pi(\mathcal{S}[x])^{\delta(x;T_i,X_i)} \prod_{r \in \mathcal{R}[H]} \beta(r)^{c(r;T_i,X_i)}, \tag{3}$$

where T_i denotes the ith derivation tree; X_i is the set of latent annotations of T_i represented by $X_i = \{x_i^1, x_i^2, \cdots\}$ (x_i^j is the jth annotation of T_i); $\pi(\mathcal{S}[x])$ is the probability of $\mathcal{S}[x]$ at the root position; $\beta(r)$ is the probability of the annotated production rule $r \in \mathcal{R}[H]$; $\delta(x; T_i, X_i)$ is 1 if the annotation at the root node is x in the complete tree T_i, X_i and is 0 otherwise; $c(\mathcal{S}[x] \to \alpha; T_i, X_i)$ is the number of occurrences of rule $\mathcal{S}[x] \to \alpha$ in the complete tree T_i, X_i; h is the annotation size that is specified in advance as a parameter; $\boldsymbol{\beta} = \{\beta(\mathcal{S}[x] \to \alpha) | \mathcal{S}[x] \to \alpha \in \mathcal{R}[H]\}$; and $\boldsymbol{\pi} = \{\pi(\mathcal{S}[x]) | x \in H\}$. The set of annotated rules $\mathcal{R}[H]$ is given in Equation 8. We summarized variables in Appendix B.

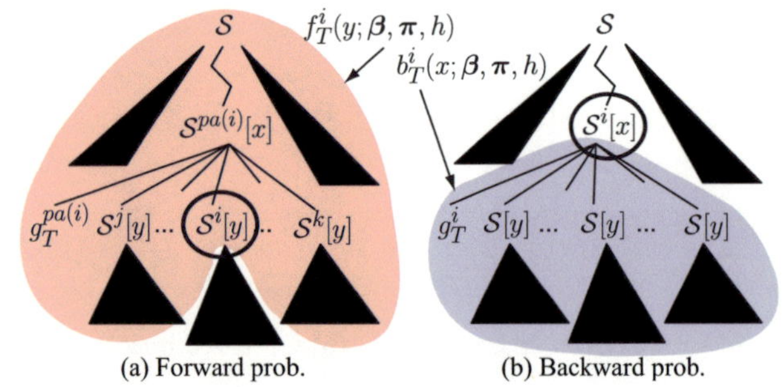

Figure 3. (a) Forward and (b) backward probabilities. The superscripts denote the indices of non-terminals (i in $\mathcal{S}^i[y]$, for example).

The likelihood of an observed tree can be calculated by summing over annotations:

$$P(T_i;\boldsymbol{\beta},\boldsymbol{\pi}) = \sum_{X_i} P(T_i, X_i;\boldsymbol{\beta},\boldsymbol{\pi}). \tag{4}$$

PCFG-LA estimates $\boldsymbol{\beta}$ and $\boldsymbol{\pi}$ using the EM algorithm. Before explaining the estimation procedure, we should note the form of production rules. In PAGE, production rules are not Chomsky normal form (CNF), as is assumed in the original PCFG-LA, because of the understandability of GP programs. Any function which can be handled with traditional GP can be represented by

$$\mathcal{S} \to g\,\mathcal{S}\,...\mathcal{S}, \tag{5}$$

which is a subset of Greibach normal form (GNF). Here $\mathcal{S} \in \mathcal{N}$ and $g \in \mathcal{T}$ ($\mathcal{N}$ and $\mathcal{T}$ are the sets of non-terminal and terminal symbols in CFG; see Section 3). A terminal symbol g in CFG is a function node ($+, -,$ $\sin, \cos \in \mathfrak{F}$) or a terminal ($v, w \in \mathfrak{T}$) in GP ($\mathfrak{F}$ and $\mathfrak{T}$ denote set of GP functions and terminals, respectively). Annotated production rules are

$$\mathcal{S}[x] \to g\,\mathcal{S}[z_1]\,...\mathcal{S}[z_{a_{\max}}], \tag{6}$$

where $x, z_m \in H$ and $a_{\max}$ is the arity of g in GP. If g has $a_{\max}$ arity, the number of parameters for the production rule $\mathcal{S} \to g\,\mathcal{S}...\mathcal{S}$ with annotations is $h^{a_{\max}+1}$, which increases exponentially as the arity number increases. In order to reduce the number of parameters, we assume that all the right-hand side non-terminal symbols have the same annotation, that is

$$\mathcal{S}[x] \to g\,\mathcal{S}[y]\,\mathcal{S}[y]...\mathcal{S}[y]. \tag{7}$$

With this assumption, the number of parameters can be reduced to h^2, which is tractable. Let $\mathcal{R}[H]$ be the set of annotated rules expressed by Equation 8. $\mathcal{R}[H]$ is defined by

$$\mathcal{R}[H] = \{\mathcal{S}[x] \to g\,\mathcal{S}[y]\,\mathcal{S}[y]...\mathcal{S}[y] | x, y, \in H, g \in \mathcal{T}\}. \tag{8}$$

4.2. Forward–backward probability

We explain forward and backward probabilities for PCFG-LA in this section. PCFG-LA ([17]) adopted forward and backward probabilities to apply the EM algorithm ([5]). The backward probability $b_T^i(x;\boldsymbol{\beta},\boldsymbol{\pi})$ represents the probability that the tree beneath the ith non-terminal $\mathcal{S}[x]$ is generated ($\boldsymbol{\beta}$ and $\boldsymbol{\pi}$ are parameters, Fig. 3 (b)), and the forward probability $f_T^i(y;\boldsymbol{\beta},\boldsymbol{\pi})$

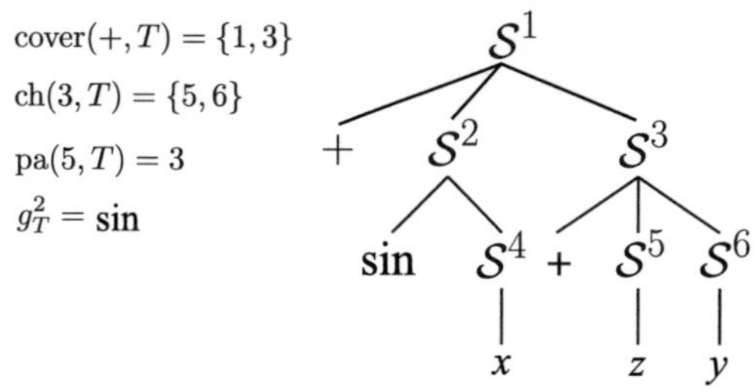

Figure 4. Example of a derivation tree and values of the specific functions. The superscripts denote the indices of non-terminals.

represents the probability that the tree above the ith non-terminal $\mathcal{S}[y]$ is generated (Fig. 3 (a)). Forward and backward probabilities can be recursively calculated as follows:

$$b_T^i(x;\boldsymbol{\beta},\boldsymbol{\pi}) = \sum_{y\in H} \beta(\mathcal{S}[x] \to g_T^i\, \mathcal{S}[y]...\mathcal{S}[y]) \prod_{j\in \mathrm{ch}(i,T)} b_T^j(y;\boldsymbol{\beta},\boldsymbol{\pi}), \tag{9}$$

$$f_T^i(y;\boldsymbol{\beta},\boldsymbol{\pi}) = \sum_{x\in H} f_T^{\mathrm{pa}(i,T)}(x;\boldsymbol{\beta},\boldsymbol{\pi})\beta(\mathcal{S}[x] \to g_T^{\mathrm{pa}(i,T)}\, \mathcal{S}[y]...\mathcal{S}[y]) \times \prod_{j\in \mathrm{ch}(\mathrm{pa}(i,T),T), j\neq i} b_T^j(y;\boldsymbol{\beta},\boldsymbol{\pi}) \quad (i \neq 1), \tag{10}$$

$$f_T^i(y;\boldsymbol{\beta},\boldsymbol{\pi}) = \pi(\mathcal{S}[y]) \quad (i = 1), \tag{11}$$

where $\mathrm{ch}(i,T)$ is a function that returns the set of non-terminal children indices of the ith non-terminal in T, $\mathrm{pa}(i,T)$ returns the parent index of the ith non-terminal in T, and g_T^i is a terminal symbol in CFG and is connected to the ith non-terminal symbol in T. For example, for the tree shown in Fig. 4, $\mathrm{ch}(3,T) = \{5,6\}$, $\mathrm{pa}(5,T) = 3$, and $g_T^2 = \mathrm{sin}$.

Using the forward–backward probabilities, $P(T;\boldsymbol{\beta},\boldsymbol{\pi})$ can be expressed by the following two equations:

$$P(T;\boldsymbol{\beta},\boldsymbol{\pi}) = \sum_{x\in H} \pi(\mathcal{S}[x]) b_T^1(x;\boldsymbol{\beta},\boldsymbol{\pi}), \tag{12}$$

$$P(T;\boldsymbol{\beta},\boldsymbol{\pi}) = \sum_{x,y\in H} \Big\{\beta(\mathcal{S}[x] \to g\, \mathcal{S}[y]...\mathcal{S}[y]) f_T^i(x;\boldsymbol{\beta},\boldsymbol{\pi}) \times \prod_{j\in \mathrm{ch}(i,T)} b_T^j(y;\boldsymbol{\beta},\boldsymbol{\pi})\Big\}. \quad (i \in \mathrm{cover}(g,T)) \tag{13}$$

Here, $\mathrm{cover}(g,T_i)$ represents a function that returns a set of non-terminal indices at which the production rule generating g without annotations is rooted in T_i. For example, if $g = +$ and T is the tree represented in Fig. 4, then $\mathrm{cover}(+,T) = \{1,3\}$.

4.3. Parameter update formula

We describe the parameter estimation in PCFG-LA. Because PCFG-LA contains latent variables X, the parameter estimation is carried out with the EM algorithm. Let $\boldsymbol{\beta}$ and $\boldsymbol{\pi}$

be current parameters $\overline{\boldsymbol{\beta}}$ and $\overline{\boldsymbol{\pi}}$ be nextstep parameters. The $\mathcal{Q}$ function to optimize in the EM algorithm can be expressed as follows:

$$\mathcal{Q}(\overline{\boldsymbol{\beta}},\overline{\boldsymbol{\pi}}|\boldsymbol{\beta},\boldsymbol{\pi}) = \sum_{i=1}^{N}\sum_{X_i} P(X_i|T_i;\boldsymbol{\beta},\boldsymbol{\pi}) \log P(T_i, X_i;\overline{\boldsymbol{\beta}},\overline{\boldsymbol{\pi}}), \tag{14}$$

where N is the number of learning data (promising solutions in EDA). A set of learning data is represented by $\mathcal{D} \equiv \{T_1, T_2, \cdots, T_N\}$. Using the forward–backward probabilities and maximizing $\mathcal{Q}(\overline{\boldsymbol{\beta}},\overline{\boldsymbol{\pi}}|\boldsymbol{\beta},\boldsymbol{\pi})$ under constraints $\sum_{\alpha}\beta(\mathcal{S}[x] \to \alpha) = 1$ and $\sum_{x}\pi(\mathcal{S}[x]) = 1$, we obtain the following update formula:

$$\overline{\pi}(\mathcal{S}[x]) \propto \pi(\mathcal{S}[x]) \sum_{i=1}^{N} \frac{b^1_{T_i}(x;\boldsymbol{\beta},\boldsymbol{\pi})}{P(T_i;\boldsymbol{\beta},\boldsymbol{\pi})}, \tag{15}$$

$$\begin{aligned}&\overline{\beta}(\mathcal{S}[x] \to g\,\mathcal{S}[y]...\mathcal{S}[y]) \propto \beta(\mathcal{S}[x] \to g\,\mathcal{S}[y]...\mathcal{S}[y]) \\ &\times \sum_{i=1}^{N}\left[\frac{1}{P(T_i;\boldsymbol{\beta},\boldsymbol{\pi})}\sum_{j\in\mathrm{cover}(g,T_i)}\left\{f^j_{T_i}(x;\boldsymbol{\beta},\boldsymbol{\pi})\prod_{k\in\mathrm{ch}(j,T_i)} b^k_{T_i}(y;\boldsymbol{\beta},\boldsymbol{\pi})\right\}\right].\end{aligned} \tag{16}$$

The EM algorithm maximizes the log-likelihood given by

$$\mathcal{L}(\boldsymbol{\beta},\boldsymbol{\pi};\mathcal{D}) = \sum_{i=1}^{N} \log P(T_i;\boldsymbol{\beta},\boldsymbol{\pi}). \tag{17}$$

By iteratively performing Equations 15–16, the log-likelihood monotonically increases and we obtain locally maximum likelihood estimation parameters. For the case of the EM algorithm, the annotation size h has to be given in advance. Because the EM algorithm is a point estimation method, this algorithm cannot estimate the optimum annotation size. For the case of models that do not include latent variables, a model selection method such as Akaike information criteria (AIC) or Bayesian information criteria (BIC) is often used. However, these methods take advantage of the asymptotic normality of estimators, which is not satisfied in models that include latent variables. In Ref. ([12]), we derived variational Bayesian (VB) ([2]) based inference for PCFG-LA, which can estimate the optimal annotation size. Because the derivation of the VB-based algorithm is much more complicated than that of the EM algorithm and because such explanation is outside the scope of this chapter, we do not explain the details of the VB-based algorithm. For details of VB-based PAGE, please read Ref. ([12]).

The procedures of PAGE are listed below.

1. Generate initial population
   Initial population $\mathcal{P}_0$ is generated by randomly creating M individuals.
2. Select promising solutions
   N individuals $\mathcal{D}_g$ are selected from a population of gth generation $\mathcal{P}_g$. In our implementation, we use the truncation selection.
3. Parameter estimation
   Using a parameter update formula (Equations 15–16), converged parameters $(\boldsymbol{\beta}_*, \boldsymbol{\pi}_*)$ are estimated with learning data $\mathcal{D}_g$.

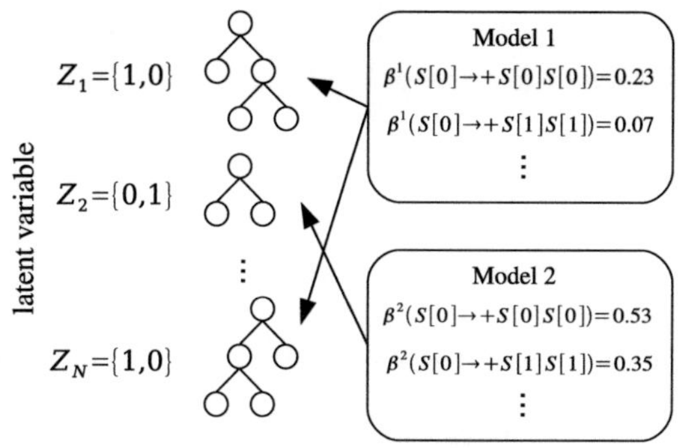

Figure 5. Illustrative description of PCFG-LAMM used in UPAGE.

4. Generation of new individuals
   EDA generates new individuals by sampling from the predictive posterior distributions, namely
   $$P(T, X|\mathcal{D}_g) = P(T, X; \boldsymbol{\beta}_*, \boldsymbol{\pi}_*).$$
   Since the EM algorithm is a point estimation method, new individuals can be generated with probabilistic logic sampling which is computationally efficient. The details of the sampling procedures are summarized below (note, when at the maximum depth limitation, select terminal nodes unconditionally).
   (a) A root node is selected following probability distribution $\boldsymbol{\pi}_* = \{\pi_*(\mathcal{S}[x])|x \in H\}$.
   (b) If there are non-terminal symbols $\mathcal{S}[x]$ $(x \in H)$ in a derivation tree, select a production rule according to the probability distribution
   $$\beta_*(\mathcal{S}[x]) = \{\beta_*(\mathcal{S}[x] \to \alpha)|\mathcal{S}[x] \to \alpha \in \mathcal{R}[H]\}.$$
   Repeat (b) until there are no non-terminal symbols left in the derivation tree.

5. Unsupervised PAGE

In this section, we introduce UPAGE ([11]) which is a mixture model extension of PAGE. UPAGE uses PCFG-LAMM as a baseline grammar, and we explain details of PCFG-LAMM and a parameter update formula in this section.

5.1. PCFG-LAMM

Although PCFG-LA is suitable for estimating local dependencies among nodes, it cannot consider global contexts behind individuals. Suppose there are two optimal solutions represented by $F_1(x)$ and $F_2(x)$. In this case, a population includes solution candidates for $F_1(x)$ and $F_2(x)$ at the same time. Since building blocks for two optimal solutions are different, model and parameter learning with one model results in slow convergence due to the mixed learning data. Furthermore in GP, there are multiple optimal structures even if the problems to be solved are not multimodal. For instance, if an optimum includes a substructure represented by $\sin(2x)$, $\sin(2x)$ as well as $2\sin(x)\cos(x)$ which are mathematically equivalent can be building blocks, where their tree representations are different. When modeling such a mixed population, it is very difficult for PCFG-LA to estimate these multiple structures separately as in the multimodal case. We have proposed a PCFG-LAMM which is a mixture model extension of PCFG-LA and have also proposed UPAGE based on PCFG-LAMM.

PCFG-LAMM assumes that the probability distributions are a mixture of more than two PCFG-LA models. In PCFG-LAMM, each solution is considered to be sampled from either of the PCFG-LA models (Figure 5). We introduce a latent variable z_i^k, where z_i^k is 1 when the ith derivation tree is generated from the kth model and 0 otherwise ($Z_i = \{z_i^1, z_i^2, \cdots, z_i^\mu\}$). We summarized variables in Appendix B. As a consequence, PCFG-LAMM handles X_i and Z_i as latent variables. The likelihood of complete data is given by

$$\begin{aligned} P(T_i, X_i, Z_i; \boldsymbol{\beta}, \boldsymbol{\pi}, \boldsymbol{\zeta}) &= \prod_{k=1}^{\mu} \left\{ \zeta^k P(T_i, X_i; \boldsymbol{\beta}^k, \boldsymbol{\pi}^k) \right\}^{z_i^k} \\ &= \prod_{k=1}^{\mu} \left\{ \zeta^k \prod_{x \in H} \pi^k(\mathcal{S}[x])^{\delta(x;T_i,X_i)} \prod_{r \in \mathcal{R}[H]} \beta^k(r)^{c(r;T_i,X_i)} \right\}^{z_i^k}, \end{aligned} \tag{18}$$

where ζ^k is the mixture ratio of the kth model ($\boldsymbol{\zeta} = \{\zeta^1, \zeta^2, \cdots, \zeta^\mu\}$ where $\sum_k \zeta^k = 1$). $\beta^k(r)$ and $\pi^k(\mathcal{S}[x])$ denote the probabilities of production rule r and root $\mathcal{S}[x]$ of the kth model, respectively. By calculating the marginal of Equation 18 with respect to X_i and Z_i, the likelihood of observed tree T_i is calculated as

$$\begin{aligned} P(T_i; \boldsymbol{\beta}, \boldsymbol{\pi}, \boldsymbol{\zeta}) &= \sum_{k=1}^{\mu} \left\{ \zeta^k P(T_i; \boldsymbol{\beta}^k, \boldsymbol{\pi}^k) \right\} \\ &= \sum_{k=1}^{\mu} \left\{ \zeta^k \sum_{x \in H} \pi^k(\mathcal{S}[x]) b_{T_i}^1(x; \boldsymbol{\beta}^k, \boldsymbol{\pi}^k) \right\}. \end{aligned} \tag{19}$$

5.2. Parameter update formula

As in PCFG-LA, the parameter inference of PCFG-LAMM is carried out via the EM algorithm because PCFG-LAMM contains latent variables X_i and Z_i. Let $\boldsymbol{\beta}$, $\boldsymbol{\pi}$ and $\boldsymbol{\zeta}$ be current parameters $\overline{\boldsymbol{\beta}}$, $\overline{\boldsymbol{\pi}}$ and $\overline{\boldsymbol{\zeta}}$ be nextstep parameters. The $\mathcal{Q}$ function of the EM algorithm is given by

$$\mathcal{Q}(\overline{\boldsymbol{\beta}}, \overline{\boldsymbol{\pi}}, \overline{\boldsymbol{\zeta}} | \boldsymbol{\beta}, \boldsymbol{\pi}, \boldsymbol{\zeta}) = \sum_{i=1}^{N} \sum_{X_i} \sum_{Z_i} P(X_i, Z_i | T_i; \boldsymbol{\beta}, \boldsymbol{\pi}, \boldsymbol{\zeta}) \log P(T_i, X_i, Z_i; \overline{\boldsymbol{\beta}}, \overline{\boldsymbol{\pi}}, \overline{\boldsymbol{\zeta}}). \tag{20}$$

By maximizing $\mathcal{Q}(\overline{\boldsymbol{\beta}}, \overline{\boldsymbol{\pi}}, \overline{\boldsymbol{\zeta}} | \boldsymbol{\beta}, \boldsymbol{\pi}, \boldsymbol{\zeta})$ under constraints ($\sum_k \zeta^k = 1$, $\sum_\alpha \beta^k(\mathcal{S}[x] \to \alpha) = 1$ and $\sum_x \pi^k(\mathcal{S}[x]) = 1$), a parameter update formula can be obtained as follows (see Appendix B):

$$\begin{aligned} \overline{\beta}^k(\mathcal{S}[x] \to g\,\mathcal{S}[y] \cdots \mathcal{S}[y]) \propto \sum_{i=1}^{N} \Bigg\{ & \frac{\beta^k(\mathcal{S}[x] \to g\,\mathcal{S}[y] \cdots \mathcal{S}[y])}{P(T_i; \boldsymbol{\beta}, \boldsymbol{\pi}, \boldsymbol{\zeta})} \zeta^k \\ & \times \sum_{\ell \in \mathrm{cover}(g, T_i)} f_{T_i}^{\ell}(x; \boldsymbol{\beta}^k, \boldsymbol{\pi}^k) \prod_{j \in \mathrm{ch}(\ell, T_i)} b_{T_i}^{j}(y; \boldsymbol{\beta}^k, \boldsymbol{\pi}^k) \Bigg\}, \end{aligned} \tag{21}$$

$$\overline{\pi}^k \propto \sum_{i=1}^{N} \left\{ \frac{\pi^k(\mathcal{S}[x])}{P(T_i; \boldsymbol{\beta}, \boldsymbol{\pi}, \boldsymbol{\zeta})} \zeta^k b_{T_i}^1(x; \boldsymbol{\beta}^k, \boldsymbol{\pi}^k) \right\}, \tag{22}$$

$$\overline{\zeta}^k \propto \sum_{i=1}^{N} \left\{ \frac{\zeta^k P(T_i; \boldsymbol{\beta}^k, \boldsymbol{\pi}^k)}{P(T_i; \boldsymbol{\beta}, \boldsymbol{\pi}, \boldsymbol{\zeta})} \right\}. \tag{23}$$

The parameter inference starts from some initial values and converges to a local optimum using Equations 21–23. A log-likelihood is given by

$$\mathcal{L}(\boldsymbol{\beta}, \boldsymbol{\pi}, \boldsymbol{\zeta}; \mathcal{D}) = \sum_{i=1}^{N} \log P(T_i; \boldsymbol{\beta}, \boldsymbol{\pi}, \boldsymbol{\zeta}). \tag{24}$$

The procedures of UPAGE are listed below.

1. Generate initial population
   Initial population $\mathcal{P}_0$ is generated by randomly creating M individuals. In our implementation, the ratio between production rules of function nodes (e.g. $\mathcal{S}[x] \to + \mathcal{S}[y]\,\mathcal{S}[y]$) and those of terminal nodes (e.g. $\mathcal{S}[x] \to + \mathcal{S}[y]\,\mathcal{S}[y]$) are set to $4:1$.
2. Select promising solutions
   N individuals $\mathcal{D}_g$ are selected from a population of gth generation $\mathcal{P}_g$. In our implementation, we used the truncation selection.
3. Parameter estimation
   Using a parameter update formula (Equations 21–23), converged parameters $(\boldsymbol{\beta}_*, \boldsymbol{\pi}_*, \boldsymbol{\zeta}_*)$ are estimated with learning data $\mathcal{D}_g$.
4. Generation of new individuals
   EDA generates new individuals by sampling from the predictive posterior distributions, namely
   $$P(T, X, Z|\mathcal{D}_g) = P(T, X, Z; \boldsymbol{\beta}_*, \boldsymbol{\pi}_*, \boldsymbol{\zeta}_*).$$
   Since the EM algorithm is a point estimation method, new individuals can be generated with probabilistic logic sampling, which is computationally cheap. The details of the sampling procedures are summarized below (note, when at the maximum depth limitation, select a terminal node unconditionally).
   (a) Select a model following probability distribution $\boldsymbol{\zeta}_* = \{\zeta_*^1, \zeta_*^2, \cdots, \zeta_*^\mu\}$.
   (b) Let the selected model index be ℓ. A root node is selected following probability distribution $\boldsymbol{\pi}_*^\ell = \{\pi_*^\ell(\mathcal{S}[x])|x \in H\}$.
   (c) If there are non-terminal symbols $\mathcal{S}[x]$ $(x \in H)$ in a derivation tree, select a production rule following the probability distribution
   $$\beta_*^\ell(\mathcal{S}[x]) = \{\beta_*^\ell(\mathcal{S}[x] \to \alpha)|\mathcal{S}[x] \to \alpha \in \mathcal{R}[H]\}.$$
   Repeat (c) until there are no non-terminal symbols left in the derivation tree.

5.3. Computer experiments

In order to show the effectiveness of UPAGE, we analyze UPAGE from the viewpoint of the number of fitness evaluations. We applied UPAGE to three benchmark problems: the royal tree problem (Section 5.3.1), the bipolar royal tree problem (Section 5.3.2) and the deceptive MAX (DMAX) problem (Section 5.3.3). Because we want to study the effectiveness of the mixture model versus PCFG-LA, we specifically compared UPAGE with PAGE. In each benchmark test, we employed the parameter settings shown in Table 1, where UPAGE and

PAGE and UPAGE				
	Meaning	Royal Tree	Bipolar Royal Tree	DMAX
M	Population size	1000	3000	3000
P_s	Selection rate	0.1	0.1	0.1
P_e	Elite rate	0.01	0.01	0.01

UPAGE				
	Meaning	Royal Tree	Bipolar Royal Tree	DMAX
h	Annotation size	11	22	22
μ	The number of mixtures	2	2	2

PAGE				
	Meaning	Royal Tree	Bipolar Royal Tree	DMAX
h	Annotation size	16	32	32

Table 1. Main parameter settings of UPAGE and PAGE.

PAGE used the same population size, elite rate and selection rate. For the method-specific parameters of PAGE and UPAGE, we determined h and μ so that the number of parameters to be estimated is almost the same in UPAGE and PAGE. In the three benchmark problems, we carried out UPAGE and PAGE 30 times to compare the number of fitness evaluations and also performed the Welch t-test (two-tailed) to determine the statistical significance.

5.3.1. Royal tree problem

We apply UPAGE to the royal tree problem ([22]), which has only one optimal solution. The royal tree problem is a popular benchmark problem in GP. The royal tree problem is suitable for analyzing GP because the optimal structure of the royal tree is composed of smaller substructures (building blocks), and hence it well reflects the behavior of GP.

The royal tree problem defines the state *perfect tree* at each level. The perfect tree at a given level is composed of the perfect tree that is one level smaller than the given level. Thus, the perfect tree of level c is composed of the perfect tree of level b. In perfect trees, alphabets of functions descend by one from a root to leaves in a tree. A function a has a terminal x. The fitness function of the royal tree problem is given by

$$Score(\mathcal{X}_i) = wb_i \sum_j (wa_{ij} \times Score(\mathcal{X}_{ij})), \tag{25}$$

where $\mathcal{X}_i$ is the ith node in tree structures, and $\mathcal{X}_{ij}$ denotes the jth child of $\mathcal{X}_i$. The fitness value of the royal tree problem is calculated recursively from a root node. In Equation 25, wb_i and wa_{ij} are weights which are defined as follows:

- wa_{ij}
  - $Full\ Bonus = 2$
    If a subtree rooted at $\mathcal{X}_{ij}$ has a correct root and is a perfect tree.

	Average number of fitness evaluations	Standard deviation
UPAGE	6171	28
PAGE	6237	18

P-value of t-test (Welch, two-tailed)
0.74

Table 2. The number of fitness evaluations, standard deviation and P-value of t-test in the royal tree problem.

- *Partial Bonus* $= 1$
  If a subtree rooted at $\mathcal{X}_{ij}$ has a correct root but is not a perfect tree.
- *Penalty* $= 1/3$
  If $\mathcal{X}_{ij}$ is not a correct root.

- wb_i
  - *Complete Bonus* $= 2$
    If a subtree rooted at $\mathcal{X}_i$ is a perfect tree.
  - *Otherwise* $= 1$

In the present chapter, we employ the following GP functions and terminals:

$$\mathfrak{F} = \{a, b, c, d\},$$
$$\mathfrak{T} = \{x\}.$$

Here, $\mathfrak{F}$ and $\mathfrak{T}$ denote function and terminal sets, respectively, of GP. For details of the royal tree problem, please see Ref. ([22]).

Table 2 shows the average number of fitness evaluations (along with their standard deviation) and the P-value of a t-test (Welch, two-tailed). As can been seen with Table 2, there is no noticeable difference between UPAGE and PAGE in the average number of fitness evaluations, which is confirmed by the P-value of t-test. The royal tree problem is not multimodal, and hence the optimal solution has only one tree expression. Consequently, we do not have to consider global contexts behind optimal solutions, which is an advantage of UPAGE over PAGE.

5.3.2. Bipolar royal tree problem

We next apply UPAGE to the bipolar royal tree problem. In the field of GA-EDAs, a mixture model based method UEBNA was proposed, and it was reported that UEBNA is especially effective in multimodal problems such as two-max problem. Consequently, we apply UPAGE to a bipolar problem having two optimal solutions, which is a multimodal extension of the royal tree problem. In order to make the royal tree problem multimodal, we set $\mathfrak{T} = \{x, y\}$ and $Score(x) = Score(y) = 1$. With this setting, the royal tree problem has two optimal solutions of x (Fig. 7(a)) and y (Fig. 7(b)). PAGE and UPAGE stop when either of the two optimal solutions is obtained.

Table 3 shows the average number of fitness evaluations along with their standard deviation. We see that UPAGE can obtain an optimal solution with a smaller number of fitness

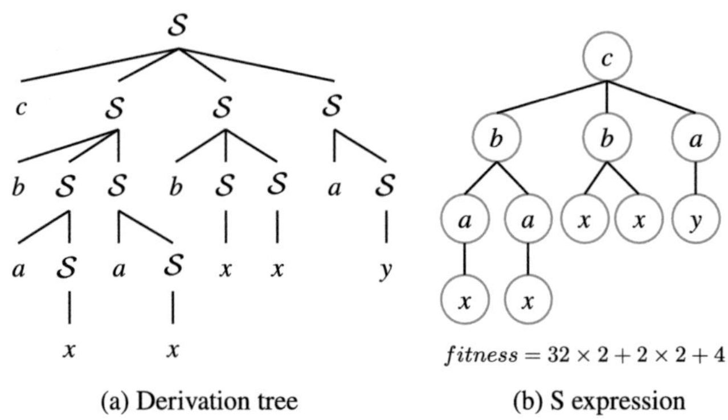

Figure 6. Example of fitness calculation in the bipolar royal tree problem. (a) Derivation tree and (b) S-expression.

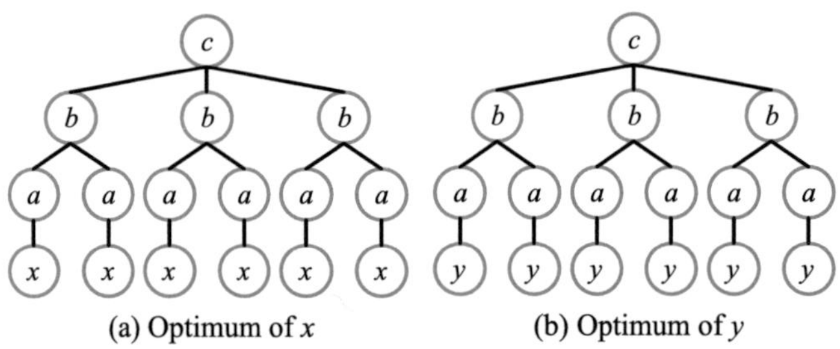

Figure 7. (a) Optimum structure of x and (b) that of y in the bipolar royal tree problem. These two structures have the same fitness value.

evaluations than PAGE. Table 3 gives the P-value of a t-test (Welch, two-tailed), which allows us to say that the difference between UPAGE and PAGE is statistically significant.

Because the bipolar royal tree problem has two optimal solutions (x and y), PAGE learns the production rule probabilities with learning data containing solution candidates of both x and y optima. Let us consider the annotation size required to express optimal solutions of the bipolar royal tree problem of depth 5. For the case of PAGE, the minimum annotation size to be able to learn the two optimal solutions separately is 10. In contrast, UPAGE can express the two optimal solutions with mixture size 2 and annotation size 5, which results in a smaller number of parameters. This consideration shows that a mixture model is more suitable for this class of problems.

Figure 8 shows the increase in the log-likelihood for the bipolar royal tree problem, in particular, the transitions at generation 0 and generation 5. As can been seen from the figure, the log-likelihood converges after about 10 iterations. The log-likelihood improvement at generation 5 is larger than that at generation 0 because the tree structures have converged toward the end of the search.

5.3.3. DMAX Problem

We apply UPAGE to the DMAX problem ([8, 10]), which has deceptiveness when it is solved with GP. The main objective of the DMAX problem is identical to that of the original MAX problem: to find the functions that return the largest *real* value under the limitation of a

	Average number of fitness evaluations	Standard deviation
UPAGE	25839	4737
PAGE	31878	4333

P-value of t-test (Welch, two-tailed)
4.49×10^{-6}

Table 3. The number of fitness evaluations, standard deviation and P-value of t-test in the bipolar royal tree problem.

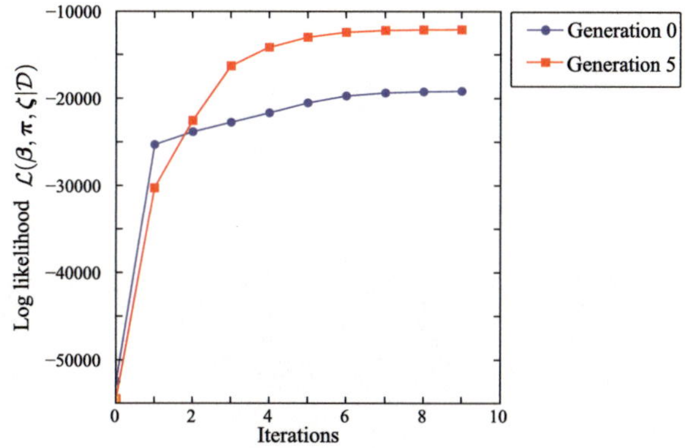

Figure 8. Transitions of loglikelihood of UPAGE in the bipolar royal tree problem.

maximum tree depth. However, the symbols used in the DMAX problem are different from those used in the MAX problem. The DMAX problem has three parameters, and the difficulty of the problem can be tuned using these three parameters. For the problem of interest in the present chapter, we selected $m = 3$ and $r = 2$, whose deceptiveness is of medium degree. In this setting, the GP terminals and functions are

$$\mathfrak{F} = \{+_3, \times_3\},$$
$$\mathfrak{T} = \{0.95, -1\},$$

where $+_3$ and $\times_3$ are 3 arity addition and multiplication operators, respectively. The optimal solution in the present setting is given by

$$(-1 \times 3)^{26}(0.95 \times 3) \fallingdotseq 7.24 \times 10^{12}. \tag{26}$$

Table 4 shows the average number of fitness evaluations along with their standard deviation for the DMAX problem. We can see that UPAGE obtained the optimal solution with a smaller number of fitness evaluations compared to PAGE. Table 4 gives the P-value of a t-test (Welch and two-tailed) and allows us to say that the difference in the averages of UPAGE and PAGE is statistically significant.

In the bipolar royal tree problem, expressions of the two optimal solutions (x or y) are different, and thus building blocks of the optima are also different. In contrast, the DMAX problem has mathematically only one optimal solution, which are represented by Equation 26. Although the DMAX problem is a unimodal problem, the DMAX problem has different expressions for the optimal solution due to commutative operators such as $+_3$ and $\times_3$. From this experiment, we see that UPAGE is superior to PAGE for this class of benchmark problems.

	Average number of fitness evaluations	Standard deviation
UPAGE	36729	3794
PAGE	38709	2233

P-value of t-test (Welch, two-tailed)
1.94×10^{-2}

Table 4. The number of fitness evaluations, standard deviation and P-value of t-test in the DMAX problem.

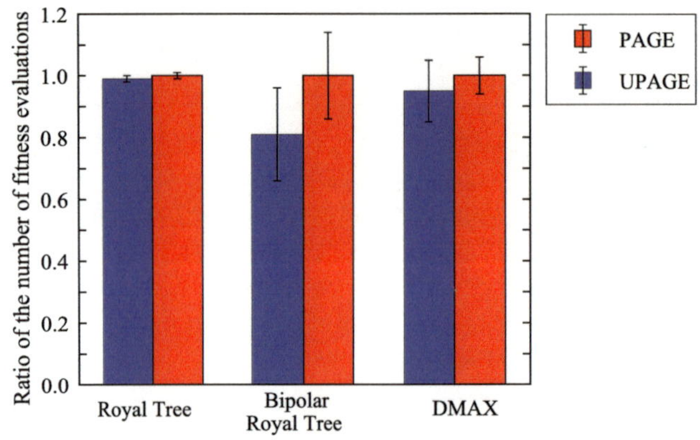

Figure 9. The average number of fitness evaluations (smaller is better) in royal tree problem, bipolar royal tree problem and DMAX problem relative to those of PAGE (i.e. the PAGE results are normalized to 1).

Common parameters in PAGE and UPAGE		
	Meaning	Bipolar Royal Tree
M	Population size	6000
P_s	Selection rate	0.3
P_e	Elite rate	0.1

UPAGE		
	Meaning	Bipolar Royal Tree
h	Annotation size	16
μ	The number of mixtures	4

PAGE		
	Meaning	Bipolar Royal Tree
h	Annotation size	32

Table 5. Parameter settings for a multimodal problem.

5.4. Multimodal problem

In the preceding section, we evaluated the performance of UPAGE from the viewpoint of the average number of fitness evaluations. In this section, we show the effectiveness of UPAGE in terms of its capability for obtaining multiple solutions of a multimodal problem. Because there are two optimal solutions in the bipolar royal tree problem (see Fig. 7(a) and (b)), we

	Successful runs / Total runs
UPAGE	10/15
PAGE	0/15

Table 6. The number of runs which could obtain both optimal solutions. We carried out 15 runs in total.

show that UPAGE can obtain both optimal solutions in a single run. Parameter settings are shown in Table 5.

Table 6 shows the number of successful runs in which both optimal solutions are obtained in a single run. As can been seen in Table 6, UPAGE succeeded in obtaining both optimal solutions in 10 out of 15 runs, whereas PAGE could not obtain them at all.

Table 7 shows production rule probabilities of UPAGE in a successful run. Although the mixture size is $\mu = 4$, we have only presented probabilities of Model = 0 and Model = 3, which are related to optimal solutions of y (Fig. 7(b)) and x (Fig. 7(a)), respectively (i.e. Model = 1 and Model = 2 are not shown). Because we see in Model = 0 that the probabilities generating y are very high, we consider that the optimal solution of y was generated by Model = 0. On the other hand, it is estimated that the optimal solution of x was generated by Model = 3. From this probability table, we can confirm that UPAGE successfully estimated the mixed population separately, because Model = 3 and 0 can generate optimal solutions of x and y with relatively high probability. It is very difficult for PAGE to estimate multiple solutions because PCFG-LA is not a mixture model and it is almost impossible to learn the distributions separately. As was shown in Section 5.3, UPAGE is superior to PAGE in terms of the number of fitness evaluations. From Table 7, it is considered that this superiority is due to UPAGE's capability of learning distributions in a separate way.

6. Discussion

In the present chapter, we have introduced PAGE and UPAGE. PAGE is based on PCFG-LA, which takes into account latent annotations to weaken the context freedom assumption. By considering latent annotations, dependencies among nodes can be considered. We reported in Ref. ([12]) that PAGE is more powerful for several benchmark tests than other GP-EDAs, including GMPE and POLE.

Although PCFG-LA is suitable for estimating dependencies among local nodes, it cannot consider global contexts (contexts of entire tree structures) behind individuals. In many real-world problems, not only local dependencies but also global contexts have to be taken into account. In order to consider the global contexts, we have proposed UPAGE by extending PCFG-LA into a mixture model (PCFG-LAMM). In the bipolar royal tree problem, there are two optimal structures of x and y and the global contexts represent which optima (x or y) each tree structure comes from. From Table 7, the mixture model of UPAGE successfully worked and UPAGE could estimate mixed population separately. We have also shown that a mixture model is effective not only in multimodal problems but also in some unimodal problems, namely in the DMAX problem. Although the optimal solution of the DMAX problem is represented by mathematically one expression, the tree expressions are not unique, due to commutative operators ($\times_3$ and $+_3$). Consequently, the mixture model is also effective in the DMAX problem (see Section 5.3.3), and this situation where there exists the expression diversity often arises in real world problems. When obtaining multiple optimal solutions in a single run, UPAGE succeeded in cases for which PAGE obtained only one of the

Model = 0	Pr
ζ^0	0.11
$\mathcal{S}[1]$	1.00
$\mathcal{S}[0] \to a\,\mathcal{S}[10]$	0.20
$\mathcal{S}[0] \to a\,\mathcal{S}[2]$	0.18
$\mathcal{S}[0] \to a\,\mathcal{S}[5]$	0.28
$\mathcal{S}[1] \to d\,\mathcal{S}[4]\,\mathcal{S}[4]\,\mathcal{S}[4]\,\mathcal{S}[4]$	1.00
$\mathcal{S}[10] \to x$	0.14
$\mathcal{S}[10] \to y$	0.86
$\mathcal{S}[11] \to x$	0.14
$\mathcal{S}[11] \to y$	0.86
$\mathcal{S}[12] \to a\,\mathcal{S}[10]$	0.17
$\mathcal{S}[12] \to a\,\mathcal{S}[2]$	0.18
$\mathcal{S}[12] \to a\,\mathcal{S}[5]$	0.32
$\mathcal{S}[13] \to x$	0.21
$\mathcal{S}[13] \to y$	0.79
$\mathcal{S}[14] \to b\,\mathcal{S}[7]\,\mathcal{S}[7]$	0.10
$\mathcal{S}[14] \to c\,\mathcal{S}[10]\,\mathcal{S}[10]\,\mathcal{S}[10]$	0.15
$\mathcal{S}[15] \to x$	0.12
$\mathcal{S}[15] \to y$	0.88
$\mathcal{S}[2] \to x$	0.25
$\mathcal{S}[2] \to y$	0.75
$\mathcal{S}[3] \to a\,\mathcal{S}[10]$	0.21
$\mathcal{S}[3] \to a\,\mathcal{S}[15]$	0.18
$\mathcal{S}[3] \to a\,\mathcal{S}[2]$	0.17
$\mathcal{S}[3] \to a\,\mathcal{S}[5]$	0.22
$\mathcal{S}[4] \to c\,\mathcal{S}[8]\,\mathcal{S}[8]\,\mathcal{S}[8]$	1.00
$\mathcal{S}[5] \to y$	0.97
$\mathcal{S}[6] \to y$	1.00
$\mathcal{S}[7] \to x$	0.52
$\mathcal{S}[7] \to y$	0.48
$\mathcal{S}[8] \to b\,\mathcal{S}[0]\,\mathcal{S}[0]$	0.50
$\mathcal{S}[8] \to b\,\mathcal{S}[12]\,\mathcal{S}[12]$	0.17
$\mathcal{S}[8] \to b\,\mathcal{S}[3]\,\mathcal{S}[3]$	0.31
$\mathcal{S}[9] \to x$	0.14
$\mathcal{S}[9] \to y$	0.86

Model = 3	Pr
ζ^3	0.52
$\mathcal{S}[11]$	1.00
$\mathcal{S}[0] \to a\,\mathcal{S}[13]$	0.16
$\mathcal{S}[0] \to a\,\mathcal{S}[2]$	0.29
$\mathcal{S}[0] \to a\,\mathcal{S}[5]$	0.32
$\mathcal{S}[1] \to b\,\mathcal{S}[0]\,\mathcal{S}[0]$	0.13
$\mathcal{S}[1] \to b\,\mathcal{S}[14]\,\mathcal{S}[14]$	0.19
$\mathcal{S}[1] \to b\,\mathcal{S}[3]\,\mathcal{S}[3]$	0.15
$\mathcal{S}[1] \to b\,\mathcal{S}[7]\,\mathcal{S}[7]$	0.17
$\mathcal{S}[1] \to b\,\mathcal{S}[8]\,\mathcal{S}[8]$	0.32
$\mathcal{S}[10] \to c\,\mathcal{S}[1]\,\mathcal{S}[1]\,\mathcal{S}[1]$	1.00
$\mathcal{S}[11] \to d\,\mathcal{S}[10]\,\mathcal{S}[10]\,\mathcal{S}[10]\,\mathcal{S}[10]$	1.00
$\mathcal{S}[12] \to a\,\mathcal{S}[4]$	0.13
$\mathcal{S}[12] \to c\,\mathcal{S}[13]\,\mathcal{S}[13]\,\mathcal{S}[13]$	0.34
$\mathcal{S}[12] \to x$	0.13
$\mathcal{S}[13] \to x$	0.72
$\mathcal{S}[13] \to y$	0.28
$\mathcal{S}[14] \to a\,\mathcal{S}[15]$	0.16
$\mathcal{S}[14] \to a\,\mathcal{S}[4]$	0.10
$\mathcal{S}[14] \to a\,\mathcal{S}[5]$	0.45
$\mathcal{S}[14] \to a\,\mathcal{S}[6]$	0.13
$\mathcal{S}[15] \to x$	0.89
$\mathcal{S}[15] \to y$	0.11
$\mathcal{S}[2] \to x$	0.99
$\mathcal{S}[3] \to a\,\mathcal{S}[13]$	0.11
$\mathcal{S}[3] \to a\,\mathcal{S}[15]$	0.14
$\mathcal{S}[3] \to a\,\mathcal{S}[2]$	0.20
$\mathcal{S}[3] \to a\,\mathcal{S}[5]$	0.44
$\mathcal{S}[4] \to x$	0.68
$\mathcal{S}[4] \to y$	0.32
$\mathcal{S}[5] \to x$	0.92
$\mathcal{S}[6] \to x$	0.93
$\mathcal{S}[7] \to a\,\mathcal{S}[13]$	0.23
$\mathcal{S}[7] \to a\,\mathcal{S}[2]$	0.31
$\mathcal{S}[7] \to a\,\mathcal{S}[4]$	0.10
$\mathcal{S}[7] \to a\,\mathcal{S}[5]$	0.29
$\mathcal{S}[8] \to a\,\mathcal{S}[2]$	0.17
$\mathcal{S}[8] \to a\,\mathcal{S}[4]$	0.18
$\mathcal{S}[8] \to a\,\mathcal{S}[5]$	0.41
$\mathcal{S}[8] \to a\,\mathcal{S}[6]$	0.16
$\mathcal{S}[9] \to a\,\mathcal{S}[13]$	0.19
$\mathcal{S}[9] \to a\,\mathcal{S}[4]$	0.19
$\mathcal{S}[9] \to a\,\mathcal{S}[5]$	0.38

Table 7. Estimated parameters by UPAGE in a successful run. Although the number of mixtures is $\mu = 4$, we only show Model = 0 and Model = 3 related to optimal solutions of y and x, respectively. Due to limited space, we do not show parameters of production rules which are smaller than 0.1.

Method	Estimation of interaction among nodes	Position independent model	Consideration of global contexts
Scalar SG-GP	No	Yes	No
Vectorial SG-GP	Partially	No	No
GT-EDA	Yes	No	No
GMPE	Yes	Yes	No
PAGE	Yes	Yes	No
UPAGE	Yes	Yes	Yes

Table 8. Classification of GP-EDAs and their capabilities.

optima. This result shows that UPAGE is more effective than PAGE not only quantitatively but also qualitatively. We also note that UPAGE is more powerful than PAGE in terms of computational time. In our computer experiments, we set the number of parameters in UPAGE and PAGE to be approximately the same. Figure 10 shows the relative computational time per generation of UPAGE and PAGE (the computational time of PAGE is normalized to 1) and we see that UPAGE required only sixty percent of the time required by PAGE. Although we have shown in Section 5.3.1 that UPAGE and PAGE required approximately the same number of fitness evaluations to obtain the optimal solution in the royal tree problem, UPAGE is more effective even for the royal tree problem if the actual computational time is considered.

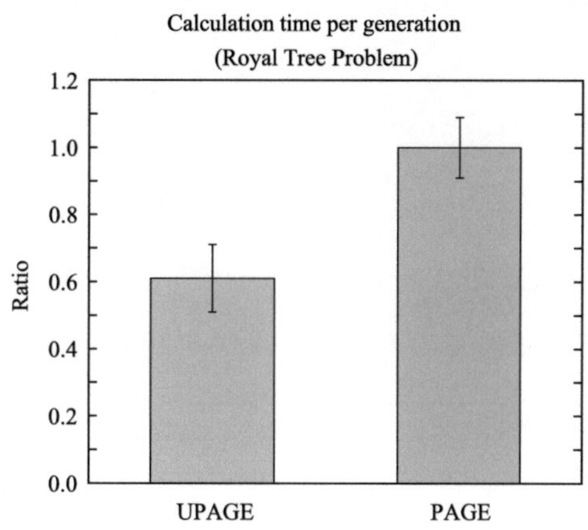

Figure 10. The computational time per generation of UPAGE and PAGE (smaller is better). The time of PAGE is normalized to 1.

Table 8 summarizes functionalities of several GP-EDAs. SG-GP employs the conventional PCFG and hence it cannot estimate dependencies among nodes. Although GT-EDA, GMPE and PAGE adopt different types of grammar models, they belong to the same class in the sense that these three methods can take into account dependencies among nodes, which is enabled by a use of specialized production rules depending on contexts. However, these methods cannot consider global contexts, and consequently, they are not suitable for estimating problems having complex distributions. In contrast, in addition to local dependencies among nodes, UPAGE can consider global contexts of tree structures. The model of UPAGE is the most flexible among these GP-EDAs, and this flexibility is reflected by the search performance.

In the present implementation of UPAGE, we had to set the mixture size μ and the annotation size h in advance because UPAGE employed the EM algorithm. However, it is desirable to estimate μ and h, as well as β, π and ζ during search. In the case of PAGE, we proposed PAGE-VB in Ref. ([12]), which adopted VB to estimate the annotation size h. In a similar fashion, it is possible to apply VB to UPAGE to enable the inference of μ and h.

We have shown the effectiveness of PAGE and UPAGE with benchmark problems not having intron structures. However, in real-world applications, problems generally include intron structures, which make the model and parameter inference much more difficult. For such problems, we consider that intron removal algorithms ([13, 30]) are effective, and application of such algorithms to GP-EDAs is left as a topic of future study.

7. Conclusion

We have introduced a probabilistic program evolution algorithm named PAGE and its extension UPAGE. PAGE takes advantage of latent annotations that enables consideration of dependencies among nodes, and UPAGE incorporates a mixture model for taking into account global contexts. By applying UPAGE to computational experiments, we have confirmed that a mixture model is highly effective for obtaining solutions in terms of the number of fitness evaluations. At the same time, UPAGE is more advantageous than PAGE in the sense that UPAGE can obtain multiple solutions for multimodal problems. We hope that it will be possible to apply PAGE and UPAGE to a wide class of real-world problems, which is an intended future area of study.

Author details

Yoshihiko Hasegawa
The University of Tokyo, Japan

Appendix A: Parameter list

We summarized parameters used in PAGE and UPAGE in the following table.

Target model	Parameter	Meaning
PAGE and UPAGE	$\delta(x;T,X)$	Frequency of a root $\mathcal{S}[x]$ in a complete tree (0 or 1)
	$c(r;T,X)$	Frequency of a production rule r in a complete tree
	h	Annotation size
	H	Set of annotation $H = \{0, 1, \cdots h-1\}$
	T_i	Observed derivation tree
	x_i^j	jth latent annotation in T_i
	$\mathcal{R}[H]$	Set of production rules
	$\mathcal{N}$	Set of non-terminals in CFG
	$\mathcal{T}$	Set of terminals in CFG
	$\mathfrak{F}$	Set of function nodes in GP
	$\mathfrak{T}$	Set of terminal nodes in GP
PAGE	$\pi(\mathcal{S}[x])$	Probability of a root $\mathcal{S}[t]$
	$\beta(r)$	Probability of a production rule r
UPAGE	ζ^k	Mixture ratio of kth model.
	$\pi^k(\mathcal{S}[x])$	Probability of a root $\mathcal{S}[t]$ in kth model.
	$\beta^k(r)$	Probability of a production rule r in kth model
	z_i^k	$z_k^k = 1$, if ith individual belongs to kth model
	μ	Mixture size

Appendix B: Derivation of a parameter update formula for UPAGE

We here explain details of the parameter update formula for UPAGE (see Section 4.1). By separating $\mathcal{Q}(\overline{\boldsymbol{\beta}},\overline{\boldsymbol{\pi}},\overline{\boldsymbol{\zeta}}|\boldsymbol{\beta},\boldsymbol{\pi},\boldsymbol{\zeta})$ into terms containing $\overline{\boldsymbol{\beta}}$, $\overline{\boldsymbol{\pi}}$ and $\overline{\boldsymbol{\zeta}}$, a parameter update formula for $\overline{\boldsymbol{\beta}}$, $\overline{\boldsymbol{\pi}}$ and $\overline{\boldsymbol{\zeta}}$ can be calculated separately.

We here derive $\overline{\boldsymbol{\beta}}$. Maximization of $\mathcal{Q}(\overline{\boldsymbol{\beta}},\overline{\boldsymbol{\pi}},\overline{\boldsymbol{\zeta}}|\boldsymbol{\beta},\boldsymbol{\pi},\boldsymbol{\zeta})$ under a constraint $\sum_\alpha \overline{\beta}^k(\mathcal{S}[x] \to \alpha) = 1$ can be performed by the method of Lagrange multipliers:

$$\frac{\partial \mathscr{L}}{\partial \overline{\beta}^k(\mathcal{S}[x] \to \alpha)} = 0, \tag{27}$$

with

$$\mathscr{L} = \mathcal{Q}(\overline{\boldsymbol{\beta}},\overline{\boldsymbol{\pi}},\overline{\boldsymbol{\zeta}}|\boldsymbol{\beta},\boldsymbol{\pi},\boldsymbol{\zeta}) + \sum_{k,x} \xi_{k,x} \left(1 - \sum_\alpha \overline{\beta}^k(\mathcal{S}[x] \to \alpha)\right), \tag{28}$$

where $\xi_{k,x}$ denote Lagrange multipliers. By calculating Equation 27, we obtain the following update formula:

$$\begin{aligned}\overline{\beta}^k(\mathcal{S}[x] \to g\,\mathcal{S}[y] \cdots \mathcal{S}[y]) \propto \sum_{i=1}^{N} \sum_{X_i} \sum_{Z_i} \Big\{ & P(X_i, Z_i | T_i; \boldsymbol{\beta}, \boldsymbol{\pi}, \boldsymbol{\zeta}) z_i^k \\ & \times c(\mathcal{S}[x] \to g\,\mathcal{S}[y] \cdots \mathcal{S}[y]; T_i, X_i) \Big\}. \end{aligned} \tag{29}$$

Because Equation 29 includes summation in terms of X_i, direct calculation is intractable due to exponential increase of computational cost. Consequently, we use forward–backward probabilities. Let $c^k(\mathcal{S}[x] \to g\,\mathcal{S}[y] \cdots \mathcal{S}[y]; T_i)$ be

$$\begin{aligned} & c^k(\mathcal{S}[x] \to g\,\mathcal{S}[y] \cdots \mathcal{S}[y]; T_i) \\ & = \sum_{X_i} \sum_{Z_i} P(X_i, Z_i | T_i; \boldsymbol{\beta}, \boldsymbol{\pi}, \boldsymbol{\zeta}) z_i^k c(\mathcal{S}[x] \to g\,\mathcal{S}[y] \cdots \mathcal{S}[y]; T_i, X_i). \end{aligned}$$

By differentiating the likelihood of complete data (Equation 18) with respect to $\beta^k(\mathcal{S}[x] \to g\,\mathcal{S}[y] \cdots \mathcal{S}[y])$, we have

$$\begin{aligned} & c^k(\mathcal{S}[x] \to g\,\mathcal{S}[y] \cdots \mathcal{S}[y]; T_i) \\ & = \frac{\beta^k(\mathcal{S}[x] \to g\,\mathcal{S}[y] \cdots \mathcal{S}[y])}{P(T_i; \boldsymbol{\beta}, \boldsymbol{\pi}, \boldsymbol{\zeta})} \sum_{X_i} \sum_{Z_i} \frac{\partial P(T_i, X_i, Z_i; \boldsymbol{\beta}, \boldsymbol{\pi}, \boldsymbol{\zeta})}{\partial \beta^k(\mathcal{S}[x] \to g\,\mathcal{S}[y] \cdots \mathcal{S}[y])}. \end{aligned}$$

The last term is calculated as

$$\begin{aligned} \sum_{X_i} \sum_{Z_i} \frac{\partial P(T_i, X_i, Z_i; \boldsymbol{\beta}, \boldsymbol{\pi}, \boldsymbol{\zeta})}{\partial \beta^k(\mathcal{S}[x] \to g\,\mathcal{S}[y] \cdots \mathcal{S}[y])} & = \zeta^k \sum_{X_i} \frac{\partial P(T_i, X_i; \boldsymbol{\beta}^k, \boldsymbol{\pi}^k)}{\partial \beta^k(\mathcal{S}[x] \to g\,\mathcal{S}[y] \cdots \mathcal{S}[y])} \\ & = \zeta^k \sum_{\ell \in \mathrm{cover}(g, T_i)} f_{T_i}^{\ell}(x; \boldsymbol{\beta}^k, \boldsymbol{\pi}^k) \prod_{j \in \mathrm{ch}(\ell, T_i)} b_{T_i}^{j}(y; \boldsymbol{\beta}^k, \boldsymbol{\pi}^k). \end{aligned}$$

By this procedure, the update formula for β is expressed with Equation 21, and the update formula for π is calculated in a similar way (and much easier). The update formula for ζ is given by

$$\begin{aligned}
\overline{\zeta}^k &\propto \sum_{i=1}^{N} \sum_{X_i} \sum_{Z_i} P(X_i, Z_i | T_i; \boldsymbol{\beta}, \boldsymbol{\pi}, \boldsymbol{\zeta}) z_i^k \\
&= \sum_{i=1}^{N} \frac{1}{P(T_i; \boldsymbol{\beta}, \boldsymbol{\pi}, \boldsymbol{\zeta})} \sum_{X_i} \sum_{Z_i} \left\{ z_i^k P(T_i, X_i, Z_i; \boldsymbol{\beta}, \boldsymbol{\pi}, \boldsymbol{\zeta}) \right\} \\
&= \sum_{i=1}^{N} \frac{1}{P(T_i; \boldsymbol{\beta}, \boldsymbol{\pi}, \boldsymbol{\zeta})} \sum_{X_i} \left\{ \zeta^k P(T_i, X_i; \boldsymbol{\beta}^k, \boldsymbol{\pi}^k) \right\} \\
&= \sum_{i=1}^{N} \frac{\zeta^k P(T_i; \boldsymbol{\beta}^k, \boldsymbol{\pi}^k)}{P(T_i; \boldsymbol{\beta}, \boldsymbol{\pi}, \boldsymbol{\zeta})}.
\end{aligned}$$

8. References

[1] Abbass, H. A., Hoai, X. & Mckay, R. I. [2002]. AntTAG: A new method to compose computer programs using colonies of ants, *Proceedings of the IEEE Congress on Evolutionary Computation*, pp. 1654–1659.

[2] Attias, H. [1999]. Inferring parameters and structure of latent variable models by variational Bayes, *the 15th Conference of Uncertainty in Artificial Intelligence*, Morgan Kaufmann, Stockholm, Sweden, pp. 21–30.

[3] Baluja, S. [1994]. Population-based incremental learning: A method for integrating genetic search based function optimization and competitive learning, *Technical Report CMU-CS-94-163*, Pittsburgh, PA.
URL: *citeseer.ist.psu.edu/baluja94population.html*

[4] Bosman, P. A. N. & de Jong, E. D. [2004]. Grammar transformations in an EDA for genetic programming, *Technical Report UU-CS-2004-047*, Institute of Information and Computing Sciences, Utrecht University.

[5] Dempster, A., Laird, N. & Rubin, D. [1977]. Maximum likelihood from incomplete data via the EM algorithm, *Journal of the Royal Statistical Society, Series B* 39(1): 1–38.

[6] Goldberg, D. E., Deb, D. & Kargupta, H. [1993]. Rapid, accurate optimization of difficult problems using fast messy genetic algorithms, *in* S. Forrest (ed.), *Proc. of the Fifth Int. Conf. on Genetic Algorithms*, Morgan Kaufman, San Mateo, pp. 56–64.

[7] Harik, G. [1999]. Linkage learning via probabilistic modeling in the ECGA, *IlliGAL Report* (99010).

[8] Hasegawa, Y. & Iba, H. [2006]. Estimation of Bayesian Network for Program Generation, *Proceedings of The Third Asian-Pacific Workshop on Genetic Programming*, Hanoi, Vietnam, pp. 35–46.

[9] Hasegawa, Y. & Iba, H. [2007]. Estimation of distribution algorithm based on probabilistic grammar with latent annotations, *Proceedings of IEEE Congress of Evolutionary Computation*, IEEE press, Singapore, pp. 1143–1150.

[10] Hasegawa, Y. & Iba, H. [2008]. A Bayesian network approach for program generation, *IEEE Transactions on Evoluationary Computation* 12(6): 750–764.

[11] Hasegawa, Y. & Iba, H. [2009a]. Estimation of distribution algorithm based on PCFG-LA mixture model, *Transactions of the Japanese Society for Artificial Intelligence (in Japanese)* 24(1): 80–91.

[12] Hasegawa, Y. & Iba, H. [2009b]. Latent variable model for estimation of distribution algorithm based on a probabilistic context-free grammar, *IEEE Transactions on Evolutionary Computation* 13(4): 858–878.
[13] Hooper, D. & Flann, N. S. [1996]. Improving the accuracy and robustness of genetic programming through expression simplification, *Proceedings of the First Annual Conference*, MIT Press, Stanford University, CA, USA.
[14] Larrañaga, P. & Lozano, J. A. [2002]. *Estimation of Distribution Algorithms*, Kluwer Academic Publishers.
[15] Looks, M. [2005]. Learning computer programs with the Bayesian optimization algorithm. Master thesis, Washington University Sever Institute of Technology.
[16] Looks, M. [2007]. Scalable estimation-of-distribution program evolution, *GECCO '07: Proceedings of the 9th annual conference on Genetic and evolutionary computation*, ACM, New York, NY, USA, pp. 539–546.
[17] Matsuzaki, T., Miyao, Y. & Tsujii, J. [2005]. Probabilistic CFG with latent annotations, *In Proceedings of the 43rd Meeting of the Association for Computational Linguistics (ACL)*, Morgan Kaufmann, Michigan, USA, pp. 75–82.
[18] Nordin, P. [1994]. A compiling genetic programming system that directly manipulates the machine code, *Advances in genetic programming*, MIT Press, Cambridge, MA, USA, chapter 14, pp. 311–331.
[19] Pelikan, M. & Goldberg, D. E. [2001]. Escaping hierarchical traps with competent genetic algorithms, *GECCO '01: Proceedings of the 2001 conference on Genetic and evolutionary computation*, ACM Press, New York, NY, USA, pp. 511–518.
[20] Pelikan, M., Goldberg, D. E. & Cantú-Paz, E. [1999]. BOA: The Bayesian optimization algorithm, *Proceedings of the Genetic and Evolutionary Computation Conference GECCO-99*, Vol. I, Morgan Kaufmann Publishers, San Fransisco, CA, Orlando, FL, pp. 525–532.
[21] Poli, R. & McPhee, N. F. [2008]. A linear estimation-of-distribution GP system, *Proceedings of Euro GP 2008*, Springer-Verlag, pp. 206–217.
[22] Punch, W. F. [1998]. How effective are multiple populations in genetic programming, *Genetic Programming 1998: Proceedings of the Third Annual Conference*, Morgan Kaufmann, University of Wisconsin, Madison, Wisconsin, USA, pp. 308–313.
[23] Ratle, A. & Sebag, M. [2001]. Avoiding the bloat with probabilistic grammar-guided genetic programming, *Artificial Evolution 5th International Conference, Evolution Artificielle, EA 2001*, Vol. 2310 of *LNCS*, Springer Verlag, Creusot, France, pp. 255–266.
[24] Regolin, E. N. & Pozo, A. T. R. [2005]. Bayesian automatic programming, *Proceedings of the 8th European Conference on Genetic Programming*, Vol. 3447 of *Lecture Notes in Computer Science*, Springer, Lausanne, Switzerland, pp. 38–49.
[25] Sałustowicz, R. P. & Schmidhuber, J. [1997]. Probabilistic incremental program evolution, *Evolutionary Computation* 5(2): 123–141.
[26] Sastry, K. & Goldberg, D. E. [2003]. Probabilistic model building and competent genetic programming, *Genetic Programming Theory and Practise*, Kluwer, chapter 13, pp. 205–220.
[27] Sato, H., Hasegawa, Y., Bollegala, D. & Iba, H. [2012]. Probabilistic model building GP with belief propagation, *Proceedings of IEEE Congress on Evolutionary Computation (CEC 2012)*. accepted for publication.
[28] Shan, Y., McKay, R. I., Abbass, H. A. & Essam, D. [2003]. Program evolution with explicit learning: a new framework for program automatic synthesis, *Proceedings of the 2003 Congress on Evolutionary Computation CEC2003*, IEEE Press, Canberra, pp. 1639–1646.
[29] Shan, Y., McKay, R. I., Baxter, R., Abbass, H., Essam, D. & Hoai, N. X. [2004]. Grammar model-based program evolution, *Proceedings of the 2004 IEEE Congress on Evolutionary Computation*, IEEE Press, Portland, Oregon, pp. 478–485.

[30] Shin, J., Kang, M., McKay, R. I., Nguyen, X., Hoang, T.-H., Mori, N. & Essam, D. [2007]. Analysing the regularity of genomes using compression and expression simplification, *Proceedings of Euro GP 2007*, Springer-Verlag, pp. 251–260.

[31] Tanev, I. [2004]. Implications of incorporating learning probabilistic context-sensitive grammar in genetic programming on evolvability of adaptive locomotion gaits of snakebot, *GECCO 2004 Workshop Proceedings*, Seattle, Washington, USA.

[32] Tanev, I. [2005]. Incorporating learning probabilistic context-sensitive grammar in genetic programming for efficient evolution and adaptation of Snakebot, *Proceedings of EuroGP 2005*, Springer Verlag, Lausanne, Switzerland, pp. 155–166.

[33] Whigham, P. A. [1995]. Grammatically-based genetic programming, *Proceedings of the Workshop on Genetic Programming : From Theory to Real-World Applications*, Tahoe City, California USA, pp. 44–41.

[34] Whigham, P. A. [1996]. Search bias, language bias, and genetic programming, *Genetic Programming 1996: Proceedings of the First Annual Conference*, MIT Press, Stanford University, CA, USA, pp. 230–237.

[35] Whigham, P. A. & Science, D. O. C. [1995]. Inductive bias and genetic programming, *In Proceedings of First International Conference on Genetic Algorithms in Engineering Systems: Innovations and Applications*, pp. 461–466.

[36] Wineberg, M. & Oppacher, F. [1994]. A representation scheme to perform program induction in a canonical genetic algorithm, *Parallel Problem Solving from Nature III*, Vol. 866 of *LNCS*, Springer-Verlag, Jerusalem, pp. 292–301.

[37] Yanai, K. & Iba, H. [2003]. Estimation of distribution programming based on Bayesian network, *Proceedings of the 2003 Congress on Evolutionary Computation CEC2003*, IEEE Press, Canberra, pp. 1618–1625.

[38] Yanai, K. & Iba, H. [2005]. Probabilistic distribution models for EDA-based GP, *GECCO 2005: Proceedings of the 2005 conference on Genetic and evolutionary computation*, Vol. 2, ACM Press, Washington DC, USA, pp. 1775–1776.

[39] Yanase, T., Hasegawa, Y. & Iba, H. [2009]. Binary encoding for prototype tree of probabilistic model building gp, *Proceedings of 2009 Genetic and Evolutionary Computation Conference (GECCO 2009)*, pp. 1147–1154.

Chapter 4

Genetically Programmed Regression Linear Models for Non-Deterministic Estimates

Guilherme Esmeraldo, Robson Feitosa,
Dilza Esmeraldo and Edna Barros

Additional information is available at the end of the chapter

http://dx.doi.org/10.5772/48156

1. Introduction

Symbolic regression is a technique which characterizes, through mathematical functions, response variables with basis on input variables. Their main features include: need for no (or just a few) assumptions about the mathematical model; the coverage of multidimensional data, frequently unbalanced with big or small samples. In order to find the plausible Symbolic Regression Models (SRM), we used the genetic programming (GP) technique [1].

Genetic programming (GP) is a specialization of genetic algorithms (GA), an evolutionary algorithm-based methodology inspired by biological evolution, to find predictive functions. Each GP individual is evaluated by performing its function in order to determine how its output fits to the desired output [2,3].

However, depending on the problem, one may notice that the estimates of the SRM found from the GP may present errors [4], affecting the precision of the predictive function. To deal with this problem, some studies [5,6] substitute the predictive functions, which are deterministic mathematical models, by linear regression statistical models (LRM) to compose the genetic individual models.

LRM, as well as the traditional mathematical models, can be used to model a problem and make estimates. Their great advantage is the possibility of controlling the estimate errors. Nevertheless, the studies available in the literature [5,6] have considered only information criteria, such as the sum of least squares [7] and AIC [8], as evaluation indexes with respect to the dataset and comparison of the solution candidate models. Despite the models obtained through this technique generate good indexes, sometimes the final models may not be representative, since the model structure assumptions were not verified, bringing some incorrect estimates [9].

So, in this study we propose the use of statistical inference and residual analysis to evaluate the final model, obtained through GP, where we check the assumptions about the structure of the model. In order to evaluate the proposed approach, we carried out some experiments with the prediction of performance of applications in embedded systems.

This chapter is organized as follows. In Section 2, we briefly introduce the theoretical basis of the regression analysis. In Section 3, we detail the main points of the proposed approach. In Section 4, we introduce the application of the proposed approach through a case study. Section 5 shows the experimental results of the case study. Finally, in Section 6, we raise the conclusions obtained with this work.

2. Linear regression background

Like most of the statistical analysis techniques, the objective of the linear regression analysis is to summarize, through a mathematical model called Linear Regression Model (LRM), the relations among variables in a simple and useful way [10]. In some problems, they can also be used to specify how one of the variables, in this case called response variable or dependent variable, varies as a function of the change in the values of the other variables of the relation, called predictive variables, regressive variables or systematic variables.

The predictive variables can be quantitative or qualitative. The quantitative variables are those which can be measured through a quantitative scale (i.e., they have a measurement unit). On the other hand, the qualitative variables are divided in classes. The individual classes of a classification are called *levels* or *classes* of a factor. In the classification of data in terms of factors and levels, the important characteristic that is observed is the extent of the variables of a factor which can influence the variable of interest [11]. These factors are often represented by dummy variables [12].

Let D be a factor with five levels. The jth dummy variable U_j for the factor D, with $j=1,...,5$, has the ith value u_{ij}, for $i=1,...,n$, given by

$$u_{ij} = \begin{cases} 1, & if \quad D_i = j^{th} \quad category \quad of \quad D \\ 0, & otherwise \end{cases} . \tag{1}$$

For instance, let there be a variable, which supports a certain characteristic x, as a two-level factor D. Taking a sample, shown in Table 1, with 5 different configurations, we can represent the factor D with the dummy variables of Table 2.

	Support to characteristic *x*
1	Yes
2	No
3	Yes
4	No
5	No

Table 1. Sample with size 5, with several pipeline support configurations.

	u1	u2
1	1	0
2	0	1
3	1	0
4	0	1
5	0	1

Table 2. Representation of the sample of Table 1, through dummy variables.

We can see in Table 2 that the configurations with support to the characteristic x had values $u1=1$ and $u2=0$, and that the configurations without support had values $u1=0$ and $u2=1$.

LRMs may also consider the combination of two or more factors. When the LRM has more than one factor, the effect of the combination of two or more factors is called *interaction effect*. Interactions occur when the effect of a factor varies according to the level of another factor [10]. In contrast, the effect of a simple factor, that is, without interaction, is called *main effect*. The interaction concept is given as follows: if the change in the mean of the response variable between two levels of a factor A is the same for different levels of a factor B, then we can say that there is no interaction; but if the change is different for different levels of B, then we say that there is interaction. Interactions report the effect that factors have over the risk of the model, and which are not reported in the analysis of correlation between the factors.

So, considering the relations between the dependent variables and the predictive variables, the statistical linear regression model will be comprised of two functions, one for the mean and another for the variance, defined by the following equations, respectively:

$$E(Y \mid X = x) = \beta_0 + \beta_1 x \tag{2}$$

$$Var(Y \mid X = x) = \sigma^2 \tag{3}$$

where the parameters in the *mean* function are the intercept β_0, which is the value of the mean $E(Y|X=x)$ when x is equal to zero, and the slope β_1, which is the rate of change in $E(Y|X=x)$ for a change of values of X, as we can see in Figure 1. Varying these parameters, it is possible to obtain all the line equations. In most applications, these parameters are unknown and must be estimated with basis on the problem data. So, we assume that the *variance* function is constant, with a positive value σ^2 which is normally unknown.

Differently from the mathematical models, which are deterministic, linear regression models consider the errors between the observed values and these estimated by the line equation. So, due to the variance $\sigma^2>0$, the values observed for the ith response y_i are typically different from the expected values $E(Y|X=x_i)$. In order to consider the error between the observed and the expected data, we have the concept of statistical error, or e_i, for the case i implicitly defined by the equation:

$$y_i = E(Y \mid X = x_i) + e_i \tag{4}$$

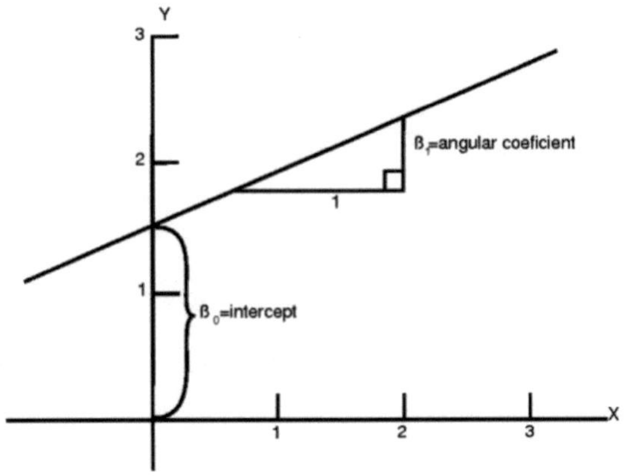

Figure 1. Graphic of the line equation $E(Y|X=x)=\beta_0+\beta_1 x$.

or explicitly by:

$$e_i = y_i - E(Y|X = x_i) \tag{5}$$

The e_i errors depend on the unknown parameters of the *mean* function and are random variables, corresponding to the vertical distance between the point y_i and the function of the mean $E(Y|X=x_i)$.

We make two important assumptions about the nature of the errors. First, we assume that $E(e_i|x_i)=0$. The second assumption is that the errors must be independent, which means that the value of the error for one case does not generate information about the value of the error for another case. In general, we assume that the errors are normally distributed (statistical Gaussian distribution), with mean zero and variance σ^2, which is unknown.

Assuming n pairs of observations $(x_1, y_1), (x_2, y_2), \ldots, (x_n, y_n)$, the estimates $\hat{\beta}_0$ and $\hat{\beta}_1$ of β_0 and β_1, respectively, must result in a line that best fits to the points. Many statistical methods are suggested to obtain estimates of the parameters of a model. Among these models, we can highlight the Least Squares and Maximum Likelihood methods. The first one stands out for being the most used estimator [13]. So, the Least Squares methods is intended to minimize the sum of the squares of the residuals e_i, which will be defined next, where the estimators are given by the equations:

$$\hat{\beta}_1 = \frac{\sum_{i=1}^{n} y_i x_i - \frac{(\sum_{i=1}^{n} y_i)(\sum_{i=1}^{n} x_i)}{n}}{\sum_{i=1}^{n} x_i^2 - \frac{(\sum_{i=1}^{n} x_i)^2}{n}} \tag{6}$$

$$\hat{\beta}_0 = \overline{y} - \hat{\beta}_1 \overline{x} \tag{7}$$

where $\overline{x}$ and $\overline{y}$ are given by:

$$\overline{x} = \frac{\sum_{i=1}^{n} x_i}{n} \tag{8}$$

$$\overline{y} = \frac{\sum_{i=1}^{n} y_i}{n} \tag{9}$$

With the estimators, the regression line (or model) is given by:

$$\hat{y} = \hat{\beta}_0 + \hat{\beta}_1 x \tag{10}$$

where each pair of observations meets the relation:

$$y_i = \hat{\beta}_0 + \hat{\beta}_1 x_i + e_i, \quad for \quad i = 1,2,..,n \tag{11}$$

From the above equation, we can then define the residual as:

$$r = \hat{e}_i = y_i - \hat{y}_i \tag{12}$$

where $\hat{e}_i$ is the error in the fitness of the model for the ith observation of y_i.

The residuals $\hat{e}_i$ are used to obtain an estimate of the variance σ^2 through the sum of the squares of $\hat{e}_i$:

$$\hat{\sigma}^2 = \frac{\sum_{i=1}^{n} \hat{e}_i^2}{n-2} \tag{13}$$

According to [14], the traditional project flow for modeling through LRMs can be divided into three stages: (i) formulation of models; (ii) fitness and (iii) inference.

LRMs are a very useful tool, since they are very flexible in stage (i), are simply computable in (ii) and have reasonable criteria in (iii). These stages are performed in this sequence. In the analysis of complex data, after the inference stage, we may go back to stage (i) and choose other models with basis on more detailed information obtained from (iii).

The first stage, formulation of models, covers the choice of options for the distribution of probabilities of the response variable (random component), predictive variables and the function that links these two components. The response variable used in this work consists in the estimate of the performance of the communication structure of the platform. The predictive variables are the configuration parameters of the buses contained in the space of the communication project. For this study, we analyzed several linking functions, and empirically chose the *identity* function, because it represents the direct mapping between bus configurations and their respective estimated performances.

The fitness stage consists in the process of estimation of the linear parameters of the generalized linear models. Several methods can be used to estimate the LRM parameters, such as the Least Squares and Maximum Likelihood methods.

Finally, the inference stage has the main objective of checking the adequateness of the model and performing a detailed study about the unconformities between the observations and the estimates given by the model. These unconformities, when significant, may imply in the choice of another linear model, or in the acceptance of aberrant data. Anyway, the whole methodology will have to be repeated. The analyst, in this stage, must check the precision and the interdependence of the performance estimates, build trust regions and tests about the parameters of interest, statistically analyze the residuals and make predictions.

3. Description of the proposed approach

The GP algorithm herein used follows the same guidelines of the traditional GP approaches: representation of solutions as genetic individuals; selection of the training set; generation of the starting population of genetic individuals that are solution candidates; fitness of the solution candidates to the training set; selection of parents; evolution, through selection, crossover and mutation operators [2]. Besides these activities, this work includes two new stages, which consist in the evaluation of the final model, as shown in the flow of Figure 1.

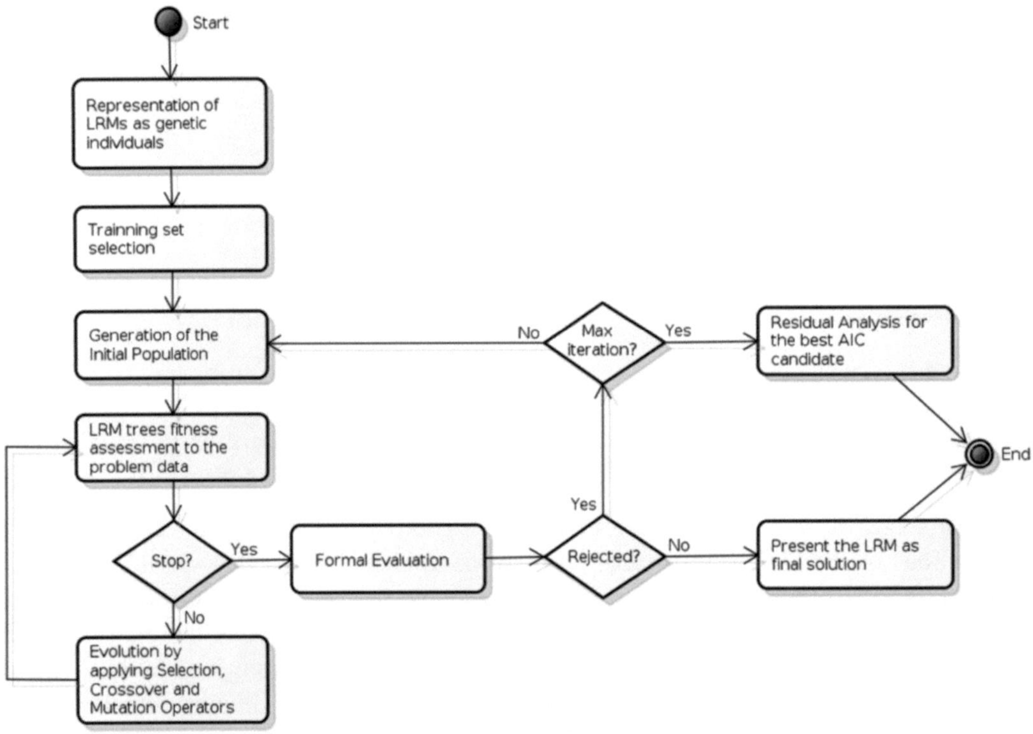

Figure 2. Flow of the proposed PG approach with LRM.

When the processing of the GP algorithms ends, due to some stop criterion, (e.g. the maximum number of generations is reached), the fittest genetic individual to the data is selected to be formally evaluated through statistical inference, with the application of the test of assumptions. Depending on the result of the evaluation, the GP algorithm can either start a new iteration, generating a new starting population, or present the LRM as a final solution.

If no candidate is approved in the formal evaluation, at the end of the iterations (limited to a maximum number as the second stop criterion), the best candidate among all the iterations may be reevaluated through residual diagnosing. In this other evaluation method, the assumptions about the model may be less formal, becoming, this way, a more subjective kind of analysis.

Each one of the activities presented in the Flow of Figure 1 will be detailed in the next subsections.

3.1. Representation of solutions as genetic individuals

GP normally uses trees as data structures [15] because the solutions are, commonly, mathematical expressions, and then it is necessary to keep their syntactic structure (trees are largely used to represent syntactic structures, defined according to some formal grammar [16]).

As seen in the previous subsection, linear regression models are statistical models comprised of two elements: a response variable and the independent variables. So, these models are structured, in the proposed approach, also as trees, called *expression trees*, where the internal nodes are either linking operators (represented by the arithmetic operator of addition) or iteration operators (represented by the arithmetic operator of multiplication) acting between the predictive variables, which are located in the leaves of the tree, as shown in Figure 3.

$$y=\beta_o+\beta_1 . X_1+\beta_2 X_2+\beta_3 . X_3$$

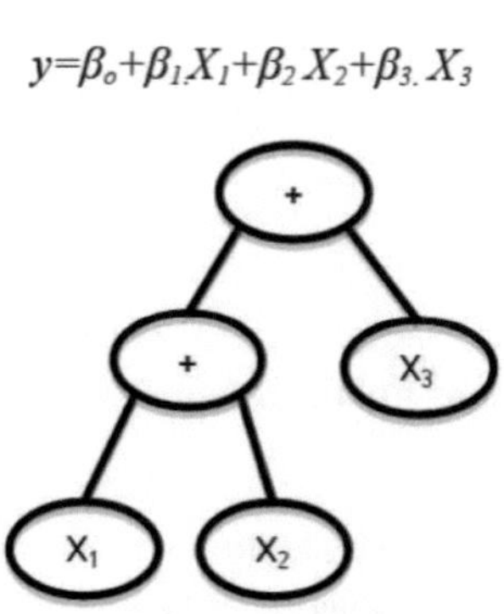

Figure 3. Example of LRM modeled as a genetic individual.

It can be seen, in the top of Figure 3, an LRM, and right below, the respective model in the form of a tree, which is the structure of a genetic individual. In this individual, we have, in the roots of the tree and of the sub-tree in the left, the linking operator, and in the leaves we have the predictive variables X_1, X_2 and X_3.

Formally, an LRM modeled as a genetic individual can be defined as a tree containing a finite set of one or more nodes, where:

i. there is a special node called *root*.
ii. the rest of the nodes form:
    1. two distinct sets where
    2. each one of these sets is also a tree which, in this case, is also called *sub-tree*. The sub-trees may be either left or right.
iii. the roots of the tree, and of the adjacent sub-trees, is either a linking or an iteration operator.
iv. the leaves are independent variables.

Once we define the data structure that will be used to represent the LRMs as genetic individuals, the next task, as defined in the flow of Figure 2, is the selection of the points of the project space that will be used to form the training set for the GP algorithm. The following subsection gives more details about the technique chosen to select points.

3.2. Selection of the training set

The selection of the elements that will compose the training set can be done in many ways, but techniques like random sampling do not guarantee a distributed sample, and variance-based sampling does not allow to collect the whole dataset of the sample, and then the selected set may not be enough to obtain a linear regression model which enables accurate estimates. So, in this work, we use the Design of Experiment technique [17] for the selection of points that will compose the training space.

Design of experiments, also known in statistics as Controlled Experiment, refers to the process of planning, designing and analyzing an experiment so that valid and objective conclusions can be extracted effectively and efficiently. In general, these techniques are used to collect the maximum of relevant information with the minimum consumption of time and resources, and to obtain optimal solutions, even when it is impossible to have a functional mathematical (deterministic) model [17-20]

The design of experiment technique adopted in this work is known as *Audze-Eglais Uniform Latin Hypercube* [21,22]. The Audze-Eglais method is based on the following analogy to Physics:

> *Assume a system composed of points of mass unit which exert repulsive forces among each other, causing the system to have potential energy. When the points are freed, from a starting state, they move. These points will achieve equilibrium when the potential energy of the repulsive forces of the masses is minimal. If the magnitude of the repulsive forces is inversely proportional to the square of the distance between the points, then the minimization of equation below will produce a system of distributed points, as uniform as possible.*

$$U = \sum_{p=1}^{P} \sum_{q=p+1}^{P} \frac{1}{L_{pq}^{2}} \tag{14}$$

where U is the potential energy and is the distance between the points p and q, and $p \neq q$.

The points of the project space are comprised of the parameters of the system to be modeled, and each point is a combination of the values that these parameters can receive. The Audze-Eglais method can be applied to these project spaces, provided that we consider the intervals (the distances) between the values of each parameter of the system, and that these values are taken together, in order to minimize the objective function.

The minimization of the above equation can be performed through some optimization technique or by verification of every possible combination. The use of the second approach may be unviable, since the search for each possible combination in project spaces with many points has a high computational cost. So, in this study, we used the GPRSKit [23] tool, which uses genetic programming techniques to minimize the equation, and outputs the points of the project space identified in the optimization of the equation.

Once defined the training set, the next task is the generation of a starting population of genetic individuals, which are LRMs candidate to solution, so the genetic algorithm can evolve them.

3.3. Generation of the starting population of genetic individuals

There must be a starting population so that the evolution algorithm can act, through the application of the selection, crossover and evolution operators. For this, aiming at the variability of individuals and consequent improvement on the precision of results, we adopted the *Ramped Half-and-Half* [24] technique.

This technique selects, initially, a random value to be the maximum depth of the tree to be generated. Next, the method for generation of the new tree is selected. *Ramped Half-and-Half* uses two generation methods, where each one generates half of the population. They are described below:

- **Growing**: this method creates new trees of several sizes and shapes, regarding the depth limit previously defined. Figure 4(a) shows an example of a tree created with the application of this method. In it, we see that the leaves have different depths.
- **Complete**: a tree created with this method has its leaves with the same depth, which is also selected at random, but respects the depth limit initially selected. Figure 4(b) shows a tree created with this method. Notice that all leaves have the same depths.

3.4. Description of the utility function (Fitness)

The fitness of a candidate LRM is evaluated with basis on the quality of the estimates that it generates compared to the data obtained from the problem data. The quality of an LRM can be quantified through its fitness and its complexity, measured, in this study, by the *Akaike Information Criterion* (AIC) [8], since it is one of the most used criteria [10].

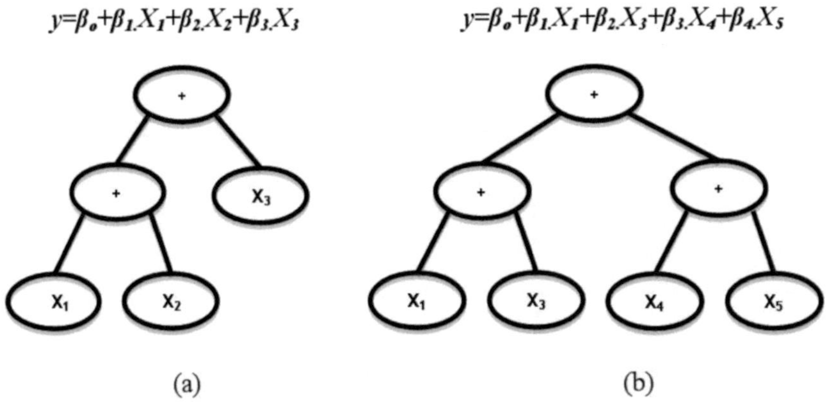

Figure 4. Examples of trees generated from (a) complete generation method and (b) generation by growing.

The AIC can be given by the following equation:

$$AIC = 2.tc - 2.\ln(L) \tag{15}$$

where tc is the number of terms of the model and L is the likeliness, which is the pooled density of all the observations. Considering an independent variable with normal distribution with mean $\beta_0 + \beta_1 x_i$ and variance σ^2, the likeliness can be given by:

$$L(\beta_0, \beta_1, \sigma^2) = \frac{1}{\sigma^2(\sqrt{2\pi})^n} e^{-\frac{1}{2}.\frac{\sum_{i=1}^{n}(y_i - \beta_0 - \beta_1 x_i)^2}{\sigma^2}} \tag{16}$$

3.5. Evolution

In this stage we apply, to the solution candidate genetic individuals, the selection, mutation and evolution operations. The first operation is responsible for the selection of individuals that will compose the set of parents. In this set, the genetic crossover function will act, so that the genetic content of each individual will be transferred to another one, generating new solution candidates. The objective is to group the best characteristics in certain individuals, forming better solutions. The mutation function will select some of the individuals to have their genetic content randomly changed, to cause genetic variability in the populations, avoiding the convergence of the algorithm to a local maximum.

The selection, crossover and mutation operations are described next.

3.5.1. Parents selection

The method for selection of parents must simulate the natural selection mechanism that acts on the biological species: the most qualified parents, those which better fits to the problem data, generate a large number of children, while the less qualified can also have descendents, so avoiding premature genetic convergence. Consequently, we focus on individuals highly fitted, without completely discarding those individuals with very low degree of fitness.

In order to build a set of parent LRMs, we use the tournament selection method [25]. In this approach, a predetermined number of solution candidate LRMs are randomly chosen to compete against each other. With this selection technique, the best LRMs of the population will only have advantage over the worst, *i.e.*, they will only win the tournament if they are chosen. Tournament parameters, like tournament size and generations number, are dependent on the problem domain. In this work, they are described in case study section.

The proposed approach for GP also uses the technique of selection by elitism [26]. In this approach, only the individual having the best fitness function value is selected. With this, we guarantee that the results of the GP approach will always have a progressive increase at each generation.

3.5.2. Crossover and mutation

In order to find the LRM that best fits to the data obtained with communication graphs, the crossover and mutation operators are applied to the genetic individuals, the LRM trees, as shown in Figure 5. The crossover and mutation operators, in genetic programming, are similar to those present in conventional genetic algorithms.

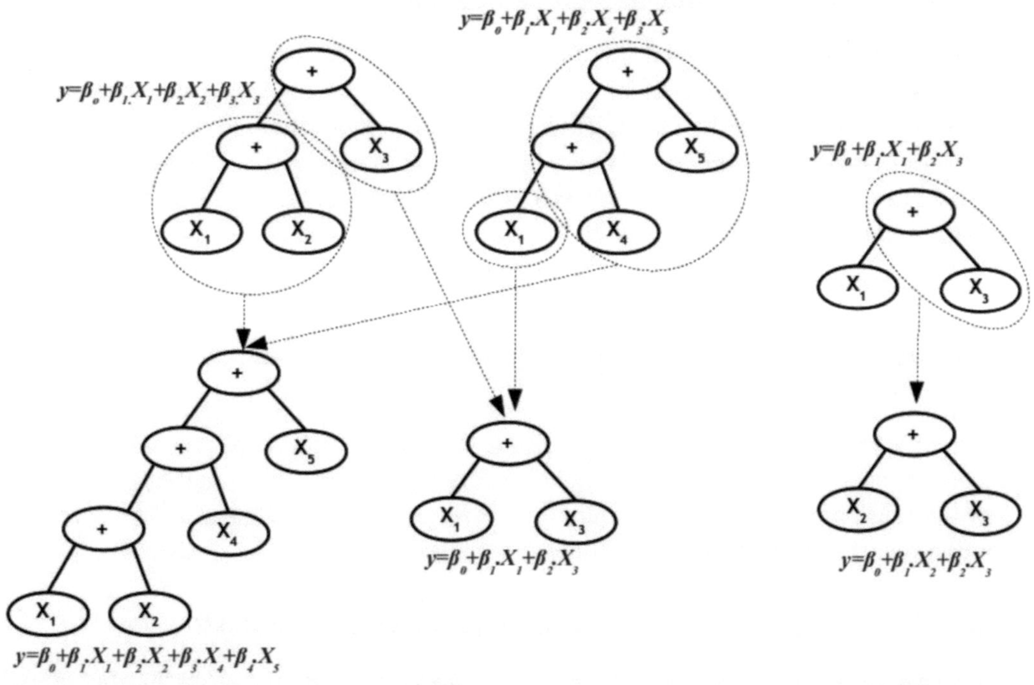

Figure 5. Expression trees representing LRMs under the operations of (a) crossover and (b) mutation.

In the first operator, represented in Figure 5 (a), the candidates are selected for reproduction according to their fitness (fittest candidates have higher probabilities of being selected) and, next, exchange their genetic content (sub-trees), randomly chosen, between each other. Figure 5(b) illustrates the crossover of the parents $y=\beta_0+ \beta_1.X_1 +\beta_2.X_2 + \beta_3.X_3$ and $y=\beta_0+ \beta_1.X_1 +\beta_2.X_4 + \beta_3.X_5$, generating the children $y=\beta_0+ \beta_1.X_1 +\beta_2.X_2 + \beta_3.X_4+ \beta_4.X_5$ and $y=\beta_0+ \beta_1.X_1 +\beta_2.X_3$.

With mutation, represented in Figure 5 (b), after a crossover operation, it is randomly generated a mutation factor for each new genetic individual. If the mutation factor exceeds a predetermined boundary, a sub-tree is selected at random in the LRM and mutated to a new different sub-tree. Figure 5 illustrates the mutation of the model $y=\beta_0+ \beta_1.X_1 + \beta_2.X_3$ to $y=\beta_0+ \beta_1.X_2 + \beta_2.X_3$, where it can be noticed that there was a mutation in the genetic content X_1 to X_2.

In the approach proposed in this work, we used the two-point crossover operator [27], because this way it combines the largest number of chromosomal schemes and, consequently, increases the performance of the technique. On the other hand, for mutation, we used the simple operator [27], because the mutation prevents the stagnation of the search with low mutation factor, but if this rate is too high, the search becomes excessively random, because the highest its value is, larger is the substituted part of the population, which may lead to the less of highly qualified structures.

3.6. Formal evaluation of a linear regression model

Once an iteration of the proposed GP algorithm is ended, the best solution found in the iteration is formally evaluated. In linear regression, assumptions about the fitted model must be considered so that the results can be reliable. So, the evaluation process consists in verifying, by residual inference, the assumptions of normality, homoscedasticity and independence about the distribution of errors of the fitted LRM. We used the following adherence tests:

- *Shapiro-Wilk* [30] to check the assumption of normality;
- *Breusch-Pagan* [31] to check the assumption homoscedasticity;
- and *Durbin-Watson* [32] to check the independence (absence of autocorrelation) among the errors.

If the result of any of these tests is not positive and the maximum number of iterations was not reached, the GP algorithm will start a new evolution iteration through the generation of a new starting population and will follow the flow presented in Figure 2. Otherwise, the algorithm presents the LRM as final solution.

3.7. Residual Analyses for the genetic individual with the best AIC

At the end of all the iterations, if no genetic individual is approved in the formal evaluations, the GP algorithm will select the solution with the best AIC for residual analysis. The residual analysis allows the evaluation of the assumptions about a model [12].

So, in this work, the residual analysis is divided in two stages:

1. Residual diagnostic plots, where we build the following diagrams:
   - Diagram of distribution of accumulated errors, to quantify the distance between the estimates given by the LRM and the data of the training set;
   - Q-Q Plots and Histograms, to check the assumptions about the error probability distributions;
   - Diagram of residuals dispersion against the fitted values, the check the assumption of homoscedasticity;
   - Diagram of dispersion of the residuals, to check the absence of autocorrelation among the errors.
2. Application of the statistical test of *Mann-Whitney-Wilcoxon* [29] to the data of the training set and the respective estimates given by the LRM found. The *Mann-Whitney-Wilcoxon* test is a non-parametric [28] statistical hypothesis test used to check whether the data of two independent sets tend to be equal (null hypothesis) or different (alternative hypothesis). With these same sets, we still perform the computation of the global mean errors, as a measurement for the central location of the set of residuals, maximums and minimums. These measurements are used to check the precision of the estimates and the possibility of presence of *outliers*.

4. Case study

In order to validate the proposed approach, we have used a case study where we predict the performance of an embedded system. The case study includes an application of the SPLASH benchmark[1] [33] for a simulation model of an embedded hardware platform. This application, which consists in the sorting a set of integers through radix [34], has two processes. The first one allocates, in a shared memory, a data structure (list), comprised of a set of integers, randomly chosen, some control flags and a *mutex* (to manage the mutually exclusive access). Once the data structure is allocated, both processes will sort the integers list, concurrently.

For the execution of the application, we designed a simulation model of a hardware platform, described in the language for modeling embedded systems, SystemC [35], comprised of two models of MIPS processors, one for each process of the application of sorting by radix, a shared memory, to stores program and application data, as well as shared data, and a ARM Amba AHB [36] shared bus model.

This model allows us to explore the bus configurations to optimize the performance of the application of radix sort.

The experiment methodology was based on the comparison between the execution times of the application, obtained by the simulation model with the estimates acquired from an LRM obtained by the proposed method. The objective is to show that the obtained models may bring highly precise estimates.

---

[1] Set of multiprocessed applications, used to study the following properties: computational load balance, computation rates and traffic requirements in communications, besides issues related to spatial locations and how these properties can be scalable with the size of the problems and the number of processors.

We considered the following configuration parameters for the Amba AHB bus: data bus width, fixed priority arbitrage mechanisms, operation frequency and transference types. With the combination of the possible values for these parameters, we built a project space with 72 distinct configurations.

In the representation of the LRMs, in the proposed GP algorithm, the configuration parameters of the bus ware characterized as predictive variables and the execution time of the embedded application, as the independent variable. The table below describes each one of these variables.

Variable	Representation in the LRM	Values
Data bus width	bw	8, 16, 32 (bits)
Transference type	ty	With preemption, without preemption
Operation frequency	fr	100, 166, 200 (MHz)
Priority of the first process	p1	Higher, lower (priority)
Priority of the second process	p2	Higher, lower (priority)
Execution time of the application	te	Time measured in ns

Table 3. Candidate variables to the linear regression model.

It can be seen in Table 3 that all the predictive variables have discrete values, and then they are classified as factors. In the LRMs, the predictive variables are represented as dummy variables.

With the increase in the training set, the probability of distortion on the estimates may increase, because the possibility of existence of outliers in this set may also increase. On the other hand, larger training sets may be more significant for the obtainment of a more precise model. For this reason, we used three training sets, with distinct sizes, to check these assumptions. So, we selected three sets, using the technique introduced in Subsection 3.2, with 10% (7 samples), 20% (14 samples) and 50% (36 samples) of the project space. The rest of the points were grouped in test sets, used to evaluate the precision of the estimates given by the obtained models.

According to [2], on average, 50 generations are sufficient to find an acceptable solution, and larger populations have higher probability of finding a valid solution. So, for the GP algorithm, we considered the following parameters: 1000 candidates for each generation of LRM trees; the maximum number of generations was limited in 50; and stop condition of the algorithm consisting of an LRM which is the fittest candidate for 30 consecutive generations.

For each generation, 999 tournaments were carried out, where 50 LRMs were randomly chosen to participate. During the tournament the AIC index is computed, in order to evaluate each one of the participants. So, the winners, those with the best AIC indexes, are selected for crossover. For mutation, a mutation factor is randomly computed in all the LRM trees generated by crossover. If the computed value for each tree is below 5% - index demonstrated in [37] as qualified to find good solutions in several problem types - then the three will mutate and, next, selected to make part of the next generation. Finally, the fittest LRM trees of the present generation are automatically selected, through elitism, to complete the number of individuals of the next generation. Finally, the maximum number of iterations was limited to 50.

After the validation stages, the final models found, for the training set, had their estimates, given by prediction, compared to those of the respective training sets, as described in the next section.

5. Experimental results

As described in the previous section, we used three training sets for validation of the proposed approach. However, the application of this approach brought different results for these sets.

For the first set, that with 10% if the project space, which we will call Set A, the final model was approved in the formal evaluation, right in the first iteration. For Set B (the set with 20% of the design space), the final model was also approved in the formal evaluation, but needed five iterations. The results of the formal tests for the models selected for the Sets A and B can be seen in Table 4.

Measurement	**P-Value**		
Set	**A**	**B**	**C**
***Shapiro-Wilk* test(Normality)**	14.44%	65.69%	3.2%
***Breusch-Pagan* test (Homoscedasticity)**	53.66%	47.34%	1e-03%
***Durbin-Watson* test (Independence)**	87.2%	56.80%	82.80%

Table 4. Formal test results for verification of assumptions about the LRMs selected for the Sets A, B and C.

The test results for Sets A and B, presented in Table 4, show indexes (p-values) above the significance level, defined in this work as 5%. So, the structures of the errors of the selected LRMs, for the sets A and B, tend to have normalized errors, with constant variances and independent from each other.

Finally, for the Set C, the last training set, no model was approved in the formal evaluation. Table 4 also shows the tests results for the final model found (best AIC) for the Set C. The p-values for the *Shapiro-Wilk* and *Breusch-Pagan* tests are below the significance level, being necessary to do residual analysis. The final results of the residual analysis are shown in the graphics of Figure 6.

Figure 6 presents the graphics of (a) Q-Q Plot and (b) Residuals histograms, as well as (c) of dispersion of the values observed in the Set C versus residuals and (d) of the order of collection of residuals. Analyzing Figure 6 (b), we may notice that the errors presented by the LRM selected for the Set C do not follow a normal distribution, violating the assumption of normality of the model structure. However, it can be seen that the distribution of the errors tends to be normal, since the points are distributed around the diagonal line of the Q-Q Plot diagram shown in Figure 6 (a). In Figure 6 (c), in turn, the assumption of homoscedasticity can be confirmed, since the maximum dispersion of the points is constant around the line. Finally, the last assumption, independence among the errors, can be verified in Figure 6 (d), since there is no apparent linear pattern in the distribution of points.

So, in the diagrams of residual analysis, we could verify that all the assumptions – normality, homoscedasticity and independence of the errors – about the structures of the errors of the LRM selected for the Set C were met.

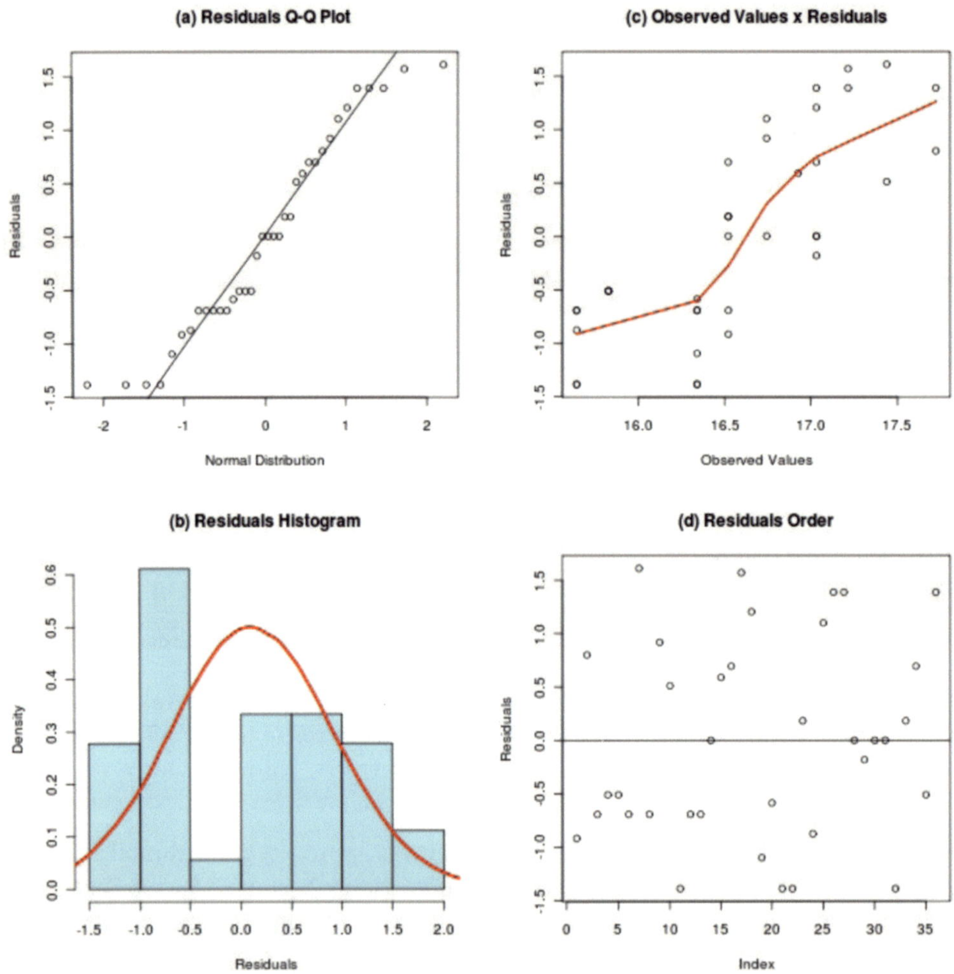

Figure 6. Graphics for analysis of assumptions about the distribution of errors for the training set with 50% of the project space.

Measurement	**Set A**	**Set B**	**Set C**
***Mann-Whitney-Wilcoxon* test (P-Value)**	100%	100%	79.12%
Global mean error	7.81e-08%	0%	7.15e-06%
Maximum error	1.43e-07%	0%	4.52e-05%
Minimum error	0%	0%	1.88e-08%

Table 5. Testing the fitness to the data from the training set and global mean, maximum and minimum errors for the LRMs selected for the Sets A, B and C.

In order to check the adherence of the LRMs to the data of the respective training sets, we performed the *Mann-Whitney-Wilcoxon* test, besides the computation of the global mean, maximum and minimum errors. The results can be seen in Table 5.

According to the result of the *Mann-Whitney-Wilcoxon* test, presented in Table 5, we can see that the estimates, given by the LRMs selected for the Sets A, B and C, tend to be equal to the data in the respective training sets, since the p-values are above the significance level, defined in the test as 5%. Analyzing Table 5, still, we notice that the selected LRMs presented accurate estimates, since the mean global, maximum and minimum errors were almost zero.

Still analyzing the precision of the estimates, with respect to the Set C, the diagram of accumulated errors is presented in Figure 7. It shows the cumulative error (x axis) for percentages of the training set (y axis). The accumulated errors indicate the deviation between the estimates given by the LRM and the data from the training set. In this case, the estimates given by the selected LRM differed by a maximum of 5e-07.

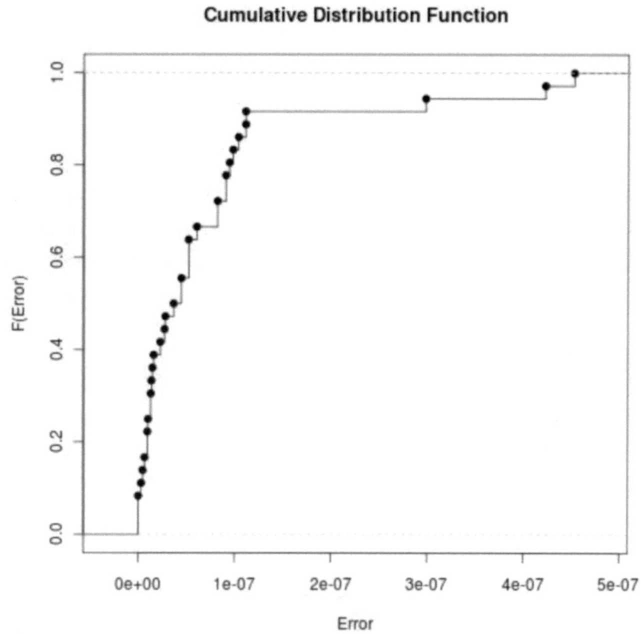

Figure 7. Graphic of accumulated errors for the LRM selected for the Set C.

Finally, in order to evaluate the precision of the predictions, which are the estimates given for the respective test sets of the Sets A, B and C, the selected LRMS were submitted to the *Mann-Whitney-Wilcoxon* test. Besides this test, the global mean, maximum and minimum errors were computed. The results can be seen in Table 6.

In Table 6, according to the results of the *Mann-Whitney-Wilcoxon* test, defined with a significance index of 5%, for the three sets, the estimates given by the selected LRMs tend to be equal to the data of the respective test sets. The three models had values for the global mean and minimum errors very close. For the maximum errors, there was a little variation, with the LRMs selected for the sets B and C, obtaining the highest and the lowest indexes, respectively.

Measurement	Results		
Set	**A**	**B**	**C**
***Mann-Whitney-Wilcoxon* test (P-Value)**	53.05%	69.11%	59.25%
Mean global error	4.12%	4.15%	4.75%
Maximum error	11.11%	14.21%	9.23%
Minimum error	4.905e-05%	9.171e-02%	8.27e-06%

Table 6. Test of fitness to the data of the test set and the global mean, maximum and minimum errors.

Still analyzing the results of the measurements presented in Table 6, we notice that the indexes obtained for the three sets, were comparatively very close. Such results may be explained by the used of the technique of selection of the training sets, which returns samples with high representative power.

In general, the use of the approach proposed in this work, which added methods for evaluation of the LRMs selected by the GP algorithm and the technique of selection of the elements of the training sets, allows the obtainment of solutions capable of providing precise estimates, even with the use of small samples.

6. Conclusions

This work has described an approach for obtainment and formal validation of LRMs, by means of the combination of genetic programming with statistical models. Our approach used the Audze-Eglais Uniform Latin Hypercube technique for the selection of samples with high representative power to form the training set. In order to evaluate the LRMs found with the introduced technique, we used statistical tests of hypothesis and residual analysis, aiming to verify the assumptions about the structures of the errors of these models.

In order to validate the proposed approach, we used a case study, with the prediction of performance in embedded systems. The problem of the case study consisted in exploring the configurations of a data bus in order to optimize the performance of the embedded application of sorting a set of integers by radix. So, with the use of the proposed technique, we generated LRMs capable of estimating the performance for all of the bus configurations.

The validation stages allowed us to realize that the LRMs found are adequate to the prediction of performance of the application, since all the assumptions about the structures of the errors were verified. So, the final LRMs were able to estimate the performances accurately, presenting mean global errors below 5%.

Author details

Guilherme Esmeraldo[1,3,*], Robson Feitosa[1], Dilza Esmeraldo[2], Edna Barros[3]
[1]*Federal Institute of Ceará, Crato,*
[2]*Catholic College of Cariri, Crato,*
[3]*Federal University of Pernambuco, Recife, Brazil*

[*] Corresponding Author

Acknowledgement

This paper has been supported by the Brazilian Research Council - CNPq under grant number 309089/2007-7.

7. References

[1] Augusto D.A (2000) Symbolic Regression Via Genetic Programming. In Proceedings of Sixth Brazilian Symposium on Neural Networks, Rio de Janeiro.
[2] Koza J.R (1992) Genetic Programming: On the Programming of Computers by Means of Natural Selection, MIT Press.
[3] Spector L, Goodman E, Wu A, Langdon W.B, Voigt H.M, Gen M, Sem S, Dorigo M, Pezeshk S, Garzon M, Burke E (2001) Towards a New Evolutionary Computation: Advances in the Estimation of Distribution Algorithms. In Proceedings of the Genetic and Evolutionary Computation Conference, Morgan Kaufmann.
[4] Keijzer M (2003) Improving Symbolic Regression with Interval Arithmetic and Linear Scaling.In Ryan C, Soule T, Keijzer M, Tsang E, Poli R., Costa E, editors. Heidelberg: Springer. 70-78 pp.
[5] Esmeraldo G, Barros E (2010) A Genetic Programming Based Approach for Efficiently Exploring Architectural Communication Design Space of MPSOCS. In Proceedings of VI Southern Programmable Logic Conference.
[6] Paterlini S, Minerva T (2010) Regression Model Selection Using Genetic Algorithms, Proceedings of the 11th WSEAS International Conference on RECENT Advances in Neural Networks, Fuzzy Systems & Evolutionary Computing.
[7] Wolberg J (2005) Data Analysis Using the Method of Least Squares: Extracting the Most Information from Experiments. Springer.
[8] Sakamoto Y, Ishiguro M, Kitagawa G (1986) Akaike Information Criterion Statistics. D. Reidel Publishing Company.
[9] Seber G. A. F, Lee A.J (2003) Linear Regression Analysis. Hoboken: Wiley.
[10] Weisberg S (2005) Applied Linear Regression, Third Edition. Hoboken: Wiley.
[11] McCulloch C.E, Searle S.R (2001) Generalized, Linear and Mixed Models. New York: Willey.
[12] Anderson D, Feldblum S, Modlin C, Schirmacher D, Schirmacher E, Thandi E (2004) A Practitioner's Guide to Generalized Linear Models. Watson Wyatt Worldwide.
[13] Hausmana J, Kuersteinerb G (2008) Difference in Difference Meets Generalized Least Squares: Higher Order Properties of Hypotheses Tests. In Journal of Econometrics, 144: 371-391.
[14] Nelder J.A, Wedderburn R.W (1972) Generalized linear models. Journal of the Royal Statistical Society Series A, 135 (3): 370–384.
[15] Chellapilla K (1997) Evolving Computer Programs Without Subtree Crossover. In IEEE. Transactions on Evolutionary Computation, 1(3):209–216.
[16] Aho A.V, Lam M.S, Sethi R, Ullman J.D (2006) Compilers: Principles, Techniques, and Tools, Second Edition. Prentice Hall.

[17] Antony J (2003) Design of Experiments for Engineers and Scientists. Butterworth-Heinemann.
[18] Cox D.E (2000) The Theory of the Design of Experiments. Chapman and Hall/CRC.
[19] Mitchell M (1999) An Introduction to Genetic Algorithms. MIT Press.
[20] Dean A, Voss D (1999) Design and Analysis of Experiements. Springer.
[21] Audze P, Eglais V (1977) A new approach to the planning out of experiments. Problems of dynamics and strength, volume 35, 1977.
[22] Bates J.S, Sienz J, Langley D.S (2003) Formulation of the Audze-Eglais Uniform Latin Hypercube Design of Experiments. Adv. Eng. Software, 34(8): 493-506.
[23] GPRSKit. Genetically Programmed Respone Surfaces Kit. Available: http://www.cs.berkeley.edu/~hcook/gprs.html. Accessed 2012 April 13.
[24] Koza J.R (1998) Genetic Programming On the Programming of Computers by Means of Natural Selection. MIT Press.
[25] Gen M, Cheng R (2000) Genetic algorithms and engineering optimization.Wiley.
[26] Ahn C.W, Ramakrishna R.S (2003) Elitism-Based Compact Genetic Algorithms. IEEE Transactions On Evolutionary Computation, 7(4).
[27] Koza J.R, Poli R (2005) Genetic Programming, In Edmund Burke and Graham Kendal, editors. Search Methodologies: Introductory Tutorials in Optimization and Decision Support Techniques. Springer.
[28] Sprent N, Smeeton N.C (2007) Applied Nonparametric Statistical Methods, Fourth Edition. Chapman and Hall/CRC.
[29] Fay M.P, Proschan M.A (2010) Wilcoxon-Mann-Whitney or t-test? On assumptions for hypothesis tests and multiple interpretations of decision rules. Statistics Survey, 4: 1-39 pp.
[30] Shapiro S.S, Wilk M.B (1965) An analysis of variance test for normality (complete samples). Biometrika 52 (3-4): 591–611 pp.
[31] Breusch T.S, Pagan A.R (1979) Simple test for heteroscedasticity and random coefficient variation. Econometrica (The Econometric Society) 47 (5): 1287–1294 pp.
[32] Savin N.E, White K.J (1977) The Durbin-Watson Test for Serial Correlation with Extreme Sample Sizes or Many Regressors. Econometrica 45(8): 1989-1996 pp.
[33] Woo S.C, Ohara M, Torrie E, Singh J.P, Gupta A (1995) The SPLASH-2 Programs: Characterization and Methodological Considerations. In Proceedings of the 22nd International Symposium on Computer Architecture Santa Margherita: 24-36 pp.
[34] Cormen T.H, Leiserson C.E, Rivest R.L, Stein C (2001) Introduction to Algorithms. McGraw-Hill and The Mit Press.
[35] Black D.C, Donovan J (2004) SystemC: From the Groung Up. Kluwer Academic Publishers.
[36] ARM AMBA (1999) AMBA Specification rev. 2.0, IHI-0011A, May 1999. Available: http://www.arm.com/products/system-ip/amba/amba-open-specifications.php. Accessed 2012 April 13.
[37] Madar J, Abonyi J, Szeifert F (2005) Genetic Programming for the Identification of Nonlinear Input–Output Models. In Industrial and Engineering Chemistry Research, 44: 3178 – 3186 pp.

Chapter 5

Parallel Genetic Programming on Graphics Processing Units

Douglas A. Augusto, Heder S. Bernardino and Helio J.C. Barbosa

Additional information is available at the end of the chapter

http://dx.doi.org/10.5772/48364

1. Introduction

In program inference, the evaluation of how well a candidate solution solves a certain task is usually a computationally intensive procedure. Most of the time, the evaluation involves either submitting the program to a simulation process or testing its behavior on many input arguments; both situations may turn out to be very time-consuming. Things get worse when the optimization algorithm needs to evaluate a population of programs for several iterations, which is the case of genetic programming.

Genetic programming (GP) is well-known for being a computationally demanding technique, which is a consequence of its ambitious goal: to automatically generate computer programs—in an arbitrary language—using virtually no domain knowledge. For instance, evolving a classifier, a program that takes a set of attributes and predicts the class they belong to, may be significantly costly depending on the size of the training dataset, that is, the amount of data needed to estimate the prediction accuracy of a single candidate classifier.

Fortunately, GP is an inherently parallel paradigm, making it possible to easily exploit any amount of available computational units, no matter whether they are just a few or many thousands. Also, it usually does not matter whether the underlying hardware architecture can process simultaneously instructions and data ("MIMD") or only data ("SIMD").[1] Basically, GP exhibits three levels of parallelism: (i) *population-level* parallelism, when many populations evolve simultaneously; (ii) *program-level* parallelism, when programs are evaluated in parallel; and finally (iii) *data-level* parallelism, in which individual training points for a single program are evaluated simultaneously.

Until recently, the only way to leverage the parallelism of GP in order to tackle complex problems was to run it on large high-performance computational installations, which are normally a privilege of a select group of researchers. Although the multi-core era has emerged and popularized the parallel machines, the architectural change that is probably going to

[1] MIMD stands for *Multiple Instructions Multiple Data* whereas SIMD means *Single Instruction Multiple Data*.

revolutionize the applicability of GP started about a decade ago when the GPUs began to acquire general-purpose programmability. Modern GPUs have an astonishing theoretical computational power, and are capable of behaving much like a conventional multi-core CPU processor in terms of programmability. However, there are some intrinsic limitations and patterns of workload that may cause huge negative impact on the resulting performance if not properly addressed. Hence, this paper aims at presenting and discussing efficient ways of implementing GP's evaluation phase, at the program- and data-level, so as to achieve the maximum throughput on a GPU.

The remaining of this chapter is organized as follows. The next Section, 2, will give an overview of the GPU architecture followed by a brief description of the open computing language, which is the open standard framework for heterogeneous programming, including CPUs and GPUs. Section 3 presents the development history of GP in the pursuit of getting the most out of the GPU architecture. Then, in Section 4, three fundamental parallelization strategies at the program- and data-level will be detailed and their algorithms presented in a pseudo-OpenCL form. Finally, Section 5 concludes the chapter and points out some interesting directions of future work.

2. GPU programming

The origin of graphics processing units dates back to a long time ago, when they were built exclusively to execute graphics operations, mainly to process images' pixels, such as calculating each individual pixel color, applying filters, and the like. In video or gaming processing, for instance, the task is to process batches of pixels within a short time-frame—such operation is also known as *frame rendering*—in order to display smooth and fluid images to the spectator or player.

Pixel operations tend to be very independent among them, in other words, each individual pixel can be processed at the same time as another one, leading to what is known as *data parallelism* or SIMD. Although making the hardware less general, designing an architecture targeted at some specific type of workload, like data parallelism, may result in a very efficient processor. This is one main reason why GPUs have an excellent performance with respect to power consumption, price, and density. Another major reason behind such a performance is attributed to the remarkable growing of the game industry in the last years and the fact that computer games have become more and more complex, pressing forward the development of GPUs while making them ubiquitous.

It turned out that at some point the development of GPUs was advancing so well and the architecture was progressively getting more ability to execute a wider range of sophisticated instructions, that eventually it earned the status of a general-purpose processor—although still an essentially data parallel architecture. That point was the beginning of the exploitation of the graphics processing unit as a parallel accelerator for a much broader range of applications besides video and gaming processing.

2.1. GPU architecture

The key design philosophy responsible for the great GPU's efficiency is the maximization of the number of transistors dedicated to actual computing—i.e., arithmetic and logic units (ALU)—which are packed as many small and relatively simple processors [26]. This is rather different from the modern multi-core CPU architecture, which has large and complex cores, reserving a considerable area of the processor die for other functional units, such as control units (out-of-order execution, branch prediction, speculative execution, etc.) and cache memory [21].

This design difference reflects the different purpose of those architectures. While the GPU is optimized to handle data-parallel workloads with regular memory accesses, the CPU is designed to be more generic and thus must manage with reasonable performance a larger variety of workloads, including MIMD parallelism, divergent branches and irregular memory accesses. There is also another important conceptual difference between them. Much of the extra CPU complexity is devoted to reduce the latency in executing a single task, which classifies the architecture as *latency-oriented* [14]. Conversely, instead of executing single tasks as fast as possible, GPUs are *throughput-oriented* architectures, which means that they are designed to optimize the throughput, that is, the amount of completed tasks per unit of time.

2.2. Open Computing Language – OpenCL

The Open Computing Language, or simply OpenCL, is an open specification for heterogeneous computing released by the Khronos Group[2] in 2008 [25]. It resembles the NVIDIA CUDA[3] platform [31], but can be considered as a superset of the latter; they basically differ in the following points. OpenCL (i) is an open specification that is managed by a set of distinct representatives from industry, software development, academia and so forth; (ii) is meant to be implemented by any compute device vendor, whether they produce CPUs, GPUs, hybrid processors, or other accelerators such as digital signal processors (DSP) and field-programmable gate arrays (FPGA); and (iii) is portable across architectures, meaning that a parallel code written in OpenCL is guaranteed to correctly run on every other supported device.[4]

2.2.1. Hardware model

In order to achieve code portability, OpenCL employs an abstracted device architecture that standardizes a device's processing units and memory scopes. All supported OpenCL devices must expose this minimum set of capabilities, although they may have different capacities and internal hardware implementation. Illustrated in Figure 1 is an OpenCL general device abstraction. The terms SPMD, SIMD and PC are mostly GPU-specific, though; they could be safely ignored on behalf of code portability, but understanding them is important to write efficient code for this architecture, as will become clear later on.

An OpenCL device has one or more *compute units* (CU), and there is at least one *processing element* (PE) per compute unit, which actually performs the computation. Such layers are meant (i) to encourage better partitioning of the problem towards fine-grained granularity and low communication, hence increasing the scalability to fully leverage a large number of CUs when available; and (ii) to potentially support more restricted compute architectures, by

[2] `http://www.khronos.org/opencl`

[3] CUDA is an acronym for *Compute Unified Device Architecture*, the NVIDIA's toolkit for GP-GPU programming.

[4] It is worthy to note that OpenCL only guarantees *functional portability*, i.e., there is no guarantee that the same code will perform equally well across different architectures (performance portability), since some low-level optimizations might fit a particular architecture better than others.

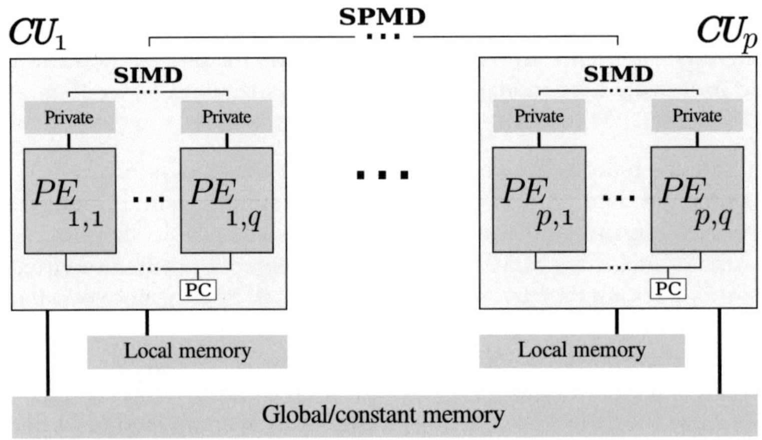

Figure 1. Abstraction of a modern GPU architecture

not strictly enforcing parallelism among CUs while still ensuring that the device is capable of doing synchronism, which can occur among PEs within each CU [15].

Figure 1 shows four scopes of memory, namely, *global*, *constant*, *local*, and *private* memories. The global memory is the device's main memory, the biggest but also the slowest of the four in terms of bandwidth and latency, specially for irregular accesses. The constant memory is a small and slightly optimized memory for read-only accesses. OpenCL provides two really fast memories: local and private. Both are very small; the main difference between them is the fact that the former is shared among all the PEs within a CU—thus very useful for communication—and the latter is even smaller and reserved for each PE.

Most of modern GPUs are capable of performing not only SIMD parallelism, but also what is referred to as SPMD parallelism (literally *Single Program Multiple Data*), which is the ability to simultaneously execute *different* instructions of the *same* program on many data. This feature is closely related to the capability of the architecture in maintaining a record of multiple different instructions within a program being executed which is done by *program counter* (PC) registers. Nowadays GPUs can usually guarantee that at least among compute units there exists SPMD parallelism, in other words, different CUs can execute different instructions in parallel. There may exist SPMD parallelism within CUs also, but they occur among blocks of PEs.[5] For the sake of simplicity, the remaining of this chapter will ignore this possibility and assume that all PEs within a CU can only execute one instruction at a time (SIMD parallelism), sharing a single PC register. A strategy of parallelization described in Section 4.4 will show how the SPMD parallelism can be exploited in order to produce one of the most efficient parallel algorithms for genetic programming on GPUs.

2.2.2. *Software model*

OpenCL specifies two code spaces: the *host* and *kernel* code. The former holds any user-defined code, and is also responsible for initializing the OpenCL platform, managing the device's memory (buffer allocation and data transfer), defining the problem's parallel

[5] Those blocks are known as *warps* [32] or *wavefronts* [1].

partitioning, submitting commands, and coordinating executions. The latter, the kernel code, is the actual parallel code that is executed by a compute device.

An OpenCL kernel is similar to a C function[6]. Due to architectural differences across devices, it has some restrictions, such as prohibiting recursion, but also adds some extensions, like vector data types and operators, and is intended to be executed in parallel by each processing element, usually with each instance working on a separate subset of the problem. A kernel instance is known as *work-item* whereas a group of work-items is called a *work-group*.

Work-items within a work-group are executed on a unique compute unit, therefore, according to the OpenCL specification, they can share information and synchronize. Determining how work-items are divided into work-groups is a critical phase when decomposing a problem; a bad division may lead to inefficient use of the compute device. Hence, an important part of the parallel modeling concerns defining what is known as *n-dimensional computation domain*. This turns out to be the definition of the *global size*, which is the total amount of work-items, and the *local size*, the number of work-items within a work-group, or simply the work-groups' size.

In summary, when parallelizing the GP's evaluation phase, the two most important modeling aspects are the *kernel* code and the n-dimensional computation domain. Section 4 will present these definitions for each parallelization strategy.

3. Genetic programming on GPU: A bit of history

It is natural to begin the history of GP on GPUs referring to the first improvements obtained by parallelization of a GA on programmable graphics hardware. The first work along this line seems to be [41], which has proposed a genetic algorithm in which crossover, mutation, and fitness evaluation were performed on graphic cards achieving speedups up to 17.1 for large population sizes.

Other GA parallelization on GPUs was proposed in [39] which followed their own ideas explored in [40] for an evolutionary programming technique (called FEP). The proposal, called Hybrid GA, or shortly HGA, was evaluated using 5 test-functions, and CPU-GPU as well as HGA-FEP comparisons were made. It was observed that their GA on GPU was more effective and efficient than their previous parallel FEP.

Similarly to [41], [24] performed crossover, mutation, and fitness evaluation on GPU to solve the problem of packing many granular textures into a large one, which helps modelers in freely building virtual scenes without caring for efficient usage of texture memory. Although the implementation on CPU performed faster in the cases where the number of textures was very small (compact search space), the performance of the implementation on GPU is almost two times faster when compared to execution on CPU.

The well-known satisfiability problem, or shortly SAT, is solved on graphic hardware in [30], where a cellular genetic algorithm was adopted. The algorithm was developed using NVIDIA's C for Graphics (Cg) programming toolkit and achieved a speedup of approximately 5. However, the author reports some problems in the implementation process, like the nonexistence of a pseudo-random number generator and limitations in the texture's size.

[6] The OpenCL kernel's language is derived from the C language.

Due the growing use of graphics cards in the scientific community, in general, and particularly in the evolutionary computation field, as described earlier, the exploration of this high-performing solution in genetic programming was inevitable. Ebner et al. published the first work exploring the GPU capacity in GP [11]. Although a high level language was used in that case (Cg), the GPU was only used to generate the images from the candidate programs (vertex and pixel shaders). Then the created images are presented to the user for his evaluation.

However, it was in 2007 that the extension of the technique of general purpose computing using graphics cards in GP was more extensively explored [2, 9, 17, 18]. Two general purpose computation toolkits for GPUs were preferred in these works: while [2, 9] implemented their GP using Cg, Harding and Banzhaf [17, 18] chose Microsoft's Accelerator, a .Net's library which provides access to the GPU via DirectX's interface.

The automatic construction of tree-structural image transformation on GPU was proposed in [2], where the speedup of GP was explored in different parallel architectures (master-slave and island), as well as on single and multiple GPUs (up to 4). When compared with its sequential version, the proposed approach obtained a speedup of 94.5 with one GPU and its performance increased almost linearly by adding GPUs.

Symbolic regression, fisher iris dataset classification, and 11-way multiplexer problems composed the computational experiments in [9]. The results demonstrated that although there was little improvement for small numbers of fitness cases, considerable gains could be obtained (up to around 10 times) when this number becomes much larger.

The classification between two spirals, the classification of proteins, and a symbolic regression problem were used in [17, 18] to evaluate their Cartesian GP on GPU. In both works, each GP individual is compiled, transferred to GPU, and executed. Some benchmarks were also performed in [18] to evaluate floating point as well as binary operations. The rules of a cellular automaton with the von Neumann neighborhood and used to simulate the diffusion of chemicals were generated by means of Cartesian GP in [17]. The best obtained speedup in these works was 34.63.

Following the same idea of compiling the candidate solutions, [16] uses a Cartesian GP on GPU to remove noise in images. Different types of noise were artificially introduced into a set of figures and performance analyses concluded that this sort of parallelism is indicated for larger images.

A simple instruction multiple data interpreter was developed using RapidMind and presented in [28], where a performance of one Giga GP operations per second was observed in the computational experiments. In contrast to [16–18] where the candidate programs were compiled to execute on GPUs, [28] showed a way of interpreting the trees. While the previous presented approach requires that programs are large and run many times to compensate the cost of compilation and transference to the GPU, the interpretable proposal of [28] seems to be more consistent because it achieved speed ups of more than an order of magnitude in the Mackey-Glass time series and protein prediction problems, even for small programs and few test cases.

The same solution of interpreting the candidate programs was used in [27], but a predictor was evolved in this case. Only the objective function evaluation was performed on GPU, but this step represents, in that study, about 85% of the total run time.

Another study exploring the GPU capacity in GP is presented in [29]. RapidMind is used to implement a GP solution to solve a cancer prediction problem from a dataset containing a million inputs. A population of 5 million programs evolves executing about 500 million GP operations per second. The author found a 7.6 speed up during the computational experiments, but their discussion indicates that the increment in the performance was limited by the access to the 768 Mb of the training data (the device used had 512Mb).

Since these first works were published, improving GP performance by using GP-GPU becomes a new research field. Even the performance of GP on graphic devices of video game consoles was analyzed [36–38], but PC implementations of GP have demonstrated to be faster and more robust. However, it was with the current high level programming languages [4, 34], namely NVIDIA's CUDA and OpenCL, that GP implementations using GP becomes popular, specially in much larger/real world applications. Also, TidePowerd's GPU.NET was studied for speed up Cartesian GP [19].

Genetic programming is used in [10] to search, guided by user interaction, in the space of possible computer vision programs, where a real-time performance is obtained by using GPU for image processing operations. The objective was evolving detectors capable of extracting sub-images indicated by the user in multiple frames of a video sequence.

An implementation of GP to be executed in a cluster composed by PCs equipped with GPUs was presented in [20]. In that work, program compilation, data, and fitness execution are spread over the cluster, improving the efficiency of GP when the problem contains a very large dataset. The strategy used is to compile (C code into NVIDIA CUDA programs) and to execute the population of candidate individuals in parallel. The GP, developed in GASS's CUDA.NET, was executed in Microsoft Windows (during the tests) and Gentoo Linux (final deployment), demonstrating the flexibility of that solution. That parallel GP was capable of executing up to 3.44 (classification problem of network intrusion) and 12.74 (image processing problem) Giga GP operations per second.

The computational time of the fitness calculation phase was reduced in [7, 8] by using CUDA. The computational experiments included ten datasets, which were selected from well-known repositories in the literature, and three GP variants for classification problems, in which the main difference between them is the criterion of evaluation. Their proposed approach demonstrated good performance, achieving a speedup of up to 820.18 when compared with their own Java implementation, as well as a speedup of up to 34.02 when compared with BioHEL [13].

Although with much less articles published in the GP field, OpenCL deserves to be highlighted because, in addition of being non-proprietary, it allows for heterogeneous computing. In fact, up to now only [4] presents the development of GP using OpenCL, where the performance of both types of devices (CPU and GPU) was evaluated over the same implementation. Moreover, [4] discusses different parallelism strategies and GPU was up to 126 times faster than CPU in the computational experiments.

The parallelism of GP techniques on GPU is not restricted only to linear, tree, and graph (Cartesian) representations. The improvement in performance of other kinds of GP, such as Grammatical Evolution [33], is just beginning to be explored. However, notice that no papers were found concerning the application of Gene Expression Programming [12] on GPUs. Some complementary information is available in [3, 6].

4. Parallelization strategies

As mentioned in Section 2.2, there are two distinct code spaces in OpenCL, the host and kernel. The steps of the host code necessary to create the environment for the parallel evaluation phase are summarized as follows [4]:[7]

1. **OpenCL initialization**. This step concerns identifying which OpenCL implementation (platform) and compute devices are available. There may exist multiple devices on the system. In this case one may opt to use a single device or, alternatively, all of them, where then a further partitioning of the problem will be required. Training data points, programs or even whole populations could be distributed among the devices.
2. **Calculating the n-dimensional computation domain**. How the workload is decomposed for parallel processing is of fundamental importance. Strictly speaking, this phase only determines the *global* and *local* sizes in a one-dimensional space, which is enough to represent the domain of training data points or programs. However, in conjunction with a kernel, which implements a certain strategy of parallelization, the type of parallelism (at data and/or program level) and workload distribution are precisely defined.
3. **Memory allocation and transfer**. In order to speedup data accesses, some content are allocated/transferred directly to the compute device's memory and kept there, thus avoiding as much as possible the relatively narrow bandwidth between the GPU and the computer's main memory. Three memory buffers are required to be allocated on the device's global memory in order to hold the training data points, population of programs, and error vector. Usually, the training data points are transferred only once, just before the beginning of the execution, remaining then unchanged until the end. The population of programs and error vector, however, are dynamic entities and so they need to be transferred at each generation.
4. **Kernel building**. This phase selects the kernel with respect to a strategy of parallelization and builds it. Since the exact specification of the target device is usually not known in advance, the default OpenCL behavior is to compile the kernel just-in-time. Although this procedure introduces some overhead, the benefit of having more information about the device—and therefore being able to generate better optimized kernel object—usually outweighs the compilation overhead.
5. **GP's evolutionary loop**. Since this chapter focuses on accelerating the evaluation phase of genetic programming by parallelizing it, the iterative evolutionary cycle itself is assumed to be performed sequentially, being so defined in the host space instead of as an OpenCL kernel. [8] The main iterative evolutionary steps are:
   (a) **Population transfer**. Changes are introduced to programs by the evolutionary process via genetic operators, e.g. crossover and mutation, creating a new set of derived programs. As a result, a population transfer needs to be performed from host to device at each generation.

[7] This chapter will not detail the host code, since it is not relevant to the understanding of the parallel strategies. Given that, and considering that the algorithms are presented in a pseudo-OpenCL form, the reader is advised to consult the appropriate OpenCL literature in order to learn about its peculiarities and fill the implementation gaps.

[8] However, bear in mind that a full parallelization, i.e. both evaluation and evolution, is feasible under OpenCL. That could be implemented, for instance, in such a way that a multi-core CPU device would perform the evolution in parallel while one or more GPUs would evaluate programs.

(b) **Kernel execution**. Whenever a new population arrives on the compute device, a kernel is launched in order to evaluate (in parallel) the new programs with respect to the training data points. For any non-trivial problem, this step is the most computationally intensive one.

(c) **Error retrieval**. Finally, after all programs' errors have been accumulated, this vector is transferred back to the host in order to guide the evolutionary process in selecting the set of parents that will breed the next generation.

Regarding the kernel code, it can be designed to evaluate programs in different parallel ways: (i) training points are processed in parallel but programs sequentially; or (ii) the converse, programs are executed in parallel but training points are processed sequentially; or finally (iii) a mixture of these two, where both programs and training points are processed in parallel.

Which way is the best will depend essentially on a combination of the characteristics of the problem and some parameters of the GP algorithm. These strategies are described and discussed in Sections 4.2, 4.3 and 4.4.

4.1. Program interpreter

The standard manner to estimate the fitness of a GP candidate program is to execute it, commonly on varying input arguments, and observe how well it solves the task at hand by comparing its behavior with the expected one. To this end, the program can be *compiled* just before the execution, generating an intermediate object code, or be directly *interpreted* without generating intermediate objects. Both variations have pros and cons. Compiling introduces overhead, however, it may be advantageous when the evaluation of a program is highly demanding. On the other hand, interpretation is usually slower, but avoids the compilation cost for each program. Moreover, interpretation is easy to accomplish and, more importantly, is much more flexible. Such flexibility allows, for example, to emulate a MIMD execution model on a SIMD or SPMD architecture [23]. This is possible because what a data-parallel device actually executes are many instances of the *same* interpreter. Programs, as has always been the case with training points, become data or, in other words, arguments for the interpreter.

A program interpreter is presented in Algorithm Interpreter. It is assumed that the program to be executed is represented as a *prefix linear tree* [5], since a linear representation is very efficient to be operated on, specially on the GPU architecture. An example of such program is:

$+$	sin	x	3.14

which denotes the infix expression $\sin(x) + 3.14$.

The program interpretation operates on a single training data point at a time. The current point is given by the argument n, and $X_n \in \Re^d$ is a d-dimensional array representing the n-th variables (training point) of the problem.

The command `INDEX` extracts the class of the current operator (*op*), which can be a function, constant or variable. The value of a constant is obtained by the `VALUE` command; for variables, this command returns the variable's index in order to get its corresponding value in X_n.

Function Interpreter(*program*, *n*)

```
for op ← program_size − 1 to 0 do
    switch INDEX( program[op] ) do
        case ADD:
            PUSH( POP + POP );
        case SUB:
            PUSH( POP − POP );
        case MUL:
            PUSH( POP × POP );
        case DIV:
            PUSH( POP ÷ POP );
        case IF-THEN-ELSE:
            if POP then
                PUSH( POP );
            else
                POP; PUSH( POP );
        ⋮
        case CONSTANT:
            PUSH( VALUE( program[op] ) );
        otherwise
            PUSH( X_n[VALUE( program[op] )] );
return POP;
```

The interpreter is stack-based; whenever an operand shows up, like a constant or variable, its value is pushed onto the stack via the PUSH command. Conversely, an operator obtains its operands' values on the stack by means of the POP command, which removes the most recently stacked values. Then, the value of the resulting operation on its operands is pushed back onto the stack so as to make it available to a parent operator.

As will be seen in the subsequent sections, whatever the parallel strategy, the interpreter will act as a central component of the kernels, doing the hard work. The kernels will basically set up how the interpreter will be distributed among processing elements and which program and training point it will operate on at a given time.

4.2. Data-level Parallelism – DP

The idea behind the data-level parallelism (DP) strategy is to distribute the training data points among the processing elements of a compute device. This is probably the simplest and most natural way of parallelizing GP's evaluation phase when the execution of a program on many independent training points is required.[9] Despite its obviousness, DP is an efficient

[9] However, sometimes it is not possible to trivially decompose the evaluation phase. For instance, an evaluation may involve submitting the program through a simulator. In this case one can try to parallelize the simulator itself or, alternatively, opt to use a program- or population-level kind of parallelism.

strategy, specially when there are a large number of training data points—which is very common in complex problems. Moreover, given that this strategy leads to a data-parallel SIMD execution model, it fits well on a wide range of parallel architectures. Figure 2 shows graphically how the training data points are distributed among the PEs.[10]

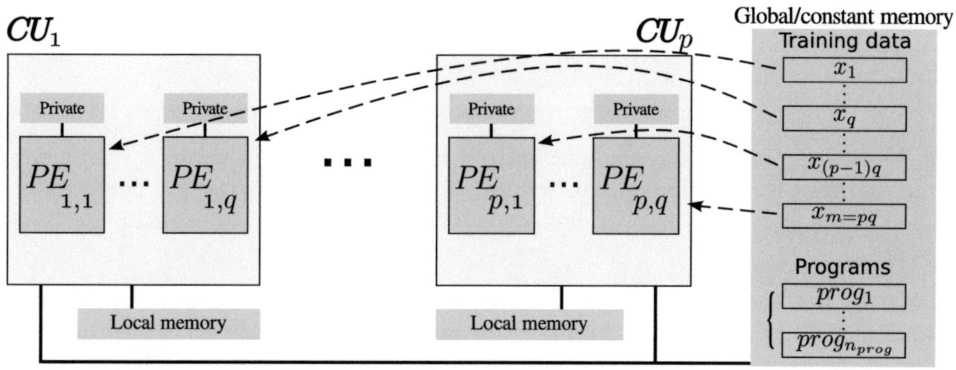

Figure 2. Illustration of the data-level parallelism (DP).

As already mentioned, to precisely define a parallelization strategy in OpenCL, two things must be set up: the *n*-dimensional domain, more specifically the global and local sizes, and the kernel itself. For the data-level parallelism, it is natural to assign the global computation domain to the training data points domain as a one-to-one correspondence; that is, simply

$$global_{size} = dataset_{size}, \tag{1}$$

where *dataset size* is the number of the training data points. OpenCL lets the programmer to choose whether he or she wants to explicitly define the local size, i.e. how many work-items will be put in a work-group. The exact definition of the local size is only really needed when the corresponding kernel assumes a particular work-group division, which is not the case for DP. Therefore, no local size is explicitly defined for DP, letting then the OpenCL runtime to decide on any configuration it thinks is the best.

Algorithm 1 presents in a pseudo-OpenCL language the DP's kernel. As with any OpenCL kernel, there will be launched $global_{size}$ instances of it on the compute device.[11] Hence, there is one work-item per domain element, with each one identified by its global or local position through the OpenCL commands `get_global_id` and `get_local_id`, respectively. This enables a work-item to select what portion of the compute domain it will operate on, based on its absolute or relative position.

For the DP's kernel, the $global_{id}$ index is used to choose which training data point will be processed, in other words, each work-item will be in charge of a specific point. The *for loop* iterates sequentially over each program of the population (the function `NthProgram` returns the *p*-th program), that is, every work-item will execute the same program at a given time. Then, the interpreter (Section 4.1) is called to execute the current program, but each work-item will provide a different index, which corresponds to the training data point it took

[10] To simplify, in Figures 2, 4 and 5 it is presumed that the number of PEs (or CUs) coincides with the number of training data points (or programs), but in practice this is rarely the case.

[11] It is worthy to notice that the actual amount of work-items executed in parallel by the OpenCL runtime will depend on the device's capabilities, mainly on the number of processing elements.

Algorithm 1: GPU DP's OpenCL kernel

$global_{id} \leftarrow$ `get_global_id();`

for $p \leftarrow 0$ **to** $population_{size} - 1$ **do**
  $program \leftarrow$ `NthProgram(`p`);`
  $error \leftarrow |$`Interpreter(` $program, global_{id}$ `)` $- Y[global_{id}]|$;
  $E[p] \leftarrow$ `ErrorReduction(`$0, \ldots, global_{size} - 1$`);`

responsibility for. Once interpreted, the output returned by the program is then compared with the expected one for that point, whose value is stored in array Y. This results in a prediction error; however, the overall error is what is meaningful to estimate the fitness of a program.

Note however that the errors are spread among the work-items, because each work-item has processed a single point and has computed its own error independently. This calls for what is known in the parallel computing literature as the *reduction* operation [22]. The naive way of doing that is to sequentially cycle over each element and accumulate their values; in our case it would iterate from work-item indexed by 0 to $global_{size} - 1$ and put the total value in $E[p]$, the final error relative to the p-th program. There is however a clever and parallel way of doing reduction, as exemplified in Figure 3, which decreases the complexity of this step from $O(N)$ to just $O(log_2 N)$ and still assures a nice coalesced memory access suited for the GPU architecture [1, 32].[12]

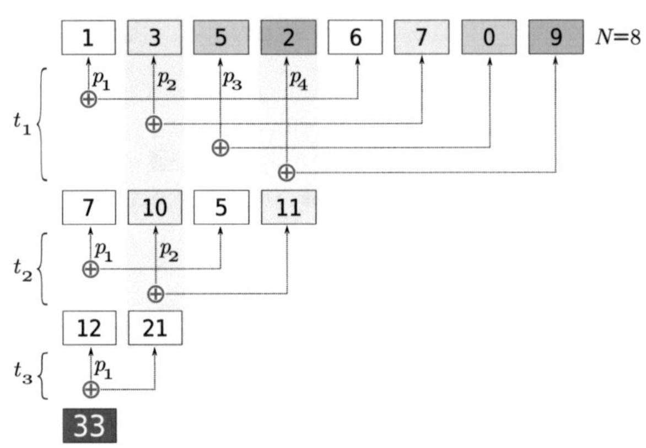

Figure 3. $O(log_2 N)$ parallel reduction with sequential addressing.

4.3. Program-level Parallelism – PP

One serious drawback of the data-level parallelism strategy is that when there are few training data points the compute device may probably be underutilized. Today's high-end GPUs have thousands of processing elements, and this number has increased at each new hardware generation. In addition, to achieve optimal performance on GPUs, multiple work-items should be launched for each processing element. This helps, for instance, to hide memory

[12] This chapter aims at just conveying the idea of the parallel reduction, and so it will not get into the algorithmic details on how reduction is actually implemented. The reader is referred to the given references for details.

access latencies while reading from or writing to the device's global memory [1, 32]. Therefore, to optimally utilize a high-end GPU under the DP strategy, one should prefer those problems having tens of thousands of training data points. Unfortunately, there are many real-world problems out there for which no such amount of data is available.

Another limitation of the DP strategy is that sometimes there is no easy way to decompose the evaluation of a program into independent entities, like data points. Many program evaluations that need a simulator, for example, fall into this category, where a parallel implementation of the simulator is not feasible to accomplish.

An attempt to overcome the DP limitations, particularly what concerns the desire of a substantially large amount of training data points, is schematically shown in Figure 4. This parallelization strategy is here referred to as program-level parallelism (PP), meaning that programs are executed in parallel, each program per PE [4, 35]. Assuming that there are enough programs to be evaluated, even a few training data points should keep the GPU fully occupied.

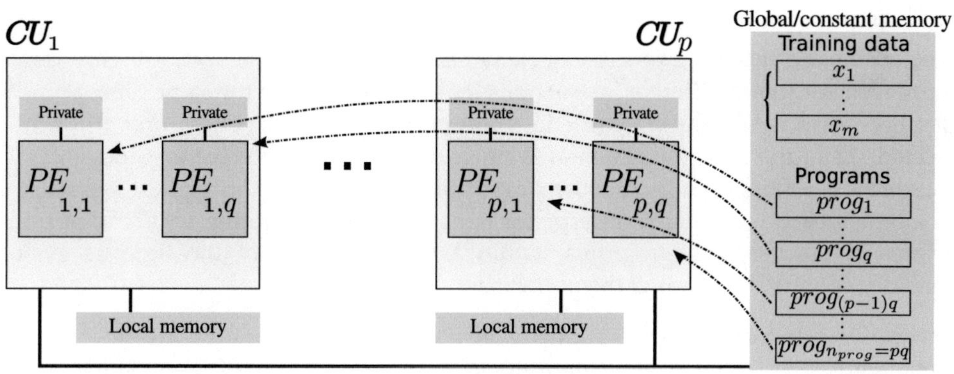

Figure 4. Illustration of the program-level parallelism (PP).

In PP, while programs are interpreted in parallel, the training data points within each PE are processed sequentially. This suggests a computation domain based on the number of programs, in other words, the global size can be defined as:

$$global_{size} = population_{size} \tag{2}$$

As with DP, PP does not need to have control of the number of work-items within a work-group, thus the local size can be left untouched.

A pseudo-OpenCL code for the PP kernel is given in Algorithm 2. It resembles the DP's algorithm, but in PP what is being parallelized are the programs instead of the training data points. Hence, each work-item takes a different program and interpret it iteratively over all points. A positive side effect of this inverse logic is that, since the whole evaluation of a program is now done in a single work-item, all the partial prediction errors are promptly available locally. Put differently, in PP a final reduction step is not required.

4.4. Program- and Data-level Parallelism – PDP

Unfortunately, PP solves the DP's necessity of large training datasets but introduces two other problems: (i) to avoid underutilization of the GPU a large population of programs should now

Algorithm 2: GPU PP's OpenCL kernel

$global_{id} \leftarrow$ `get_global_id();`
$program \leftarrow$ `NthProgram(`$global_{id}$`);`

$error \leftarrow 0.0$;
for $n \leftarrow 0$ **to** $dataset_{size} - 1$ **do**
  $error \leftarrow error + |$`Interpreter(` $program, n$ `)` $- Y[n]|$;

$E[global_{id}] \leftarrow error$;

be employed; and, more critically, (ii) the PP's execution model is not suited for an inherently data-parallel architecture like GPUs.

While (i) can be dealt with by simply specifying a large population as a parameter choice of a genetic programming algorithm, the issue pointed out in (ii) cannot be solved for the PP strategy.

The problem lies on the fact that, as mentioned in Section 2, GPUs are mostly a SIMD architecture, specially among processing elements within a compute unit. Roughly speaking, whenever two (or more) different instructions try to be executed at the same time, a hardware conflict occurs and then these instructions are performed sequentially, one at a time. In the related literature, this phenomenon is often referred to as *divergence*. Since in PP each PE interprets a different program, the degree of divergence is the highest possible: at a given moment each work-item's interpreter is potentially interpreting a different primitive. Therefore, in practice, the programs within a CU will most of the time be evaluated sequentially, seriously degrading the performance.

However, observing the fact that modern GPUs are capable of simultaneously executing different instructions at the level of compute units, i.e. the SPMD execution model, one could devise a parallelization strategy that would take advantage of this fact. Such strategy exists, and it is known here as program- and data-level parallelism, or simply PDP [4, 35]. Its general idea is illustrated in Figure 5. In PDP, a single program is evaluated per compute unit—this

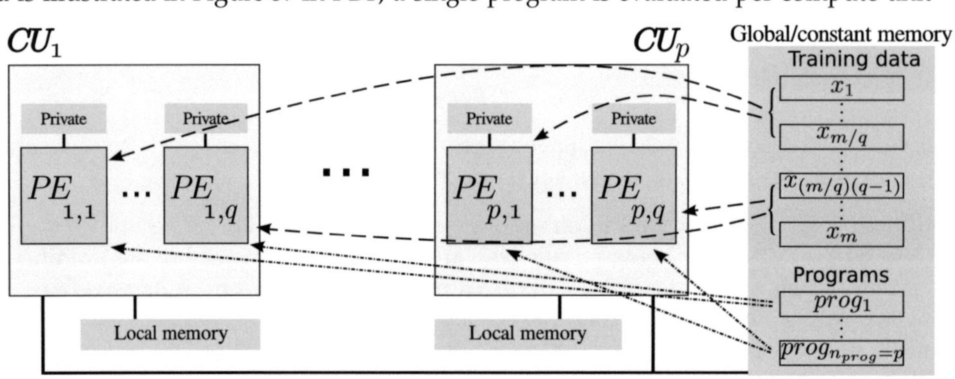

Figure 5. Illustration of the program- and data-level parallelism (PDP).

prevents the just mentioned problem of divergence—but within each CU all the training data points are processed in parallel. Therefore, there are two levels of parallelism: a program-level parallelism among the compute units, and a data-level parallelism on the processing elements.

Indeed, PDP can be seen as a mixture of the DP and PP strategies. But curiously, PDP avoids all the drawbacks associated with the other two strategies: (i) once there are enough data to saturate just a single CU, smaller datasets can be used at no performance loss; (ii) large populations are not required either, since the number of CUs on current high-end GPUs is in the order of tens; and (iii) there is no divergence with respect to program interpretation.[13]

In order to achieve both levels of parallelism, a fine-tuned control over the computation domain is required; more precisely, both local and global sizes must be properly defined.

Since a work-group should process all training data points for a single program and there is a population of programs to be evaluated, one would imagine that setting $local_{size}$ as $dataset_{size}$ and $global_{size}$ as $population_{size} \times dataset_{size}$ would suffice. This is conceptually correct, but an important detail makes the implementation not as straightforward as one would expect. The OpenCL specification allows any compute device to declare an upper bound regarding the number of work-items within a work-group. This is not arbitrary. The existence of a limit on the number of work-items per work-group is justified by the fact that there exists a relation between the maximum number of work-items and the device's capabilities, with the latter restricting the former. Put differently, an unlimited number of work-items per work-group would not be viable, therefore a limit, which is provided by the hardware vendor, must be taken into account.

With the aforementioned in mind, the local size can finally be set to

$$local_{size} = \begin{cases} dataset_{size} & \text{if } dataset_{size} < local_{max\_size} \\ local_{max\_size} & \text{otherwise} \end{cases}, \tag{3}$$

which limits the number of work-items per work-group to the maximum supported, given by the variable $local_{max\_size}$, when the number of training data points exceeds it. This implies that when such a limit takes place, a single work-item will be in charge of more than one training data point, that is, the work granularity is increased. As for the global size, it can be easily defined as

$$global_{size} = population_{size} \times local_{size}, \tag{4}$$

meaning that the set of work-items defined above should be replicated as many times as the number of programs to be evaluated.

Finally, algorithm 3 shows the OpenCL kernel for the PDP strategy. Compared to the other two kernels (Algorithms 1 and 2), it comes as no surprise its greater complexity, as this kernel is a combination of the other two and still has to cope with the fact that a single instance, i.e. a work-item, can process an arbitrary number of training data points. The command `get_group_id`, which returns the work-group's index of the current work-item, has the purpose of indexing the program that is going to be evaluated by the entire group. The *for loop* is closely related to the local size (Equation 3), and acts as a way of iterating over multiple training data points if the work-item (indexed locally by $local_{id}$) is in charge of many of them; when the dataset size is less or equal to the local size, only one iteration will be performed. Then, an index calculation is done in order to get the index (n) of the current training data

[13] Notice, though, that divergence might still occur if two (or more) training data points can cause the interpreter to take different paths for the same program. For instance, if the conditional *if-then-else* primitive is used, a data point could cause an interpreter's instance to take the *then* path while other data could make another instance to take the *else* path.

Algorithm 3: GPU PDP's OpenCL kernel

$local_{id} \leftarrow$ `get_local_id();`
$group_{id} \leftarrow$ `get_group_id();`
$program \leftarrow$ `NthProgram(`$group_{id}$`);`

$error \leftarrow 0.0$;
for $i \leftarrow 0$ **to** $\lceil dataset_{size}/local_{size} \rceil - 1$ **do**
  $n \leftarrow i \times local_{size} + local_{id}$;
  if $n < dataset_{size}$ **then**
    $error \leftarrow error + |$`Interpreter(`$program, n$`)` $- Y[n]|$;

$E[group_{id}] \leftarrow$ `ErrorReduction(`$0,\ldots,local_{size}-1$`);`

point to be processed.[14] Due to the fact that the dataset size may not be evenly divisible by the local size, a range check is performed to guarantee that no out-of-range access will occur. Finally, since the prediction errors for a given program will be spread among the local work-items at the end of the execution, an error reduction operation takes place.

5. Conclusions

This chapter has presented different strategies to accelerate the execution of a genetic programming algorithm by parallelizing its costly evaluation phase on the GPU architecture, a high-performance processor which is also energy efficient and affordable.

Out of the three studied strategies, two of them are particularly well-suited to be implemented on the GPU architecture, namely: (i) data-level parallelism (DP), which is very simple and remarkably efficient for large datasets; and (ii) program- and data-level parallelism (PDP), which is not as simple as DP, but exhibits the same degree of efficiency for large datasets and has the advantage of being efficient for small datasets as well.

Up to date, only a few large and real-world problems have been solved by GP with the help of the massive parallelism of GPUs. This suggests that the potential of GP is yet under-explored, indicating that the next big step concerning GP on GPUs may be its application to those challenging problems. In several domains, such as in bio-informatics, the amount of data is growing quickly, making it progressively difficult for specialists to manually infer models and the like. Heterogeneous computing, combining the computational power of different devices, as well as the possibility of programming uniformly for any architecture and vendor, is also an interesting research direction to boost the performance of GP. Although offering both advantages, OpenCL is still fairly unexplored in the field of evolutionary computation.

Finally, although optimization techniques have not been thoroughly discussed in this chapter, this is certainly an important subject. Thus, the reader is invited to consult the related material found in [4], and also general GPU optimizations techniques from the respective literature.

Acknowledgements

The authors would like to thank the support provided by CNPq (grants 308317/2009-2 and 300192/2012-6) and FAPERJ (grant E-26/102.025/2009).

[14] The careful reader will note that this index calculation leads to an efficient coalesced memory access pattern [1, 32].

Author details

Douglas A. Augusto and Heder S. Bernardino
Laboratório Nacional de Computação Científica (LNCC/MCTI), Rio de Janeiro, Brazil

Helio J. C. Barbosa
Laboratório Nacional de Computação Científica (LNCC/MCTI), Rio de Janeiro, Brazil
Federal University of Juiz de Fora (UFJF), Computer Science Dept., Minas Gerais, Brazil

6. References

[1] Advanced Micro Devices [2010]. *AMD Accelerated Parallel Processing Programming Guide - OpenCL.*

[2] Ando, J. & Nagao, T. [2007]. Fast evolutionary image processing using multi-gpus, *Proc. of the International Conference on Systems, Man and Cybernetics*, pp. 2927 –2932.

[3] Arenas, M. G., Mora, A. M., Romero, G. & Castillo, P. A. [2011]. Gpu computation in bioinspired algorithms: a review, *Proc. of the international conference on Artificial neural networks conference on Advances in computational intelligence*, Springer-Verlag, pp. 433–440.

[4] Augusto, D. A. & Barbosa, H. J. [2012]. Accelerated parallel genetic programming tree evaluation with opencl, *Journal of Parallel and Distributed Computing* (0): –.
URL: *http://www.sciencedirect.com/science/article/pii/S074373151200024X*

[5] Augusto, D. A. & Barbosa, H. J. C. [2000]. Symbolic regression via genetic programming, *Proceedings of the VI Brazilian Symposium on Neural Networks*, IEEE Computer Society, Los Alamitos, CA, USA, pp. 173–178.

[6] Banzhaf, W., Harding, S., Langdon, W. B. & Wilson, G. [2009]. Accelerating genetic programming through graphics processing units., *Genetic Programming Theory and Practice VI*, pp. 1–19.
URL: *http://dx.doi.org/10.1007/978-0-387-87623-8_15*

[7] Cano, A., Zafra, A. & Ventura, S. [2010]. Solving classification problems using genetic programming algorithms on gpus, *Lecture Notes in Computer Science (including subseries Lecture Notes in Artificial Intelligence and Lecture Notes in Bioinformatics)* 6077 LNAI(PART 2): 17–26.

[8] Cano, A., Zafra, A. & Ventura, S. [2012]. Speeding up the evaluation phase of gp classification algorithms on gpus, *Soft Computing* 16(2): 187–202.

[9] Chitty, D. M. [2007]. A data parallel approach to genetic programming using programmable graphics hardware, *in* D. Thierens, H.-G. Beyer, J. Bongard, J. Branke, J. A. Clark, D. Cliff, C. B. Congdon, K. Deb, B. Doerr, T. Kovacs, S. Kumar, J. F. Miller, J. Moore, F. Neumann, M. Pelikan, R. Poli, K. Sastry, K. O. Stanley, T. Stutzle, R. A. Watson & I. Wegener (eds), *GECCO '07: Proceedings of the 9th annual conference on Genetic and evolutionary computation*, Vol. 2, ACM Press, London, pp. 1566–1573.
URL: *http://www.cs.bham.ac.uk/ wbl/biblio/gecco2007/docs/p1566.pdf*

[10] Ebner, M. [2009]. A real-time evolutionary object recognition system, *Lecture Notes in Computer Science (including subseries Lecture Notes in Artificial Intelligence and Lecture Notes in Bioinformatics)* 5481 LNCS: 268–279. cited By (since 1996) 1.
URL: *http://www.scopus.com/inward/record.url?eid=2-s2.0-67650697120&partnerID=40&md5=1a9de902eb5649a01e3e87c222a79ee3*

[11] Ebner, M., Reinhardt, M. & Albert, J. [2005]. Evolution of vertex and pixel shaders, *Proceedings of the European Conference on Genetic Programming Genetic Programming – EuroGP*, Vol. 3447 of *LNCS*, Springer Berlin / Heidelberg, pp. 142–142.

[12] Ferreira, C. [2006]. *Gene Expression Programming: Mathematical Modeling by an Artificial Intelligence*, 2 edn, Springer.

[13] Franco, M. A., Krasnogor, N. & Bacardit, J. [2010]. Speeding up the evaluation of evolutionary learning systems using gpgpus, *Proceedings of the 12th annual conference on Genetic and evolutionary computation*, GECCO '10, ACM, New York, NY, USA, pp. 1039–1046.
URL: *http://doi.acm.org/10.1145/1830483.1830672*

[14] Garland, M. & Kirk, D. B. [2010]. Understanding throughput-oriented architectures, *Commun. ACM* 53: 58–66.

[15] Gaster, B., Kaeli, D., Howes, L., Mistry, P. & Schaa, D. [2011]. *Heterogeneous Computing With OpenCL*, Elsevier Science.
URL: *http://books.google.com.br/books?id=qUJVU8RH3jEC*

[16] Harding, S. [2008]. Evolution of image filters on graphics processor units using cartesian genetic programming, pp. 1921–1928. cited By (since 1996) 3.
URL: *http://www.scopus.com/inward/record.url?eid=2-s2.0-55749093400&partnerID=40&md5=fddf39574ff1025ad80adf204ccb451f*

[17] Harding, S. & Banzhaf, W. [2007a]. Fast genetic programming and artificial developmental systems on gpus, *Proc. of the International Symposium on High Performance Computing Systems and Applications*, p. 2.

[18] Harding, S. & Banzhaf, W. [2007b]. Fast genetic programming on GPUs, *Proc. of the European Conference on Genetic Programming – EuroGP*, Vol. 4445 of *LNCS*, Springer, Valencia, Spain, pp. 90–101.

[19] Harding, S. & Banzhaf, W. [2011]. Implementing cartesian genetic programming classifiers on graphics processing units using gpu.net, *Proceedings of the Conference Companion on Genetic and evolutionary computation – GECCO*, ACM, pp. 463–470.

[20] Harding, S. L. & Banzhaf, W. [2009]. Distributed genetic programming on GPUs using CUDA, *Workshop on Parallel Architectures and Bioinspired Algorithms*, Universidad Complutense de Madrid, Raleigh, NC, USA, pp. 1–10.

[21] Hennessy, J. & Patterson, D. [2011]. *Computer Architecture: A Quantitative Approach*, The Morgan Kaufmann Series in Computer Architecture and Design, Elsevier Science.
URL: *http://books.google.com.br/books?id=v3-1hVwHnHwC*

[22] Hillis, W. D. & Steele, Jr., G. L. [1986]. Data parallel algorithms, *Commun. ACM* 29: 1170–1183.

[23] Juille, H. & Pollack, J. B. [1996]. Massively parallel genetic programming, *in* P. J. Angeline & K. E. Kinnear, Jr. (eds), *Advances in Genetic Programming* 2, MIT Press, Cambridge, MA, USA, chapter 17, pp. 339–358.

[24] Kaul, K. & Bohn, C.-A. [2006]. A genetic texture packing algorithm on a graphical processing unit, *Proceedings of the International Conference on Computer Graphics and Artificial Intelligence*.

[25] Khronos OpenCL Working Group [2011]. *The OpenCL Specification, version 1.2.*
URL: *http://www.khronos.org/registry/cl/specs/opencl-1.2.pdf*

[26] Kirk, D. & Hwu, W. [2010]. *Programming Massively Parallel Processors: A Hands-On Approach*, Applications of GPU Computing Series, Morgan Kaufmann Publishers.
URL: *http://books.google.com.br/books?id=qW1mncii_6EC*

[27] Langdon, W. [2008]. Evolving genechip correlation predictors on parallel graphics hardware, pp. 4151–4156. cited By (since 1996) 0.
URL: *http://www.scopus.com/inward/record.url?eid=2-s2.0-55749103342&partnerID=40&md5=028c81cb3bb1b8380f2f816b8e50b1f4*

[28] Langdon, W. & Banzhaf, W. [2008]. A SIMD interpreter for genetic programming on GPU graphics cards, *Genetic Programming*, pp. 73–85.

[29] Langdon, W. & Harrison, A. [2008]. Gp on spmd parallel graphics hardware for mega bioinformatics data mining, *Soft Computing* 12(12): 1169–1183. cited By (since 1996) 13.
URL: *http://www.scopus.com/inward/record.url?eid=2-s2.0-49049115131&partnerID=40&md5=4d332814a77dc0233bed7ff3184a6ccb*

[30] Luo, Z. & Liu, H. [2006]. Cellular genetic algorithms and local search for 3-sat problem on graphic hardware, *Proc. of the Congress on Evolutionary Computation – CEC*, pp. 2988 –2992.

[31] NVIDIA Corporation [2007]. *NVIDIA CUDA Compute Unified Device Architecture - Programming Guide.*
URL: *http://developer.download.nvidia.com/compute/cuda/1_0/NVIDIA_CUDA_Programming_Guide_1.0.pdf*

[32] NVIDIA Corporation [2010]. *OpenCL Best Practices Guide.*

[33] Pospichal, P., Murphy, E., O'Neill, M., Schwarz, J. & Jaros, J. [2011]. Acceleration of grammatical evolution using graphics processing units: Computational intelligence on consumer games and graphics hardware, pp. 431–438. cited By (since 1996) 0.
URL: *http://www.scopus.com/inward/record.url?eid=2-s2.0-80051950282&partnerID=40&md5=46bb1910d0121a948a804f8aa62308eb*

[34] Robilliard, D., Marion-Poty, V. & Fonlupt, C. [2008]. Population parallel gp on the g80 gpu, *Artificial Intelligence and Lecture Notes in Bioinformatics* 4971: 98–109.

[35] Robilliard, D., Marion, V. & Fonlupt, C. [2009]. High performance genetic programming on gpu, *Proceedings of the 2009 workshop on Bio-inspired algorithms for distributed systems*, BADS '09, ACM, New York, NY, USA, pp. 85–94.

[36] Wilson, G. & Banzhaf, W. [2008]. Linear genetic programming gpgpu on microsoft's xbox 360, *2008 IEEE Congress on Evolutionary Computation, CEC 2008*, pp. 378–385. cited By (since 1996) 4.
URL: *http://www.scopus.com/inward/record.url?eid=2-s2.0-55749108355&partnerID=40&md5=304d6784cd00eac6e253229092ba7788*

[37] Wilson, G. & Banzhaf, W. [2009]. Deployment of cpu and gpu-based genetic programming on heterogeneous devices, *Proceedings of the Conference Companion on Genetic and Evolutionary Computation Conference*, Late Breaking Papers, ACM, pp. 2531–2538.

[38] Wilson, G. & Banzhaf, W. [2010]. Deployment of parallel linear genetic programming using gpus on pc and video game console platforms, *Genetic Programming and Evolvable Machines* 11(2): 147–184. cited By (since 1996) 2.
URL: *http://www.scopus.com/inward/record.url?eid=2-s2.0-77954814128&partnerID=40&md5=8e8091dedc7d49dfccc20e0f569af0ce*

[39] Wong, M.-L. & Wong, T.-T. [2006]. Parallel hybrid genetic algorithms on consumer-level graphics hardware, *Proc. of the Congress on Evolutionary Computation*, pp. 2973 –2980.

[40] Wong, M., Wong, T. & Fok, K. [2005]. Parallel evolutionary algorithms on graphics processing unit, *Evolutionary Computation, 2005. The 2005 IEEE Congress on*, Vol. 3, pp. 2286–2293 Vol. 3.

[41] Yu, Q., Chen, C. & Pan, Z. [2005]. Parallel genetic algorithms on programmable graphics hardware, *Proc. of the international conference on Advances in Natural Computation*, Springer-Verlag Berlin, pp. 1051–1059.

Section 2

Successful Applications

Chapter 6

Structure-Based Evolutionary Design Applied to Wire Antennas

Giovanni Andrea Casula and Giuseppe Mazzarella

Additional information is available at the end of the chapter

http://dx.doi.org/10.5772/48249

1. Introduction

Antennas are 3D structures, so, at variance of other MW subsystems like filters and couplers, their design has been a matter of intuition and brute-force computations from the beginning (Silver, 1949; Elliott, 1981 just to remember a few). Therefore, an antenna design has been faced at different levels, from simple formulas (Collin, 1985) to sophisticated synthesis techniques (Orchard et al., 1985; Bucci et al., 1994), and from simple heuristic models (Carrel, 1961) to modern global random optimizations, such as GA (Linden & Altshuler, 1996, 1997; Jones & Joines, 1997) and PSO (Baskar et al., 2005), with their heavy computational loads.

Moreover, an antenna design problem is typically divided into two phases, namely an external problem (the evaluation of the antenna currents from the field requirements) and an internal problem (the design of the feed structure needed to achieve those currents, and the input match) (Bucci et al., 1994). In many cases these two phases are almost independent, but for some mutual constraints, as in reflector (Collin, 1985) and slot (Costanzo et al., 2009; Montisci, 2006) or patch (Montisci et al., 2003) array synthesis, since in these cases there is a clear boundary separating the feeding and radiating part of the antenna. In other problems, as in wire antennas design (Johnson & Jasik, 1984), such phases are strictly interconnected, since no clear-cut divides the two parts. For parasitic wire antennas, the interconnection is even stronger, since every element acts as feeding and radiating part at the same time.

The traditional approach to the design of wire antennas starts by choosing a well-defined structure, whose parameters are then optimized. However, a good design requires also a continuous human monitoring, mainly to trim the initial structure to better fit the antenna specifications. A trimming which requires both a deep knowledge and experience in order to effectively change the structure under design. As a matter of fact, such traditional approach is quite expensive, and therefore design techniques without human interaction are of interest, as long as they provide equal, or better, results. This can be achieved only when no initial structure is assumed, since this choice (by necessity fixed in a fully automated procedure) can constrain too strongly the final solution.

The present work proposes such an alternative technique which allows to automate the whole project (and not only its repetitive parts), and provide original solutions, not achievable using standard design techniques. This is obtained by describing the whole antenna in terms of elementary parts (wire segments, junctions, and so on), and of their spatial relations (distance, orientation), and searching for high-performance structures by distributing, in the space, groups of these elementary objects. In this way, the final antenna is sought for in an enormous search space, with a very large number of degrees of freedom which leads to better solutions both in terms of performance and overall dimensions. On the other hand, such solution space must be searched for in an effective, and automatic, way in order to get the required antenna. Aim of this work is to describe how to effectively perform an automatic design of wire antennas without an initial choice of the structure, in order to achieve higher performances than those obtainable by using classical design techniques (eg Yagi antennas and log-periodic antennas (Johnson & Jasik, 1984)).

This can be achieved using a new design technique, namely the Structure-based Evolutionary Design (SED), a new global random search method derived by the strategy first proposed by Koza (Koza, 1992). Many optimization techniques recently proposed, such as GA, share the same inspiration, though natural selection is definitely not an optimization process. As a matter of fact, Darwin stated that "the natural system is founded on the descent with modification" (Darwin, 1859), since what is commonly named natural selection is a process leading to biological units better matched to local changing environments. Therefore, from a conceptual point of view, design approaches based on natural selection should be formulated as a search for antennas fulfilling a set of antenna specifications (the *local changing environment*) rather than as optimization of a given performance index. As we will show later, SED allows following this paradigm and in a way closer to how natural selection works. Natural selection has, in fact, a number of peculiar characteristics. First, if we look at it in a functional, or effective, way it works at the organ level. Moreover, it allows an enormous variability, which is limited only by some broad-sense constraints.

Each individual in the SED approach is a "computer program", i.e., a sequential set of unambiguous instructions completely (and uniquely) describing the realization (almost in engineering terms) of the physical structure of an admissible individual. This is a marked difference with GA, where an individual is only a set of physical dimensions and other parameters. In the practical implementation of SED, populations of thousands of individuals, which are traditionally stored as tree structures, are genetically bred using the Darwinian principle of survival and reproduction of the fittest, along with recombination operations appropriate for mating computer programs. Tree structures can be easily evaluated in a recursive manner; every tree node has an operator function and every terminal node has an operand, making mathematical expressions easy to evolve and to be evaluated.

The performance, in the particular problem environment, of each individual computer program in the population is measured by its "fitness". The nature of the fitness measure depends on the problem at hand. Different fitness functions, built from different requirements, can lead to completely different results, each one best fitted to the corresponding original requirements.

The only information which the design process requires to advance in its search within the space of possible solutions are the current population and the fitness of all its individuals. A new population is then generated, by applying simple rules inspired by natural evolution.

The main (meta)-operators used in SED are reproduction, crossover and mutation.

- The reproduction simply reproduces in the new population, without any change, a predetermined number of individuals among those who obtained the best fitness.
- Crossover is applied on an individual by simply switching one of its nodes with another node from another individual in the population. With a tree-based representation, replacing a node means the replacement of the whole branch. This adds greater effectiveness to the crossover operation, since it exchanges two actual sub-individuals with different dimensions. The expressions resulting from a single crossover can be either quite close or very different from their initial parents. The sudden jump from an individual to a very different one is a powerful trap-escaping mechanism.
- Mutation affects an individual in the population, replacing a whole node in the selected individual, or just the node's information. To maintain integrity, operations must be fail-safe, i.e. the type of information the node holds must be taken into account.

Since each individual in the SED approach is a set of unambiguous instructions describing the realization of a generic physical structure, the presented procedure can be extended, in principle, to any 3D structure.

Before entering into the SED description, some considerations on the name chosen (Casula et al., 2011a) are in order. Koza, in his 1992 paper, coined the name "genetic programming" for his approach. Actually, this name resembles too closely another optimization approach, but with marked differences with the Koza approach, namely the genetic algorithms (GA). We decided to use a different name, better linked to the approach we use, to avoid any ambiguity between very different approaches. In order to better grasp the differences between SED and GA, we can say that GA works on the "nucleotide" (i.e. bit) level, in the sense that the structure is completely defined from the beginning, and only a handful of parameters remain to be optimized. On the other hand, the approach used in SED assumes no "a priori" structure, and it builds up the structure of the individuals as the procedure evolves. Therefore it operates at the "organ" (i.e. physical structure) level, a far more powerful level: it acts on subparts of the whole structure, thus allowing an effective exploration of a far more vast solution space than other design techniques. SED is able to determine both the structure shape and dimensions as an outcome of the procedure, and is therefore a powerful tool for the designer. As a consequence, its solution space has the power of the continuum, while the GA solution space is a discrete one, so it is a very small subspace of the former. Moreover, the typical evolution operators work on actual physical structures, rather than on sequences of bits with no intuitive link to the structure shape. The enormous power of SED fully allows the exploration of more general shapes for the structure. The main drawback is the ill-posedness of the SED, which calls for a regularization procedure.

The rest of this chapter is organised as follows:

- Section 2 starts with a general description of the Structure-based Evolutionary Design, and of the main steps of the evolutionary process.
- SED is then specifically applied to the design of broadband parasitic wire arrays (Sections 2.1-2.3): a suitable tree representation of wire antennas is devised, appropriate antenna requirements are set, a suitable fitness is derived and the evaluation procedure for each individual is described.
- In Section 3 several examples are presented: for each set of requirements, a suitable fitness function must be derived, and some suggestions are given to choose the best fitness for the problem at hand.
- The results obtained with SED are finally compared with other algorithms like Particle Swarm Optimization and Differential Evolution, showing that the performances obtained by SED are significantly higher.

2. Description of the Structure-based Evolutionary Design

SED is a global random search procedure, looking for individuals best fitting a given set of specifications. These individuals are described as instruction sets, and internally represented as trees. The main steps of the whole evolutionary design can be summarized in the flowchart of Fig.1:

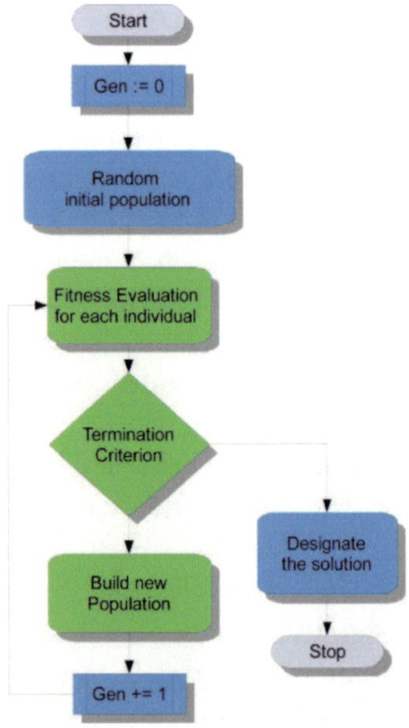

Figure 1. Flowchart of the Evolutionary Design.

After an initial step, where N individuals are picked up at random, an iterative procedure starts, which includes the evaluation of the fitness (appropriate for the problem at hand) for each individual, and the building of the next generation of the population. A larger probability of breeding is assigned to individuals with the highest fitness. The generation of new populations ends only when opportune stopping rules are met (i.e. when the individual-antenna fulfils, to a prescribed degree, the stated requirement).

The solution space, i.e., the set of admissible solutions in which the procedure looks for the optimum, has the power of the continuum. This is the main advantage of SED, since it allows exploring, and evaluating, general structure configurations, but, on the other hand, it can lead to a severely ill-conditioned synthesis problem. As a consequence, a naive implementation usually does not work, since different starting populations lead to completely different final populations, possibly containing only individuals poorly matched to the requirements (a phenomenon similar to the occurrence of traps in optimization procedures).

A suitable stabilization is therefore needed. This role can be accomplished by suitable structure requirements, or forced by imposing further constraints, not included in the structure requirements. Whenever possible, the former ones are the better choice, and should be investigated first.

Typically, a high number N of individuals for a certain number of generations must be evaluated in order to obtain a good result from the design process. Since each individual can be evaluated independently from each other, the design process is strongly parallelizable, and this can significantly reduce the computation time.

2.1. SED applied to the design of wire antennas

The Structure-Based Evolutionary Design, based on evolutionary programming, has been devised and applied to the design of broadband parasitic wire arrays for VHF-UHF bands. This requires first to devise a suitable tree representation of wire antennas, well tailored to the SED meta-operators, and then suitable antenna requirements. We consider only antennas with a symmetry plane, and with all element centres on a line. Therefore, each "wire" is actually a symmetric pair of metallic trees, and only one of them must be described.

In antenna design, the most intuitive fitness function can be built as the "distance" between actual and required far-field behaviour (Franceschetti et al., 1988) or, even more simply, as the antenna gain or SNR (Lo et al., 1966). However, this is not the case for SED. The solution space, i.e., the set of admissible solution in which the procedure looks for the optimum, is composed, in our case, of every Parasitic Dipole Array (PDA) antenna with no limit on the number of wire segments, nor on the size or orientation, represented as real numbers. The design problem is therefore strongly ill-conditioned and, in order to stabilize it, appropriate suitable antenna requirements must be set. Far-field requirements are unable to stabilize the problem, since the far-field degrees of freedom are orders of magnitude less than those of the solution space (Bucci & Franceschetti, 1989), so that a huge number of different antennas gives the same far field. As a matter of fact, a wire segment whose length is a small fraction of the wavelength can be added or eliminated without affecting the far field. We must therefore revert to near-field requirements. Among them, the easiest to implement, and probably the most important, is a requirement on the input impedance over the required bandwidth. Since this constraint is a "must-be" in order to get a usable solution, we get the required stabilization at virtually no additional cost. As a further advantage, a low input reactance over the bandwidth prevents from superdirective solutions (Collin, 1985) even when a reduced size is forced as a constraint.

The performances of each individual (antenna) of the population are evaluated by its fitness function. The details of the fitness function we have chosen for PDA design are widely described in the next section. However, at this point it must be stressed that the fitness function depends in an essential way on the electromagnetic behaviour of the individual.

Since we are interested in assessing SED as a viable, and very effective, design tool, we accurately try to avoid any side-effect stemming out from the electromagnetic analysis of our individuals. Therefore we rely on known, well-established and widely used antenna analysis programs. Since our individuals are wire antennas, our choice has fallen on NEC-2 (Burke et al., 1981).

The Numerical Electromagnetics Code (NEC-2) is a MoM-based, user-oriented computer code for the analysis of the electromagnetic response of wire antennas and other metallic structures (Lohn et al., 2005). It is built around the numerical solution of the integral equations for the currents induced on the structure. This approach allows taking well into account the main second-order effects, such as conductor losses and the effect of lossy ground on the far field. Therefore we are able to evaluate the actual gain, and not the array directivity, with a two-fold advantage. First of all, the gain is the far-field parameter of interest and, second, this prevents from considering superdirective antennas, both during the evolution and as final solution, which is even worse. NEC has been successfully used to model a wide range of antennas, with high accuracy (Burke & Poggio, 1976a, 1976b, 1981; Deadrick et al., 1977) and is now considered as one of the reference electromagnetic software (Lohn et al., 2005; Linden & Altshuler, 1996, 1997). However, since SED is by no means linked, or tailored, to NEC, a different, and most effective, EM software could be used, to reduce the total computational time, further improving the accuracy of the simulation.

2.2. Construction and evaluation of each parasitic dipole array

Each PDA is composed of a driven element and a fixed number of parasitic elements. In order to get transverse dimensions close to those of Yagi and LPDA, and to ease the realization, the centers of the elements are arranged on a line, with the driven element at the second place of the row. In Yagi terminology, we use a single reflector. We actually have experimented with more reflectors but, exactly as in standard Yagi, without any advantage over the single-reflector configuration. Each element is symmetric w.r.t its center, and the upper part is represented, in the algorithm, as a tree.

Each node of the tree is an operator belonging to one of the following classes:

a. add a wire according to the present directions and length
b. transform the end of the last added wire in a branching point
c. modify the present directions and length
d. stretch (or shrink) the last added wire

This mixed representation largely increases the power of the standard genetic operations (mutation and cross-over), since each element can evolve independently from the others. Of course, after each complete PDA is generated, its geometrical coherency is verified, and incoherent antennas (e.g., an antenna with two elements too close, or even intersecting) are discarded.

The SED approach has been implemented in Java, while the analysis of each individual has been implemented in C++ (using the freeware source code Nec2cpp) and checked using the freeware tool 4nec2. The integration with NEC-2 has mainly been achieved through three classes:

1. a parser for the conversion of the s-expressions, represented as n-ary trees, in the equivalent NEC input files;
2. a NecWrapper which writes the NEC listing to a file, launches a NEC2 instance in a separate process, and parses the output generated by NEC;
3. an Evaluator which calculates the fitness using the output data generated by NEC.

In order to better grasp the representation chosen, the S-expression for the simple Yagi antenna of Fig.2 follows.

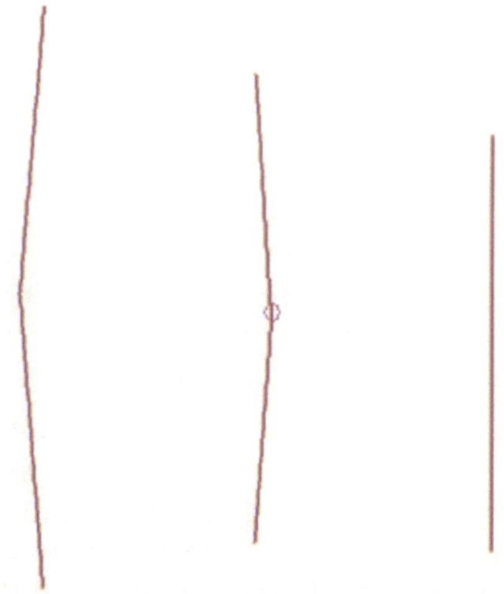

Figure 2. Antenna Structure corresponding to the S-expression of the example

S-expression:

Tree 0:

(StretchAlongZ 1.3315124586134857 (Wire 0.42101090906114413 1.0

(StretchAlongX 0.5525837649288541 (StretchAlongY 1.4819461053740617

(RotateWithRespectTo_Y 0.3577743384222999 END)))))

Tree 1:

(Wire 0.5581593081319647 1.0 (RotateWithRespectTo_X -0.44260816356142224

(RotateWithRespectTo_Z 0.08068272691709244 (StretchAlongZ 0.7166185389610261

(StretchAlongX 1.42989629787443 (StretchAlongZ 1.346598788775623

END))))))

Tree 2:

(Wire 0.3707701115469606 1.0 (RotateWithRespectTo_X 0.5262591815805174

(RotateWithRespectTo_Z -0.7423883999218206 (RotateWithRespectTo_Z 0.07210315212202911

END))))

The corresponding NEC-2 input file is:

GW 1 17 0.00E00 0.00E00 0.00E00 -1.34E-02 1.44E-02 1.33E-01 1.36E-03

GW 2 22 -1.38E-01 0.00E00 0.00E00 -1.25E-01 0.00E00 1.66E-01 1.36E-03

GW 3 15 1.21E-01 0.00E00 0.00E00 1.21E-01 0.00E00 1.18E-01 1.36E-03

GX 4 001

GE

2.3. Fitness function

The fitness function must measure how closely the design meets the desired requirements. To achieve our design goal, a fitness should be developed, which is to direct the evolution process on a structure with reduced size, with the highest end-fire gain, and with an input match as better as possible in the widest frequency range. Actually, the increase in a parameter (i.e. the gain) usually results in a reduction in the other ones (i.e. frequency bandwidth and input matching), thus the algorithm must manage an elaborate trade-off between these conflicting goals. Therefore, the form of the fitness function can be a critical point, since only a suitable fitness can lead the design process to significant results. Moreover, depending on the used fitness, the computation time can be largely reduced (i.e. a good result can be obtained with less generations).

After evaluation of different fitness structures, we have chosen a fitness function composed by three main terms suitably arranged as:

$$Fitness = \left(F_M + F_G\right) \cdot F_S \tag{1}$$

The first term (F_M) takes into account the input matching of the antenna, the second term (F_G) takes into account the antenna gain including the effect of ohmic losses, and the last term (F_S) takes into account the antenna size.

In (2.1):

$$F_M = \left|1 - \overline{SWR}\right| \cdot \alpha_M; \qquad F_G = \left|\frac{G_{MAX}}{\overline{G}}\right| \cdot \alpha_G; \qquad F_S = 1 + \frac{D_{REAL} - D_{MAX}}{D_{MAX}} \cdot \alpha_S \tag{2}$$

wherein α_M, α_G and α_S are suitable weights, while $\overline{SWR}$ and $\overline{G}$ are the mean values of SWR and gain over the bandwidth of interest, D_{REAL} represents the real antenna size and D_{MAX} is the maximum allowed size for the antenna.

The requirement of a given, and low, VSWR all over the design bandwidth is obviously needed to effectively feed the designed antenna. However it has an equally important role. The VSWR requirement (a near-field requirement) stabilizes the problem, at virtually no additional cost.

The evaluation procedure for each individual (i.e. for each antenna) can be described by the flowchart in Fig.3.

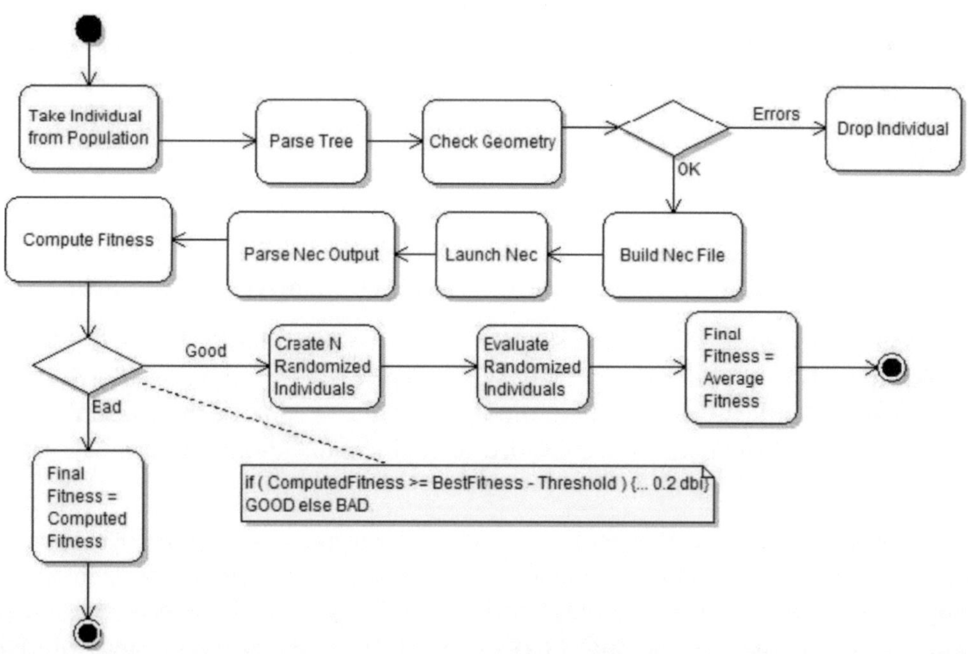

Figure 3. Flowchart of the evaluation procedure for each individual of the population.

The process requires, as inputs, the required frequency range of the antenna, the number of frequency points N_F to be evaluated, the metal conductivity and the maximum size of the antenna. Actually, the generated antenna can overcome the bounding box dimensions, but with a penalty directly proportional to the excess size.

The proposed fitness functions try to perform a trade-off between contrasting objectives, through the relative weights.

In this sense, we can say that the selected individuals are the best adapted to the (present) antenna requirements. However, a different view would be the association of each (different) requirement to a different fitness, thus leading to a multi-objective design.

In fact, generic evolutionary algorithms, like SED, PSO, DE, GA are a very powerful tool for solving difficult single objective problems, but they can also be applied to solving many multi-objective problems. Actually, real-world problems usually include several conflicting objectives, and a suitable trade-off must be found. An interesting topic is therefore the study of Multi-Objective optimization methods (Chen, 2009), and in solving such multi-objective problems the adopted optimization method must provide an approximation of the Pareto set such that the user can understand the trade-off between overlapped and conflicting objectives, in order to make the final decision. Usually, a decomposition method is implemented to convert a multi-objective problem into a set of mono-objective problems, and an optimal Pareto front is approximated by solving all the sub-problems together (Carvalho, 2012), and this requires insight not only of the algorithmic domain, but also knowledge of the application problem domain.

In design methods dealing with a set of individuals, like SED, such point of view could lead to better ways to explore the solution space, and is a promising direction for future investigations.

3. Results

The automated design of wire antennas using SED has been applied to several PDAs, with different maximum sizes, number of elements, and operation frequencies, and with different requirements both on Gain and input matching, always obtaining very good results.

We present here only a few examples, chosen also to show the flexibility of SED. All designed antennas have been compared with known antennas. However, since our antennas are wide-band 3D structures, it has been difficult to device a suitable comparison antenna. To get a meaningful comparison, we decided to compare our designed antennas with an antenna of comparable size.

The first presented antenna (Casula et al., 2009), shown in Fig.4a, has been obtained by constraining the evolution of each individual only in two directions (i.e. horizontally and vertically). This limitation is a hard limitation, and significantly affects the antenna performances. This compromise leads anyway to antennas easy to realize, and with good performances.

The designed antenna works at the operation frequency of 800 MHz, and the requested bandwidth is of 70 MHz (i.e. 9%, from 780 MHz to 850 MHz). The best designed antenna is represented in Fig.1a. The antenna size is $0.58\lambda_0$ x $0.67\lambda_0$ x $1.2\lambda_0$, λ_0 being the space wavelength at the operation frequency of 800 MHz, its gain is above 11.6 dB (see Fig.5) and its SWR is less than 2 in the whole bandwidth of 70 MHz (see Fig.1b). No additional matching network is therefore required.

The chosen comparison antenna has been a 4-elements dipole array, with the same H-plane size of our antenna. This array, shown in Fig.4b, is composed of 4 vertical elements, with a length of $1.2\lambda_0$ and spacing of $0.58\lambda_0$ in the H-plane and of $0.67\lambda_0$ in the E-plane, and its gain is within +/- 1 dB with respect to our antenna. The latter, therefore, uses in an effective way its size. However, it must be stressed that our antenna has a single, and well-matched, feed point, while the array needs a BFN to produce the correct feeding currents of the array elements, which have also a quite large Q. The array realization is therefore more complex.

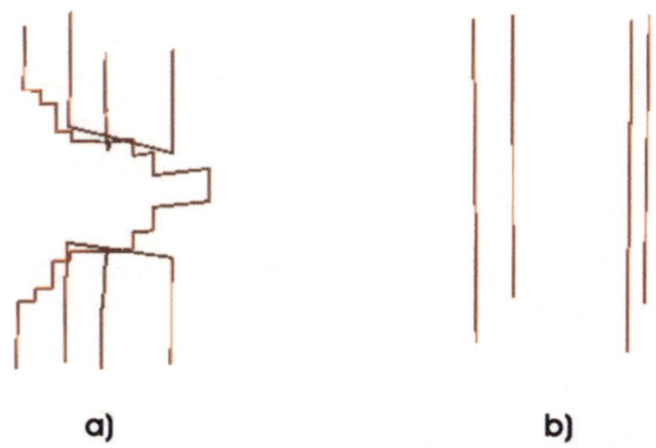

Figure 4. a) SED designed antenna; b) Reference Planar Array with 4 elements and the same size (in the H-plane).

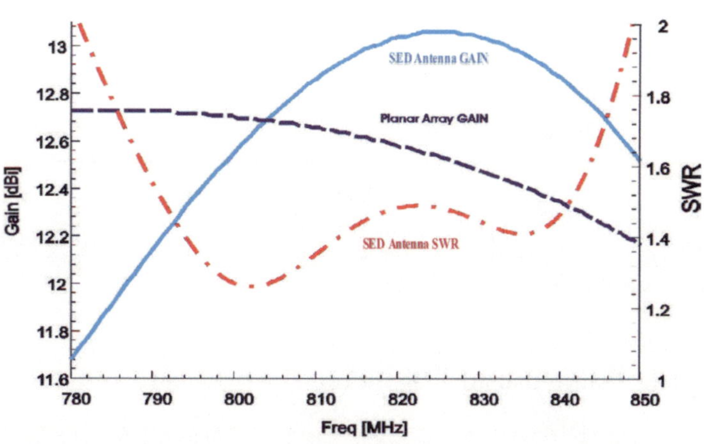

Figure 5. Gain and SWR of the GP designed antenna compared to the Gain of the reference Planar Array with 4 elements and the same size (in the H-plane).

Note that we have considered the antenna made of perfectly conducting (PEC) wires. The VSWR constraint has prevented to fall in a super-directive solution, but the robustness of a designed ideal antenna respect to conductor losses has not been checked.

The second example removes the constraints of right-angle junctions made in the first example, and will be used also to evaluate the role of the conductor losses on the SED performances. As a matter of fact, this can be easily done by designing an optimal antenna assuming PEC (Antenna 2A) and another one, assuming a finite conductivity σ (antenna 2B), in this case equal to that of pure copper (σ=5.8*10^7 S/m). Then the first antenna is analysed by including also the finite conductivity of the wires (Casula et al., 2011b).

For the 2A antenna, at the operation frequency of 500 MHz, requiring a bandwidth of 60 MHz (i.e. 12%, from 470 MHz to 530 MHz), SED designs the antenna shown in Fig.6a. The performances of the antenna 2A are shown in Table 1.

Antenna 2A has been analysed also assigning to the conductors a finite conductivity equal to the pure copper (σ=5.8*10^7 S/m). The results show a significant degradation of the antenna performances, since even using a very good conductor as material, the dissipations due to the finite conductivity are very large, making the antenna unusable (in fact NEC2 gives similar values for the SWR, but a very low efficiency). In other words, such antenna is actually close to a super-directive one.

On the other side, asking SED to design an antenna with the same specifications of antenna 2A, but assuming σ=5.8*10^7 S/m, we obtain an antenna with similar performances with respect to the 2A antenna, but with a larger size (Antenna 2B). The designed antenna is shown in Fig.6b, and, since the losses affect the antenna gain, the finite conductivity effect is already included in the fitness. The performances of the antenna 2B are shown in Table 1.

This antenna shows similar performances with respect to the antenna shown in Fig.6a, but it has a larger size ($0.1833\lambda_0^3$ with respect to $0.03\lambda_0^3$). Nevertheless, unlike the antenna shown in Fig.6a, it is feasible.

Antenna	**Conductivity σ (S/m)**	**Design Shown**	**Antenna Size**	**Bandwidth (SWR<2)**	**MAX Directivity Gain (dBi)**	**Efficiency (%)**
2A	$+\infty$ (PEC)	Fig.6a	$0.33\lambda_0$x $0.22\lambda_0$ x $0.4\lambda_0$	70 MHz (14%)	26	100
2B	5.8*10^7 (pure copper)	Fig.6b	$0.47\lambda_0$ x $0.3\lambda_0$ x $1.3\lambda_0$	90 MHz (18%)	20	90.09

Table 1. Performances of the antennas 2A and 2B.

The frequency responses of both antennas are shown in Fig. 7 and 8. Also from these responses, we easily deduce that antenna 2A (designed and analysed using PEC) is almost superdirective.

The presented results show that the introduction of a finite value of metal conductivity allows to obtain antennas with similar performances with respect to the antennas designed with perfect conductors, but with a larger size. On the other hand, antennas designed assuming perfect conductors are characterized by collected and closer branches and tend to be super-directive.

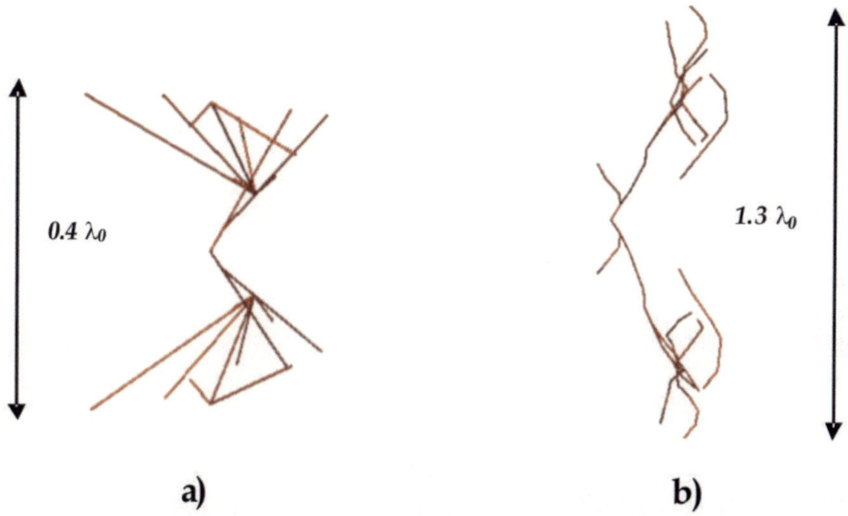

Figure 6. a) Antenna 2A, designed using perfect conductors; b) Antenna 2B, designed using finite metal conductivity.

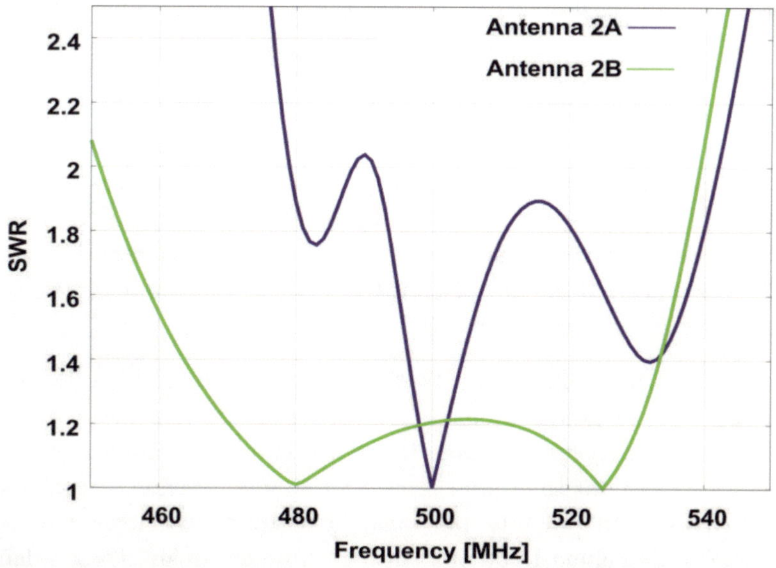

Figure 7. SWR of the antennas 2A and 2B.

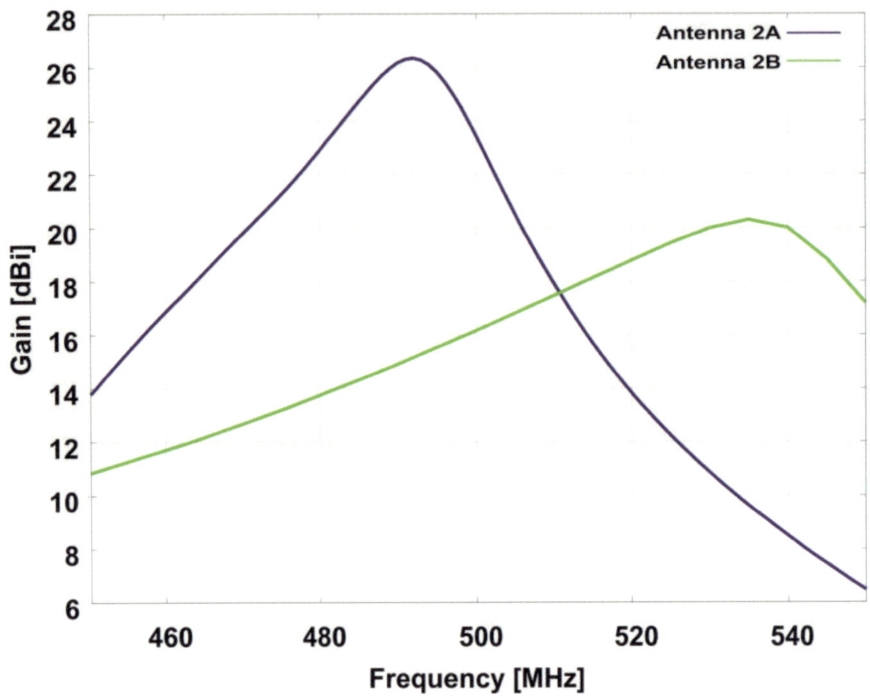

Figure 8. Gain of the antennas 2A and 2B.

Material	Conductivity σ (S/m)	Efficiency (%)	Max Directivity Gain (dB)
PEC	+∞	100	20.35
Copper	$5.8*10^7$	90.09	20.3
Aluminium	$3.77*10^7$	87.71	20.29
Stainless Steel	$0.139*10^7$	34.84	20.01

Table 2. Performances of the antenna designed using pure copper (shown in Fig.6b) for different values of conductivity.

In Table 2, the antenna shown in Fig.6b, designed supposing the metal to be copper, has been analysed for different values of conductivity. While the maximum directivity is almost constant with respect to σ, the efficiency rapidly decreases. It is therefore required to take into account in SED the actual conductivity of the antenna material, but, doing so, the designed antennas will show similar performances to the antenna designed using copper, with an acceptable value for the efficiency.

The last presented antenna (Casula et al., 2011a) is a broadband parasitic wire array for VHF-UHF bands with a significant gain, showing significant improvements over existing solutions (Yagi and LPDA) for the same frequency bands. In order to fulfil these strict requirements, we had to devise a quite complicate fitness function, composed by several secondary objectives overlapped to the main goal; these objectives are expressed by appropriate weights modelling trade-offs between different goals. These relative weights have been modelled by linear relations to avoid discontinuities and thus reducing the probability of local maxima of the fitness, which trap the evolution process. The robustness respect to realization errors is also evaluated and taken into account in the fitness.

We choose to maximize gain as the main goal of the fitness. Since we want to maximize the end-fire gain, the radiation pattern has been divided into 4 regions:

1. The endfire direction:

   $\theta = 90°;\ \varphi = 0°$

2. The back direction:

   $\theta = 90°;\ \varphi = 180°$

3. The FRONT region:

   $|\theta| > 90° + 2\Delta\theta;\ 0° + 2\Delta\varphi < \varphi \leq 90°$

   (where $\Delta\vartheta$ and $\Delta\varphi$ take into account the desired main lobe amplitude)

4. The REAR region:

   $0° \leq |\theta| \leq 180°;\ 90° \leq |\varphi| \leq 180°;$

Our goal is the maximization of the gain in the region 1 while minimizing the gains in the other 3 regions, with all the gains expressed in dB. Since we want to optimize the antenna in a certain frequency bandwidth, we start computing a suitable weighted average gain G_{AW1} on region 1:

$$G_{AW1} = \frac{1}{N_F} \sum_{i=1}^{N_F} w_i \cdot G_{Ei} \tag{3}$$

wherein the average is taken over the N_F frequency points, spanning the whole bandwidth of interest. In (3.1) G_{Ei} is the endfire gain and w_i depends on the input impedance of the PDA:

$$w_i = \begin{cases} 0.2 & \text{If } [(Re\,(ZIN) < 35\ \Omega) \text{ or } (Re\,(ZIN) > 400\ \Omega)] \\ \alpha_i & \\ 1 & \text{If } [(35\Omega \leq Re(ZIN) \leq 400\ \Omega)] \text{ and } [(Im(ZIN) > Re\,(ZIN))] \end{cases}$$

α_i is a weight proportional to the difference between the imaginary part X_{IN}^A and the real part R_{IN}^A of the array input impedance.

The average gains over all other regions, namely G_{BGR} in the back direction, G_{FGR} in the front region and G_{RGR} in the rear region, are then computed. An "effective" endfire gain G_{AW} is then obtained properly weighting each gain:

$$G_{AW}=G_{AW1}\cdot\frac{1}{1+\alpha_{BGR}*G_{BGR}}\cdot\frac{1}{1+\alpha_{FGR}*G_{FGR}}\cdot\frac{1}{1+\alpha_{RGR}*G_{RGR}} \tag{4}$$

The weigths α_{BGR}, α_{FGR} and α_{RGR} are chosen through a local tuning in order to get the maximum gain in the end-fire direction and an acceptable radiation pattern in the rest of the space. In our case, we obtained the following values: α_{BGR}=0.08, α_{FGR}=0.14 and α_{RGR}=0.02.

In order to design a wideband antenna, we must add some parameters taking into account the antenna input matching, and therefore we introduced suitable weights connected to the antenna input impedance. Holding gain weights fixed, the other parameters concerning input matching are added one by one choosing each weight through a further local tuning.

The G_{AW} is therefore furthermore modified taking into account:

a. The values of R_{IN}^A, X_{IN}^A (averaged over the BW), and their normalized variance;

b. The SWR over all the required bandwidth

according to the following guidelines:

1. A step is introduced, with a weight α_{XR}=50 if $|X_{IN}^A| > R_{IN}^A$, and α_{XR}=0 otherwise, to boost up structures with $R_{IN}^A > |X_{IN}^A|$;
2. A weight α_{XX}=0.03 is introduced, related to $|X_{IN}^A|$, forcing the evolution process to structures with an $|X_{IN}^A|$ as small as possible;
3. A weight α_{RX}=0.1 is introduced, related to $R_{IN}^A - |X_{IN}^A|$, to advantage structures with a low Q factor;
4. A weight α_{RR}=0.055 is introduced, related to R_{IN}^A, to boost up structures with a high real part of the input impedance (as long as it is lower than 300 Ω);
5. Weights $\alpha_{VR}=\alpha_{VX}$=0.015 are introduced, inversely related to the normalized variance of R_{IN}^A and X_{IN}^A, to advantage structures with a regular impedance behaviour;
6. A sequence of small steps, related to the SWR (with a weight α_{SWR} between 30 for an SWR>20 and 0.005 for an SWR<4), is introduced to first boost up and then hold the evolution in areas of the evolution space with good SWR values.

At this point we have a modified average gain G_M, expressed by:

$$G_M=G_{AW}\cdot\left(\frac{1}{1+\alpha_{XR}}\right)\cdot\left(\frac{1}{1+\alpha_{XX}\left|X_{IN}^A\right|}\right) \tag{5}$$

$$\cdot\left(\frac{1}{1+\alpha_{RX}\dfrac{R_{IN}^A-\left|X_{IN}^A\right|}{R_{IN}^A}}\right)\cdot\left(\frac{1}{1+\alpha_{RR}*\dfrac{\left|R_{IN}^A-300\right|}{R_{IN}^A}}\right)\cdot\left(\frac{1}{1+\alpha_{VX}\cdot\sigma_R^2}\right)\cdot\left(\frac{1}{1+\alpha_{VR}\cdot\sigma_X^2}\right)\cdot\left(\frac{1}{1+\alpha_{SWR}}\right)$$

where σ_R^2 and σ_X^2 are the normalized variance of R_{IN}^A and of X_{IN}^A, respectively.

The difference G_R-G_M (where G_R is a suitably high gain, needed only to work with positive fitness values) is then modulated taking into account both the Q factor (obtained as the ratio between the imaginary part and the real part of the array input impedance at the central frequency) and the structure size to get a particular fitness f_1. The individual generated by the genetic process associated to a fitness f_1 higher or very close to the best fitness obtained as yet, are then perturbed (assigning random relocations to array elements) and analysed to assess their robustness respect to random modification of the structure. Two different random perturbed antennas are considered for each individual, and the final fitness f_2 is the partial fitness f_1 averaged over all the initial and perturbed configurations. This random relocation allows getting robust structures respect to both constructive errors and bad weather conditions (for example movements due to wind effect). On the other hand, this robustness test is quite time-consuming. Therefore it is performed only on antennas already showing good performances. The final population is graded according to their f_2 value.

The antenna designed using the fitness expressed by (3.3) is a PDA with 20 elements: 1 reflector, 1 driven element and 18 directors. The operation frequency is 500 MHz, and the requested bandwidth is of 70 MHz (i.e. 14%, from 475 MHz to 545 MHz). The best antenna is represented in Fig.9, and its shape is typical of all antennas designed using our SED optimization technique. The antenna size is very small, since it fits in a box large 1.72 λ_0 x 0.03 λ_0 x 0.57 λ_0, being λ_0 the space wavelength at the operation frequency of 500 MHz. Its SWR is less than 2 in the whole bandwidth of 70 MHz, and its gain is above 18 dB.

Figure 9. Designed Antenna Structure.

The antenna has been designed using a population size of 1000 individuals, with a crossover rate set to 60%, and a mutation rate set to 40%. Its convergence plot is shown in Fig.10, and it appears that 300 generations are enough to reach convergence.

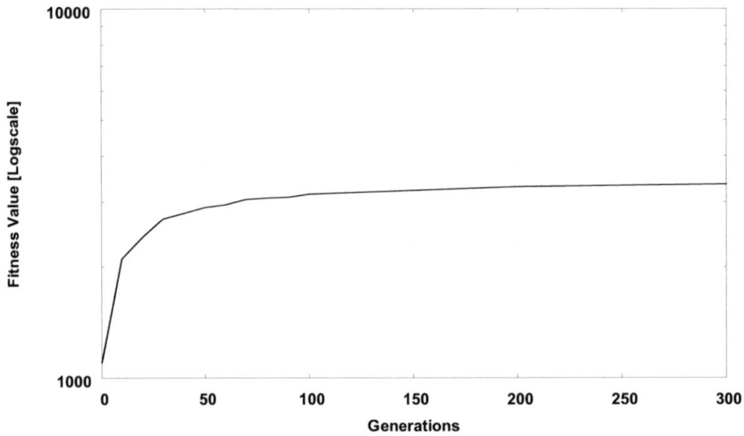

Figure 10. Plot of convergence of the designed antenna in Fig.9.

To assess the performances of our designed PDA, we need a comparison antenna. The best candidate is an existing Yagi but its choice is by no means obvious. Since, for a parasitic antenna, an increase in the number of elements adds little to the antenna complexity, we think that the most significant comparison is a gain comparison with a standard Yagi with the same size of our PDA (about $1.72\lambda_0$ in the endfire direction), and a size comparison with an Yagi with the same number of elements as our PDA. The first standard Yagi is composed of only 9 elements, and its gain and SWR, compared to our optimized PDA, are shown in Fig. 11. The standard Yagi bandwidth (SWR<2) is about 35 MHz (7% compared to 14%) with a gain between 12 and 13 dB, i.e. at least 5 dB less than ours, over the whole bandwidth.

A standard Yagi antenna with the same number of elements than our PDA, i.e., 20 has been selected for the second comparison. Though this antenna is very large (its size is about $6\lambda_0$x $0.5\lambda_0$), it has (see Fig.12) a quite narrow bandwidth (its gain is above 15 dB in a bandwidth smaller than 10%, and even its SWR is less than 2 in a bandwidth of about 9%) if compared with our PDA.

The PDA antenna of Fig. 11 and 12 has been designed choosing a fitness which pushes individuals toward higher Gain giving a smaller importance to input matching. As a further example, it is possible, by suitably choosing the fitness weights, to design a PDA antenna which favours individuals with better input matching. The performances of such an antenna are shown in Fig.13. The bandwidth (with SWR<2) has increased to 150 MHZ (30%), and its gain is only a few dB less than the first optimized PDA antenna. It is important to highlight that the size of the antenna with a larger input bandwidth is the same of the antenna with a higher gain.

In Fig. 14 we show also the F/B ratio of both the PDA designed antennas, which is very close also to standard Yagis' F/B. This comparison shows that, though the PDA we have designed appear to be more difficult to realize than a standard Yagi, they allow significantly better performances in a larger bandwidth, both on input matching, gain and F/B ratio. Furthermore, it is significantly smaller than standard Yagis.

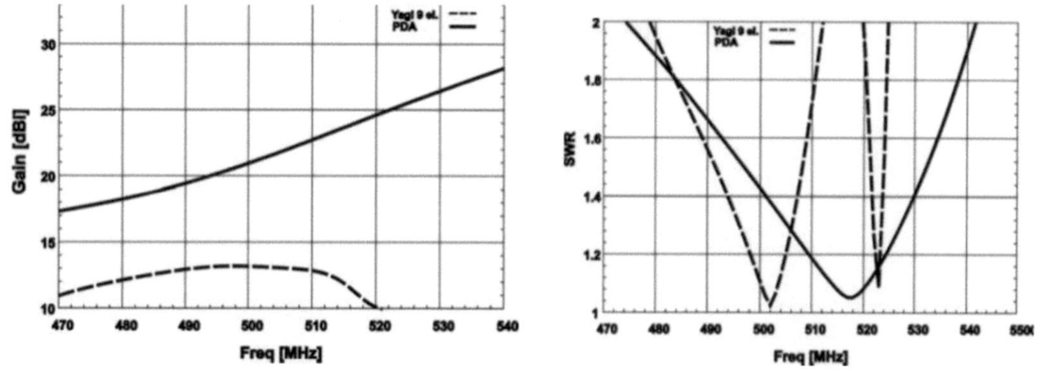

a) b)

Figure 11. (a) Gain and (b) SWR comparison between the PDA Designed Antenna and a standard Yagi with the same size (and 9 elements); (b): SWR comparison between the PDA Designed Antenna and a standard Yagi with the same size (and 9 elements).

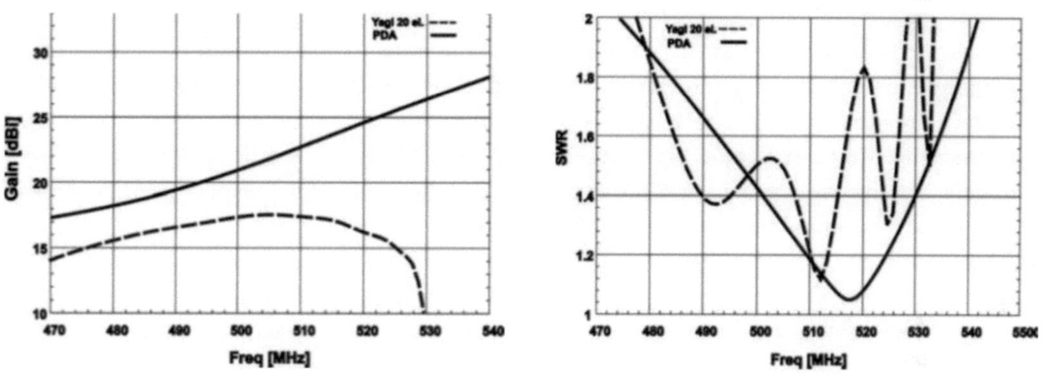

a) b)

Figure 12. (a) Gain and (b) SWR comparison between the PDA Designed Antenna and a standard Yagi with the same number of elements, 20, and a far larger size (6 λ_0 vs 1.72 λ_0).

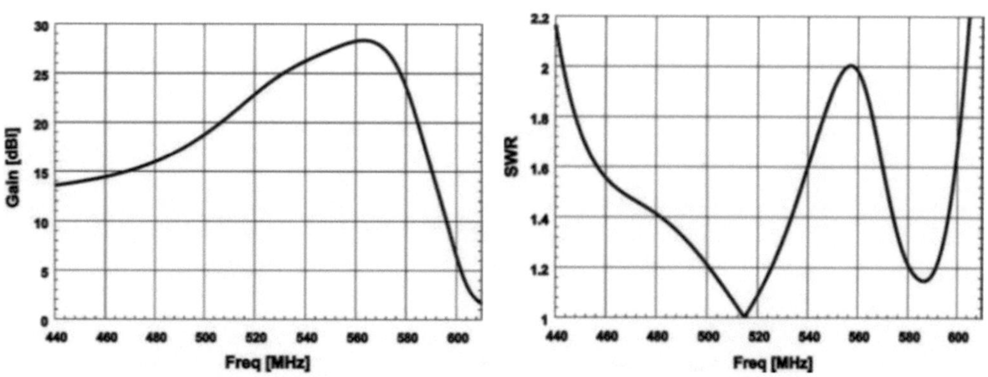

a) b)

Figure 13. (a) Gain and (b) SWR of the PDA Designed Antenna with a fitness pushing towards a larger SWR bandwidth

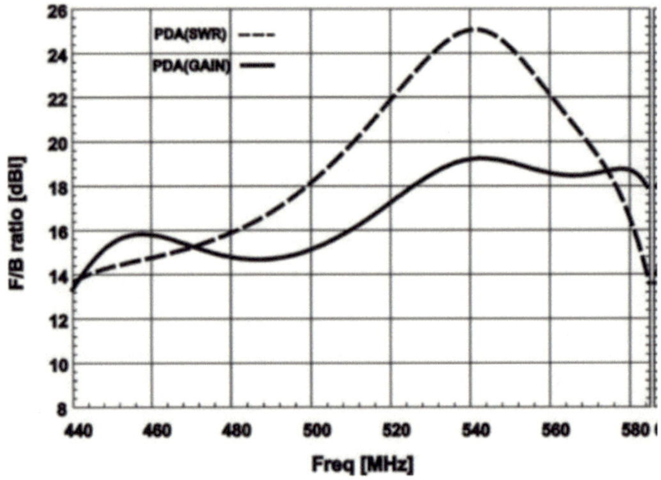

Figure 14. F/B ratio comparison between the PDA Designed Antenna with a fitness pushing towards a larger Gain bandwidth and one towards a larger SWR bandwidth.

In order to demonstrate that the inclusion of the antenna robustness into the fitness using our simple device works well, we have tested a hundred random perturbations of the reference antenna of Fig.9. These have been obtained perturbing the ends of each arm of the antenna with a random value between -2 and 2 mm. The standard deviations of the SWR and gain are shown in Fig.15 and are expressed in percentage with respect to the values of the unperturbed antenna shown in Fig.9. Despite of such huge perturbation, the designed PDA is so robust that the behaviour of all perturbed antennas is essentially the same of the unperturbed one. Therefore, despite of its (relative) low computational cost, the approach we have devised to include robustness in the fitness allows to design antennas which are very robust respect to realization errors.

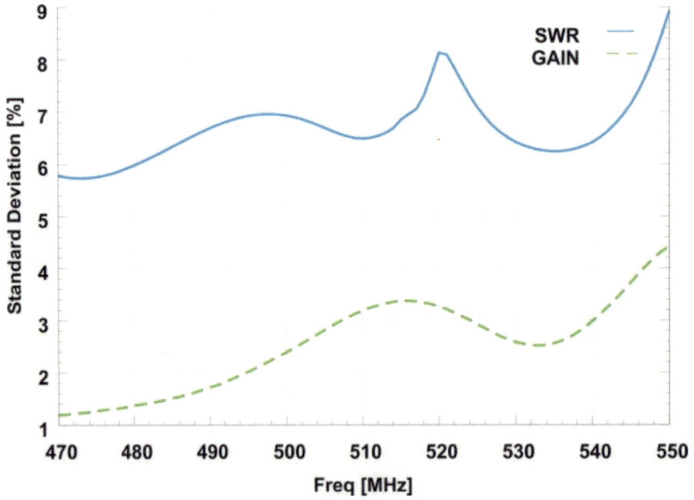

Figure 15. Standard Deviation of SWR and Gain of the PDA Designed Antenna in Fig.9, considering 100 randomly perturbed configurations.

Finally, we consider the computational issue. The computational cost of SED, like that of many other random optimization techniques, is the computational cost required to evaluate each individual. Therefore different techniques, such as SED and standard GA, can have different cost as long as they evaluate a different number of individuals, or more complex ones.

For the example presented in Fig.10, SED requires $3*10^5$ NEC evaluations of individuals. GA with comparable antenna size (such as the one described in (Jones & Joines, 1997)) requires a likely, or even larger, number of NEC evaluations. Since also the number of NEC unknown is more or less the same for both approaches, depending essentially on the antenna size, we can conclude that SED has a computational cost comparable, or slightly larger than standard GA. On the other hand, SED allows to explore a far larger solution space. If we consider as computational effectiveness of a design approach the size of the solution space explored for a given computational cost, we can conclude that SED is computationally more effective and with more performing antennas than GA.

A comparison between SED and other algorithms like Particle Swarm Optimization and Differential Evolution, shows that both the computational cost and the complexity are of the same order of magnitude, also in these cases. But, again, the performances obtained by them are not as good as the ones obtained using SED.

In Table 3, we show the results obtained by our PDA, designed using SED, compared with the results obtained by:

(Baskar et al., 2005), who used PSO to optimize the element spacing and lengths of a Yagi–Uda antenna;

(Goudos et al., 2010) who used Generalized Differential Evolution applied to Yagi-Uda antenna design;

(Li, 2007), who used Differential Evolution to optimize the geometric parameters of Yagi-Uda antennas;

(Yan et al., 2010), who designed a wide-band Yagi-Uda antenna with X-shape driven dipoles and parasitic elements using differential evolution algorithm, obtaining a bandwidth of 20%.

	N° Elements	Size	Gain at center frequency (dB)	VSWR at center frequency	Bandwidth (VSWR<2)
Baskar 2005 (PSO)	15	0.239x4.115 λ_0	16.4	1.05	-
Goudos 2010 (DE)	15	0.239x4.943 λ_0	17.58	1.1	-
Yan 2010 (DE)	11	0.527x1.391 λ_0	12.5	1.8	20%
Li 2007 (DE)	15	0.459x4.664 λ_0	16.59	1.085	-
SED	20	0.57x1.72 λ_0	21	1.4	30%

Table 3. Comparison between the performances reached by SED, PSO and DE in the design of a Parasitic Wire Dipole Array.

Both (Baskar et al., 2005), (Goudos et al., 2010) and (Li, 2007) decide to perform the optimization only at the center frequency, and this is a simpler task and can lead to better results than an optimization over the whole antenna bandwidth, which is the choice we made in our SED design. Nonetheless, the results obtained by SED are better than the ones obtained by PSO and DE even at the center frequency.

In fact we are able to get a wideband antenna with a very high gain, i.e. we both maximize antenna gain and minimize SWR and antenna size within the whole bandwidth (which is a wide bandwidth, equal to 30%).

Therefore, SED can lead to better results if compared with PSO and DE, both in terms of performances and of overall size. This is probably due to the fact that the solution space of SED is larger than the corresponding solution spaces of PSO and DE, and hence a proper choice of the fitness function can push the evolution process to more performing antennas.

4. Conclusion

In this chapter a new design technique, namely the Structure-based Evolutionary Design (SED) has been described in detail. This is a new global random search method based on the evolutionary programming concept. The proposed technique has been compared with the standard genetic algorithms (GA), a widely used design technique, showing the numerous advantages of our approach with respect to standard ones. Its main advantage is the ability to explore a far larger solution space than standard optimization algorithms. Moreover, SED assumes no "a priori" structure, but it builds up the structure of the individuals as the procedure evolves, being able to determine both the structure shape and dimensions as an outcome of the procedure. Inclusion of input matching requirements prevents from ill-posedness, a danger always present when the solution space is so large. The described procedure has been used to design wire antennas, and several examples are presented, showing very good results. The goal of the design process is to develop wire antennas fulfilling the desired requirements for both Gain and VSWR in a frequency band as wide as possible, and with the smallest size. For each set of requirements, a suitable fitness function must be derived, and some suggestions are given to choose the best fitness for the problem at hand. The results obtained with SED are finally compared with other global search algorithms showing that both the computational cost and the complexity are of the same order of magnitude, but the performances obtained by SED are significantly higher.

Author details

Giovanni Andrea Casula and Giuseppe Mazzarella
Università degli Studi di Cagliari/Dipartimento di Ing. Elettrica ed Elettronica, Piazza d'Armi, Cagliari, Italy

Acknowledgement

Work supported by Regione Autonoma della Sardegna, under contract number CRP1_511, with CUP F71J09000810002, titled *"Valutazione e utilizzo della Genetic Programming nel progetto di strutture a radiofrequenza e microonde"* .

5. References

Baskar, S.; Alphones, A.; Suganthan, P.N.; Liang, J.J. (2005). Design of Yagi-Uda antennas using comprehensive learning particle swarm optimization, *Microwaves, Antennas and Propagation*, IEE Proceedings, vol. 152, issue 5.

Bucci, O. M.; Franceschetti , G. (1989). On the degrees of freedom of Scattered Fields, *IEEE Transactions on Antennas and Propagation*, vol. 37, pp. 918-926.

Bucci, O. M.; D'Elia, G.; Mazzarella, G.; Panariello, G. (1994). Antenna pattern synthesis: a new general Approach, *Proc. IEEE* , 82, pp. 358–371.

Burke, G. J. ; Poggio, A. J. (1976a). Computer Analysis of the Twin-Whip, *UCRL-52080,* Lawrence Livermore Laboratory, CA.

Burke, G. J. ; Poggio, A. J. (1976b). Computer Analysis of the Bottom-Fed FM Antenna, *UCRL-52109,* Lawrence Livermore Laboratory, CA.

Burke, G. J. ; Poggio, A. J. (1981). Numerical Electromagnetics Code -Method of Moments, *Tech. Rep. UCID-18834,* Lawrence Livermore National Laboratory.

Carrel, R. (1961). The Design of Log-Periodic Dipole Antennas, *IRE International Convention Record*, Vol.9, pp. 61-75.

Carvalho, R.; Saldanha, R. R.; Gomes, B. N.; Lisboa, A.C.; Martins, A. X. (2012). A Multi-Objective Evolutionary Algorithm Based on Decomposition for Optimal Design of Yagi-Uda Antennas, *IEEE TRANSACTIONS ON MAGNETICS, VOL. 48, NO. 2.*

Casula, G.A.; Mazzarella, G.; Sirena N. (2009). Genetic Programming design of wire antennas, *Antennas and Propagation Society International Symposium.*

Casula, G.A.; Mazzarella, G.; Sirena N. (2011a). Evolutionary Design of Wide-Band Parasitic Dipole Arrays, *IEEE Transactions on Antennas and Propagation*, vol. 59; p. 4094-4102.

Casula, G.A.; Mazzarella, G.; Sirena N. (2011b). On the Effect of the Finite Metal Conductivity in the design of Wire Antennas using Evolutionary Design, *Antennas and Propagation Society International Symposium.*

Chen, C.; Chen, Y.; Zhang, Q. (2009). Enhancing MOEA/D with guided mutation and priority update for multi-objective, *CEC MOEA Competition, Trondheim, Norway.*

Collin, R.E. (1986). *Antennas and radiowave propagation*, McGraw-Hill.

Costanzo, S.; Casula, G.A.; Borgia, A.; Montisci, G.; Di Massa, G.; Mazzarella, G. (2009). Synthesis of Slot Arrays on Integrated Waveguides, *IEEE Antennas and Wireless Propagation Letters*, vol. 9; p. 962-965.

Darwin, C. (1859). *The Origin of Species*, J. Murray, London, Chapter XIII.

Deadrick, J.; Burke, G. J.; Poggio, A. J. (1977). Computer Analysis the Trussed-Whip and Discone-Cage Antennas, *UCRL-52201.*

Elliott, R.S. (1981). *Antenna theory and design*, Prentice-Hall, N.Y.

Franceschetti, G.; Mazzarella, G.; Panariello, G. (1988). Array synthesis with excitation constraints, *Proc. IEE, pt.H*, Vol.135.

Hansen, R.C. (1990). Superconducting Antennas, *IEEE Transactions on Aerospace Aerospace and Electronics Systems*, Vol. 26.

Hansen, R.C. (1991). Antenna Applications of Superconductors, *IEEE Transactions on Microwave Theory and Techniques*, Vol. 39.

Goudos, S.K.; Siakavara, K.; Vafiadis, E.E.; Sahalos, J.N. (2010). *Pareto optimal Yagi-Uda antenna design using multi-objective differential evolution*, Progress In Electromagnetics Research, Vol. 105, pp 231-251.

Johnson, R.C.; Jasik, H. (1984). *Antenna Engineering Handbook – Second Edition*, Mc Graw – Hill.

Jones, E. A.; Joines, W.T. (1997). Design of Yagi-Uda Antennas Using Genetic Algorithms, *IEEE Trans. On Antennas and Propagation*, Vol.45 n°9, pp.1386-1392.

Koza, J. R. (1992). *Genetic Programming: On the Programming of Computers by Means of Natural Selectio* , MIT Press.

Li, J. Y. (2007). Optimizing Design of Antenna Using Differential, *Proceedings of Asia-Pacific Microwave Conference.*

Linden, D.; Altshuler, E. (1996). Automating Wire Antenna Design using Genetic Algorithms, *Microwave Journal*, vol. 39, no. 3, pp. 74-86.

Linden, D.; Altshuler, E. (1997). Wire-Antenna designs using genetic algorithms, *Antennas and Propagation Magazine*, IEEE, vol.39, no.2, pp.33-43.

Lo, Y. T.; Lee, S. W.; Lee, Q. H. (1966). Optimization of directivity and signal-to-noise ratio of an arbitrary antenna array, *Proc. IEEE*, vol. 54, pp. 1033–1045.

Lohn, J. D.; Hornby, G. S.; Linden, D. S. (2005). An Evolved Antenna For Deployment on NASA's Space Technology 5 Mission, in Genetic Programming Theory And Practice II, *Springer*.

Montisci, G.; Casula, G.A.; Galia, T.; Mazzarella, G. (2003) Design of series-fed printed arrays, *Journal of Electromagnetic Waves and Applications.*

Montisci, G. (2006). Design of circularly polarized waveguide slot linear arrays, *IEEE Transactions on Antennas and Propagation*, 54 (10), pp. 3025-3029.

Orchard, H.J.; Elliott, R.S.; Stern, G.J. (1985). Optimising the synthesis of shaped beam antenna patterns, *Microwaves, Antennas and Propagation, IEE Proceedings H*, Vol. 132 , pp 63 - 68.

Silver, S. (1949). *Microwave Antenna Theory and Design*, Mc Graw – Hill.

Yan, Ya-li; Fu Guang; Gong, Shu-xi; Chen, Xi; Li, Dong-chao. (2010). Design of a wide-band Yagi-Uda antenna using differential evolution algorithm, *International Symposium on Signals Systems and Electronics (ISSSE).*

Chapter 7

Dynamic Hedging Using Generated Genetic Programming Implied Volatility Models

Fathi Abid, Wafa Abdelmalek and Sana Ben Hamida

Additional information is available at the end of the chapter

http://dx.doi.org/10.5772/48148

1. Introduction

One challenge posed by financial markets is to correctly forecast the volatility of financial securities, which is a crucial variable in trading and risk management of derivative securities. Dynamic hedging is very sensitive to volatility forecast and good hedges require accurate estimate of volatility. Implied volatilities, generated from option markets, can be particularly useful in such contents as they are forward-looking measures of the market's expected volatility during the remaining life of an option [1, 2]. Since there is no explicit formula available to compute directly the implied volatility, the latter can be obtained by inverting the option pricing model. On the contrary, the genetic programming offers explicit formulas which can compute directly the implied volatility. This volatility forecasting method should be free of strong assumptions regarding underlying price dynamics and more flexible than parametric methods. This paper proposes a non parametric approach based on genetic programming to improve the accuracy of the implied volatility forecast and consequently the dynamic hedging.

Genetic Programming [3] is an optimization technique which extends the basic genetic algorithms [4] to process non-linear problem structure. In genetic programming, solutions are represented as tree structures that can vary in size and shape, rather than fixed length character strings as in genetic algorithms. This means that genetic programming can be used to perform optimization at a structural level. In the standard genetic programming, the entire population of function-trees is evaluated against the entire training data set, so the number of function-tree evaluations carried out per generation is directly proportional to both the population size and the size of the training set. Genetic programming can encounter the problem of managing training sets which are too large to fit into the memory of computers, and then the realization of predictors. In machine learning, the practiced solution to learn large data set is the application of resampling techniques, such as, bagging

[5], boosting [6] and arcing [7]. However, these techniques require that the entire data sets be stored in the main memory. When applied to large data sets, this approach could be impractical. In this paper, we proposed to split data into smaller subsets. First, the genetic programming is run separately on all training sub-samples. Such approach is called static training-subset selection method [8]; it might provide local solutions not adaptive to the entire enlarged data set. Alternatively, a dynamic training approach is developed. It allows genetic programming to learn simultaneously on all training sub-samples and it implies a new parameter added to the basic genetic programming algorithm which is the number of generations to change sample. This approach lightens the training task for the genetic programming and favors the discovery of solutions that are more robust across different learning data samples and seem to have better generalization ability. Comparison between generated models using static and dynamic selection methods reveals that, the dynamic approach improves the forecasting performance of the generated models using genetic programming. The best forecasting implied volatility models are selected according to total MSE criterion. They are used to compute hedge factors and implement dynamic hedging strategies. According to the average hedging errors, the genetic programming presented accurate hedging performance compared to that of Black-Scholes model.

The rest of the paper is organized as follows: section 2 provides background information regarding related works in forecasting volatility and dynamic hedging, section 3 describes research design and methodology used in this paper, section 4 reports experimental results and finally section 5 concludes.

2. Related works

Traditional parametric methods have limited success in estimating and forecasting volatility as they are dependent on restrictive assumptions and difficult to estimate. Several machine learning techniques have been recently used to overcome these difficulties such as artificial neural networks and evolutionary computation algorithms. In particular, genetic programming has been successfully applied to forecast financial time series [9,10].

This paper makes an initial attempt to test whether the hedger can benefit more by using generated genetic programming implied volatilities instead of Black-Scholes implied volatilities in conducting dynamic hedging strategies.

Changes in asset prices is not the only risk faced by market participants, instantaneous changes in market implied volatility can also bring a hedging portfolio significantly out of balance. Extensive research during the last two decades has demonstrated that the volatility of stocks is not constant over time [11]. The Autoregressive Conditional Heteroskedasticiy (ARCH) and the Generalized ARCH (GARCH) models are introduced [12,13] to describe the evolution of the asset price's volatility in discrete time. Econometric tests of these models clearly reject the hypothesis of constant volatility and find evidence of volatility clustering over time. In the financial literature, stochastic volatility models have been proposed to model these effects in a continuous-time setting [14-17]. Although these models improve the benchmark Black-Scholes model, they are complex because they require strong assumptions and computational effort to estimate parameters and stochastic process. As mentioned in [18], traditional financial engineering methods based on parametric models such as the GARCH model family, seem to have difficulty to improve the accuracy in volatility forecasting due to their rigid as well as linear structure. Using its basic and flexible tree-structured representation, genetic programming is capable of solving non-linear problems. In the context of forecasting volatility, most of research papers have focused on forecasting historical volatility based on past returns in different markets. Using historical returns of Nikkei 225 and S&P500 indices, Chen and Yeh [19] have applied a recursive genetic programming approach to estimate volatility by simultaneously detecting and adapting to structural changes. Results have shown that the recursive genetic programming is a promising tool for the study of structural changes. Using high frequency foreign exchange USD-CHF and USD-JPY time series, Zumbach et al. [20] have compared the genetic programming forecasting accuracy to that of historical volatilities, the GARCH (1,1), FIGARCH and HARCH models. According to the root-mean squared errors, the generated genetic programming volatility models did consistently outperform the benchmarks. Similarly, Neely and Weller [21] have tested the forecasting performance of genetic programming for USD-DEM and USD-YEN daily exchange rates against that of GARCH (1,1) model and a related RiskMetrics volatility forecast over different time horizons, using various accuracy criteria. While the genetic programming rules did not usually match the GARCH (1,1) or RiskMetrics models' MSE or R^2, its performance on those measures was generally close. But, the genetic programming did consistently outperform the GARCH model on mean absolute error (MAE) and model error bias at all horizons. Overall, on some dimensions the genetic programming has produced significantly superior results. Applying a combination of theory and techniques such as wavelet transform, time series data mining, Markov chain based discrete stochastic optimization, and evolutionary algorithms genetic algorithms and genetic programming, Ma et al. [22,23] have proposed a systematic approach to address specifically non linearity problems in the forecast of financial indices using intraday data of S&P100 and S&P500 indices. As a result, accuracy of forecasting has reached an average of over 75% surpassing other publicly available results on the forecast of any financial index. Abdelmalek et al. [8] have extended the studies mentioned earlier by forecasting the implied volatility of Black-Scholes from the S&P500 index call options instead of historical volatility using a static training of genetic programming. The performance of generated genetic programming volatility forecasting models is compared between time series samples and moneyness-time to maturity classes. Using Total and out-of-sample mean squared errors (MSE) as forecasting performance measures, the time series model seems to be more accurate in forecasting implied volatility than moneyness-time to maturity models.

Option contracts prices are affected by new information and changes in expectations as much as they are by changes in the value of the underlying index. If traders have perfect foresight on forward volatility, then dynamic hedging would be essentially riskless. In practice, continuous hedging is impossible, but the convexity of option contract allows for adjustments in the exposure to higher-order sensitivities of the model, such as gamma, vega, etc. Most of the existing literature on hedging a target contract using other exchange-traded options focuses on static strategies, motivated at least in part by the desire to avoid the high costs of frequent trading. The goal of static hedging is to construct a buy-and-hold portfolio of exchange traded claims that perfectly replicates the payoff of a given over-the-counter product [24,25]. The static hedging strategy does not require any rebalancing and therefore, it does not incur significant transaction costs. Unfortunately, the odds of coming up with a perfect static hedge for a given over-the-counter claim are small, given the limited number of exchange listed option contracts with sufficient trading volume. In other words, the static hedge can only be efficient if traded options are available with sufficiently similar maturity and moneyness as the over-the-counter product that has to be hedged. Under a stochastic volatility, a perfect hedge can in principle be constructed with a dynamically rebalanced portfolio consisting of the underlying and one additional option. In practice, the dynamic replication strategy for European options will only be perfect if all of the assumptions underlying the Black-Scholes formula hold. For general contingent claims on a stock, under market frictions, the delta might still be used as first-order approximation to set up a riskless portfolio. However, if the volatility of the underlying stock varies stochastically, then the delta hedging method might fail severely. A simple method to limit the volatility risk is to consider the volatility sensitivity vega of the contract. The portfolio will have to be rebalanced frequently to ensure delta-vega neutrality. With transaction costs, frequent rebalancing might result in considerable losses. In practice, investors can rebalance their portfolios only at discrete intervals of time to reduce transactions costs.

Non parametric hedging strategies as an alternative to the existing parametric model based-strategies, have been proposed [26,27]. Those studies estimated pricing formulas by nonparametric or semi-parametric statistical methods such as neural networks and kernel regression, and they measured their performance in terms of delta-hedging. Few researches have focused on the dynamic hedging using genetic programming, however. Chen et al. [28] have applied genetic programming to price and hedge S&P500 index options. By distinguishing the case in-the-money from the case out-of-the-money, the performance of genetic programming is compared with the Black-Scholes model in terms of hedging accuracy. Based on the post-sample performance, it is found that in approximately 20% of the 97 test paths, genetic programming has lower tracking error than the Black-Scholes formula.

Based on the literature survey, one can conclude that the genetic programming could be used to efficiently forecast volatility and implement accurate dynamic hedging strategies, which opens up an alternative path besides other data-based approaches.

3. Research design and methodology

Accurate volatility forecasting is an essential element in conducting good dynamic hedging strategies. The first thrust of this paper deals with generation of implied volatility from option markets using static and dynamic training of genetic programming, respectively. While the static training [8] is characterized by training the genetic programming independently on a single Sub-sample, the dynamic training allows the genetic programming to train on the entire data sub samples simultaneously rather than just a single subset by changing the training Sub-sample during the run process. This permits to improve the robustness of genetic programming to generate general models adaptive to all training samples. The second thrust of this paper is to study the accuracy of the generated genetic programming implied volatility models in terms of dynamic hedging. Since the true volatility is unobservable, it is impossible to assess the accuracy of any particular model; forecasts can only be related to realized volatility. In this paper, we assume that the implied volatility is a reasonable proxy for realized volatility, to generate forecasting implied volatility models using genetic programming and then to analyze the implications of this predictability for hedging purposes.

Figure 1 illustrates the operational procedure to implement the proposed approach.

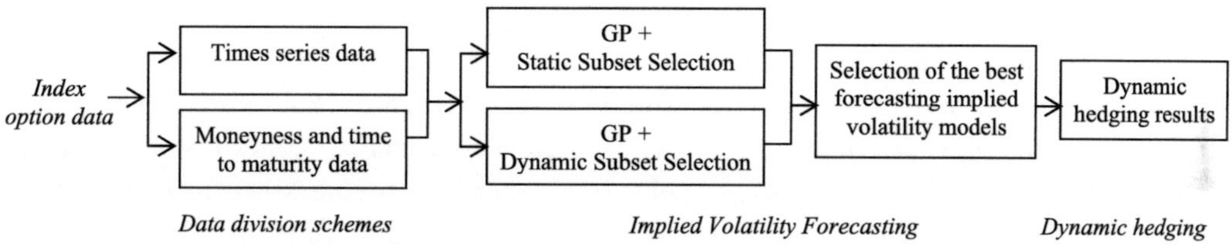

Figure 1. Description of the proposed approach's implementation

The operational procedure consists of the following steps: The first step is devoted for the data division schemes. The second step deals with the implementation of genetic programming[1] (GP), the application of training subset selection methods and the selection of the best forecasting implied volatility models. The last step is dedicated to dynamic hedging results.

3.1. Data division schemes

Data used in this study consist of daily prices for the European-style S&P 500 index calls and puts options traded on the Chicago Board of Options Exchange from 02 January to 29 August 2003. The data base include the time of the quote, the expiration date, the exercise price and the daily bid and ask quotes for call and put options. Similar information for the underlying S&P 500 index is also available on a daily basis. S&P500 index options are among the most actively traded financial derivatives in the world. The minimum tick for series trading below 3 is 1/16 and for all other series 1/8. Strike price intervals are 5 points, and 25 points for far months. The expiration months are three near term months followed by three additional months from the March quarterly cycle (March, June, September, and December). Following a standard practice, we used the average of an option's bid and ask price as a stand-in for the market value of the option. The risk free interest rate is approximated by using 3 month US Treasury bill rates. It is assumed that there are no transaction costs and no dividend.

---

1 GP system is built around the Evolving Object library, which is an ANSI-C++ evolutionary computation Framework (EO library).

To reduce the likelihood of errors, data screening procedures are used [29,30]. We apply four exclusion filters to construct the final option sample. First, as implied volatilities of short-term options are very sensitive to small errors in the option price and may convey liquidity-related biases, options with time to maturity less than 10 days are excluded. Second, options with low quotes are eliminated to mitigate the impact of price discreteness on option valuation. Third, deep-in-the-money and deep-out-of-the money option prices are also excluded due to the lack of trading volume. Finally, option prices not satisfying the arbitrage restriction [31], $C \geq S - Ke^{-r\tau}$, are not included.

The final sample contains 6670 daily option quotes, with at-the-money (ATM), in-the-money (ITM) and out-of-the money (OTM) options respectively taking up 37%, 34% and 29% of the total sample.

In this paper, two data division schemes are used. The full sample is sorted first, by time series (TS) and second by moneyness-time to maturity (MTM). For time series, data are divided into 10 successive samples (S_1, S_2…S_{10}), each contains 667 daily observations. The first nine samples are used as training sub-samples. For moneyness-time to maturity, data are divided into nine classes with respect to moneyness and time to maturity criteria. According to moneyness criterion: A call option is said out-of-the money (OTM) if $S/K < 0.98$; at-the-money (ATM) if $S/K \in \left[0.98, 1.03\right[$; and in-the-money (ITM) if $S/K \geq 1.03$. According to time to maturity criterion: A call option is Short Term (ST) if $\tau < 60$ days; Medium Term (MT) if $\tau \in \left[60, 180\right]$ days; and Long Term (LT) if $\tau > 180$ days. Each class C_i is divided on training set C_i^L and test set C_i^T, which produces respectively nine training and nine test MTM sub-classes. Figure 2 illustrates the two division schemes.

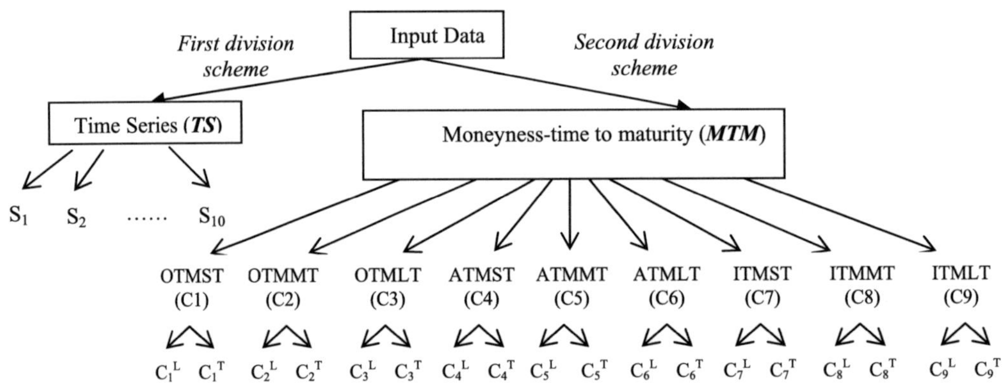

Figure 2. Data division schemes

3.2. Implied volatility forecasting using genetic programming:

This subsection describes the design of genetic programming and the experiments accomplished using the genetic programming method to forecast implied volatility. In the first experiment, the genetic programming is trained using static training-subset selection method; in the second one, we used dynamic training-subset selection methods. We describe training and test samples used in these experiments.

3.2.1. *The design of genetic programming:*

Our genetic programming software is referred to as symbolic regression written in C++ language. It is designed to find a function that relates a set of inputs to an output without making any assumptions about the structure of that function. Symbolic regression was one of the earliest applications of genetic programming [3], and has continued to be widely studied [32-35]. The following pseudo code describes the genetic programming's algorithm structure used in this paper.

```
Initialize population
While (termination condition not satisfied) do
Begin
        Evaluate the performance of each individual according to the fitness criterion
        Until the offspring population is fully populated do
           - Select individuals in the population using the selection algorithm
           - Perform crossover and mutation operations on the selected individuals
           - Insert new individuals in the offspring population
    Replace the existing population by the new population
End while
Report the best solution found
End
```

Algorithm 1 Pseudo code of genetic programming

The genetic programming's algorithm structure consists of the following steps: nodes definition, initialization, fitness evaluation, selection, genetic operators (crossover and mutation) and termination condition.

Nodes Definition: The nodes in the tree structure of genetic programming can be classified into terminal (leaf) nodes and function (non-terminal) nodes. The terminal and function sets used are described in Table 1.

The terminal set includes the inputs variables, notably, the option price divided by strike price ($\frac{C}{K}$ for calls and $\frac{P}{K}$ for puts), the index price divided by strike price $\frac{S}{K}$ and time to maturity τ. The function set includes unary and binary nodes. Unary nodes consist of mathematical functions, notably, cosinus function (cos), sinus function (sin), log function (ln), exponential function (exp), square root function ($\sqrt{\ }$) and the normal cumulative distribution function (Φ). Binary nodes consist of the four basic mathematical operators, notably, addition (+), subtraction (-), multiplication ($\times$) and division (%). The basic division operation is protected against division by zero and the log and square root functions are protected against negative arguments.

Expression		Definition
Terminal Set	C/K	Call price / Strike price
	S/K	Index price / Strike price
	τ	Time to maturity
Function Set	+ (plus)	Addition
	- (minus)	Subtraction
	* (multiply)	Multiplication
	$\%$ (divide)	Protected division: $x \% y = 1$ if $y=0$; $x \% y = x \% y$ otherwise
	ln	Protected natural log: $\ln(x) = \ln(\lvert x \rvert)$
	Exp	Exponential function: $\exp(x) = e^x$
	Sqrt	Protected square root: $\sqrt{x} = \sqrt{\lvert x \rvert}$
	Ncdf	Normal cumulative distribution function Φ

Table 1. Terminal set and function set

Individuals are encoded as LISP S-expressions which can also be depicted as a parse tree. The search space for genetic programming is the space of all possible parse trees that can be recursively created from the terminal and function sets.

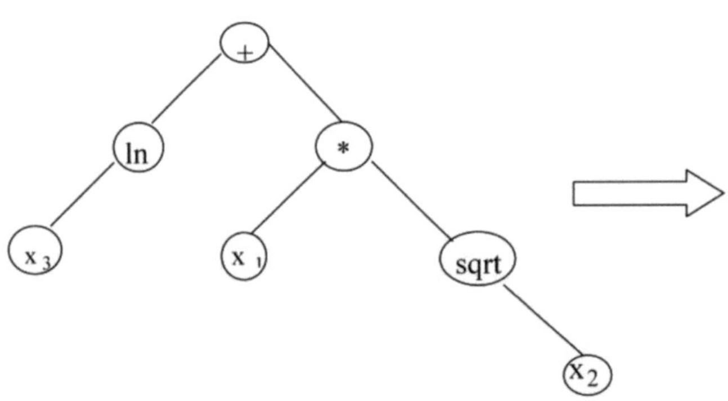

$$\hat{y} = \ln(x_3) + x_1 * \sqrt{x_2}$$

Figure 3. Example of a tree structure for GP and the corresponding functions

Initialization: The generated genetic programming volatility models are performed using a ramped half and half as initialization method [3]. This method involves generating an equal number of trees using a maximum initial depth that ranges from 2 to 6, as specified in Table 2. For each level of depth, 50% of the initial trees are generated via the full method and the other 50% are generated via the grow method. In the full method, the initial trees have the property that every path from root to endpoint is of maximum depth. In the grow method, initial trees can be of various depths, subject to the constraint that they do not exceed the maximum depth.

Fitness function: The fitness function assigned to a particular individual in the population must reflect how closely the output of an individual program comes to the target function. In this paper, the Black-Scholes implied volatility σ_t^{BS} is used as target output. It is defined as the standard deviation which equates the Black-Scholes price C_{BS} [2] to the market option price C_t^* [36]:

$$\begin{aligned} \exists! \quad & \sigma_t^{BS}(K,T) \succ 0, \\ & C_{BS}\left(S_t, K, \tau, \sigma_t^{BS}(K,T)\right) = C_t^*(K,T) \end{aligned} \tag{1}$$

The generated genetic programming trees provide at each time t the forecast value $\hat{\sigma}_t$, and the fitness function used to measure the accuracy of forecast is the mean squared error (MSE) between the target (σ_t^{BS}) and forecasted ($\hat{\sigma}_t$) output volatility, computed as follows:

$$MSE = \frac{1}{N}\sum_{t=1}^{N}\left(\sigma_t^{BS} - \hat{\sigma}_t\right)^2 \tag{2}$$

Where, N is the number of data sample.

Selection: Based on the fitness criterion, the selection of the individuals for reproduction is done with the tournament selection algorithm. A group of individuals is selected from the population with a uniform random probability distribution. The fitness values of each member of this group are compared and the actual best is selected. The size of the group is given by the tournament size which is equal to 4, as indicated in Table 2.

Genetic operators: Crossover and mutation are the two basic operators which are applied to the selected individuals in order to generate new individuals for the next generation. As described in Figure 4, the subtree crossover creates new offspring trees from two selected parents by exchanging their sub-trees. As indicated in Table 2, the crossover operator is used to generate about 60% of the individuals in the population. The maximum tree size (measured by depth) allowed after the crossover is 17. This is a popular number used to limit the size of tree [3]. It is large enough to accommodate complicated formulas and works in practice.

---

[2] $C_{BS} = SN(d_1) - Ke^{-r\tau}N(d_2), d_1 = \dfrac{\ln\left(\dfrac{S}{K}\right) + \left(r + 0.5\sigma^2\right)\tau}{\sigma\sqrt{\tau}}, d_2 = d_1 - \sigma\sqrt{\tau}$.

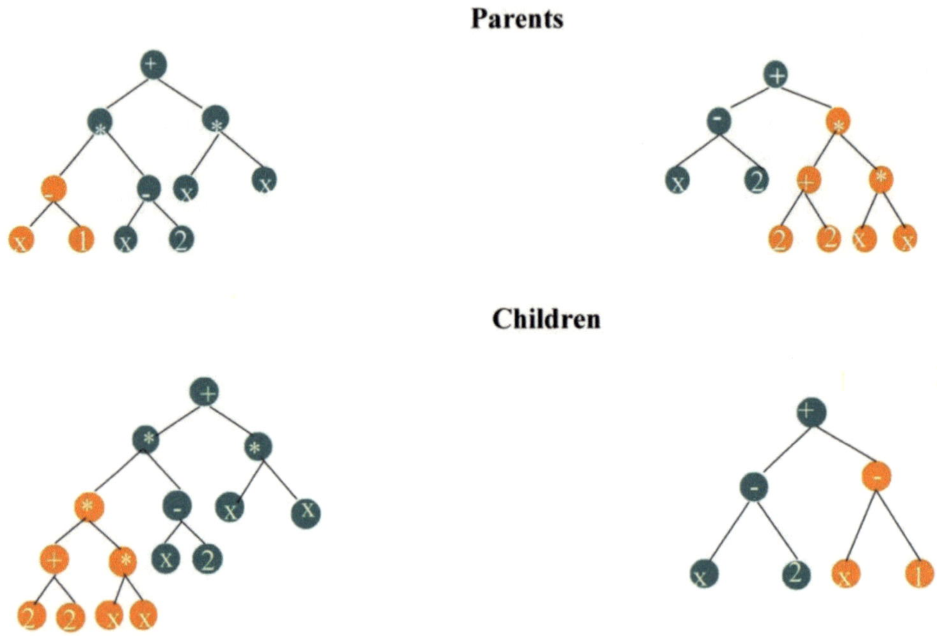

Figure 4. Example of subtree crossover

The mutation operator randomly changes a tree by randomly altering nodes or sub-trees to create a new offspring. Often multiple types of mutation are beneficially used simultaneously [37,38]. In this paper, three mutation operators are used simultaneously, they are described below:

Branch (or subtree) mutation operator randomly selects an internal node in the tree, and then it replaces the subtree rooted at that node with a new randomly-generated subtree [3].

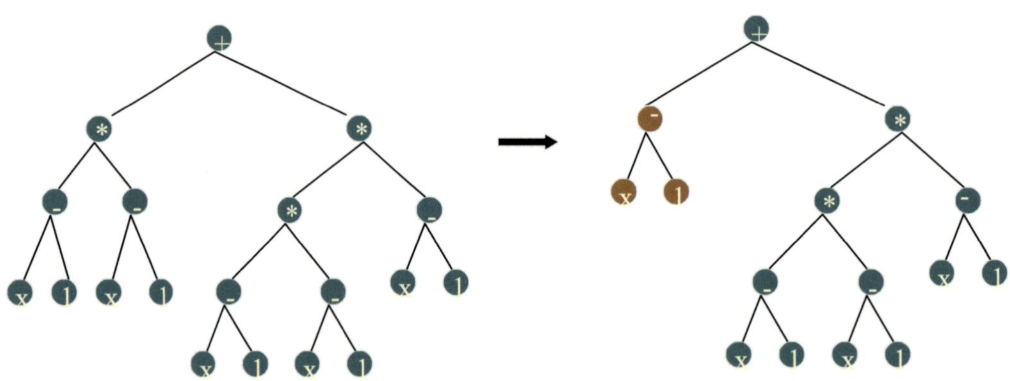

Figure 5. Example of subtree mutation

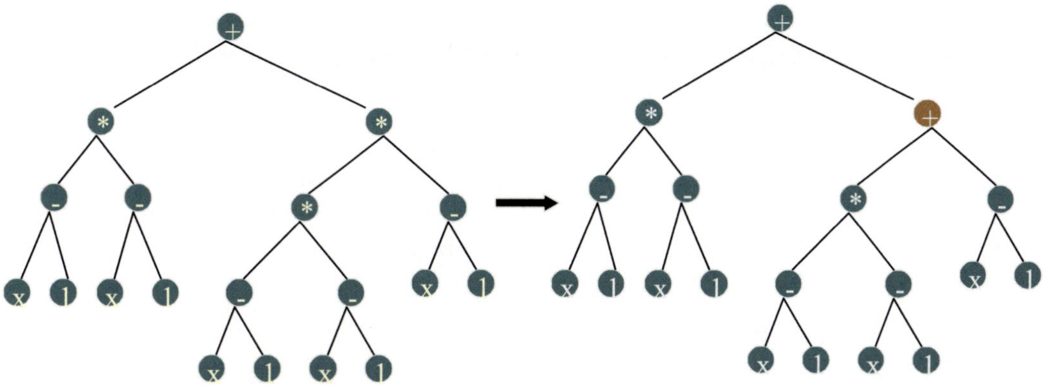

Figure 6. Example of point mutation

Point mutation operator consists of replacing a single node in a tree with another randomly-generated node of the same arity [39].

Expansion mutation operator randomly selects a terminal node in the tree, and then replaces it with a new randomly-generated subtree.

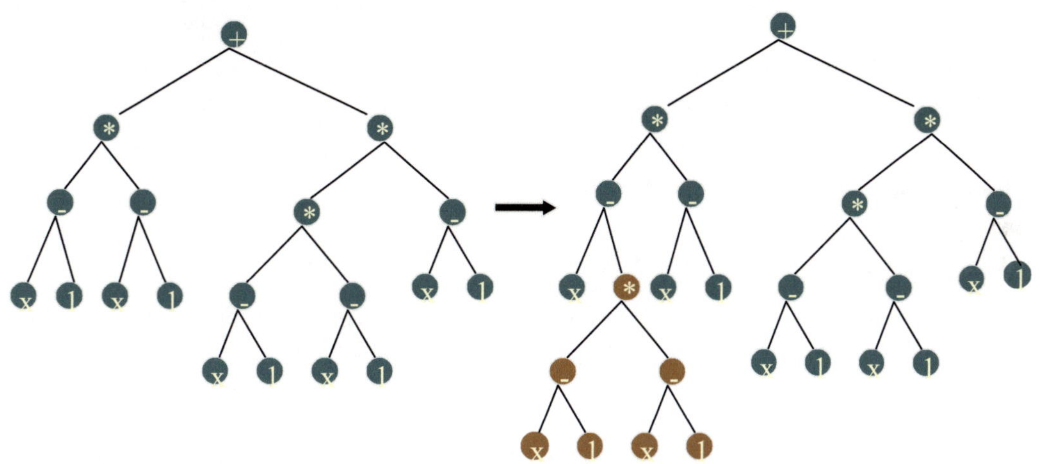

Figure 7. Example of expansion mutation

As indicated in Table 2, Branch mutation is applied with a rate of 20%; Point and Expansion mutations are applied with a rate of 10%, respectively.

Replacement: The method of replacing parents for the next generation is comma replacement strategy [40], which selects the best offspring to replace the parents. It assumes that offspring size is higher than parents' size. If μ is the population size and λ is the number of the new individuals (which can be larger than μ), the population is constructed using the best μ out of the λ new individuals.

Termination criterion: The stopping criterion is the maximum number of generations. It is fixed at 400 and 1000 for static and dynamic training- subset selection, respectively. In the dynamic training- subset selection approach, the maximum number of generations is increased to allow the genetic programming to train on the maximum of samples simultaneously. The number of generations to change sample varied between 20 and 100 generations.

The implementation of genetic programming involves a series of trial and error experiments to determine the optimal set of genetic parameters which is listed in Table 2. By varying genetic parameters, each program is run ten times with ten different random seeds. The choice of the best genetic program is made according to the mean and median of Mean Squared Errors (MSE) for training and testing sets.

Population size:	100
Offspring size:	200
Maximum number of generations for static method:	400
Maximum number of generations for dynamic method:	1000
Generations' number to change sample	20-100
Maximum depth of new individual:	6
Maximum depth of the tree:	17
Tournament size:	4
Crossover probability:	60%
Mutation probability:	40%
Branch mutation:	20%
Point mutation:	10%
Expansion mutation:	10%

Table 2. Summary of genetic programming parameters

3.2.2. Dynamic training-subset selection method

As data are divided in several sub-samples, the genetic programming is trained, first, independently on each sub-sample relative to each data division scheme (algorithm 1). This approach is called static training-subset selection method [8]. Second, the genetic programming is trained simultaneously on the entire data sub-samples relative to each data division scheme, rather than just a single subset by changing the training sub-sample during the run process. This approach is called dynamic training-subset selection method. The main goal of this method is to make genetic programming adaptive to all training samples and able to generate general models and solutions that are more robust across different learning data samples. In the context of evolutionary algorithms, there are at least three approaches for defining the frequency of resampling [41]. The first approach called "individual-wise" consists of extracting a new sample of data instances from the training set for each individual of the population. As a result, different individuals will probably be evaluated on different data samples, which cast some doubts on the fairness of the selection procedure of the evolutionary algorithm. The second approach called "run-wise" consists of extracting a single fixed sample of data instances from the training set used to evaluate the fitness of all individuals throughout the evolutionary run, which will probably reduce significantly the robustness and predictive accuracy of the evolutionary algorithm. The third approach called "generation-wise" consists of extracting a single fixed sample of data instances from the training set at each generation, and all individuals of that generation will have their fitness evaluated on that data sample. This method avoids the disadvantages of the two previous approaches, and as such seems more effective. In particular, an individual will only survive for several generations if it has a good predictive accuracy across different data samples. The dynamic approach proposed in this study differs from the three previous approaches as it doesn't extract a fixed sample of data instances from the training set, but selects it from the whole sub-samples data which are already built up and use it to evaluate the fitness of all individuals when the generations' number to change sample is reached. In this paper, we proposed four dynamic training-subset selection methods: *Random Subset Selection* method (*RSS*), *Sequential Subset Selection* method (*SSS*), *Adaptive-Sequential Subset Selection* method (ASSS) and *Adaptive-Random Subset Selection* method (*ARSS*). The *RSS* and *SSS* allow the genetic programming to learn on all training samples in turn (*SSS*) or randomly (*RSS*). However, with these methods, there is no certainty that genetic programming will focus on the samples which are difficult to learn. Then, the *ASSS* and the *ARSS*, which are variants of *the adaptive subset selection (ASS)*, are introduced to focus the genetic programming's attention onto the difficult samples i.e. having the greatest MSE and then to improve the learning algorithm.

Dynamic subset selection is easily added to the basic GP algorithm with no additional computational cost according to the static subset selection.

Let S be the set of training samples $S_{i\ (i=1...k)}$, where k is the total number of samples. A selection probability P (S_i) is allocated to each sample S_i from S. The training sample S_i is changed each g generations (g is the number of generations to change sample) according to this selection probability and the dynamic training-subset selection method used. Once a new training sample is selected, the best individuals are used as population for the next training samples. This procedure is repeated until the maximum number of generations is reached. This permits genetic programming to adapt its generating process to changing data in response to feedback from the fitness function which is the mean squared error computed as in static approach. By the end of the evolution, only individuals with the desirable characteristics that are well adapted to the environmental changes will survive.

a. Random training-Subset Selection method (RSS):

It selects randomly the training samples with replacement. At each g generations, all the samples from S have the same probability to be selected as the current training sample: P (S_i) $=1/k$, $1 \leq i \leq k$. This method differs from that proposed by Gathercole and Ross [42] as random selection concerns training samples which are already constructed according to data division scheme, rather than data instances.

As selection of training samples is random, the performance of the current population changes with the training sample used for evolving the genetic program. Figure 8 illustrates an example of the best fitness (MSE) curve along evolution using RSS method. With the sample change, the MSE may increase, but it is improved during the following generations, the time that the population adapts itself to the new environment.

Figure 8 shows that some training samples could be duplicated, but some others could be eliminated.

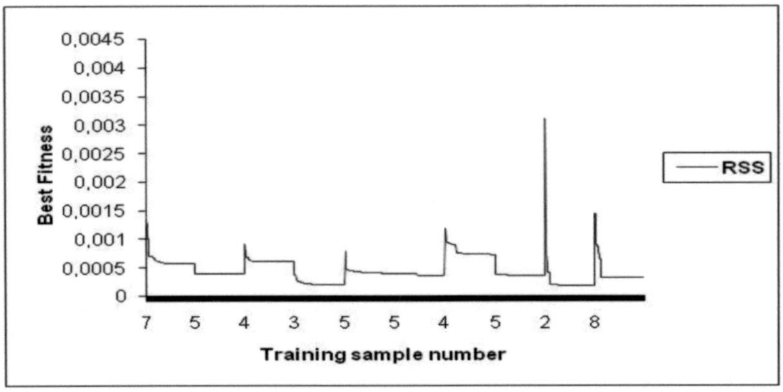

Figure 8. Example of fitness curve of the best individuals generated by genetic programming using RSS method for time series samples

b. Sequential training-Subset Selection method (SSS)

It selects all the training samples in the order. If, at generation g-1, the current training sample is S_i, then at generation g: P (S_j) = 1, with j= i+1 if i<k, or j=1 if i=k.

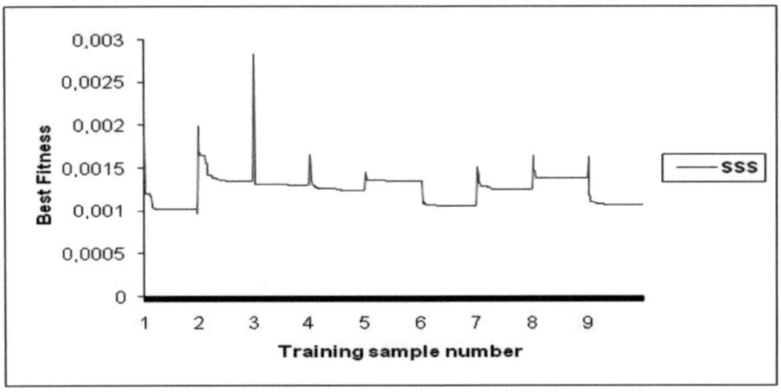

Figure 9. Example of curve fitness of the best individuals generated by genetic programming using SSS method for moneyness-time to maturity classes

As illustrated in Figure 9, all the learning subsets are used during the evolution in an iterative way.

c. Adaptive training-Subset Selection method (ASS):

Instead of selecting a training subset data in a random or sequential way, one can use an adaptive approach to dynamically select difficult training subsets data which are frequently misclassified. This approach is inspired from the dynamic subset selection method proposed by Gathercole and Ross [42] which is based on the idea of dynamically selecting instances, not training samples, which are difficult and/or have not been selected for several generations. Selection is made according to a weight computed proportionally to the sample's average fitness. Each g generations, the weights are updated as follows:

$$W(S_i) = \frac{\sum_{t=1}^{g}\sum_{j=1}^{M} f(X_j)}{M * g} \tag{3}$$

Where, M is the size of S_i ($X_j \in S_i$), g is the number of generations to change sample, and $f(X_j)$ is the MSE of the individual X_j.

At each g generations, training samples are re-ordered, so that the most difficult training samples, which have higher weights, will be moved to the beginning of the ordered training list, and the easiest training samples, which have smaller weights, will be moved to the end of the ordered training list.

1. Adaptive-Sequential training-Subset Selection method (ASSS):

It uses the following procedure (step 1 to step 3):

Step 1. Let the first generation t be set to 0. Each training sample is assigned an equal weight, i.e., $W(S_i) = 1$ for $1 \le i \le k$.

Step 2. The probability P (S_i) that a training sample S_i is selected to be included in the training set and evolve genetic programming is determined using the Roulette wheel selection scheme.

$$P(S_i) = \frac{w(S_i)}{\sum w(S_i)}$$

Where, the summation is over all training samples.

Moreover, the probability P (S_i) is positively related to the fitness of the parse tree generated relative to the corresponding training sample.

$$P(S_i) = \frac{f(S_i)}{\sum f(S_i)}$$

Where, $f(S_i)$ is the average fitness of individuals relative to the training sample.

Compute a fitness function which is the mean squared error for each individual in the training sample and then the average fitness. Update the weights: $W(S_i) = \frac{\sum_{t=1}^{g}\sum_{j=1}^{M} f(X_j)}{M * g}$

Step 3. t=t+g. If t<T (T is the total number of generations), then go to step 2.

As illustrated in Figure 10, selection of training samples is made in the order for the first t generations using the SSS method. Some training samples could be duplicated to improve the genetic programming learning. Later, samples are selected for the next run according to the adaptive approach based on the re-ordering procedure.

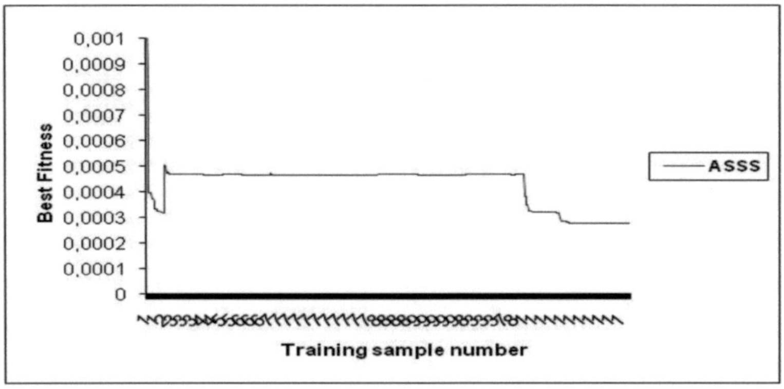

Figure 10. Example of curve fitness of the best individuals generated by genetic programming using ASSS method for time series samples

2. Adaptive-Random training-Subset Selection method (ARSS):

The ARSS method uses the same procedure as the ASSS method, except that the initial weights are generated randomly in the start of running, rather than initialized with a constant: For t=0, $W(S_i) = \tilde{P}_i, \tilde{P}_i \in [0,1], 1 \le i \le k.$ Then, for the few first generations, samples are selected using *RSS* method. After, the selection of samples is made using the adaptive approach based on the re-ordering procedure.

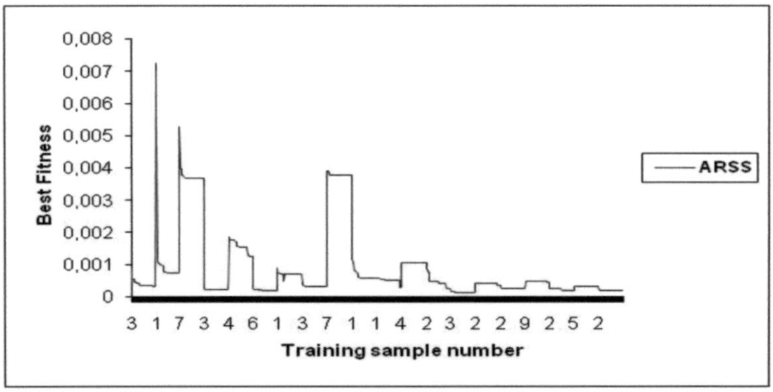

Figure 11. Example of curve fitness of the best individuals generated by genetic programming using ARSS method for moneyness-time to maturity classes

3.2.2. Training and test samples

Different forecasting genetic programming volatility models are estimated from the training set and judged upon their performance on the test set. Table 3 summarizes the training and test data samples used for static and dynamic training-subset selection methods, respectively.

In static training-subset selection approach, first, the genetic program is trained separately on each of the first nine TS sub-samples (S_1,..., S_9) using ten different seeds and is tested on the subset data from the immediately following date (S_2,..., S_{10}). Second, using the same genetic parameters and random seeds applied for TS data, the genetic programming is trained separately on each of the first nine MTM sub-classes (C_1^L,..., C_9^L) and is tested on the second nine MTM sub-classes (C_1^T,..., C_9^T).

Subset Selection	Learning data sample	Test data sample
Static Subset Selection	$S_i \in$ TS samples (S_1, ..., S_9) *(1 subset for a run)*	The successive TS sample S_j, j=i+1
	$C_i^L \in$ MTM training samples (C_1^L, ..., C_9^L) *(1 subset for a run)*	The corresponding MTM test samples C_i^T
Dynamic Subset Selection (RSS/SSS/ASSS/ ARSS)	TS samples S_1, ..., S_9 *(9 subsets for a run)*	The last subset in TS samples set (S_{10})
	MTM samples C_1^L, ..., C_9^L *(9 subsets for a run)*	The nine MTM test samples ($C_1^T + C_2^T \ldots + C_9^T$)
	TS samples + MTM samples (S_1, ..., S_9 ; C_1^L, ..., C_9^L) *(18 subsets for a run)*	The last TS sample with the nine MTM test samples ($S_{10} + C_1^T + C_2^T \ldots + C_9^T$)

Table 3. Definition of training and test data samples for static and dynamic training-subset selection methods

In dynamic training-subset selection approach, first, the genetic program is trained on the first nine TS sub-samples simultaneously (S_1,..., S_9) using ten different seeds and it is tested only on the tenth sub-sample data (S_{10}). Second, the genetic programming is trained on the first nine MTM sub-classes simultaneously (C_1^L,..., C_9^L) and it is tested on the second nine MTM sub-classes regrouped in one test sample data ($C_1^T + C_2^T \ldots + C_9^T$). Third, the genetic programming is trained on both the nine TS sub-samples and the nine MTM sub-classes simultaneously (S_1, ..., S_9 ; C_1^L, ..., C_9^L) and it is tested on one test sample data composed of the TS and MTM test data ($S_{10} + C_1^T + C_2^T \ldots + C_9^T$).

Based on the training and test MSE, the best generated genetic programming volatility models relative to static and dynamic training-subset selection methods respectively are selected. These models are then compared with each other according to the MSE total and the best ones are used to implement the dynamic hedging strategies as described in the following section.

3.3. Dynamic hedging

To assess the accuracy of selected generated genetic programming volatility models in hedging with respect to Black-Scholes model, three dynamic hedging strategies are employed, notably, delta-neutral, delta-gamma neutral and delta-vega neutral strategies.

For delta hedging, at date zero, a delta hedge portfolio consisting of a short position in one call (or put) option and a long (short) position in the underlying index is formed. At any time t, the value of the delta hedge portfolio $\mathrm{P}(t)$ is given by:

$$P(t) = V(t) + \Delta_V(t)S(t) + \beta(t) \tag{4}$$

Where, $P(t)$, $V(t)$, $S(t)$, $\Delta_V(t)$ and $\beta(t)$ denote the values of the portfolio, hedging option (call or put), underlying, delta hedge factor and bond (money market account) respectively.

The portfolio is assumed self-financed, so the initial value of the hedge portfolio at the beginning of the hedge horizon is zero:

$$\mathrm{P}(0) = V(0) + \Delta_V(0)S(0) + \beta(0) = 0 \tag{5}$$

$$\Rightarrow \beta(0) = -(V(0) + S(0)\Delta_V(0)) \tag{6}$$

A dynamic trading strategy is performed in underlying and bond to hedge the option during the hedge horizon. The portfolio rebalancing takes place at intervals of length δt during the hedge horizon $\left[0,\tau\right]$, $o < \tau \leq T$, where T is the maturity of the option. At each rebalancing time t_i, the hedge factor $\Delta_v(t_i)$ is recomputed and the money market account is adjusted:

$$\beta(t_i) = e^{r\delta t}\beta(t_{i-1}) - S(t_i)(\Delta_V(t_i) - \Delta_V(t_{i-1})) \tag{7}$$

The delta hedge error is defined as the absolute value of the delta hedge portfolio at the end of the hedge horizon of the option, $\left|P(\tau)\right|$.

For delta-gamma hedging, a new position in a traded option is required. Then, the delta-gamma hedge portfolio is formed with:

$$P(t) = V(t) + x(t)S(t) + y(t)V_1(t) + B(t) \tag{8}$$

Where, $V_1(t)$ is the value of an additional option which depends on the same underlying, with the same maturity but different strike price than the hedging option $V(t)$. $x(t)$ and $y(t)$ are the proportions of the underlying and the additional option respectively. They are chosen such that the portfolio $\mathrm{P}(t)$ is both delta and gamma neutral:

$$\begin{cases} \mathit{Delta}\ \text{neutral:} \Delta_V(t) + x(t) + y(t)\Delta_{V1}(t) = 0 \\ \mathit{Gamma}\ \text{neutral:} \Gamma_V(t) + y(t)\Gamma_{V_1}(t) = 0 \end{cases} \tag{9}$$

$$\Rightarrow \begin{cases} y(t) = \dfrac{-\Gamma_V(t)}{\Gamma_{V_1}(t)} \\ x(t) = -\Delta_V(t) - y(t)\Delta_{V1}(t) \end{cases} \tag{10}$$

Where, the values of $\Delta_V(t)$ and $\Gamma_V(t)$ are the delta and gamma factors for the option $V(t)$; the values $\Delta_{V_1}(t)$ and $\Gamma_{V_1}(t)$ are the delta and gamma factors for the option $V_1(t)$.

At the beginning of the hedge horizon, the value of the hedge portfolio is zero:

$$P(0) = V(0) + x(0)S(0) + y(0)V_1(0) + B(0) = 0 \tag{11}$$

$$\Rightarrow B(0) = -(V(0) + x(0)S(0) + y(0)V_1(0)) \tag{12}$$

At each rebalancing time t_i, both delta and gamma hedge factors are recomputed and the money market account is adjusted:

$$B(t_i) = e^{r\delta t}B(t_{i-1}) - (x(t_i) - x(t_{i-1}))S(t_i) - (y(t_i) - y(t_{i-1}))V_1(t_i) \tag{13}$$

The delta-gamma hedge error is defined as the absolute value of the delta-gamma hedge portfolio at the end of the hedge horizon of the option, $|P(\tau)|$.

For delta-vega hedging, a new position in a traded option is required as in the delta-gamma hedging. The proportions of the underlying $x(t)$ and the additional option $y(t)$ are chosen such that the portfolio $P(t)$ is both delta and vega neutral:

$$\begin{cases} \textit{Delta}\text{ neutral:}\Delta_V(t) + x(t) + y(t)\Delta_{V1}(t) = 0 \\ \textit{Vega}\text{ neutral:}\vartheta_V(t) + y(t)\vartheta_{V_1}(t) = 0 \end{cases} \tag{14}$$

$$\Rightarrow \begin{cases} y(t) = \dfrac{-\vartheta_V(t)}{\vartheta_{V_1}(t)} \\ x(t) = -\Delta_V(t) - y(t)\Delta_{V1}(t) \end{cases} \tag{15}$$

Where, $\vartheta_V(t)$ and $\vartheta_{V_1}(t)$ are the vega factors for the options $V(t)$ and $V_1(t)$ respectively.

As in delta-gamma hedging, at each rebalancing time t_i, both delta and vega hedge factors are recomputed and the money market account is adjusted. The delta-vega hedge error is defined as the absolute value of the delta-vega hedge portfolio at the end of the hedge horizon of the option, $|P(\tau)|$.

35 option contracts are used as hedging options and 35 other contracts which depend on the same underlying, with the same maturity but different strike prices are used as additional options. Contracts used to implement the hedging strategies are divided according to moneyness and time to maturity criteria, which produces nine classes.

The delta, gamma and vega hedge factors are computed using the Black-Scholes formula by taking the derivative of the option value with respect to index price, the derivative of delta with respect to index price and the derivative of the option value with respect to volatility respectively. For the genetic programming models, the hedge ratios are computed using the same formulas replacing the Black-Scholes implied volatilities with the generated genetic programming volatilities. Two rebalancing frequencies are considered: 1-day and 7 days revision.

The average hedging error is used as performance measure. For a particular moneyness-time to maturity class, the tracking error is given by:

$$\begin{cases} \varepsilon_M = \dfrac{\sum_{i=1}^{n} \varepsilon_i(\tau)}{n} \\ \varepsilon_i = e^{-rT} \times \dfrac{|P_i(\tau)|}{N \times V(0)} \end{cases} \tag{16}$$

Where, n is the number of options corresponding to a particular moneyness-time to maturity class and $\varepsilon_i(\tau)$ is the present value of the absolute hedge error of the portfolio $|P(\tau)|$ over the observation path N (as a function of rebalancing frequency), divided by the initial option price $V(0)$.

4. Result analysis and empirical findings

4.1. Selection of the best genetic programming-implied volatility forecasting models

Selection of the best generated genetic programming volatility model, relative to each training set, for TS, MTM, and both TS and MTM classifications, is made according to the training and test MSE. For static training-subset selection method, nine generated genetic programming volatility models are selected for TS (M1S1…M9S9) and similarly nine generated genetic programming volatility models are selected for MTM classification (M1C1…M9C9). The performance of these models is compared according to the MSE Total, computed using the same formula as the basic MSE for the enlarged data sample.

Table 4 reports the MSE total and the standard deviation (in parentheses) of the generated genetic programming volatility models, using static training-subset selection method, relative to the TS samples and the MTM classes.

TS Models	MSE Total	MTM Models	MSE Total
M1S1	0,002723 (0,004278)	M1C1	2,566 (20,606)
M2S2	0,005068 (0,006213)	M2C2	0,006921 (0,032209)
M3S3	0,003382 (0,004993)	M3C3	0,030349 (0,076196)
M4S4	**0,001444 (0,002727)**	**M4C4**	**0,001710 (0,004624)**
M5S5	0,002012 (0,003502)	M5C5	1,427142 (33,365115)
M6S6	0,001996 (0,003443)	**M6C6**	**0,002357 (0,004096)**
M7S7	0,001901 (0,003317)	M7C7	0,261867 (0,303256)
M8S8	0,002454 (0,004005)	M8C8	0,004318 (0,008479)
M9S9	0,002419 (0,004095)	M9C9	0,002940 (0,010490)

Table 4. Performance of the generated genetic programming volatility models using static training-subset selection method, according to MSE total for the TS samples and the MTM classes

Table 4 shows that, the generated genetic programming volatility models M4S4, M4C4 and M6C6 present the smallest MSE on the enlarged sample for TS and MTM samples respectively. Comparison between these models reveals that the TS model M4S4 seems to be more performing than MTM models M4C4 and M6C6 for the enlarged sample. Furthermore, results show that the performance of TS models is more uniform than that of MTM models. MTM models are not able to fit appropriately the entire data sample as well as the TS models as they have large Total MSE. Indeed, the MSE total exceed 1 with some MTM classes, however it does not reach 0.006 for all TS samples. Figure 12 describes the evolution's pattern of the squared errors given by TS models and MTM models for all observations in the enlarged data sample. Some extreme MSE values for MTM data are not shown in this figure.

It appears throughout Figure 12 that, the TS models are adaptive not only to training samples, but also to the enlarged sample. In contrast, the MTM models such as M1C1 are adaptive to training classes, but not all to the enlarged sample. A first plausible explanation of these unsatisfied results is an insufficient search intensity inducing difficulty to obtain general model suitable for the entire benchmark input data. To enhance exploration intensity during learning and thus improve the genetic programming performance, we introduced to the evolution procedure the dynamic subset selection, which aims to obtain a general model that can be adaptive to both TS and MTM classes simultaneously.

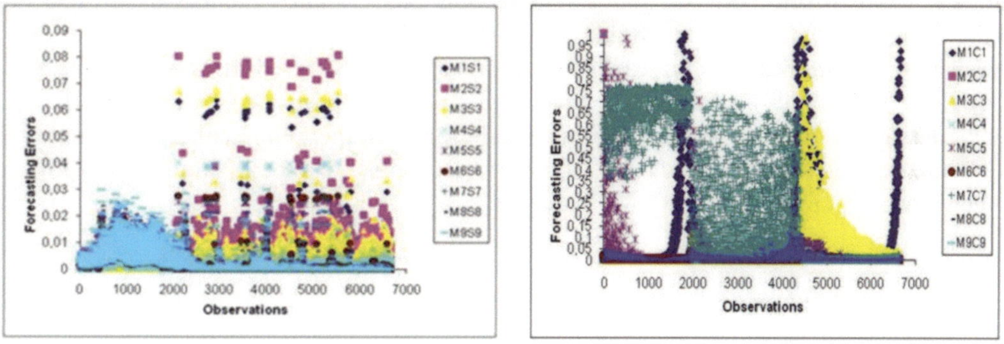

(a) MSE pattern for TS samples (b) MSE pattern for MTM classes

Figure 12. Evolution of the squared errors for total sample of the best generated GP volatility models, using static training-subset selection method, relative to TS samples(a) and MTM classes (b).

For dynamic training-subset selection methods (RSS, SSS, ASSS and ARSS), four generated genetic programming volatility models are selected for TS classification (MSR, MSS, MSAS and MSAR). Similarly, four generated genetic programming volatility models are selected for MTM classification (MCR, MCS, MCAS and MCAR) and four generated genetic programming volatility models are selected for global classification, both TS and MTM classes (MGR, MGS, MGAS and MGAR). Table 5 reports the best generated genetic programming volatility models, using dynamic training-subset selection, relative to TS samples, MTM classes and both TS and MTM data.

TS Models	MSE Total	MTM Models	MSE Total	Global Models	MSE Total
MSR	0.002367 (0.003934)	MCR	0.002427 (0.003777)	MGR	0.002034 (0.003501)
MSS	**0.002076 (0.004044)**	MCS	0.007315 (0.025811)	MGS	0.002492 (0.003013)
MSAS	0.002594 (0.003796)	MCAS	0.002831 (0.004662)	MGAS	0.001999 (0.003587)
MSAR	0.002232 (0.003782)	**MCAR**	**0.001424 (0.003527)**	**MGAR**	**0.001599 (0.003590)**

Table 5. Performance of the generated genetic programming volatility models, using dynamic training-subset selection method, according to MSE total for the TS samples, the MTM classes and both TS and MTM samples

Based on the MSE total as performance criterion, the generated genetic programming volatility models MSS, MCAR and MGAR are selected. They seem to be more accurate in forecasting implied volatility than the other models because they have the smallest MSE in enlarged sample. However, the MTM model MCAR and the global model MGAR outperform the TS model MSS. Figure 13 describes the evolution's pattern of the squared errors for these generated volatility models.

Figure 13 shows that almost all models relative to each data's group are performing on the enlarged sample and present forecasting errors which are small and very closed. Forecasting errors are higher for the MTM classes than for the TS samples and both TS and MTM samples. Comparison between models generated using static training-subset selection method (Figure 12) and dynamic training-subset selection methods (Figure 13) respectively, reveals that the amplitude of forecasting errors relative to TS and MTM classes respectively is lower for the models generated using dynamic training-subset selection methods than for the models generated using static training-subset selection method. Actually, the quality of the generated genetic programming forecasting models has been improved with the dynamic training, in particular for MTM classes.

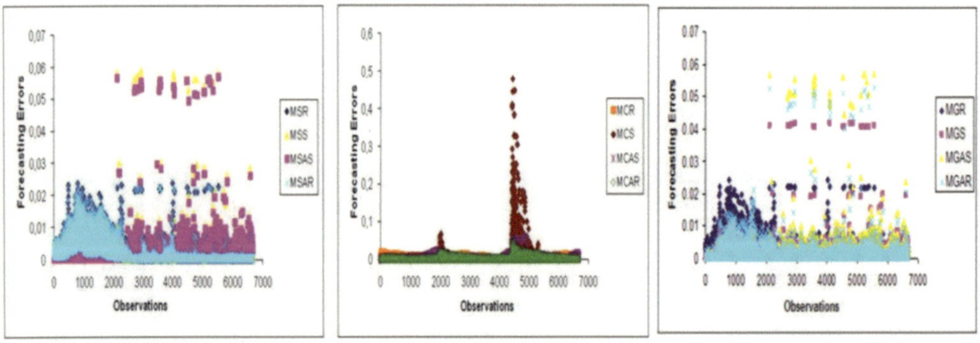

(a) MSE pattern for TS samples

(b) MSE pattern for MTM classes

(c) MSE pattern for TS+MTM

Figure 13. Evolution of the squared errors for total sample of the best generated GP volatility models, using dynamic training-subset selection methods, relative to TS samples (a), MTM classes (b) and both TS and MTM samples (c).

The best generated genetic programming volatility models selected, relative to dynamic training-subset selection method, are compared to the best generated genetic programming volatility model, relative to static training-subset selection method. Results are reported in Table 6.

Models	MSE total
M4S4	0,001444 (0,002727)
MCAR	0.001424 (0.003527)
MGAR	**0.001599 (0.003590)**

Table 6. Comparison between best models generated by static and dynamic selection methods for call options

Comparison between models reveals that the best models generated respectively by static (M4S4) and dynamic selection methods (MCAR and MGAR) present total MSE small and very close. While the generated genetic programming volatility models M4S4 and MCAR have total MSE smaller than the MGAR model, the latest seems to be more accurate in forecasting implied volatility than the other models. This can be explained by the fact that, on one hand, the difference between forecasting errors is small, and on the other hand, the MGAR model is more general than MCAR and M4S4 models because it is adaptive to all TS and MTM classes simultaneously. In fact, the MGAR model, generated using ARSS method, is trained on all TS and MTM classes simultaneously. Whereas, the MCAR model, generated using ARSS method, is trained only on MTM classes simultaneously; and the M4S4 model, generated using static training-subset selection method, is trained separately on each subset of TS.

As the adaptive-random training subset selection method is considered the best one to generate implied volatility model for call options, it is applied to put options. The decoding of volatility forecasting formulas generated for call and put options as well as their forecasting errors are reported in Table 7.

A detailed examination of the formulas in Table 7 shows that the implied volatilities generated by genetic programming are function of all the inputs used, namely the option price divided by strike price ($\frac{C}{K}$ for calls and $\frac{P}{K}$ for puts), the index price divided by strike price $\frac{S}{K}$ and time to maturity τ . The implied volatilities generated for calls and puts cannot be negative since they are computed using the square root and the normal cumulative distribution functions as the root nodes. Furthermore, the performance of models is uniform as they present near MSE on the enlarged sample.

4.2. Dynamic hedging results:

The performance of the best genetic programming forecasting models is compared to the Black-Scholes model in delta, gamma and vega hedging strategies. Table 8 reports the average hedging errors for call options using Black-Scholes (BS) and genetic programming (GP) models, at the 1-day and 7-days rebalancing frequencies. Values in bold correspond to the GP hedging errors which are less than the BS ones.

Option	LISP Expression	Formula	MSE Total
Call	sqrt((X0/(multiply(X,((multiply(X1,plus(X1,X2))*X1)*X1))*X1)))	$\sigma_{GP} = \sqrt{\dfrac{\dfrac{C}{K}}{\left(\dfrac{S}{K}\right)^6 + \left(\dfrac{S}{K}\right)^5 * \tau}}$	0.001599
Put	ncdf (sin ((cos (sin (minus (minus (-(cos (sin(X2))), ln(X0)), ln(X0))))-exp(X1))))	$\sigma_{GP} = \Phi\left(\sin\left(\cos\left(\sin\left(\begin{matrix}-\cos(\sin(\tau)) \\ -2 * \ln\left(\dfrac{P}{K}\right)\end{matrix}\right)\right) - \exp\left(\dfrac{S}{K}\right)\right)\right)$	0.001539

Table 7. Performance of the best generated genetic programming volatility models for call and put options and their decoding formulas $\left(X_0 = \dfrac{C}{K} or \dfrac{P}{K}, X_1 = \dfrac{S}{K}, X_2 = \tau\right)$

Results in Table 8 show that the delta hedging performance improves for out-of-the money call options at longer maturities, for at-the-money call options at medium maturities and for in-the money call options at shorter maturities, regardless of the model used at daily hedge revision frequency. The best delta hedging performance is achieved using in-the-money short term call options for all MTM classes, regardless of the option model used.

The delta-gamma hedging performance improves for all moneyness classes of call options at longer maturities, regardless of the model used at daily hedge frequency (except in-the-money call options using the genetic programming model). The best delta-gamma hedging performance is achieved, for BS model, using at-the-money long term call options for all MTM classes. However, the best delta-gamma hedging performance is achieved, for genetic programming model, using in-the-money short term call options for all MTM classes.

The delta-vega hedging performance improves for out-of-the money and in-the-money call options at longer maturities and for at-the-money call options at shorter maturities, regarding BS model at daily hedge revision frequency. However, the delta-vega hedging performance improves for out-of-the money call options at shorter maturities, for at-the-money call options at medium maturities and for in-the money call options at longer maturities, regarding genetic programming model at daily hedge revision frequency. The best delta-vega hedging performance is achieved, for BS model, using out-of-the-money long term call options for all moneyness and time to maturity classes. However, the best delta-gamma hedging performance is achieved, for genetic programming model, using at-the-money medium term call options for all MTM classes.

The percentage of cases where the hedging error of the genetic programming model is less than the BS hedging error is around 59%. In particular, the performance of genetic programming model is better than the BS model on in-the-money call options class. Further, the total of hedging errors relative to genetic programming model is about 21 percent slightly lower than 19 percent relative to BS model. Table 9 displays the average hedge errors for put options using BS and genetic programming models, at the 1-day and 7-days rebalancing frequencies. Values in bold correspond to the genetic programming hedging errors which are less than the BS ones.

			Rebalancing Frequency					
			1-day			7- days		
S/K	**Hedging strategy**	**Model**	**<60**	**60-180**	**>=180**	**<60**	**60-180**	**>=180**
<0.98	**Delta hedging**	BS	0,013119	0,001279	0,000678	0,057546	0,010187	0,005607
		GP	**0,009669**	**0,001081**	**0,000662**	**0,053777**	**0,009585**	**0,005594**
	Gamma hedging	BS	0,000596	0,000732	0,000061	0,003026	0,007357	0,000429
		GP	0,000892	0,002040	0,000075	0,003855	**0,001359**	**0,000153**
	Vega hedging	BS	0,000575	0,000050	0,000039	0,000525	0,000226	0,000099
		GP	**0,000473**	0,002035	0,004518	0,000617	0,004642	0,040071
0.98-1.03	**Delta hedging**	BS	0,002508	0,000717	0,000730	0,019623	0,005416	0,002283
		GP	**0,002506**	**0,0007**	0,001725	0,020	**0,0054**	**0,0022**
	Gamma hedging	BS	0,000069	0,000018	0,000006	0,000329	0,000169	0,000027
		GP	0,000377	0,000040	0,000029	0,000727	**0,000155**	0,000059
	Vega hedging	BS	0,000066	0,000373	0,003294	0,000527	0,023500	0,031375
		GP	0,000281	**0,000013**	**0,000207**	0,001102	**0,000147**	**0,000134**
>=1.03	**Delta hedging**	BS	0,000185	0,000906	0,001004	0,001602	0,006340	0,006401
		GP	**0,000184**	**0,000905**	**0,001**	**0,000840**	**0,005789**	**0,0064**
	Gamma hedging	BS	0,000323	0,000047	0,000028	0,001546	0,000386	0,000157
		GP	**0,000028**	0,000057	0,000036	**0,000227**	0,000429	0,000175
	Vega hedging	BS	0,000362	0,000060	0,000052	0,001757	0,002015	0,000247
		GP	**0,000067**	**0,000057**	**0,00005**	**0,000831**	**0,000864**	**0,000186**

Table 8. Average hedge errors of dynamic hedging strategies relative to BS and GP models for call options

Results in Table 9 show that the delta-gamma hedging performance improves for all moneyness classes of put options (except in-the-money put options) at longer maturities, regarding BS model at daily hedge frequency. However, the delta-gamma hedging performance improves for in-the money put options and at-the-money put options at medium maturities and for out-of-the money put options at longer maturities, regarding genetic programming model at daily hedge revision frequency. The best delta-gamma hedging performance is achieved, for BS model, using at-the-money long term put options for all MTM classes. However, the best delta-gamma hedging performance is achieved, for genetic programming model, using out-of-the-money long term put options for all MTM classes.

			Rebalancing Frequency					
			1-day			7- days		
S/K	**Hedging strategy**	**Model**	**<60**	**60-180**	**>=180**	**<60**	**60-180**	**>=180**
<0.98	**Delta hedging**	BS	0,007259	0,002212	0,001189	0,015453	0,013715	0,007740
		GP	0,064397	0,002270	0,001256	0,016872	0,013933	0,007815
	Gamma hedging	BS	0,000107	0,000043	0,000705	0,000383	0,000253	0,013169
		GP	0,000177	0,000351	**0,000676**	0,000990	0,000324	**0,009201**
	Vega hedging	BS	0,000051	0,000715	0,000612	0,000174	0,002995	0,008527
		GP	0,002800	**0,000345**	0,000625	0,018351	**0,000184**	0,008979
0.98-1.03	**Delta hedging**	BS	0,007331	0,002267	0,001196	0,170619	0,009875	0,004265
		GP	**0,0073**	**0,002219**	**0,001185**	**0,170316**	**0,009715**	**0,004260**
	Gamma hedging	BS	0,003750	0,000049	0,000027	0,032725	0,000119	0,000119
		GP	**0,003491**	**0,000031**	**0,000024**	**0,029792**	**0,000113**	**0,000103**
	Vega hedging	BS	0,035183	0,000052	0,000044	0,037082	0,000329	0,000043
		GP	**0,004343**	**0,000038**	**0,000043**	**0,037045**	**0,000190**	**0,000041**
>=1.03	**Delta hedging**	BS	0,007680	0,004469	0,000555	0,037186	0,017322	0,011739
		GP	**0,006641**	**0,004404**	**0,0005**	**0,037184**	**0,017076**	**0,011733**
	Gamma hedging	BS	0,000262	0,000204	0,000079	0,001196	0,001319	0,000369
		GP	0,000548	0,000287	0,000166	0,002034	0,001323	0,001059
	Vega hedging	BS	0,000232	0,000108	0,000025	0,000488	0,000644	0,000270
		GP	0,000312	**0,000080**	**0,00002**	0,001047	0,001186	**0,000244**

Table 9. Average hedge errors of dynamic hedging strategies relative to BS and GP models for put options

The delta-vega hedging performance improves for BS using at-the-money and out-of-the-money put options at longer maturities and in-the-money put options at shorter maturities, at daily hedge revision frequency. However, the delta-vega hedging performance improves for all moneyness classes of put options (except in-the-money put options) at longer maturities, regarding genetic programming model at daily hedge frequency. The best delta-vega hedging performance is achieved, for BS model, using out-of-the-money long term put options for all MTM classes. However, the best delta-vega hedging performance is achieved, for genetic programming model, using at-the-money long term put options for all MTM classes.

The percentage of cases where the hedging error of the genetic programming model is less than the BS hedging error is around 57%. In particular, the performance of genetic programming model is better than the BS model on at-the-money put options class. But, the total of hedging errors relative to genetic programming model is about 50 percent slightly higher than 46 percent relative to BS model.

In summary, the genetic programming model is more accurate in all hedging strategies than the BS model, for in-the-money call options and at-the-money put options. The performance of genetic programming is pronounced essentially in terms of delta hedging for call and put options. The percentage of cases where the delta hedging error of the genetic programming model is less than the BS delta hedging error is 100% for out-of-the money and in-the-money call options as well as for at-the-money and out-of-the-money put options. The percentage of cases where the delta-vega hedging error of the genetic programming model is less than the BS delta-vega hedging error is 100% for in-the-money call options as well as for at-the-money put options. The percentage of cases where the delta-gamma hedging error of the genetic programming model is less than the BS delta-gamma hedging error is 100% for at-the-money put options.

Furthermore, results exhibit that as the rebalancing frequency changes from 1-day to 7-days revision, as the hedging errors increase and vice versa. The option value is a nonlinear function of the underlying, therefore, hedging is instantaneous and hedging with discrete rebalancing gives rise to error. Frequent rebalancing can be impractical due to transactions costs. In the literature, consequences of discrete time hedging have been considered usually in conjunction with the existence of transaction costs, that's why hedgers would like to trade at least frequently as possible. Pioneered by Leland [43], asymptotic approaches are used as well [44-46]. For most MTM classes, delta-gamma and delta-vega hedging strategies are shown to perform better in dynamic hedging when compared with delta hedging strategy, regardless of the model used. The delta-gamma strategy enables the performance of a discrete rebalanced hedging to be improved. The delta-vega strategy corrects partly for the risk of a randomly changing volatility.

5. Conclusion

This paper is concerned with improving the dynamic hedging accuracy using generated genetic programming implied volatilities. Firstly, genetic programming is used to predict implied volatility from index option prices. Dynamic training-subset selection methods are applied to improve the robustness of genetic programming to generate general forecasting implied volatility models relative to static training-subset selection method. Secondly, the implied volatilities derived are used in dynamic hedging strategies and the performance of genetic programming is compared to that of Black-Scholes in terms of delta, gamma and vega hedging.

Results show that the dynamic training of genetic programming yields better results than those obtained from static training with fixed samples, especially when applied on time series and moneyness-time to maturity samples simultaneously. Based on the MSE total as performance criterion, three generated genetic programming volatility models are selected M4S4, MCAR and MGAR. However, the MGAR seems to be more accurate in forecasting implied volatility than MCAR and M4S4 models because it is more general and adaptive to all time series and moneyness-time to maturity classes simultaneously.

The main conclusion concerns the importance of implied volatility forecasting in conducting hedging strategies. Genetic programming forecasting volatility makes hedge performances higher than those obtained in the Black-Scholes world. The best genetic programming hedging performance is achieved for in-the-money call options and at-the-money put options in all hedging strategies. The percentage of cases where the hedging error of the genetic programming model is less than the Black-Scholes hedging error is around 59% for calls and 57% for puts. The performance of genetic programming is pronounced essentially in terms of delta hedging for call and put options. The percentage of cases where the delta hedging error of the genetic programming model is less than the Black-Scholes delta hedging error is 100% for out-of-the money and in-the-money call options as well as for at-the-money and out-of-the-money put options. The percentage of cases where the delta-vega hedging error of the genetic programming model is less than the Black-Scholes delta-vega hedging error is 100% for in-the-money call options as well as for at-the-money put options. The percentage of cases where the delta-gamma hedging error of the genetic programming model is less than the Black-Scholes delta-gamma hedging error is 100% for at-the-money put options.

Finally, improving the accuracy of implied volatility forecasting using genetic programming can lead to well hedged options portfolios relative to the conventional parametric models.

Our results suggest some interesting issues for further investigation. First, the genetic programming can be used to hedge options contracts using implied volatility of other models than Black-Scholes model, notably stochastic volatility models and models with jump, as a proxy for genetic programming volatility forecasting. Further, the hedge factors can be computed numerically not analytically. Second, this work can be reexamined using data from individual stock options, American style index options, options on futures, currency and commodity options. Third, as the genetic programming can incorporate known analytical approximations in the solution method, parametric models such as GARCH models can be used as a parameter in the genetic programming to build the forecasting volatility model and the hedging strategies. Finally, the genetic programming can be extended to allow for dynamic parameter choices including the form and the rates of genetic operators, the form and pressure of selection mechanism, the form of replacement strategy and the size of population. This dynamic genetic programming method can improve the performance without extra calculation costs. We believe these extensions are of interest for application and will be object of our future works.

Author details

Fathi Abid and Wafa Abdelmalek
Research Unit MODESFI, Faculty of Economics and Business, Sfax, Tunisia

Sana Ben Hamida
Research Laboratory SOIE (ISG Tunis), Paris West University, Nanterre, France

6. References

[1] Blair B.J, Poon S, Taylor S.J (2001) Forecasting S&P100 Volatility: The Incremental Information Content of Implied Volatilities and High Frequency Index Returns. Journal of Econometrics.105: 5-26.

[2] Busch T, Christensen B.J, Nielsen M.Ø (2007) The Role of Implied Volatility in Forecasting Future Realized Volatility and Jumps in Foreign Exchange, Stock, and Bond Markets. CREATES Research Paper 2007-9. Aarhus School of Business, University of Copenhagen. pp.1-39.

[3] Koza J.R (1992) Genetic programming: on the Programming of Computers by means of Natural Selection. Cambridge, Massachusetts: the MIT Press. 819 p.

[4] Holland J.H (1975) Adaptation in Natural and Artificial Systems. Ann Arbor: University of Michigan Press.

[5] Breiman L (1996) Bagging Predictors. Machine Learning. 2:123-140.

[6] Freund Y, Schapire R (1996) Experiments with a New Boosting Algorithm. In Proceedings of the 13th International Conference on Machine Learning. Morgan Kauffman Publishers. pp. 148-156.

[7] Breiman L (1998) Arcing Classifiers. Annals of Statistics. 26: 801-849.

[8] Abdelmalek W, Ben Hamida S, Abid F (2009) Selecting the Best Forecasting-Implied Volatility Model using Genetic programming. Journal of Applied Mathematics and Decision Sciences (Special Issue: Intelligent Computational Methods for Financial Engineering). Hindawi Publishing Corporation. Available: http:// www.hindawi.com/journals/jamds/2009/179230.html

[9] Tsang E, Yung P, Li J (2004) EDDIE-Automation, a Decision Support Tool for Financial Forecasting. Decision Support Systems. 37: 559–565.Available: http://sci2s.ugr.es/keel/pdf/specific/.../ science2_4.pdf

[10] Kaboudan M (2005) Extended Daily Exchange Rates Forecasts using Wavelet Temporal Resolutions. New Mathematics and Natural Computing. 1: 79-107. Available: http://www.mendeley.com/.../extended-daily-... - États-Unis

[11] Bollerslev T, Chou R.Y, Kroner K.F (1992) ARCH Modelling in Finance: a Review of the Theory and Empirical Evidence. Journal of Econometrics. 52: 55-59.

[12] Engle R.F (1982) Autoregressive Conditional Heteroscedasticity with Estimates of the Variance of U.K. Inflation. Econometrica. 50: 987-1008.

[13] Bollerslev T (1986) Generalized Autoregressive Conditional Heteroscedasticity. Journal of Econometrics. 31: 307-327.

[14] Hull J, White A (1987) The Pricing of Options on Assets with Stochastic Volatilities. Journal of Finance. 42: 218-300.

[15] Scott L (1987) Option Pricing When the Variance Changes Randomly: Theory, Estimation and an Application. Journal of Financial and Quantitative Analysis. 22: 419-438. Available: http:// www.globalriskguard.com/resources/.../der6.pdf

[16] Wiggins J (1987) Option Values under Stochastic Volatility: Theory and Empirical Evidence. Journal of Financial Economics. 19: 351-372.

[17] Heston S.L (1993) A Closed-Form Solution for Options with Stochastic Volatility. Review of Financial Studies. 6: 327-344.

[18] Ma I, Wong T, Sankar T, Siu R (2004) Volatility Forecasts of the S&P100 by Evolutionary Programming in a Modified Time Series Data Mining Framework. In: Jamshidi M, editor. Proceedings of the World Automation Congress (WAC2004). 17: 567-572.

[19] Chen S.H, Yeh C.H (1997) Using Genetic programming to Model Volatility in Financial Time Series. In: Koza J.R, Deb K, Dorigo M, Fogel D.B, Garzon M, Iba H, Riolo R.L, editors. Genetic programming 1997, Proceedings of the Second Annual Conference. Morgan Kaufmann Publishers. pp. 58-63.

[20] Zumbach G, Pictet O.V, Masutti O (2002) Genetic programming with Syntactic Restrictions Applied to Financial Volatility Forecasting. In: Kontoghioghes E.J, Rustem B, Siokos S, editors. Computational Methods in Decision-Making, Economics and Finance. Kluwer Academic Publishers. pp. 557-581.

[21] Neely C.J, Weller P.A (2002) Using a Genetic Program to Predict Exchange Rate Volatility. In: Chen S.H, editor. Genetic Algorithms and Genetic programming in Computational Finance, Chapter 13. Kluwer Academic Publishers. pp. 263-279.

[22] Ma I, Wong T, Sanker T (2006) An Engineering Approach to Forecast Volatility of Financial Indices. International Journal of Computational Intelligence. 3: 23-35.

[23] Ma I, Wong T, Sanker T (2007) Volatility Forecasting using Time Series Data Mining and Evolutionary Computation Techniques. In Proceedings of the 9th Annual Conference on Genetic and Evolutionary Computation (GECCO 07). ACM New York Press.

[24] Derman E, Ergener D, Kani I (1995) Static Options Replication. The Journal of Derivatives. 2: 78-95.

[25] Carr P, Ellis K, Gupta V (1998) Static Hedging of Exotic Options. Journal of Finance. 53: 1165-1190.

[26] Hutchinson J.M, Lo A.W, Poggio T (1994) A NonParametric Approach to Pricing and Hedging Derivative Securities via Learning Network. Journal of Finance. 49: 851-889.

[27] Aït-Sahalia Y, Lo A (1998) Nonparametric Estimation for State-Price Densities Implicit in Financial Asset Prices. The Journal of Finance. 53: 499-547.

[28] Chen S.H, Lee W.C, Yeh C.H (1999) Hedging Derivative Securities with Genetic Programming. International Journal of Intelligent Systems in Accounting, Finance and Management. 4: 237-251.

[29] Harvey C.R, Whaley R.E (1991) S&P 100 Index Option Volatility. Journal of Finance. 46: 1551-1561.

[30] Harvey C.R, Whaley R.E (1992) Market Volatility Prediction and the Efficiency of the S&P100 Index Option Market. Journal of Financial Economics. 31: 43-73.

[31] Merton R.C (1973) Theory of Rational Option Pricing. Bell Journal of Economics and Management Science. 4: 141-183.
[32] Cai W, Pacheco-Vega A, Sen M, Yang K.T (2006) Heat Transfer Correlations by Symbolic Regression. International Journal of Heat and Mass Transfer. 49: 4352-4359.
[33] Gustafson S, Burke E.K, Krasnogor N (2005) On Improving Genetic programming for Symbolic Regression. In Proceedings of the IEEE Congress on Evolutionary Computation. 1: 912-919.
[34] Keijzer M (2004) Scaled Symbolic Regression. Genetic programming and Evolvable Machines. 5: 259-269.
[35] Lew T.L, Spencer A.B, Scarpa F, Worden K (2006) Identification of Response Surface Models Using Genetic programming. Mechanical Systems and Signal Processing. 20: 1819-1831.
[36] Black F, Scholes M. (1973) The Pricing of Options and Corporate Liabilities. Journal of Political Economy. 81: 637-659.
[37] Kraft D. H, Petry F. E, Buckles W. P, Sadasivan T (1994) The Use of Genetic Programming to Build Queries for Information Retrieval. In Proceedings of the 1994 IEEE World Congress on Computational Intelligence. IEEE Press. pp. 468–473.
[38] Angeline P. J (1996) An Investigation into the Sensitivity of Genetic Programming to the Frequency of Leaf Selection during Subtree Crossover. In: Koza J. R et al., editors. Genetic Programming 1996: Proceedings of the First Annual Conference. MIT Press. pp. 21–29. Available: www.natural-selection.com/Library/1996/gp96.zip.
[39] McKay B, Willis M.J, Barton G.W (1995) Using a Tree Structural Genetic Algorithm to Perform Symbolic Regression. In First International Conference on Genetic Algorithms in Engineering Systems: Innovations and Applications (GALESIA). 414: 487-492.
[40] Schwefel H.P (1995) Numerical Optimization of Computer Models. John Wiley & Sons, New York.
[41] Cavaretta M.J, Chellapilla K. (1999) Data Mining Using Genetic Programming: The Implications of Parsimony on Generalization Error. In Proceedings of the 1999 Congress on Evolutionary Computation (CEC' 99). IEEE Press. pp. 1330-1337.
[42] Gathercole C, Ross P (1994) Dynamic Training Subset Selection for Supervised Learning in Genetic Programming. Parallel Problem Solving from Nature III. 866 of LNCS: 312-321.
[43] Leland H.E. (1985) Option Pricing and Replication with Transaction Costs. Journal of Finance. 40: 1283-1301.
[44] Kabanov Y.M, Safarian M.M (1997) On Leland Strategy of Option Pricing with Transaction Costs. Finance Stochastic. 1: 239-250.
[45] Ahn H, Dalay M, Grannan E, Swindle G (1998) Option Replication with Transactions Costs: General Diffusion Limits. Ann. Appl. Prob. 8: 676-707.

[46] Grandits P, Schachinger W (2001) Leland's Approach to Option Pricing: The Evolution of Discontinuity. Math Finance. 11: 347-355.

Chapter 8

The Usage of Genetic Methods for Prediction of Fabric Porosity

Polona Dobnik Dubrovski and Miran Brezočnik

Additional information is available at the end of the chapter

http://dx.doi.org/10.5772/48188

1. Introduction

Advanced fabric production demands developing strategies with regard to new fabric constructions in which sample-production is reduced to a minimum. It is clear that a new fabric construction should have the desired end-usage properties pre-specified as project demands. Achieving such a demand is a complex task based on our knowledge of the relations between the fabric constructional parameters and the predetermined fabric end-usage properties that fit the desired quality. Individual fabric properties are difficult to predict when confronting the various construction parameters, which can be separated into the following categories: raw materials, fabric structure, design, and manufacturing parameters.

Many attempts have been made to develop predictive models for fabric properties with different modelling tools. There are essentially two types of modelling tools: deterministic (mathematical models, empirical models, computer simulation models) and non-deterministic (models based on genetic methods, neural network models, models based on chaos theory and theory of soft logic), and each of them has its advantages and disadvantages [1].

Deterministic modelling tools present the heart of conventional science and have their basis in first principles, statistical techniques or computer simulations. Mathematical models offer a deep understanding of relations between constructional parameters and predetermined fabric property, but due some simplifying assumptions large prediction errors occur. Empirical models based on statistical techniques show a much better agreement with the real values but the problems with samples preparing, process repeatability, measurements errors and extrapolation occur. They usually refer to the one type of testing method of particular fabric property. The advantage of computer simulation models is their ability to capture the randomness inherent in fabric structure so the predicted values are very near the real ones, but on the other hand they require numerous fabric samples data. The problem with extrapolation still remains. In general, when deterministic modelling is used, the obtained models are the results of strict mathematical rules and/or the models are set in advance. In this case the goal is to discover merely a set of numerical coefficients for a model whose form has been pre-specified. However, nowadays more and more processes and systems are modelled and optimized by the use of non-deterministic approaches. This is due to the high degree of complexity of the systems, and consequently, inability to study them successfully by the use of conventional methods only. In non-deterministic modelling of systems, no precise and strict mathematical rules are used [2, 3, 4, 5, 6, 7]. For example, in genetic programming, no assumptions about the form, size, and complexity of models are made in advance. They are left to the stochastic, self-organized, intelligent, and non-centralized evolutionary processes [1, 8].

Fabrics are porous materials having different porous structures as the consequence of different manufacturing techniques needed to interlace the fundamental structural elements, e.g. fibres, yarns or layers, into fibrous assembly. Fabric porosity strongly determines important physical, mechanical, sorptive, chemical, and thermal properties of the fabrics such as mechanical strength, thermal resistance, permeability (windproofness, breathability), absorption and adsorption properties (wicking, wetting), translucence, soiling propensity, UV light penetration, sound absorption ability, etc. [9, 10]. Knowledge about the fabric's porous structure is, therefore, an important step when characterising fabrics, in order to predict their behaviour under different end-usage conditions regarding a product. Hence, if porosity is estimated or predicted then when developing a new product the desired porosity parameters can be set in advance on the basis of selecting those fabric constructional factors that have an effect on porosity and, in this way sample production trials could be reduced.

This chapter gives some basic information about the porosity, porosity parameters of woven and nonwoven fabrics, and the results of the studies dealing with the prediction of porosity parameters of two types of fabrics, e.g. woven fabrics made from the 100% cotton staple yarns and needle-punched nonwovens made from the mixture of viscose/polyester fibres, using nondeterministic modelling tools, e.g. genetic programming (GP) and genetic algorithms (GA), respectively.

2. Porosity and porosity parameters

Flat textile materials, e.g. fabrics, are porous materials which allow the transmission of energy and substances and are therefore interesting materials for different applications. In general, they are used for clothing, interior and wide range of technical applications. Fabric as porous barrier between the human body an environment should support heat and water vapour exchange between the body and environment in order to keep the body temperature within the homeostasis range. Besides thermo-physiological protection, fabrics also play an important role by heat protection due to the flames or convection heat, contact heat, radiant heat as well as due to the sparks and drops of molten metal, hot gases and vapours [11].

Fabrics protect users against micro-organisms, pesticides, chemicals, hazardous particles and radiations (radioactive particles, micro-meteorites, X-rays, micro-waves, UV radiation, etc.). They act very important role also by environmental protection as filters for air and water filtrations, sound absorption and isolation materials against noise pollution, adsorption materials for hazardous gas pollution, etc. [10, 12, 13]. By all mentioned applications dedicated to absorption, desorption, filtration, drainage, vapours transmission, etc., the essential constructional parameter that influences fabric efficiency to protect human or environment is porosity. The fabric in a dry state is a two-phase media which consists of the fibrous material – solid component and void spaces containing air – gas (void) component. The porosity of a material is one of the physical properties of the material and describes the fraction of void space in the material. The porosity (or void volume fraction) is expressed as coefficient ranging between 0 and 1 or as percentage ranging between 0% and 100% (by multiplying the coefficient by 100). Mathematically, the porosity is defined as the ratio of the total void space volume to the total (or bulk) body volume [14, 15]:

$$\varepsilon = \frac{V_v}{V} \tag{1}$$

where, ε is the porosity expressed as coefficient, V_v is the volume of the total void space in cm^3, and V is the total or bulk body volume in cm^3. The total volume of the body consists of the volumes of the solid and void components as follows:

$$V = V_v + V_s \tag{2}$$

where, V is the total volume of the body in cm^3, V_v is the volume of void component in cm^3, and V_s is the volume of solid component in cm^3. If the volume of void component is exposed from the Equation 2, the Equation 1 can be further written as follows:

$$\varepsilon = \frac{V_v}{V} = \frac{V - V_s}{V} = 1 - \frac{V_s}{V} = 1 - \beta \tag{3}$$

$$\beta = \frac{V_s}{V} \tag{4}$$

where, β is the fulfilment (or solid volume fraction) which describes the fraction of solid component volume in the material expressed as coefficient ranging between 0 and 1 or as percentage. If we take into account the common equation for material density (Equation 5), and assume that the mass of the material is actually the mass of solid component (m_s=m_b), the Equation 3 could be further written in the form of Equation 6:

$$\rho = \frac{m}{V} \tag{5}$$

$$\varepsilon = 1 - \frac{V_s}{V} = 1 - \frac{m_s \rho_b}{\rho_s m_b} = 1 - \frac{\rho_b}{\rho_s} \tag{6}$$

where, ε is the porosity expressed as coefficient, V_s is the volume of solid component in cm^3, V is the volume of the body (or bulk volume) in cm^3, m_s is the mass of solid component in g, m_b is the mass of the body (or bulk mass) in g, ϱ_b is the bulk density in g/cm^3, and ϱ_s is the density of solid component in g/cm^3.

In this way exactly defined porosity of the material is useful parameter, only, when materials with the same porous structure are compared, and gives an indication which material possesses more void space in the bulk volume. It does not give any information about the porous structure of the material, so it is an insufficient parameter for describing fibre assembly characteristics [16]. Namely, the materials with the same porosity could have very different porous structure and consequently, in the case of fabrics, different protection, filtration, sound absorption, etc., properties; so the need to define porous structure and some other porosity parameters is essential. From the theoretical point of view, the porosity parameters could be easily determined on the basis of an ideal geometrical model of the material porous structure. The simpler models consider that all pores, whatever their shape, are the same and regularly arranged in a fibre assembly [16, 17]. Ideal models are based also on some other simplifying assumptions depending on the fibre assembly type. Porosity parameters calculated on the basis of ideal models of porous structures are usually not in a good correlation with the real porosity parameters. Real porous media generally have rather complex structures that are relatively difficult to define. But the advantage of ideal geometric models of porous structures is the possibility to understand the influence of porous structure on some end-usage properties of the material, which is crucial by a new product planning.

The fundamental building elements of the material porous structure are pores (also capillaries, channels, holes, free volume) [15, 18]. Pores are void spaces within the material which are separated between each other, and are classified [19, 20]:

1. according to the position in the material into:
   a. inter-pores, e.g. pores which lie between the structural elements of the material,
   b. intra-pores, e.g. pores which lie within the structural element of the material;
2. according to the pore width (the shortest pore diameter) into:
   a. macropores whose pore-width is greater than 50 nm,
   b. mesopores whose pore-width lies in the range between 2 and 50 nm, and
   c. micropores with the pore-width lower than 2 nm;
3. according to the fluid accessibility into (Figure 1):
   a. closed pores being inaccessible for fluid flow or surroundings,
   b. blind pores which are accessible for fluid but terminate inside the material and prevent fluid flow, and
   c. open (or through) pores which are open to external surface and permit fluid flow;

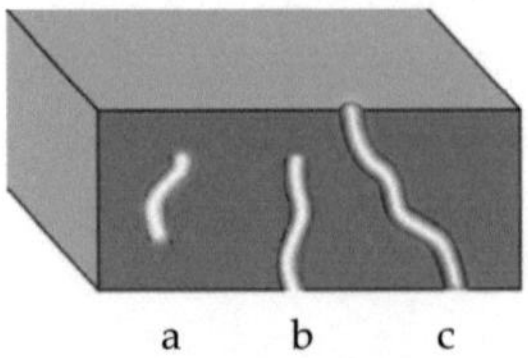

Figure 1. Types of pores according to the fluid accessibility

4. according to the pore shape into (Figure 2):
   a. cylindrical pores,
   b. slit-shape pores,
   c. cone-shape pores, and
   d. ink bottle pores;

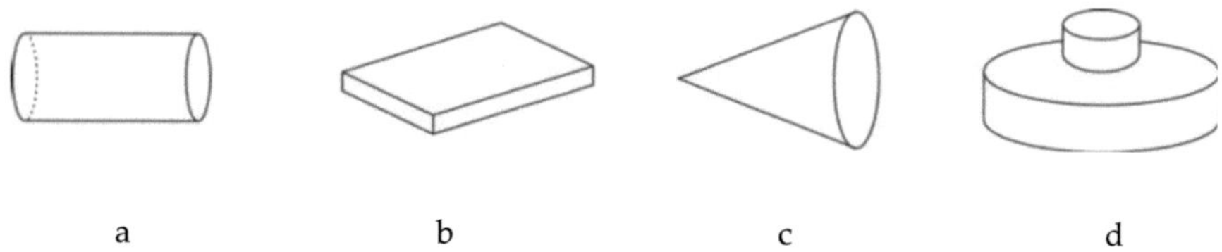

Figure 2. Types of pores according to the pore shape [19]

5. according to the geometry of pore-cross section into (Figure 3):
   a. pores with geometrically regular cross-sectional shape and
   b. pores with geometrically irregular cross-sectional shape,

Figure 3. Different shapes of pore cross-sections [20]

6. according to the uniformity of pore cross-section over the pore length into (Figure 4):
   a. pores with a permanent cross-section,
   b. pores with a different cross-sections and for which different diameters are defined (the most constricted, the largest, the mean pore diameters).

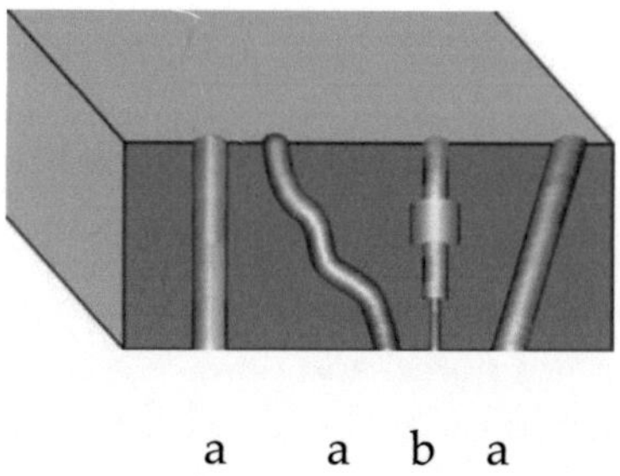

Figure 4. Pores with permanent (a) and non-permanent (b) cross-sections over their length

Four groups of pore descriptors, e.g. size, shape, orientation, and placement, are defined as important parameters [21]. Pores can be mathematically assessed on the basis of known model of pores geometry and constructional parameters of the material with the following parameters: the number of pores, pore size, pore volume, pore surface area, pore length, etc.

On the basis of an ideal geometrical model of porous structure, the pore size distribution which is also an important parameter of material porous structure can not assessed while the pores in geometrical model are usually assumed to be the same sizes. Such situation rarely occurs in the real fabrics. The further considerations of ideal geometrical models of material porous structures and porosity parameters will be focused on different types of fabrics.

Fabrics are flat textile materials which are produced by different manufacturing techniques using different fibrous forms of input material (or structural element), and consequently having different porous structures. Following basic types of fabrics are known (Figure 5):

- woven fabrics which are made by interlacing vertical warp and horizontal weft yarns at right angles to each other,
- knitted fabrics which are made by forming the yarn into loops and their interlacing in vertical (warp-knitted fabrics) or horizontal (weft-knitted fabrics) direction,
- nonwoven fabrics which are produced from the staple fibres, filaments or yarns by different web-forming, bonding and finishing techniques.

Figure 5. 2-D schematic presentations of woven-, knitted-, and nonwoven (made from staple fibres) fabrics

While this chapter is focused on the genetic methods in order to predict porosity of woven and nonwoven fabrics, only those types of fabrics and their ideal geometric models of porous structure will be presented.

2.1. Woven fabric's ideal geometric model of porous structure

When a woven fabric is treated as a three dimensional formation, different types of pores are detected [22, 23, 24]: 1. inter-pores, e.g. the pores which are situated between warp and weft yarns (macropores, interyarn pores) and pores which are situated between fibres in the yarns (mesopores, interfiber/intrayarn pores), 2. intra-pores, e.g. the pores which are situated in the fibres (micropores, intrafiber pores). The structure and dimensions of the inter- or intrayarn pores are strongly affected by the yarn structure and the density of yarns in the woven structure [22]. As fibrous materials, woven fabrics have, with regard to knitted fabrics or nonwovens, the most exactly determined an ideal geometrical model of a macro-porous structure in the form of a tube-like system, where each macropore has a cylindrical shape with a permanent cross-section over all its length (Figure 6) [25]. Because the warp density is usually greater than the weft density, the elliptical shape of the pore cross-section is used to represent the situation in Figure 6. Macropores are opened to the external surface and have the same cross-section area. They are separated by warp or weft yarns, and are uniformly distributed over the woven fabric area.

The primary constructional parameters of woven fabrics which alter the porous structure are:

- yarn fineness, e.g. the mass of 1000 meter of yarn from which the yarn diameter can be calculated,
- type of weave, e.g. the manner how the yarns are interlaced. It has an effect on the pore size as well as on the shape of pore cross-section [26],
- the number of yarns in length unit (warp and weft densities), which directly alters the pore size.

When fibre properties (fibre density, dimension, and shape) are different, two woven fabrics with similar woven structures and geometrical configurations can have distinctly different porosity [22].

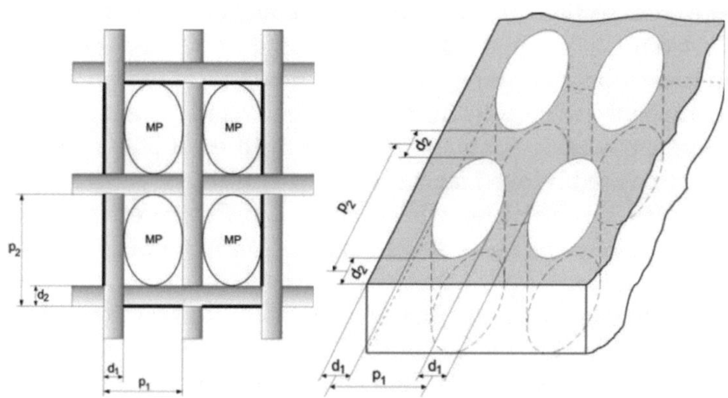

Figure 6. 2D and 3D presentations of an ideal model of the porous structure of a woven fabric [27, 28] (d – yarn thickness, p – yarn spacing, MP - macropore; 1, 2 indicates warp and weft yarns, respectively)

To compare woven fabrics with porosity, the following porosity parameters can be calculated on the basis of the woven fabric primary constructional parameters and the ideal model of porous structure in the form of a tube-like system:

- (total) porosity by using Equation 6 where the bulk density of the material is actually the woven fabric density and the density of solid component is the yarn density. If the fibre volume fraction (yarn packing factor) is exposed from the Equation 7 which represents the yarn diameter calculation, and then inserted in Equation 8 by assuming Equation 9 for woven fabric density at the same time, the porosity of woven fabrics can be then written in the form of Equation 10:

$$d = \sqrt{\frac{4T}{10^5 \pi \cdot \rho_{yarn}}} = \sqrt{\frac{4T}{1000 \cdot \pi \cdot \rho_{fib} \cdot \beta_{fib}}} \tag{7}$$

$$\rho_{yarn} = \rho_{fib} \cdot \beta_{fib} \tag{8}$$

$$\rho_{fab} = \frac{m}{D \cdot 1000} \tag{9}$$

$$\varepsilon = 1 - \frac{\rho_b}{\rho_s} = 1 - \frac{\rho_{fab}}{\rho_{yarn}} = 1 - \frac{100 \cdot m \cdot d^2 \cdot \pi}{D \cdot 4 \cdot T} \tag{10}$$

where, d is the yarn diameter in cm, T is the yarn fineness in tex, ρ_{yarn} is the yarn bulk density in g/cm^3, ρ_{fib} is the fibre density in g/cm^3, β_{fib} is the fibre volume fraction (or yarn packing factor), ρ_{fab} is the woven fabric bulk density in g/cm^3, m is the woven fabric mass per unit area in g/m^2, D is the woven fabric thickness in mm, ρ_b is the body bulk density in g/cm^3, and ρ_s is the density of solid component in g/cm^3. It is worth to mention that in this way defined porosity refers to all types of pores regarding their position in the woven fabric, e.g. inter- and intra-pores;

- area of pore cross-section which refers only on macropores in a woven fabric. The ideal model of woven fabric porous structure is based on the assumption that macropores have cylindrical shape with circular cross-section. In real woven fabrics, the macropore cross-section shape is more likely to be irregular rather regular (Figure 7) [26]. The shape of pore cross-section and consequently the area of pore cross-section depend on the type of yarns used. Woven fabrics made from filament yarns have pure macropores with rectangular cross-sections, whilst woven fabrics made from staple yarns have a small percentage of pure macropores, some of partly latticed macropores as well as fully latticed macropores (as the consequence of the phenomenon of latticed pores) with mostly irregular cross-sections. The area of pore cross-section also depends on the phenomenon of changing the position of warp threads according to the longitudinal fabric axis and the phenomenon of thread spacing irregularity [28]. For the theoretical calculations of the macropore cross-section area three types of regular pore cross-section shapes are taken into account, e.g. circular (Equation 11), rectangular (Equation 12) and elliptical (Equation 13) as follows:

$$A_{p/circular} = \frac{\pi}{16}(p_1 + p_2 - d_1 - d_2)^2 = \frac{\pi}{16}\left(\frac{10}{g_1} + \frac{10}{g_2} - d_1 - d_2\right)^2 \tag{11}$$

$$A_{p/rectangular} = (p_1 - d_1)\cdot(p_2 - d_2) = \left(\frac{10}{g_1} - d_1\right)\cdot\left(\frac{10}{g_2} - d_2\right) \tag{12}$$

$$A_{p/elliptical} = \frac{\pi}{4}\cdot(p_1 - d_1)\cdot(p_2 - d_2) = \frac{\pi}{4}\left(\frac{10}{g_1} - d_1\right)\cdot\left(\frac{10}{g_2} - d_2\right) \tag{13}$$

where, A_p is the area of macropore cross-section in mm^2, p is the yarn spacing in mm, d is the yarn diameter in mm, g is the number of yarns per unit length in threads/cm, and subscripts 1 and 2 indicate warp and weft yarns, respectively;

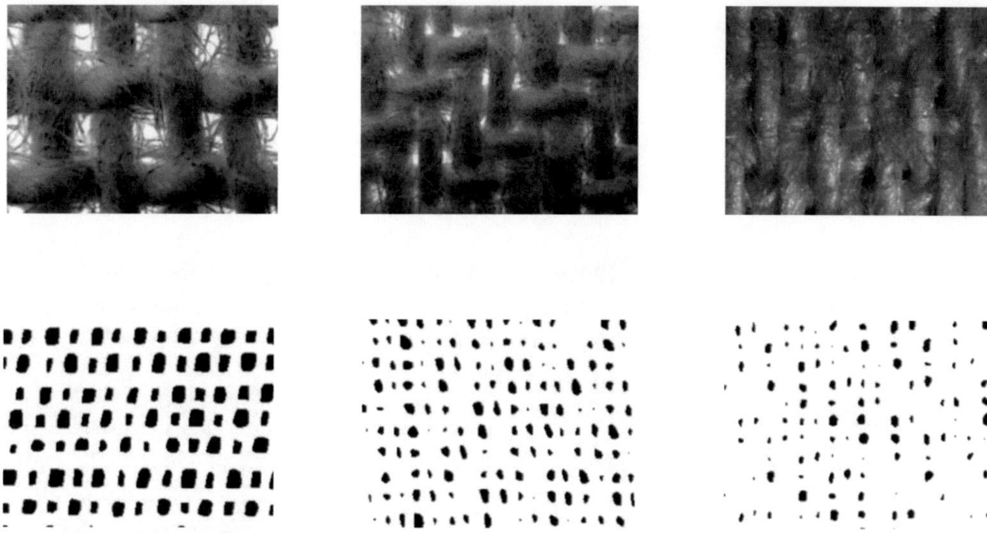

plain, 21/16 threads/cm twill, 27/22 threads/cm satin, 30/24 threads/cm

Figure 7. Real and binary images of the pore cross-section shape and the number of pores in real woven fabrics (magnification of binary images: 20 x, magnification of real images: 80 x, yarn fineness: 36 tex, fabric relative density: 83 %)

- number of macropores in the area unit (pore density). It can be seen from Figure 7, that one macropore belongs to one warp yarn and one weft yarn, so the number of macropores can be calculated on the basis of warp and weft densities using Equation 14:

$$N_p = g_1 \cdot g_2 \tag{14}$$

where, N_p is the pore density in pores/cm^2, g_1 is the warp density in threads/cm, and g_2 is the weft density in threads/cm;

- open porosity (open area) which describes the fraction of macropore cross-section area in the area unit of woven fabric. If we assume elliptical macropore cross-section area (Figure 7), the open porosity is calculated as follows:

$$\varepsilon_{open} = \frac{A_p}{A_p + A_y} = \frac{\pi(p_1 - d_1)\cdot(p_2 - d_2)}{4 \cdot p_1 \cdot p_2} \tag{15}$$

where, ε_{open} is the open porosity, A_p is the macropore cross-section area in mm^2, A_y is the projection area of warp and weft yarns, which refers to one macropore in mm^2, p is the yarn spacing in mm, d is the yarn diameter in mm, and subscripts 1 and 2 indicate warp and weft yarns, respectively. Open porosity can be calculated also on the basis of cover factor (Equation 16) or pore density (Equation 17) [26, 29]:

$$\varepsilon_{open} = 1 - K = 1 - \left[\frac{\left(d_1 g_1 + d_2 g_2 - \left\{ \frac{d_1 d_2 g_1 g_2}{10} \right\} \right)}{10} \right] \tag{16}$$

$$\varepsilon_{open} = N_p \cdot A_p \tag{17}$$

where, ε_{open} is the open porosity, K is the woven fabric cover factor, d is the yarn diameter in mm, g is the warp/weft density in threads/cm, N_p is the pore density in pores/cm^2, A_p is the area of macropore cross-section in cm^2, and subscripts 1 and 2 indicate warp and weft yarns, respectively;

- equivalent macropore-diameter. If we assume that macropore has cylindrical shape, then the area of macropore cross-section is equal to the area of circle with radius r (Equation 18). Equivalent macropore diameter is the diameter of macropore with circular cross-section whose area is the same as the area of the macropore with irregular cross-section shape (Equation 19) [30].

$$A_{circle} = \pi \cdot r^2 = \frac{\pi \cdot d^2}{4} \tag{18}$$

$$d_e = \sqrt{\frac{4 \cdot A_p}{\pi}} \tag{19}$$

where, A_{circle} is the circular cross-section macropore area in mm^2, r is the macropore radius in mm, d is the macropore diameter in mm, d_e is the equivalent macropore diameter in mm, and A_p is the macropore cross-section area of macropore with irregular shape in mm^2;

- maximal an minimal macropore diameters which refer to the elliptical shape of macropore cross-section. In the case where warp density is greater than weft density the maximal diameter is equal to p_2-d_2, while minimal diameter is equal to p_1-d_1 (Figure 7);
- macroporosity which describes the portion of macropore volume in volume unit of woven fabric. In general, it is defined using Equation 20. In the case of the elliptical macropore cross-section shape, the macroporosity, defined with Equation 21, is the same as open porosity:

$$\varepsilon_{macro} = \frac{V_p}{V_p + V_y} = \frac{A_p \cdot D}{p_1 \cdot p_2 \cdot D} = \frac{A_p}{p_1 \cdot p_2} \tag{20}$$

$$\varepsilon_{macro} = \frac{V_p}{V_p + V_y} = \frac{\pi(p_1 - d_1) \cdot (p_2 - d_2) \cdot D}{4 \cdot p_1 \cdot p_2 \cdot D} = \frac{\pi(p_1 - d_1) \cdot (p_2 - d_2)}{4 \cdot p_1 \cdot p_2} = \varepsilon_{open} \tag{21}$$

where, ε_{macro} is the macroporosity, V_p is the macropore volume in cm^3, V_y is the volume of warp and weft yarns which refers to one macropore in cm^3, p is the yarn spacing in mm, d is the yarn diameter in mm, D is the woven fabric thickness in mm, A_P is the macropore area in mm^2, ε_{open} is the open porosity, and subscripts 1 and 2 indicate warp and weft yarns, respectively.

2.2. Nonwoven fabric's ideal geometric model of porous structure

The porous structure of nonwoven fabric is a result of nonwoven construction (the type and properties of fibres or yarns as input materials, fabric mass, fabric thickness, etc.) as well as technological phases, e.g. the type of web production, bonding methods and finishing treatments. According to several different methods to produce non-woven fabrics having consequently very different porous structure, the ideal geometric model of porous structure in the form of tube-like system is partially acceptable only by those nonwovens which are thin and translucence, e.g. light polymer–laid nonwovens and some thin spun-laced or heat-bonded nonwovens (Figure 8). Such model is based on the assumptions that fibres having the same diameter are distributed only in the direction of fabric plane and the distance between fibres and the length of individual fibres is much greater than the fibre diameter. Xu [21] found out that in most nonwoven fabrics, pore shape is approximately polygonal and that pores appear more circular when the fabric density increases. Pore orientation to some extent relates to fibre orientation. If pores are elongated and predominantly oriented in one direction, fibres are likely to be oriented in that direction. The variation in pore size is inherently high. Some regions may contain more pores than others or may have larger pores than those in other regions.

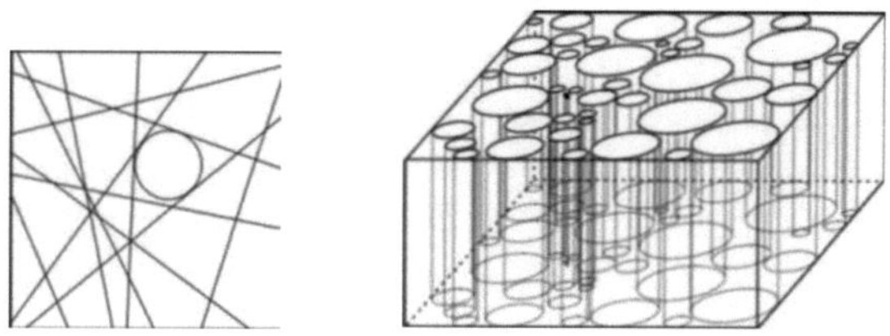

Figure 8. 2D and 3D presentations of an ideal model of the porous structure of a nonwoven fabric (with detail to define opening diameter of pore by 2D presentation)

The primary constructional parameters of nonwoven fabrics which alter the porous structure are:

- fibre fineness, e.g. the mass of 1000 meter of fibre, from which the fibre diameter can be calculated,
- web mass per unit area and
- web thicknesses.

To compare nonwoven fabrics with porosity, the following porosity parameters can be calculated on the basis of the nonwoven fabric primary constructional parameters and the ideal model of porous structure in the form of a tube-like system:

- (total) porosity by using Equation 6 where the bulk density of the material is actually the nonwoven fabric density and the density of solid component is the fibre density. The nonwoven fabric density is calculated on the basis of primary nonwoven constructional parameters, e.g. fabric mass and thickness using Equation 9 where index fab in this case refers to the nonwoven fabric. Substituting Equation 9 into Equation 6, final Equation 22 of nonwoven porosity which refers to inter- (pores between fibres in nonwovens) and intra-pores (pores inside the fibres) is obtained:

$$\varepsilon = 1 - \frac{\rho_b}{\rho_s} = 1 - \frac{\rho_{fab}}{\rho_{fib}} = 1 - \frac{m_{fab}}{D_{fab} \cdot \rho_{fib} \cdot 1000} \tag{22}$$

where, ε is the nonwoven fabric porosity, ρ_b is the body bulk density in g/cm³, ρ_s is the density of solid component in g/cm³, ρ_{fab} is the nonwoven fabric density in g/cm³, ρ_{fib} is the fibre density in g/cm³, m_{fab} is the nonwoven fabric mass per unit area in g/m², and D_{fab} is the nonwoven fabric thickness in mm;

- opening diameter which is the diameter of the maximum circle that can fit in a pore (Figure 8). It is predicted on the basis of nonwoven fabric constructional parameters and refers to the heat-bonded nonwoven fabrics, as follows [17, 21]:

$$d_o = \frac{1}{\sqrt{C \cdot L}} - d_{fib} \tag{23}$$

$$C = \frac{D_{fab}}{d_{fib}} \tag{24}$$

$$L = \frac{8 \cdot m_{fab}}{\pi \cdot D_{fab} \cdot d_{fib} \cdot \rho_{fib}} \tag{25}$$

where, d_o is the opening diameter in μm, C is the thickness factor, L is the specific total length of fibres per nonwoven unit area in mm^{-1}, d_{fib} is the fibre diameter in μm, D_{fab} is the nonwoven thickness in mm, m_{fab} is the nonwoven fabric mass per unit area in g/m², and ρ_{fib} is the fibre density in g/cm³;

- average area of pore cross-section which is for un-needled fabrics (e.g. fabrics made of layers of randomly distributed fibres) predicted using Equation 26 [17]:

$$A_p = \frac{\pi \cdot \varepsilon \cdot d_{fib}^2}{(1-\varepsilon)^2} \tag{26}$$

where, A_p is the average area of pore cross-section in mm², ε is the porosity, and d_{fib} is the fibre diameter in μm. On the basis of calculated average area of pore-cross-section, the equivalent pore diameter is then calculated using Equation 19.

Needle-punched nonwoven fabric is a sheet of fibres made by mechanical entanglement, penetrating barbed needles into a fibrous mat [31]. Needle-punched nonwovens represent the largest segment of filtration materials used as dust filters [32]. The geometrical model of three-dimensional needle-punched nonwoven fabric proposed by Mao & Rusell [33], is also known from the literature, and it is constructed on a two-dimensional fibre orientation within the fabric plane, with interconnecting fibres oriented in the z-direction (Figure 10). Such model relies on the following basic assumptions: 1. the fibres in the fabric have the same diameter, and a fraction of the fibres is distributed horizontally in the two-dimensional plane, the rest are aligned in the direction of the fabric thickness, 2. fibre distribution in both the fabric plane and the z-direction is homogeneous and uniform, 3. in each two-dimensional plane, the number of fibres oriented in each direction is not the same, but obeys the function of the fibre orientation distribution $\Omega(\alpha)$, where α is the fibre orientation angle, 4. the distance between fibres and the length of individual fibres is much greater than the fibre diameter. The basic porosity parameters which are based on the mentioned geometrical model of needle-punched nonwoven fabric are still difficult to define due to the fact that in each fabric planes fibres lie in different direction and in this way produce pores with different orientations, diameters, connectivity and accessibility to fluid flow (Figure 9). The only porosity parameters that are calculated from such model are:

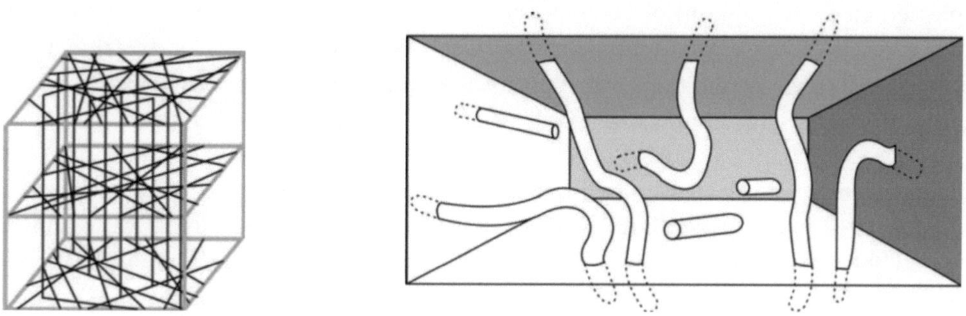

Figure 9. Geometrical models of needle-punched nonwoven fabric and porous structure [14, 34]

- total porosity (Equation 22) and
- mean pore diameter which is deduced from the fibre radius and porosity according to the following relation proposed by White [34]:

$$d_p = \frac{\varepsilon}{1-\varepsilon} \cdot \frac{d_{fib}}{2} \tag{27}$$

$$d_{fib} = 35.68 \sqrt{\frac{T}{\rho_{fib}}} \tag{28}$$

where, d_p is the mean pore diameter in μm, ε is the nonwoven fabric porosity, d_{fib} is the fibre diameter in μm, T is the fibre linear density in tex, and ρ_{fib} is the fibre density in g/cm^3.

Three kinds of pores may be present in needle-punched nonwoven fabrics, namely, closed pores, open pores, and blind pores. The important pore structure characteristics of needle-punched nonwoven fabrics as filter media are the most constricted open pore diameter (smallest detected pore diameter), the largest pore diameter (bubble point pore diameter), and mean pore diameter (mean flow pore diameter) [35].

3. The usage of genetic programming to predict woven fabric porosity parameters

Porosity parameters based on an ideal geometrical model of porous structure give woven fabric constructor some useful information about porosity by developing a new product, but they are not in a good agreement with the experimental values. In order to balance the difference between the theoretical and experimental values of porosity parameters, genetic programming was used to develop models for predicting the following macro-porosity parameters of woven fabric: the area of macro-pore cross-section, macro-pore density, open porosity, and equivalent macro-pore diameter. The genetic programming is a variant of evolutionary algorithm methods described in many sources (e.g., [2, 3, 4]). The basic information on the evolutionary algorithms is given at the beginning of the section 4. We implemented Koza's variant of genetic programming [2]. In our research, the independent input variables (the set of terminals) were: yarn fineness T (tex), weave value V, fabric tightness t (%) and denting D (ends/dent in the reed). The set of terminals also included random floating-point numbers between –10 and +10. Variegated reed denting was treated as an average value of treads, dented in the individual reed dent. The dependent output variables were: area of macro-pore cross-section A_p (10^{-3} mm^2), pore density N_p (pores/cm^2), and equivalent macro-pore diameter (μm). For all modelling, the initially set of functions included the basic mathematical operations of addition, subtraction, multiplication, and division. In the case of modelling the area of macro-pore cross-section and pore density the initially set of functions also included a power function, whereas the set of functions for modelling of equivalent macro-pore diameter included an exponential function. We then used the genetic programming system to evolve appropriate models consist of above-mentioned sets of terminals and functions. Open porosity was calculated on the basis of predicted values of the area of macro-pore cross-section and macro-pore density and Equation 17. The equivalent macro-pore diameter was calculated on the basis of predicted values of the area of macro-pore cross-section using Equation 19. The fitness measure for modelling by genetic programming was exactly the same as defined by Equation 33 in section 4. The goal of the modelling was to find such a predictive model in a symbolic form, that Equation 33 would give as low an absolute deviation as possible.

The evolutionary parameters for modelling by genetic programming were: population size 2000, maximum number of generations to be run 400, probability of reproduction 0.1, probability of crossover 0.8, probability of mutation 0.1, minimum depth for initial random organisms 2, maximum depth for initial random organisms 6, maximum depth of mutation fragment 6, and maximum permissible depth of organisms after crossover 17. The generative method for the initial random population was *ramped half-and-half*. The method of selection was tournament selection with a group size of 7. For the purpose of this research 100 independent genetic programming runs were executed. Only the results of the best runs (i.e., the models with the smallest error between the measurements and predictions) are presented in the paper.

3.1. Materials and porosity measurements

Our experiments involved woven fabrics made from staple yarns with two restrictions: first, only fabrics made from 100% cotton yarns (made by a combing and carding procedure on a ring spinning machine) were used in this research; second, fabrics were measured in the grey state to eliminate the influence of finishing processes. We believe that it is very hard, perhaps even impossible, to include all woven fabrics types to predict individual macro-porosity parameters precisely enough, and so we focused our research on unfinished staple yarn cotton fabrics. We would like to show that genetic programming can be used to establish the many relations between woven fabric constructional parameters and particular fabric properties, and that the results are more useful for fabric engineering than ideal theoretical models. The cotton fabrics varied according to yarn fineness (14 tex, 25 tex, and 36 tex), weave type (weave value), fabric tightness (55% - 65%, 65% - 75%, 75% - 85%), and denting. The constructional parameters of woven fabric samples are collected in Table 1. They were woven on a Picanol weaving machine under the same technological conditions. The weave values of plain (0.904), twill (1.188), and satin (1.379) fabrics, as well as fabric tightness, were determined according to Kienbaum's setting theory [36].

We used an optical method to measure porosity parameters of woven fabrics, since it is the most accurate technique for macro-pores with diameters of more than 10 μm. For each fabric specimen, we observed between 50 and 100 macro-pores using a Nikon SMZ-2T computer-aided stereomicroscope with special software. We measured the following macro-porosity parameters: area of macro-pore cross-section, pore density, and equivalent macro-pore diameters.

3.2. Predictive models of woven fabric porosity parameters

Equations 29 and 30 present predictive models of the area of macro-pore cross-section A_P and macro-pore density N_P, respectively [37]. Here *V* is the weave factor, *T* is the yarn linear density in tex, *t* is the fabric tightness in %, and *D* is the denting in ends per reed dent. The open porosity and equivalent diameter are calculated using Equations 17 and 19, respectively, where for Ap and Np the predicted values are taken into account. Because the model of the area of macro-pore cross-section is more complex, the functions $f_1, f_2, \ldots f_{10}$ are not presented here but are written in the appendix. When calculating the values of models, the following rules have to be taken into account: the protected division function returns to 1 if denominator is 0; otherwise, it returns to the normal quotient. The protected power function raises the absolute value of the first argument to the power specified by its second argument.

By a comparison of both GA models (Equations 29 and 30) with the theoretical ones (Equations 11-13 and 14), the complexity of GA models is obvious and derives from the factors involved in the models. Namely, factors involved in GA models don't ignore the irregularity of macro-pores cross-section area as well as the number of pores, due to the phenomenon of latticed pores in the case of staple yarns (which depends on the type of weave – factor V and fabric tightness – factor t) and the phenomenon of thread spacing irregularity (factor D), as theoretical models do. Theoretical model for the macro-pore cross-section area assumes that all macro-pores in woven structure have the same cross-section area regardless the type of used yarns, type of weave, fabric tightness and denting, whilst the theoretical model for the pore density assumes no reduction of the number of pores.

Ref.	Yarn linear density *T*, tex	Weave value *V*	Fabric tightness t, %	Denting *D*, ends/reed dent
1	14	0.904	62	2
2	14	0.904	70	2
3	14	0.904	84	2
4	14	1.188	62	3
5	14	1.188	70	3
6	14	1.188	80	3
7	14	1.379	59	5
8	14	1.379	69	5
9	14	1.379	79	5
10	25	0.904	62	2
11	25	0.904	73	2
12	25	0.904	83	2
13	25	1.188	63	2
14	25	1.188	73	2
15	25	1.188	84	2
16	25	1.379	60	2+3
17	25	1.379	70	2+3
18	25	1.379	81	2+3
19	36	0.904	62	1
20	36	0.904	71	1
21	36	0.904	83	1
22	36	1.188	63	2
23	36	1.188	72	2
24	36	1.188	83	2
25	36	1.379	58	2+3
26	36	1.379	65	2+3
27	36	1.379	79	2+3

Table 1. The constructional parameters of woven fabric samples

$$A_p = \frac{1}{V^2 t^2}\left(f_1 + \frac{t}{f_2 - f_3}\right)\cdot\left(f_8\left(f_9 + f_{10}\right) + TV\left(f_4 + f_7 + \frac{f_5 f_6}{t(T+t)}\right)\right) \tag{29}$$

$$N_p = \frac{(D+V)(D+t)\left(t + \dfrac{9+t}{T-V}\right)}{2.93+T} - \frac{D\left(t + \left(T + V - t + \dfrac{Vt}{D}\right)^{-7} + \dfrac{-1.4 + 2D + 0.95DV^{-1-T} + \dfrac{9+D+t}{-6.6+T}}{T + \dfrac{t}{D+V}}\right)}{(D+T)\left(1.055 - 0.8816V + \dfrac{D}{V\sqrt{\dfrac{T}{V^D}} - t}\right)} - \frac{D\left(\dfrac{D\left(1.05 - V - \dfrac{6.3}{(-1+D)DV^T}\right)}{DT - t} + \dfrac{t + \dfrac{T - \dfrac{t}{D}}{D+V^2}}{T + \dfrac{9.5+t}{D-T+V}}\right)}{1.055 - V + \dfrac{3.56 \cdot 5.18^V (D+T)}{V(1.05 + V + Tt)}} \tag{30}$$

Figure 10 presents a comparison of the experimental, predicted, and theoretical values of macro-porosity parameters. Theoretical values of macro-pore density are calculated on the basis of an ideal model of porous structure using Equation 14. By calculation of the theoretical values of the area of macro-pore cross-section, open porosity, and the equivalent pore diameter, the circular, rectangular, and elliptical shape of macro-pore area are taken into account.

Theoretical values of woven fabric porosity parameters deviate from experimental ones on average by 118.3% (min 8.8%, max 452.9%) for the area of the macro-pore with rectangular cross-section, 111.5% (min 14.5%, max 370.6%) for the area of the macro-pore with circular cross-section, 72.8% (min 0.2%, max 335.3%) for the area of the macro-pore with elliptical cross-section, 37.3% (min 0.0%, max 395.0%) for the macro-pore density, 232.6% (min 19.9%, max 1900.1%) for the open porosity of fabrics with rectangular pore cross-section, 221.0% (min 14.3%, max 1558.0%) for the open porosity of fabrics with circular pore cross-section, 166.3% (min 5.9%, max 1479.0%) for the open porosity of fabrics with elliptical pore cross-section, 43.7% (min 4.3%, max 135.1%) for the equivalent pore diameter where rectangular pore cross-section is taken into account, 43.7% (min 7.0%, max 116.9%) for the equivalent pore diameter where circular cross-section is taken into account, and 28.0% (min 0.1%, max 108.6%) for the equivalent pore diameter where elliptical pore cross-section is taken into account.

The results of woven fabric porosity parameters determined with models based on genetic programming show very good agreement with experimental values (Figure 11) and justify the complexity of GA models. The predicted values deviate from experimental ones on average by 1.5% (min 0.0%, max 10.2%) for the area of the macro-pore cross-section, 2.0% (min 0.0%, max 8.0%) for the macro-pore density, 3.2% (min 0.0%, max 10.1%) for the open porosity, and 0.8% (min 0.0%, max 5.2%) for the equivalent macro-pore diameter. The correlation coefficients between the predicted and experimental values are 0.9999, 0.9989, 0.9941, and 0.9997 for the area of macro-pore cross-section, macro-pore density, open porosity, and equivalent diameter, respectively.

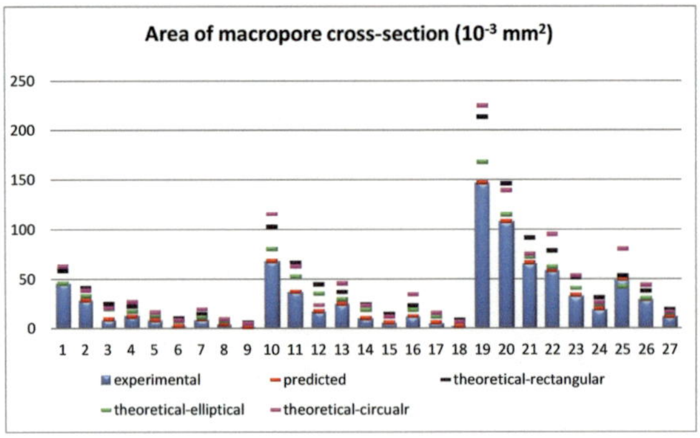

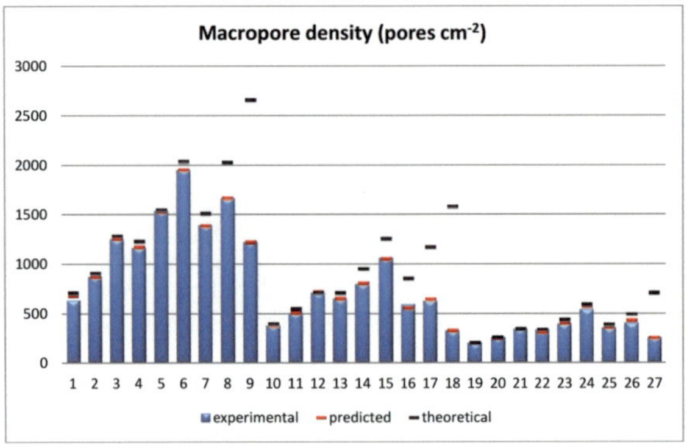

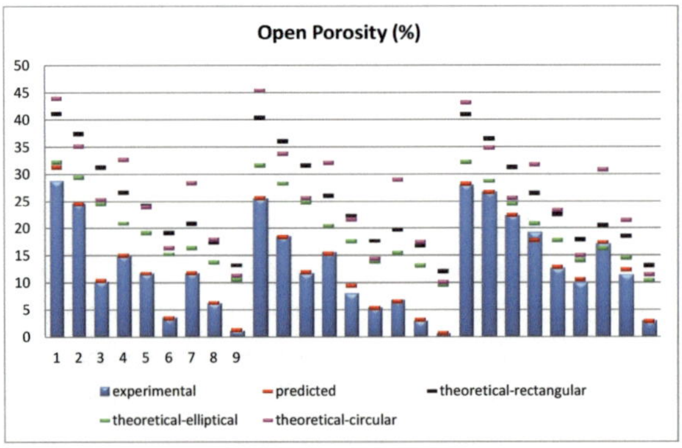

Figure 10. Results of woven fabric porosity parameters

The models are based on image analysis technique and assumption that woven samples are transparent. The boundary limits for the validity of the models are as follows: 1. the minimal values for yarn linear density, weave factor and fabric tightness, are 14 tex, 0.904, and 55%, respectively, 2. the maximal values for yarn linear density, weave factor and fabric tightness are 36 tex, 1.379, and 85%, respectively.

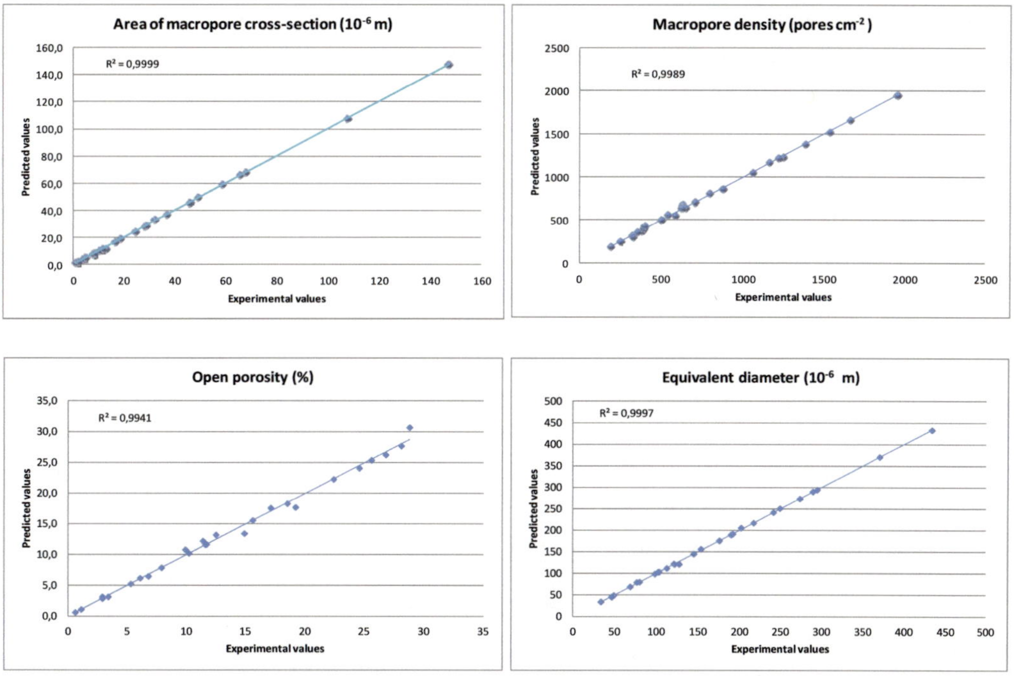

Figure 11. Scatter plots of experimental and predicted porosity parameters using GP models

4. The usage of genetic algorithm to predict nonwoven fabric porosity parameters

In this research, the genetic algorithm was used for definition of predictive models of nonwoven fabric porosity parameters. Since needle-punched nonwoven fabrics have completely different porous structure when compared to woven fabrics, it is inappropriate to focus on open porosity through the prediction of the area of macro-pore cross-section and macro-pore density. The most valuable porosity parameters for needle-punched nonwoven porous structure characterisations are total porosity and mean pore diameter, and those parameters were the subjects of our research. Since the basic steps in evolutionary computation are well-known, only a brief description follows. Firstly, the initial population *P(t)* of the random organisms (solutions) is generated. The variable *t* represents the generation time. The next step is the evaluation of population *P(t)* according to the fitness measure. Altering the population *P(t)* by genetic operations follows. The genetic operations alter one or more parental organism(s); thus, creating their offspring. The evaluation and alteration of population takes place until the termination criterion has been fulfilled. This can be the specified maximum number of generations or a sufficient quality of solutions [38]. More comprehensive information on evolutionary computation can be found in [39].

The independent input variables were fibre fineness - T (dtex), nonwoven fabric area mass - m (g/m^2), and nonwoven fabric thickness - D (mm). The dependent output variables were mean pore diameter d_p (μm) and total porosity ε (%). Since the GA approach is unsuitable for the evolution of prediction models (organisms) in their symbolic forms, it is necessary to define them in advance [38]. In this study, a quadratic polynominal equation with three variables was used as a prespecified model for the prediction of porosity parameters as follows:

$$Y = c_1 + c_2 m + c_3 D + c_4 T + c_5 m^2 + c_6 D^2 + c_7 T^2 + c_8 mD + c_9 mT + c_{10} DT + c_{11} mDT \tag{31}$$

where, Y is the dependent output variable, m is the nonwoven fabric mass per unit area in g/m², D is the nonwoven fabric thickness in mm, T is the fibre fineness in dtex, and $c_{1 \ldots 11}$ are constants. The main reasons for this selection were as follows: 1. a polynominal model is relatively simple, 2. for the problem studied we did not expect harmonic dependence of the output variables, 3. some preliminary modelling-runs with different types of prespecified models showed that the quadratic polynominal model provides very good selection in terms of prediction quality. In our research, the initial random population $P(t)$ consisted of N prespecified models (Equation 31) where N is the population size. Of course, in our computer implementation of the GA, the population $P(t)$ consisted only of the N sets of the real-valued vectors of model constants. The individual vector is equal to:

$$\mathrm{c} = (c_1, c_2, \cdots, c_{11}) \tag{32}$$

The absolute deviation $D(i,t)$ of individual model i (organism) in generation time t was introduced as a fitness measure. It was defined as:

$$D(i,t) = \sum_{j=1}^{n} \left| E(j) - P(i,j) \right| \tag{33}$$

where, $E(j)$ is the experimental value for measurement j, $P(i, j)$ is the predicted value returned by the individual model i for measurement j, and n is the maximum number of measurements. The goal of the optimisation task was to find such a predictive model (defined by Equation 31), that Equation 33 would give as low an absolute deviation as possible. Therefore, the aim was to find out appropriate real-valued constants in Equation 32. However, since it was unnecessary that the smallest values of the above equation also meant the smallest percentage deviation of this model, the average absolute percentage deviation of all measurements for individual model i was defined as:

$$\Delta(i) = \frac{D(i,t)}{| E(j) | \, n} \cdot 100\% \tag{34}$$

The Equation 33 was not used as a fitness measure for evaluating population, but only for finding the best organism within the population, after completing the run.

The altering of population $P(t)$ was effected by reproduction, crossover, and mutation. For the crossover operation, two parental vectors, e.g., c_1 and c_2 were randomly selected. Then the crossover took place between two randomly-selected parental genes having the same index. Two offspring genes were created according to the extended intermediate crossover, as considered by Mühlenbeim and Schlierkamp-Voosen [40]. During the mutation operation, one parental vector c was randomly selected. Then, the mutation took place in one randomly selected parental gene. During both the crossover and mutation processes, the numbers of crossover and mutational operations performed on parental vector(s), were randomly selected. The evolutionary parameters for modelling by genetic algorithms were: population size 300, maximum number of generations to be run 5000, probability of reproduction 0.1, probability of crossover 0.8 and probability of mutation 0.1. Tournament selection with a group size of 5 was used. For the purpose of the research 200 independent genetic algorithms runs were carried out. Only the best models are presented in the paper.

4.1. Materials and porosity measurements

Bearing in mind the fact that nonwovens have very different structures and, thus, also porosity parameters due to their sequences when web-forming, bonding, as well as finishing methods, the nonwoven fabric samples were limited to one type of nonwoven fabrics – those needle-punched nonwoven fabrics made from a mixture of polyester and viscose staple fibres. Nonwoven multi-layered webs were first obtained from the same manufacturing process by subjecting the fibre mixtures to carding and then orienting the carded webs in a cross-direction by using a cross lapper to achieve web surface mass ranges of 100-150, 150-200, 250-300, and 300-350 g/m^2, and a web volume mass range of 0.019-0.035 g/cm^3. The webs were made from a mixture of polyester (PES) and viscose (VIS) staple fibres of different content, fineness, and lengths, as follows: samples 1–3 from a mixture of 87% VIS fibres (1.7 dtex linear density, 38 mm length) and 12.5% of PES fibres (4.4 dtex linear density, 50 mm length), samples 4–7 from a mixture of 60% VIS fibres (1.7 dtex linear density, 38 mm length) and 40% PES fibres (3.3 dtex linear density, 60 mm length), samples 8–11 from a mixture of 30% VIS fibres (3.3 dtex linear density, 50 mm length), 40% PES fibres type 1 (6.7 dtex linear density, 60 mm length) and 30% of PES fibres type 2 (4.4 dtex linear density, 50 mm length), samples 12–15 from a mixture of 70% PES fibres type 1 and 30% PES type 2. Multi-layered carded webs were further subjecting to pre-needling using needle-punching machine, under the following processing parameters of one-sided pre-needle punching: stroke frequency 250/min; delivery speed 1.5 m/min; needling density 30/cm, depth of needle penetration 15 mm, and felting needles of 15x18x38x3 M222 G3017. The processing parameters of further two-sided needle-punching were as follows: stroke frequency 900/min; delivery speed 5.5 m/min; needling density 60/cm (30/cm upper and 30/cm lower), depth of upper and lower needle penetrations 12 mm, and felting needles of 15x18x32x3 M222 G3017. The webs were further processed through a pair of heated calendars at under 180 °C with different gaps between the rollers, in order to achieve further changes in fabric density and, consequently, in the porosity within the range of 80–92 %. The constructional parameters of the nonwoven fabric samples are collected in Table 2. All the nonwoven fabric samples were in a grey state to eliminate the influence of finishing treatments. The constructional parameters of the nonwoven fabric samples, e.g. the nonwoven fabric mass per unit area and thickness were measured according to ISO 9073-1 (Textiles – Test Methods for nonwovens – Part 1: Determination of mass per unit area) and ISO 9073-2 (Textiles – Test Methods for nonwovens – Part 2: Determination of thickness).

Ref.	Average fibre fineness T, dtex	Fabric mass per unit area m, g/m²	Fabric thickness D, mm
1	2.0	143	1.202
2	2.0	142	0.941
3	2.0	142	0.576
4	2.3	173	1.509
5	2.3	201	1.558
6	2.3	171	0.941
7	2.3	200	1.071
8	5.0	259	1.360
9	5.0	259	1.261
10	5.0	279	1.182
11	5.0	274	1.112
12	6.0	298	1.400
13	6.0	304	1.266
14	6.0	352	1.347
15	6.0	343	1.235

Table 2. The constructional parameters of nonwoven fabric samples

The porosity parameters of the nonwoven fabric samples were measured using the Pascal 140 computer aided mercury intrusion porosimeter, which measures pores' diameters between 3.8 - 120 μm, and operates under low pressure. The mercury intrusion technique is based on the principle that non-wetting liquid (mercury) coming in contact with a solid porous material can not be spontaneously absorbed by the pores of the solid itself because of the surface tension, but can be forced by applying external pressure. The required pressure depends on the pore-size and this relationship is commonly known as the Washburn equation [9]:

$$P = \frac{-2 \cdot \gamma \cdot \cos\theta}{r} \tag{35}$$

where, P is the applied pressure, ϒ is the surface tension of mercury, θ is the contact-angle and r is the capillary radius. The distribution of pore size, as well as the total porosity and the specific pore volume can be obtained from the relationship between the pressure necessary for penetration (the pore dimension) and the volume of the penetrated mercury (pore volume). There are certain main assumptions necessary when applying the Washburn equation: the pores are assumed to be of cylindrical shape and the sample is pressure stable.

Each nonwoven sample of known weight was placed in the dilatometer, then the air around the sample was evacuated and finally the dilatometer was filled with mercury by increasing the pressure up to the reference level. The volume and pressure measurements' data were transferred into the computer programme and the following data were detectable or calculated: the specific pore volume (mm³/g), the average pore diameter (μm) and the total porosity (%). The volume of penetrated mercury is directly the measure of the sample's pore volume expressed as a specific pore volume in mm^3/g, and is obtained by means of a capacitive reading system. The average pore diameter is evaluated at 50% of the cumulative volume of mercury.

4.2. Predictive models of nonwoven fabric porosity parameters

Equations 36 and 37 present predictive models of the total porosity ε and mean pore diameter d_p, respectively. Here T is the fibre fineness in dtex, m is the nonwoven fabric mass per unit area in g/m^2, and D is the nonwoven fabric thickness in mm.

$$\begin{aligned}\varepsilon &= 150.1 - 8.61\cdot 10^{-2} m + 3.21\cdot 10^{-2} D - 66.04\cdot T - 1.09\cdot 10^{-3} m^2 - 28.74\cdot D^2 + \\ &+0.89\cdot T^2 + 0.24\cdot m\cdot D + 0.20\cdot m\cdot T + 32.16\cdot D\cdot T - 0.10\cdot m\cdot D\cdot T\end{aligned} \tag{36}$$

$$\begin{aligned}d_p &= 103.12 - 0.39\cdot m + 6.01\cdot D - 0.73\cdot T - 2.12\cdot 10^{-3} m^2 - 30.77\cdot D^2 - 3.79\cdot T^2 + \\ &+0.46\cdot m\cdot D + 0.16\cdot m\cdot t + 1.13\cdot D\cdot T - 3.79\cdot 10^{-3}\cdot m\cdot D\cdot T\end{aligned} \tag{37}$$

Figure 12 presents a comparison of the experimental, predicted and theoretical values of porosity parameters, e.g. total porosity and mean pore diameter. The theoretical values of total porosity and mean pore diameters were calculated using Equation 22 and 27-28, respectively.

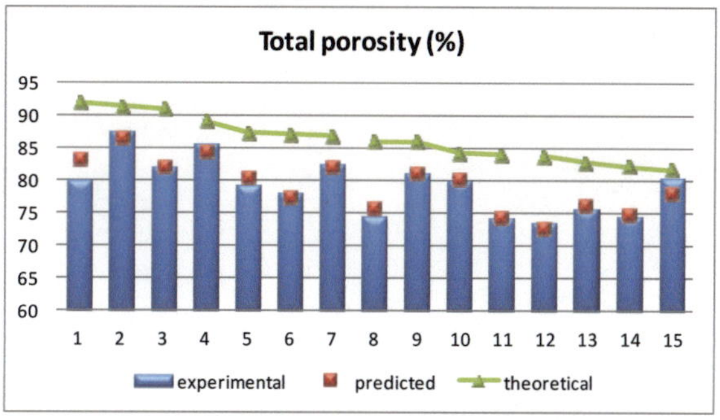

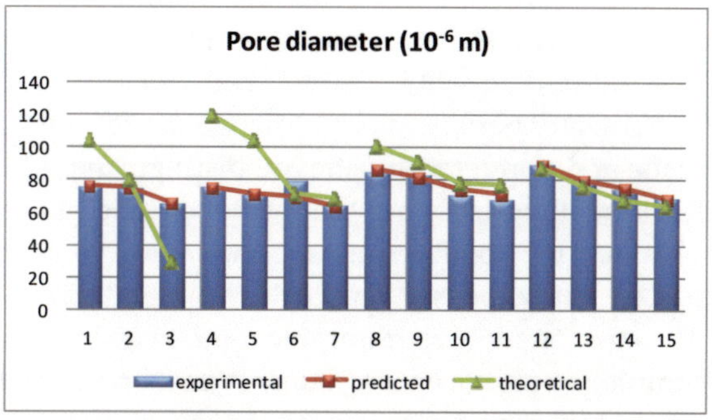

Figure 12. Results of nonwoven fabric porosity parameters

In Figure 12, the theoretical values of total porosity and mean pore diameter as well as predicted values of pore diameter are linked with lines while samples (1-3, 4-7, 8-11, and 12-15) are arranged regarding their decreased porosity. The results show that nonwovens with similar porous structure and lower porosity also have lower pore diameter. The experimental values of total porosity are for some samples not in a good agreement with theoretical ones, while samples which should have the highest porosity actually have the lowest (samples No. 1, 8, and 12). The reason may lie in fact, that these samples contain more closed pores which are not detectable with mercury porosimetry.

The results show that the theoretical values of porosity parameters deviate from experimental ones on average by 8.0% (min 0.0%, max 15.4%) for total porosity and by 19.7% (min 2.9, max 57.3%) for pore diameter, whilst the predicted values, calculated using Equations 36-37, are in better agreement with the experimental ones. The mean predicted error is: 1.1% (from 0.0% to 4.4%) for the total porosity and 1.9% (from 0.0% to 12.4%) for the average pore diameter. The correlation coefficients between the predicted and experimental values are 0.9024 and 0.8492 for the total porosity and the average pore diameter, respectively. Scatter plots of the experimental and predicted values for porosity parameters, are depicted in Figure 13.

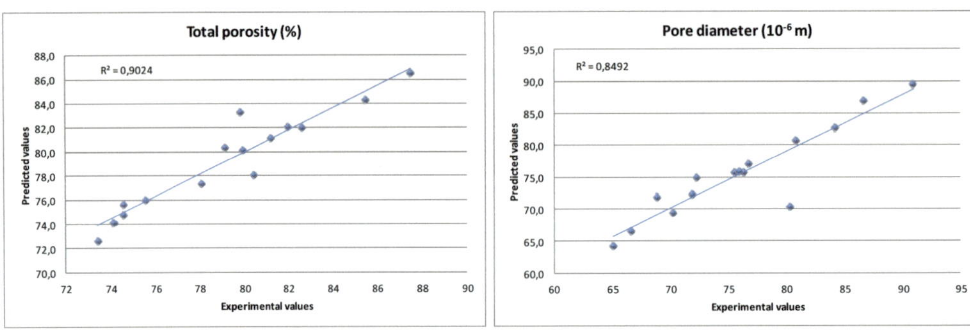

Figure 13. Scatter plots of experimental and predicted porosity parameters using GA models

5. Conclusion

By a new fabric developing, there is a need to know some relationships between the constructional parameters of fabrics and their predetermined end-usage properties in order to produce fabrics with desired quality. Fabric constructors develop a new fabric construction on the basis of their experiences or predictive models using different modelling tools of which deterministic and nondeterministic are distinguished. In general, the models obtained by deterministic modelling tools are the results of strict mathematical rules while in the case of models obtained by nondeterministic modelling tools, there are no precise, strict mathematical rules. Our study focused on the development of predictive models based on the genetic methods, e.g. genetic programming and genetic algorithms, in order to predict some porosity parameters of woven and nonwoven fabrics. Predictive models of the: 1. area of macro-pore cross-section and macro-pore density of woven fabrics based on the constructional parameters of woven fabrics (yarn linear density, weave factor, fabric tightness, denting), image analysis as testing method of porosity measurements, and genetic programming, and 2. total porosity and mean pore diameter of nonwoven fabrics based on the constructional parameters of nonwoven fabrics (fibre linear density, fabric mass per unit area, fabric thickness), mercury intrusion porosimetry as testing method of porosity measurements, and genetic algorithm, were developed. Open porosity and equivalent pore diameter of woven fabric were also predicted using values calculated on the basis of predictive models of the area of macro-pore cross-section and pore density, and known mathematical relationships. All proposed predictive models were created very precisely and could serve as guidelines for woven/nonwoven engineering in order to develop fabrics with the desired porosity parameters.

In general, for prediction of porosity parameters of woven or nonwoven samples both modelling tools can be used, e.g. GA and GP. Usually, GP method is used for more difficult problems. Our purpose was to show usability and effectiveness of both methods. By woven fabric modelling, the range of porosity parameters' measurements was substantial larger with more input variables when compared to the nonwoven fabrics (and this means more difficult problem), so the GP was used as modelling tool. By GP modelling, the models are developed in their symbolic forms, thus more precise models are developed in regard to the GA modelling, where only coefficients of prespecified models are defined. At the same time, for GP modelling more measurements data are desired for better model accuracy, while by GA modelling good results are achieved by lower number of measurements (in our case 27 measurements were available for woven fabrics and only 15 for nonwoven fabrics). The advantage of GP modelling is its excellent prediction accuracy, while its disadvantage is the complexity of the developed models. In general, by GA modelling, the developed models are simple but less accurate.

Author details

Polona Dobnik Dubrovski
Department of Textile Materials and Design, University of Maribor, Faculty of Mechanical Engineering, Slovenia

Miran Brezočnik
Department of Mechanical Engineering, University of Maribor, Faculty of Mechanical Engineering, Slovenia

Appendix

$$f_1 = 12.856 + \frac{T}{V} + \frac{T}{Dt} x \left(35.3 + D + \frac{6.43}{2D + \frac{2T^2}{Vt} - \frac{t}{D + \frac{4.74T^3}{t^2} + \frac{T(T-D)}{t}}} \right),$$

$$f_2 = -12.856 - D + T - \frac{2T^2}{Vt} + \frac{0.0727 \cdot V\ t^2}{T^2}$$

$$f_3 = T\left(\frac{7V}{T - 28.86V} + \frac{35.3 + D + \frac{0.5t}{T}}{V} + \frac{t}{\left(T - \frac{4.1739T}{V} + t\right)\left(D - \frac{4.1739T}{V} + t + \frac{0.5t}{T}\right)}\right)^{-1},$$

$$f_4 = 19.3 + 0.034\left(6.43 + T + \frac{2T^2}{V^2 t}\right) + \frac{2T^2}{Vt} - \frac{(28.86 - 2.37T - t)}{7.43 + D - 4.1739T + t + \frac{(T^2 + Dt)}{Vt}},$$

$$f_5 = T\left(\frac{T}{t} - 2.37\right)\left(77 + 4D + \frac{D + \frac{2(35.3 - D)T\left(35.3 + T + \frac{T}{V}\right)}{t^2}}{28.86 + T - \frac{4.1739T}{V} + V + t}\right), f_6 = \frac{V^2 t^2}{3.3T^2 + 28.86Vt - 0.98TVt} - T$$

$$f_7 = \frac{\frac{2T^2}{Vt} - \frac{t^3}{T^2(2T + t) + D(Tt - 2T^2 + t^2)}}{77 + 2D - Vt},$$

$$f_8 = 41.7137 + 2D + \frac{35.3 + D - \frac{4.1739T}{T^2 - 8.393t}}{V} + \frac{t}{35.3 + \frac{T}{V} - \frac{6.88T^2(35.3 + T)}{DVt^2} + t},$$

$$f_9 = \frac{35.3 + D}{V} + \left(\frac{35.3 + D + \frac{\frac{28.86}{V} + t + \frac{(T + t)(T - 0.29Vt}{V^2 t}}{T - \frac{4.1739T}{V} + t}}{6.43 + \frac{28.86T}{DV} - \frac{8.35(35.29 + 2D)T}{t}}\right)$$

$$f_{10} = \frac{28.86 + t + \frac{(28.86 - D)t - T^2}{\frac{2T^2}{V^2} - \frac{99.2Vt}{T} + t}\left(6.43 + \frac{Vt}{T - 0.24D}\left(D - \frac{4.1739T}{V} + 0.034TV + t\right)\right)}{41.7137 + D - \frac{16.786T^3}{DVt^2} - \frac{8.393T^2}{V^2 t} + \frac{Vt^2}{T(2.37T + t(V - 8.393))}}$$

6. References

[1] M. Brezočnik, The Usage of Genetic Programming in Intelligent Manufacturing Systems, Maribor: University of Maribor, Faculty of Mechanical Engineering, 2000.

[2] J.R. Koza, Genetic programming II, Massachusetts: The MIT Press, 1994.

[3] J.R. Koza, Genetic programming III, San Francisco: Morgan Kaufmann, CA, 1999.

[4] M. Brezocnik, J. Balic, "Emergence of intelligence in next-generation manufacturing systems", *Robot. Comput. Integrat. Manufact.*, Vol. 19, pp. 55-63, 2003.

[5] P. Udhayakumar and S. Kumanan, "Task Scheduling of AGV in FMS Using Non-Traditional Optimization Techniques", *Int. Journal of Simulation Modelling*, Vol. 9, pp. 28-39, 2010.

[6] N. Chakraborti, R. Sreevathsan, R. Jayakanth and B. Bhattacharya, "Tailor-made material design: An evolutionary approach using multi-objective genetic algorithms", *Computational Materials Science* , Vol. 45, pp. 1-7, 2009.

[7] S. Mohanty, B. Mahanty and P.K.J. Mohapatra, "Optimization of hot rolled coil widths using a genetic algorithm", *Materials and Manufacturing Processes* , Vol. 18, pp. 447-462, 2003

[8] M. Brezočnik and J. Balič, »A Genetic-based Approach to Simulation of Self-Organizing Assembly«, *Robot. Comput. Integrat. Manufact.*, Vol. 17, pp. 113-120, 2001.

[9] Porosimeter Pascal Instruction Manual, Milan: Thermo Electron S.p.A, 2004.

[10] K. L. Hatch, Textile Sciences, New York: West Publishing Company, 2000.

[11] P. Bajaj and A. Sengupta, »Protective Clothing«, in *Textile Progress*, Manchester, The Textile Institute, 1992, pp. 1-94.

[12] Y. Shoshani and Y. Yakubov, »A Model for Calculating the Noise Absorption Capacity of Nonwoven Fiber Webs«, *Textile Research Journal*, Vol. 69, pp. 519-526, 1999.

[13] M. Mohammadi and P. Banks-Lee, »Determing Effective Thermal Conductivity of Multilayered Nonwoven Fabrics«, *Textile Research Journal*, Vol. 73, pp. 802-808, 2003.

[14] N. Pan and P. Gibson, Thermal and moisture transport in fibrous materials, Cambridge: Woodhead Publishing Limited and CRC Press LLC, 2006.

[15] K. Dimitrovski, New Method for Assesment of Porosity in Textiles, Doctoral Disertation, Ljubljana: University of Ljubljana, Textile Department, 1996.

[16] B. Neckar and S. Ibrahim, »Theoretical Approach for Determing Pore Charachteristics Between Fibres«, *Textile Research Journal*, Vol. 73, pp. 611-619, 2003.

[17] G. Lombard, A. Rollin and C. Wolff, »Theoretical and Experimental Opening Sizes of Heat-Bonded Geotextiles«, *Textile Research Journal*, Vol. 59, pp. 208-217, 1989.

[18] M. J. Park, S. H. Kim, S. J. Kim, S. H. Jeong and J. Jaung, »Effect of Splitting and Finishing on Absorption/Adsorption Properties of Split Polyester Microfiber Fabrics«, *Textile Research Journal*, Vol. 71, pp. 831-840, 2001.

[19] K. Kaneko, »Determination of pore size and pore size distribution«, *Journal of Membrane Science*, Vol. 96, pp. 59-89, 1994.

[20] A. Jena and K. Gupta, »Liquid Extrusion Techniques for Pore Structure Evaluation of Nonwovens«, *International Nonwoven Journal*, Vol. 12, pp. 45-53, 2003.

[21] B. Xu, »Measurement of Pore Charachteristics in Nonwoven Fabrics Using Image Analysis«, *Clothing and Textiles Research Journal*, Vol. 14, pp. 81-88, 1996.

[22] Y. L. Hsieh, »Liquid Transport in Fabric Structures«, *Textile Research Journal,* Vol. 65, pp. 299-307, 1995.

[23] D. Jakšić and N. Jakšić, »Assessment of Porosity of Flat Textile Fabrics«, *Textile Research Journal,* Vol. 77, pp. 105-110, 2007.

[24] V. Nagy and L. M. Vas, »Pore Charachteristic Determination with Mercury Porosimetry in Polyester Staple Yarns«, *Fibres & Textiles in Eastern Europe,* Vol. 13, pp. 21-26, 2005.

[25] D. Jakšić, The Development of the New Method to Determine the Pore Size and Pore Size Distribution in Textile Products, Ljubljana: Faculty of Natural Sciences and Technology, Departmetn of Textile Technology, 1975.

[26] P. D. Dubrovski, The Influence of Woven Fabric Geometry on Porosity of Biaxial Fabrics, Doctoral Disertation, Maribor: University of Maribor, Faculty of Mechanical Engineeeing, 1999.

[27] P. D. Dubrovski, »Volume Porosity of Woven Fabrics«, *Textile Research Journal,* Vol. 70, pp. 915-919, 2000.

[28] P. D. Dubrovski, »A Geometrical Method to Predict the Macroporosity of Woven Fabrics«, *Journal of the Textile Institute,* Vol. 92, pp. 288-298, 2001.

[29] A. V. Kulichenko and L. Langenhove, »The Resistance to Flow Transmission of Porous Materials«, *Journal of the Textile Institute,* Vol. 83, pp. 127-132, 1992.

[30] J. C. Russ, The image Processing Handbook, CRC Press, 1996.

[31] A. T. Purdy, Needle-punching, Manchester: The Textile Institute, 1980, pp. 49.

[32] R. D. Anandjiwala and L. Boguslavsky, »Development of Needle-punched Nonwoven Fabrics from Flax Fibers for air Filtration Applications«, *Textile Research Journal,* Vol. 78, pp. 614-624, 2008.

[33] J. Mao and S. J. Rusell, »Modelling Permeability in Homogeneous Three-Dimensional Nonwoven Fabrics«, *Textile Research Journal,* Vol. 73, pp. 939-944, 2003.

[34] X. Chen, F. Vroman, M. Lewandowski and A. Perwuelz, »Study of the Influence of Fiber Diameter and Fiber Blending on Liquid Absorption Inside Nonwoven Structures«, *Textile Research Journal,* Vol. 79, pp. 1364-1370, 2009.

[35] A. Patanaik and R. Anandjiwala, »Some Studies on Water Permeability of Nonwoven Fabrics«, *Textile Research Journal,* Vol. 79, pp. 147-153, 2009.

[36] M. Kienbaum, »Gewebegeometrie and Produktenwicklung«, *Melliand Textilberichte,* Vol. 71, pp. 737-742, 1990.

[37] P. D. Dubrovski and M. Brezočnik, »Using Genetic Programming to predict the Macroporosity of Woven Cotton Fabrics«, *Textile Research Journal,* Vol. 72, pp. 187-194, 2002.

[38] M. Brezočnik, M. Kovačič and L. Gusel, »Comparison Between Genetic Algorithm and Genetic Programming Approach for Modelling the Stress Distribution«, *Material and Manufacturing Processes,* Vol. 20, pp. 497-508, 2005.

[39] T. Bäck, D. B. Fogel and Z. Michalewicz, Handbook of evalutionary computation, New York - Oxford: IOP Publishing and Oxford University Press, 1997.

[40] M. Gen and R. Cheng, Genetic algorithms and engineering design, Canada: John Wiley & Sons, Inc., 1997.

Chapter 9

Genetic Programming: A Novel Computing Approach in Modeling Water Flows

Shreenivas N. Londhe and Pradnya R. Dixit

Additional information is available at the end of the chapter

http://dx.doi.org/10.5772/48179

1. Introduction

The use of artificial intelligence in day to day life has increased since late 20th century as seen in many home appliances such as microwave oven, washing machine, camcorder etc which can figure out on their own what settings to use to perform their tasks optimally. Such intelligent machines make use of the soft computing techniques which treat human brain as their role model and mimic the ability of the human mind to effectively employ modes of reasoning that are approximate rather than exact. The conventional hard computing techniques require a precisely stated analytical model and often a lot of computational time. Premises and guiding principles of Hard Computing are precision, certainty, and rigor [1]. Many contemporary problems do not lend themselves to precise solutions such as recognition problems (handwriting, speech, objects and images), mobile robot coordination, forecasting, combinatorial problems etc. This is where soft computing techniques score over the conventional hard computing approach. Soft computing differs from conventional (hard) computing in that, unlike hard computing, it is tolerant of imprecision, uncertainty, partial truth, and approximation. The guiding principle of soft computing is to exploit the tolerance for imprecision, uncertainty, partial truth, and approximation to achieve tractability, robustness and low solution cost [1]. The principal constituents, i.e., tools, techniques of Soft Computing (SC) are Fuzzy Logic (FL), Neural Networks (NN), Evolutionary Computation (EC), Machine Learning (ML) and Probabilistic Reasoning (PR). Soft computing many times employs NN, EC, FL etc, in a complementary rather than a competitive way resulting into hybrid techniques like Adaptive Neuro-Fuzzy Interface System (ANFIS).

The application of soft computing techniques in the field of Civil Engineering started since early nineties and since encompassed almost all fields of Civil Engineering namely Structural Engineering, Construction Engineering and Management, Geotechnical

Engineering, Environmental Engineering and lastly Hydraulic Engineering which is the focus of this chapter. The technique of ANN is now well established in the field of Civil Engineering to model various random and complex phenomena. Other techniques such as FL and EL caught attention of many research workers as a complimentary or alternative technique to ANN, particularly after knowing the drawbacks of ANN [2]. The soft computing tool of Genetic Programming which is essentially classified as an Evolutionary Computation (EC) technique has found its foot in the field of Hydraulic Engineering in general and modeling of water flows in particular since last 12 years or so. Modeling of water flows is perhaps the most daunting task ever faced by researchers in the field of Hydraulic Engineering owing to the randomness involved in many natural processes associated with the water flows. In pursuit of achieving more and more accuracy in estimation/forecasting of water related variables the researchers have made of use Genetic Programming for various tasks such as forecasting of runoff with or without rainfall, forecasting of ocean waves, currents, spatial mapping of waves to name a few. The present chapter takes a stalk of the applications of GP to model water flows which will enable the future researchers who want to pursue their research in this field. The chapter is organized as follows. Next section deals with basics of GP. A review of applications of GP in the field of Ocean Engineering is presented in the next section followed by review of applications in the field of hydrology. Few applications in the field of Hydraulics are discussed in the subsequent section. It may be noted that papers published in reputed international journals are only considered for review. Two case studies are presented next which are based on publications of the first author. The concluding remarks and future scope as envisaged by the authors are discussed at the end.

2. The evolutionary computation

The paradigm of evolutionary processes distinguishes between an organism's genotype, which is constructed of genetic material that is inherited from its parent or parents, and the organism's phenotype, which is the coming to full physical presence of the organism in a certain given environment and is represented by a body and its associated collection of characteristics or phenotypic traits. Within this paradigm, there are three main criteria for an evolutionary process to occur as per [3] and they are

- Criterion of Heredity: Offspring are similar to their parents: the genotype copying process maintains a high fidelity.
- Criterion of Variability: Offspring are not exactly the same as their parents: the genotype copying process is not perfect.
- Criterion of Fecundity: Variants leave different numbers of offspring: specific variations have an effect on behavior and behavior has an effect on reproductive success.

The evolutionary techniques can be differentiated into four main streams of Evolutionary Algorithm (EA) development [4] namely Evolution Strategies (ES), Evolutionary Programming (EP), Genetic Algorithms (GA) and Genetic Programming (GP) [5]. However, all evolutionary algorithms share the common property of applying evolutionary processes in the form of selection, mutation and reproduction on a population of individual structures that undergo evolution. The criterion of heredity is assured through the application of a crossover operator, whereas the criterion of variability is maintained through the application of a mutation operator. A selection mechanism then 'favours' the more fit entities so that they reproduce more often, providing the fecundity requirement necessary for an evolutionary process to proceed.

3. Genetic programming:

Like genetic algorithm (GA) the concept of Genetic Programming (GP) follows the principle of 'survival of the fittest' borrowed from the process of evolution occurring in nature. But unlike GA its solution is a computer program or an equation as against a set of numbers in the GA and hence it is convenient to use the same as a regression tool rather than an optimization one like the GA. GP operates on parse trees rather than on bit strings as in a GA, to approximate the equation (in symbolic form) or computer program that best describes how the output relates to the input variables. A good explanation of various concepts related to GP can be found in [5] Koza (1992). GP starts with a population of randomly generated computer programs on which computerized evolution process operates. Then a 'tournament' or competition is conducted by randomly selecting four programs from the population. GP measures how each program performs the user designated task. The two programs that perform the task best 'win' the tournament. GP algorithm then copies the two winner programs and transforms these copies into two new programs via crossover and mutation operators i.e. winners now have the 'children.' These two new child programs are then inserted into the population of programs, replacing the two loser programs from the tournament. Crossover is inspired by the exchange of genetic material occurring in sexual reproduction in biology. The creation of offspring's continues (in an iterative manner) till a specified number of offspring's in a generation are produced and further till another specified number of generations are created. The resulting offspring at the end of all this process (an equation or a computer program) is the solution of the problem. The GP thus transforms one population of individuals into another one in an iterative manner by following the natural genetic operations like reproduction, mutation and cross-over. Figure 1 shows general flowchart of GP as given by [5].

The tree based GP corresponds to the expressions (syntax trees) from a 'functional programming language' [5]. In this type, Functions are located at the inner nodes; while leaves of the tree hold input values and constants. A population of random trees representing the programs is initially constructed and genetic operations are performed on these trees to generate individuals with the help of two distinct sets; the terminal set T and the function set F.

Population: These are the programs initially constructed from the data sets in the form of trees to perform genetic operations using Terminal set and Function set. The function set for a run is comprised of operators to be used in evolving programs eg. addition, subtraction, absolute value, logarithm, square root etc. The terminal set for a run is made up of the values on which the function set operates. There can be four types of terminals namely inputs, constant, temporary variables, conditional flags. The population size is the number of programs in the population to be evolved. Larger population can solve more complicated problem. The maximum size of population depends upon RAM of the computer and length of programs in the population.

4. Genetic operations

Cross over: Two individuals (programs) are chosen as per the fitness called parents. Two random nodes are selected from inside such program (parents) and thereafter the resultant sub-trees are swapped, generating two new programs. The resulting individuals are inserted into the new population. Individuals are increased by 2. The parents may be identical or different. The allowable range of cross over frequency parameter is 0 to 100%

Mutation: One individual is selected as per the fitness. A sub-tree is replaced by another one randomly. The mutant is inserted into the new population. Individuals are increased by 1. The allowable range of mutation frequency parameter is 0 to 100%

Reproduction: The best program is copied as it is as per the fitness criterion and included in the new population. Individuals are increased by 1. Reproduction rate = 100 – mutation rate – (crossover rate * [1 – mutation rate])

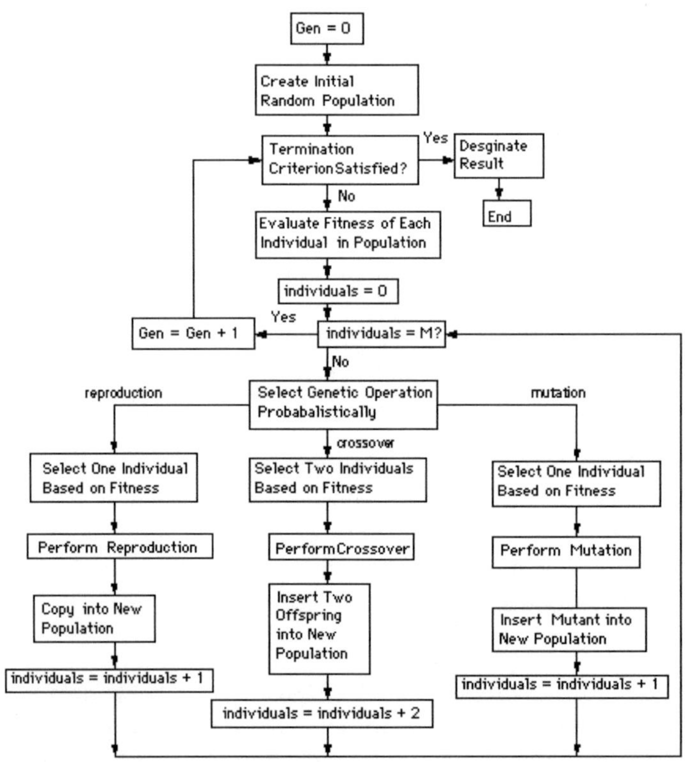

Figure 1. Flowchart of Genetic programming (Ref: [5])

The second variant of GP is Linear genetic Programming (LGP) which uses a specific linear representation of computer programs. The name 'linear' refers to the structure of the (imperative) program representation only and does not stand for functional genetic programs that are restricted to a linear list of nodes only. On the contrary, it usually represents highly nonlinear solutions. Each individual (Program) in LGP is represented by a variable-length sequence of simple C language instructions, which operate on the registers or constants from predefined sets. The function set of the system can be composed of arithmetic operations (+, - , X, /), conditional branches, and function calls (f {x, x^n, sqrt, e^x ,sin, cos, tan, log, ln }). Each function implicitly includes an assignment to a variable which facilitates use of multiple program outputs in LGP. LGP utilizes two-point string cross-over. A segment of random position and random length of an instruction is selected from each parents and exchanged. If one of the resulting children exceeds the maximum length, this cross-over is abandoned and restarted by exchanging equalized segments. An operand or operator of an instruction is changed by mutation into another symbol over the same set. The readers are referred to [7] and [8] for further details.

Gene-Expression Programming (GEP) is an extension of GP, developed by [5]. The genome is encoded as linear chromosomes of fixed length, as in Genetic Algorithm (GA); however, in GEP the genes are then expressed as a phenotype in the form of expression trees. GEP combines the advantages of both its predecessors, GA and GP, and removes their limitations. GEP is a full fledged genotype/phenotype system in which both are dealt with separately, whereas GP is a simple replicator system. As a consequence of this difference, the complete genotype/phenotype GEP system surpasses the older GP system by a factor of 100 to 60,000. In GEP, just like in other evolutionary methods, the process starts with the random generation of an initial population consisting of individual chromosomes of fixed length. The chromosomes may contain one or more than one genes. Each individual chromosome in the initial population is then expressed and its fitness is evaluated using one of the fitness function equations available in the literature. These chromosomes are then selected based on their fitness values using a roulette wheel selection process. Fitter chromosomes have greater chances of selection for passage to the next generation. After selection, these are reproduced with some modifications performed by the genetic operators. In Gene Expression Programming, genetic operators such as mutation, inversion, transposition and recombination are used for these modifications. Mutation is the most efficient genetic operator, and it is sometime used as the only means of modification. The new individuals are then subjected to the same process of modification, and the process continues until the maximum number of generations is reached or the required accuracy is achieved.

5. Why use GP in modeling water flows?

It is a known fact that many variables in the domain of Hydraulic Engineering are of random nature having a complex underlying phenomenon. For example the generation of ocean waves which are primarily functions of wind forcing is a very complex procedure. Forecasting of the ocean waves is an essential prerequisite for many ocean-coastal related activities. Traditionally this is done using numerical models like WAM and SWAN. These models are extremely complex in development and application besides being highly computation-intensive. Further they are more useful for forecasting over a large spatial and temporal domain. The accuracy levels of wave forecasts obtained through such numerical models again leaves scope for exploration of alternative schemes. These numerical models suffer from disadvantages like requirement of exogenous data, complex modeling procedure, rounding off errors and large requirement of computer memory and time and there is no guarantee that the results will be accurate. Particularly when point forecasts were required the researchers therefore used the data driven techniques namely ARMA, ARIMA and since last two decades or so the soft computing technique of Neural Networks. A comprehensive review of applications of ANN in Ocean Engineering is done by [9]. Although wave forecasting models were developed using Artificial Neural Networks by many research workers their was scope for use of another data driven techniques in that the ANN based models generally were unable to forecast extreme events with reasonable accuracy and the accuracy of forecasts decreases with increase in lead time as reported in many research papers. This became an ideal situation for the entry of another soft computing tool of GP which functions in a completely different way than ANN in that it does not involve any transfer function and evolves generations and generations of 'offspring' based on the 'fitness criteria' and genetic operations as explained in the earlier section the researchers thought, may be useful to capture the underlying trends better than ANN technique and can be used as a regressive tool. Same can be said about another important variable in hydraulic engineering "runoff or stream flow".

The rainfall -runoff modeling is very complex procedure and many numerical schemes are available as well as a large number of attempts by ANNs are also been made [2, 10, 11]. Thus Genetic Programming entered in rainfall-runoff modeling. It was also found that GP results were superior to that of M5 Model Trees another data driven modeling technique [12, 13]. Apart from these two variables the use of GP for modeling for many hydraulic engineering processes was found necessary for similar reasons. A review of these applications particularly in Ocean Engineering, Hydrology and Hydraulics (all grouped under Hydraulic Engineering) will be presented in the next three sections.

6. Applications in ocean engineering

As mentioned earlier papers published in reputed international journals are considered in this chapter. Primarily the applications of GP in Ocean Engineering were found for modeling of oceanic parameters like waves, water levels, zero cross wave periods, currents, wind, sediment transport and circular pile scour. Table 1 shows applications of GP in the field of Ocean Engineering listed chronologically followed by their review. This will facilitate the reader to have a glance of the work which would be presented next.

REF. NO.	YEAR	AUTHOR	TITLE OF PAPER	JOURNAL/PUBLICATION
14	2007	Kalra R., Deo M.C.	Genetic Programming to retrieve missing information in wave records along the west coast of India	Applied Ocean Research
25	2007	Singh, A. K., Deo M.C., Sanil Kumar V.	Combined Neural network – genetic programming for sediment transport	Journal of Maritime Engineering, The Institution of Civil Engineers, Issue MAO
16	2007	Charhate S. B., Deo M. C., Sanil Kumar V.	Soft and Hard Computing Approaches for Real Time Prediction of Currents in a Tide Dominated Coastal Area	Journal of Engineering for the Maritime Environment. Proceedings of the Institution of Mechanical Engineers, London, M4
15	2008	Ustoorikar K.S., Deo, M. C.	Filling up Gaps in wave data with Genetic Programming	Marine Structures
18	2008	Jain., P., Deo M. C.	Artificial intelligence tools to forecast ocean waves in real time	The Open Ocean Engineering Journal
22	2008	Charhate, S. B., Deo, M. C., Londhe S. N.	Inverse modeling to derive wind parameters from wave measurements	Applied Ocean Research
17	2008	Gaur, S., and Deo, M. C.	Real time wave forecasting using genetic programming	Ocean Engineering
06	2008	Londhe S. N.	Soft computing approach for real-time estimation of missing wave heights	Ocean Engineering
23	2009	Charhate, S. B., Deo, M. C., Londhe S. N.	Genetic programming for real time prediction of offshore wind	International Journal of Ships and Offshore Structures
26	2009	Guven, A., Azmathulla, H. Md., Zakaria, N.A.	Linear genetic programming for prediction of circular pile scour	Ocean Engineering
24	2009	Daga, M., Deo, M. C.	Alternative data-driven methods to estimate wind from waves by inverse Modeling	Natural Hazards, 49(2), 293-310
08	2009	Guven, A.	Linear genetic programming for time-series modelling of daily flow rate	Journal of Earth Syst. Sci., 118(2), 137-146

19	2010	Kambekar, A. R., Deo, M. C.	Wave simulation and forecasting using wind time history and data driven Methods	Ships and Offshore Structures
20	2010 a	Ghorbani, M. A. , Makarynskyy, O., Shiri, J., Makarynska, D.	Genetic Programming for Sea Level Predictions in an Island Environment	International Journal of Ocean and Climatic systems
21	2010 b	Ghorbani, M. A., Khatibi, R., Aytek, A., Makarynskyy, O., Shiri, J.	Sea water level forecasting using genetic programming and comparing the performance with Artificial Neural Networks	Computers and Geosciences
12	2012	Kambekar, A. R., Deo, M. C.	Wave Prediction Using Genetic Programming And Model Trees	Journal of Coastal Research, Doi: 10.2112/Jcoastres-D-10-00052.1, 28(1), 43-50

Table 1. Applications of GP in Ocean Engineering

One of the earlier applications was done to retrieve missing information in wave records along the west coast of India [14]. Such a need arises many times due to malfunctioning of instrument or drift of wave measuring buoy making it inoperative as a result of which data is not measured and it is lost forever. Filling up the missing significant wave height (Hs) values at a given location based on the same being collected at the nearby station(s) was done using GP. The wave heights were measured at an interval of 3 hours. Data at six locations around Indian coastline was used in this exercise. Out of the total sample size of four years the observations for the initial 25 months were used to evaluate the final or optimum GP program or equation while those for the last 23 months were employed to validate the performance and achieve gap in-filling with different quanta of missing information. It was found that both tree based and linear GP models worked in similar fashion as far as accuracy of estimation was considered. The data was made available by National Institute of Ocean Technology (NIOT) under the National Data Buoy Programme implemented by the Department of Ocean Development, Government of India from January 2000 to December 2003 (www.niot.res.in). The initial parameters selected for a GP run were as follows: initial population size = 500; mutation frequency = 95%; crossover frequency = 50%. The fitness criterion was the mean squared error.

When the similar work was also carried out using ANN it was found that GP produces results that are marginally more satisfactory than ANN. Another exercise was also carried out especially to estimate peaks by calibrating a separate model for high wave data which showed a marginal improvement in prediction of peaks. A similar exercise was carried out by [15], albeit in altogether different area of Gulf of Mexico near the USA coastline. Gaps in hourly significant wave height records at one location were filled by using the significant wave heights at surrounding 3 locations at same time instant and the soft tool of GP and

ANN. In all data spanning over 4 years was used for the study. The exercise was carried out for 4 locations in the Gulf of Mexico. The data can be downloaded from www.ndbc.noaa.gov. The typical value of the population size was 500, number of generations 15 and number of tournaments 90,00,000. The mutation and the cross-over frequency also varied for different testing exercises and it ranged from 20% to 80%. The fitness criterion was the mean squared error between actual observations and corresponding predictions.

The suitability of this approach was also tried for different gap lengths ranging from 1 day to 1 month and it was concluded on the basis of 3 error measures that the accuracy of gap filling decreases with increase in the gap length. The accuracy of the results were also judged by calculating statistical parameters of the wave records without gaps filled and with gaps filled using GP model. When the gap lengths did not exceed 1 or 5 days all the four statistics were faithfully reproduced. Compared to ANN GP produced marginally better results. In both the cases Linear Genetic Programming technique was employed.

In another earlier works of GP current predictions over a time step of twenty minutes, one hour, 3 hours, 6 hours, 12 hours and 24 hours at 2 locations in the tidal dominated area of the Gulf of Khambhat along west coast of India was carried out using two soft techniques of ANN and GP and 2 hard techniques of traditional harmonic analysis and ARIMA [16]. The work involved antecedent values of current only to forecast the current for various lead times at these locations. The fitness function selected was the mean square error, while the initial population size was 500, mutation frequency was 95%, and the crossover frequency was kept at 50%. The authors concluded that the model predictions were better for alongshore currents and small interval of times. For cross shore currents ARIMA performs better than ANN and GP even at longer prediction intervals. In general the three data driven techniques performed better than harmonic analysis. The new technique GP performed at par with ANN if not better. Perhaps the only drawback of the work was that the data (spanning over 7 months) is less than a year indicating that all possible variations in data set were not presented while calibrating the model making it susceptible when it is used at operational level.

Online wave forecasts over lead times of 3, 6, 12 and 24 hours were carried out at two locations in the gulf of Mexico using past values of wave heights (3 in number) and the soft computing technique of GP [17]. The data measured from 1999 to 2004 was available for free download on the web site of National Buoy Centre (http://www.ndbc.noaa.gov). The data belonged to the hourly wave heights measured over a period of 15 years with an extensive testing period of about 5 years which is the most in the papers reported till this time (with ANN as modeling tool). The locations chosen were differing to a large extent in that one was a deep water buoy and the other was a coastal buoy. The work was different from others in one aspect that monthly models were developed instead of routine yearly models. However any peculiar effect of this either good or bad on forecasting accuracy was not evident from the 3 error measures calculated. Though the results of GP were promising (high correlation coefficients for 3 and 6 hr forecast) the forecasting accuracy decreased for longer lead times of 12 hr and 24 hr. It was found that the results of GP were superior to ANN. For GP model the initial population size was 500 while the number of generations was 300. The mutation frequency was 90 percent while the cross over frequency was 50 percent. Values of these control parameters were selected initially and thereafter varied in trials till the best fitness measures were produced. The fitness criterion was the mean squared error between the actual and the predicted value of the significant wave height. Another exercise on real time forecasting of waves for warning times up to 72 hours at three locations along the Indian coastline using alternative techniques of ANN, GP and MT was carried out by [18]. The data was measured from 1998 to 2004 by the national data buoy program (www.niot.res.in). Forecasting waves up to 72hr and that too with reasonable accuracy is itself a specialty of this work. The data had many missing values which were filled by using temporal as well as spatial correlation approaches. Both MT and GP results were competitive with that of the ANN forecasts and hence the choice of a model should depend on the convenience of the user. The selected tools were able to forecast satisfactorily even up to a high lead time of 72 hrs. The authors have rightly stated that this accuracy was possible in the moderate ocean environment around Indian coastline where the target waves were less than around 6 m and 2.5 m for the offshore and coastal stations respectively. The paper does not provide any information about the initial parameters chosen for implementing GP. The significant wave height and average wave period at the current and subsequent 24 hr lead time were predicted from continuous and past 24-hourly measurements of wind speeds and directions as well as two soft computing techniques of GP and MT [19]. The data collected at 8 locations in Arabian Sea and Indian Ocean (www.niot.res.in) was used to develop both hind-casting and forecasting models. Both the methods, GP and MT, performed satisfactorily in the given task of wind wave simulation as reflected in high values of the error statistics of R, R^2, CE and low values of MAE, RMSE and SI. This is noteworthy since MT is not purely non-linear like GP. Although the magnitudes of these statistics did not indicate a significant difference in the relative performance of GP and MT, qualitative scatter diagrams and time histories showed the tendency of MT to better estimate the higher waves. Forecasting at higher lead times were fairly accurate compared to the same at lower ones. In general the performance of wave period was less satisfactory than that of wave height and this can be expected in view of a highly varying nature of wave period values. For details regarding the initial GP parameters involved in calibration readers are referred to the original paper where an exhaustive list of parameters is given. Lately [12], extended their earlier work by forecasting Significant wave height and zero cross wave period over time intervals of 1 to 4 days using the current and previous values of wind velocity and wind direction at 2 locations around the Indian coastline. It was found out that best results were possible when the length of the input sequence matched with that of the output lead time. As observed earlier here also it was found that the accuracy of prediction decreases with increase in lead time. However the results were satisfactory for 4 days ahead predictions also. In general it was observed that results of MT were slightly inferior to that of GP. Separate models were also developed to account for the monsoon (rainfall season in India) which showed a considerable improvement over yearly models. The models calibrated at one location when applied for another nearby locations also shown satisfactory performance provided both sites have spatial homogeneity in terms of openness, long offshore distances and deep water conditions. This work used tree based GP where as earlier mentioned three works used Linear Genetic Programming.

GP was used to forecast sea levels averaged over 12 h and 24 h time intervals for time periods from 12 to 120 h ahead at the Cocos (Keeling) Islands in the Indian Ocean [20]. The model produced high quality predictions over all considered time periods. The presented results demonstrates the suitability of GP for learning the non-linear behavior of sea level variations in terms of the R^2 (with values no lower than 0.968), MSE (with values generally smaller than 431) and MARE (no larger than 1.94%). This differs from earlier applications particularly for wave forecasting in that for forecasting of waves it was difficult to achieve higher order accuracy in terms of r, rmse and other error measures for as far as 24 hour forecast. Perhaps the recurring nature of sea water levels (the deterministic tidal component which is inherent in water level, is the reason behind this high level accuracy. In order to assess the ability of GP model relative to that of the ANN technique, a comparison was performed in terms of the above mentioned statistics. The developed GP model was found to perform better than the used ANNs. In the current work, the linear genetic programming approach was employed. The water level at Hillary's Boat Harbor, Australia was predicted three time steps ahead using time series averaged over 12hr, 24hr, 5 day and 10 day time interval and the soft tool of GP [21]. The results are compared with ANN. Total 12 years of data was used out of which 3 years of data is used for model validation. Tree based GP was used. The results of 12 hr averaged input data were found to be better than 24 hr averaged input data and in general the accuracy of prediction reduced for higher lead times. For both the cases GP results were better than ANN. For 5 day averaged inputs performance of GP was inferior to that of ANN though it improved for 10 day averaged inputs. It may be noted that the input data is averaged over 12hr, 24hr, 5days and 10 days which means there is possibility of loss of information which can be major draw back of this work. For both the above works the hourly sea-level records from a SEA-level Fine Resolutions Acoustic Measuring Equipment (SEA-FRAME) station were used. The information about initial parameters of GP is however not mentioned in both the works.

Estimation of wind speed and wind direction using the significant wave height, zero cross wave period, average wave period and the soft tools of ANN and GP was carried out at 5 locations around Indian coastline [22]. The paper has three folds in that in the first attempt both ANN and GP were tried for estimating the wind speed in which GP was found better and therefore in the second fold GP was only used to determine both wind speed and direction by calibrating the model by splitting of wind vector into two components. Two variants of GP, one based on Tree based approach and the other on Linear Genetic Programming were also tried though the accuracy of estimation for both the approaches was at par. In the third fold a network of wave buoys were formed and wind direction and wind speed at one location was estimated using the same at other locations. This was also done by combining data of all locations and making a regional model. All the attempts yielded highly satisfactory results as far as accuracy of estimation is considered. It was also confirmed that for estimation of only wind speed the non-splitting of wind velocity gives better results. Similarly wind speed and its directions were predicted for intervals of 3hr, 6hr, 9hr, 12hr and 24 hr at locations along the west coast of India using two soft computing techniques of ANN and GP and previous values of the same [23]. It was found that GP rivaled ANN predictions at all the cases and even bettered it particularly for open sea location. The results for prediction of wind speed and wind direction together were better when training of GP and ANN models was done on the basis of splitting of wind vector into two components along orthogonal directions although a separate model for wind speed alone was better (as shown by [22]). In general long interval predictions were less accurate compared to short interval predictions for both the techniques. Data for one location was for about 1.5 years while for the other location it was for 3 years. A discussion on appropriate use of statistical measures to assess the model accuracy was also presented. A similar work was carried out to estimate the wind speed at 5 locations around the Indian coastline using the wave parameters and 3 data driven techniques namely GP (program based- tree type), MT and another data driven tool of Locally weighted projection regression (LWPR) by [24]. All models showed tendency to underestimate higher values in given records. When all of the eight error statistics employed were viewed together, no single method appeared distinctly superior to others, but the use of an average evaluation index EI which they have suggested in this work gave equal weightage to each measure showed that the GP was more acceptable than other methods in carrying out the intended inverse modeling. Separate GP models were developed to estimate higher wind speeds that may be encountered in stormy conditions. At all the locations, these models indicated satisfactory performance of GP although with a fall in accuracy with increase in randomness. For all the above works the data was measured by national data buoy program of India (www.niot.res.in) however no mention is made about the initial parameters chosen for GP implementation.

The estimation of longshore sediment transport rate at an Indian location was carried out using GP and combined GP-ANN models [25]. The data was actually measured by one of the authors in his field study. The inputs were significant wave height, zero cross wave period, breaking wave height, breaking wave angle and surf zone width. The limitation of the work was the amount of data (81) used for training and testing of the models. The choice of control parameters was as follows: initial population size = 500; mutation frequency = 95%; crossover frequency = 50%. The initial trial with GP yielded reasonable results (r = 0.87). However by first training the ANN with same inputs and using the output as input for GP model yielded better results (r = 0.92). Thus the paper shows that combined ANN-GP model is more attractive than single GP model. It may be noted this is a kind of work done in the domain of Ocean Engineering wherein a different parameter (sediment transport rate) is modeled rather than the usual parameters of waves, periods etc. Another different work was carried out by [26], for prediction of scour depth due to ocean/lake waves around a pile/pier in medium dense silt and sand bed using Linear Genetic Programming and Adaptive Neuro-Fuzzy Inference system and measured laboratory data. For initial GP parameters readers are referred to actual paper where in an exhaustive list of parameters is provided. The study was carried out in both dimensional and non-dimensional form in which non-dimensional form yielded better results. The relative importance of input parameters on scour process was also investigated by first using all the influential parameters as inputs and then removing them one by one and observing the results. The drawback of the work is perhaps the small number of data used in model making (total 38 data, 28 of which is used for training the model) which may be impediment in operational use of this model. The results were found to be superior to ANFIS results.

In all the above cases where GP is compared with another data driven technique like ANN, MT or LWPR it was found that GP is superior to all of them in terms of accuracy of results. However it can be said that GP needs to be explored further particularly for prediction of extreme events like water levels, wave heights during hurricanes. A detailed study on effect of variation of GP control parameters like initial population, mutation, crossover percentage etc. on model accuracy is now need of the day. Similarly the critic on other approaches about decreasing forecasting accuracy with increase in the lead time seems to be true for GP as well. This needs more attention if GP is here to stay.

7. Applications in hydrology

Table 2 exhibits the applications of GP in Hydrology chronologically which are reviewed in this paper. The table also indicates that the applications of GP to the field of Hydrology started much earlier as compared to Ocean Engineering.

Genetic Programming is used in Hydrology (science of water) for various purposes such as modeling of phenomena like rainfall-runoff process, evapo-transpiration, flood routing, stage-discharge curve. The GP approach was applied to the flow prediction of the Kirkton catchment in Scotland (U.K.) [27]. The results obtained were compared to those attained using optimally calibrated conceptual models and an ANN. The data sets selected for the modeling process were rainfall, streamflow and Penman open water evaporation. The data used for calibration was of 610 days while that of validation was of 1705 days. The models were developed with preceding values of rainfall, evaporation and stream flow for predicting stream flow one time step ahead. Two conceptual models as well as ANN were employed for developing the stream flow forecasting model. It was observed that the rainfall data was the most influencing factor on the output. All models performed well in terms of forecasting accuracy with GP performing better. The paper does not give any details about the values of the parameters used for calibration of GP model. In another work one day ahead forecasting of runoff knowing the rainfall and runoff of the previous days and the soft computing tool of Linear Genetic Programming was carried out in Lindenborg catchment of Denmark by [28]. The models were developed for forecasting runoff as well as variation of runoff by using previous values of variation of discharge as input as well as previous values of discharge as input along with rainfall information. It was found that it was necessary to include information of discharge rather than variation of discharge. The model predicting discharge gave wrong local peaks in the low regime where as models predicting variation of discharge gave less wrong peaks in the low flow. Both the models had difficulty in predicting high peaks. The models were also developed using ANN. The author concluded that GP is more efficient in peak flow prediction where as ANNs were better in dealing with the noise. The author suggested specialized model for each type of flow to improve the

REF. NO.	YEAR	AUTHOR	TITLE OF PAPER	JOURNAL/PUBLICATION
27	1999	Savic A.D., Walters, G. A., Davidson J.W	A genetic Programming approach to rainfall-runoff modeling	Water Resources Management
28	1999	Drecourt J	Application of Neural Networks and Genetic Programming to Rainfall Runoff Modeling.	Danish Hydraulic Institute (Hydro-Informatics Techonologies - HIT)
29	2001	Whigham, P. A., Crapper, P. F.	Modeling rainfall runoff using Genetic Programming	Mathematical and Computer Modelling,
30	2001	Khu, S. T., Liong, S. U., Babovic, V., Madsen, H., Muttil, N.	Genetic Programming And Its Application In Real-Time Runoff Forecasting	Journal of American Water Resources Association
31	2002	Babovic, V., Keijzer, M.	Rainfall runoff modeling Based on Genetic programming	Nordic Hydrology
32	2007	Sivapragasam,C., Maheswaran, R., Venkatesh, V.	Genetic programming approach for flood routing in natural channels	Hydrological processes
33	2007	Parasuraman, K., Elshorbagy, A., Carey, S. K.	Modelling the dynamics of the evapotranspiration process using genetic Programming	Hydrological Sciences
34	2010	El. Baroudy, I., Elshorbagy, A., Carey, S. K., Giustolisi., O., Savic, D	Comparison of three data-driven techniques in modeling the evapotranspiration process	Journal of Hydroinformatics
13	2010	Londhe, S. N. and Charhate S. B.	Comparison of data driven modeling techniques for river flow forecasting	Hydrological sciences
35	2011	Azmathullah, MD., Ghani, A. AB., Leow, C. S., Chang., C. K., Zakaria, N. A.	Gene-Expression Programming for the Development of a Stage-Discharge Curve of the Pahang River	Water Resource Management

Table 2. Applications of GP in Hydrology

accuracy at peak prediction. He also suggested coupling of black box models with gray models. No specific information is provided about the initial values of GP parameters. The rainfall-runoff relationship in two different catchments was discovered by [29] using GP. The results obtained with a deterministic lumped parameter model, based on the unit hydrograph approach were compared with those obtained using a stochastic machine learning model of GP. For the Welsh catchment in UK, the results between the two models were similar. Since rainfall and runoff were highly correlated, the deterministic assumption underlying the IHACRES model (deterministic) was satisfied. Therefore, IHACREX could achieve a satisfactory correlation between calibration and simulation data. The GP approach which did not require any causal relationships achieved similar results. The behavior of the studied Australian catchment is very different from the Welsh catchment. The runoff ratio was very low (7%), and hence, the a priori assumptions of IHACRES (and other deterministic models) were **a** poor representation of the real world. This was demonstrated by the inability of IHACREJS to use more than one season's data for calibration purposes and only able to use data from a high rainfall period. Since the GP approach did not make any assumptions about the underlying physical processes, calibration periods over more than one season could be used. These led to significantly improved generalizations for the modeled behavior of the catchment. In summary, either approach worked satisfactorily when rainfall and runoff were correlated. However, when this correlation was poor, the CFG-GP had some advantages because it did not assume any underlying relationships. This is particularly important when considering the modeling of environmental problems, where typically the relationships are nonlinear, and are often measured at a scale which does not match with conceptual or deterministic modeling assumptions. Readers are referred to original paper for details of parameters setting for evolving the rainfall-runoff model. In their work of GP in hydrology, [30] first used a simple example of the Bernoulli equation to illustrate how GP symbolically regresses or infers the relationship between the input and output variables. An important conclusion from this study was that non-dimensionalizing the variables prior to symbolic regression process significantly enhance the success of GSR (Genetic Symbolic Regression). GP was then applied to the problem of real-time runoff forecasting for the Orgeval catchment in France. GP functions as an error updating procedure complementing the rainfall-runoff model, MIKE11/ NAM. Ten storm events were used to infer the relationship between the NAM simulated runoff and the corresponding prediction error. That relationship was subsequently used for real-time forecasting of six storm events. The results indicated that the proposed methodology was able to forecast different storm events with great accuracy for different updating intervals. The forecast hydrograph performs well even for a long forecast horizon of up to nine hours. However, it was found that for practical applications in real-time runoff forecasting, the updating interval should be less than or equal to the time of concentration of the catchment. The results were also compared with two known updating methods such as the auto-regression and Kalman filter. Comparisons showed that the proposed scheme, NAM-GSR, is comparable to these methods for real time runoff forecasting. Readers are referred to original paper for details of initial values of various parameters used in calibrating the GP model. The rainfall-runoff models were created on the basis of data alone as well as in combination with conceptual models and Genetic Programming [31]. The study was carried out in Orgeval catchment of France having an area about 104 km^2 using hourly rainfall runoff data of 10 storms for calibration and 6 storms for testing the models. The models were calibrated to forecast the temporal difference between the current and future discharge rather than absolute value of discharge for the lead times of 1 to 12 hours. In fact the paper discusses the phase lag associated with temporal time series forecasting models and removal of it by forecasting the temporal difference. The results were superior to conceptual numerical model. The model was then calibrated using a hybrid method in that the surface runoff value was first forecasted by using a conceptual forecasting model and then using the simulation error and GP to forecast the stream flow. The hybrid models provided a many fold improvement over the raw GP models. The paper in our opinion serves as a basic paper in the field of application of GP in Hydrology and readers may read the paper in original for all details about the GP models developed. The details are not produced here to save the space. Linear Genetic Programming technique was used to predict daily river discharge one day ahead using previous values of the same at Schuylkill River at Berne, PA, USA [8]. Additionally the models were developed using multilayer perceprton as well as Generalized Regression Neural Networks (GRNN). The statistical ARMA method was also used to develop the stream flow forecasting model. The results showed that both LGP and NN techniques predicted the daily time series of discharge with quite good agreement as indicated by high value of coefficient of determination and low values of error measures with the observed data. LGP models generally predicted the maximum and minimum discharge values better than the NN models though LGP results were also far from accurate. The robustness of the developed models was tested by using applied data which was neither used in training or testing and the results were judged using Akaike Information Criterion (AIC). For LGP parameters readers are requested to refer the comprehensive list presented in the paper.

The potential of the GP-based model for flood routing between two river gauging stations on river Walla in USA was explored for single peaked as well as multi-peaked flood hydrographs by [32]. The accuracy of GP models was far superior than modified Muskingum method which is a traditional physics based hydrologic flood routing model which also showed time lag in predictions. The inputs were current and antecedent discharge at upstream station and antecedent discharge at downstream station while the output was current discharge at the downstream station. The LGP was employed for the flood routing exercise. The optimal GP parameters used in this study were: crossover rate, 0.9; mutation rate, 0.5; population size, 200; number of generations, 500; and functional set, i.e. simple arithmetic functions (plus, minus, multiply, divide).

The utility of genetic programming in modeling the eddy-covariance (EC) measured evapo-transpiration flux was investigated by [33]. The performance of the GP technique was compared with artificial neural network and Penman-Monteith model estimates. EC measured evapo-transpiration fluxes from two distinct case-studies with different climatic and topographic conditions were considered for the analysis and latent heat is modeled as a function of net radiation, ground temperature, air temperature, wind speed and relative humidity. Results from the study indicated that both data-driven models (ANN and GP) performed better than the Penman-Monteith method. However, the performance of the GP model is comparable with that of ANN models. One of the important advantages of employing GP to model evapo-transpiration process is that, unlike the ANN model, GP resulted in an explicit model structure that can be easily comprehended and adopted. Another advantage of GP over ANN was found that unlike ANN, GP can evolve its own model structure with relevant inputs reducing the tedious task of identifying optimal input combinations. This work was extended by [34] where in an additional data driven tool of Evolutionary Polynomial Regression was used to model the evapo-transpiration process. Additionally the effect of previous states of input variable (lags) on modeling the EC measured AET (actual evapo-transpiration) is investigated. The evapo-transpiration is estimated using the environmental variables such as net radiation (NR), ground temperature (GT), air temperature (AT), wind speed (WS) and relative humidity (RH). It has been found out that random search and evolutionary-based techniques, such as GP and EPR techniques, do not guarantee consistent performance in all case studies e.g. good and/or bad performance for modelling AET. The authors further stated that this may be due to the practical impossibility of conducting exhaustive search, i.e. searching the entire solution space, to reach the optimal model. The results of ANN, GP and EPR were mostly at par with each other though EPR models were easier to understand. Readers may refer the original papers for above two works for the values of GP parameters.

Recently the stage –discharge relationship for the Pahang River in Malaysia was modeled using Genetic Programming (GP) and Gene Expression Programming (GEP) by [35]. The data was provided by Malaysian Department of Irrigation and Drainage (DID). Gene Expression Programming is an extension of GP. GEP is a full-fledged genotype/phenotype system in which both are dealt with separately, whereas GP is a simple replicator system. Stage and discharge data from 2 years were used to compare the performance of the GP and GEP models against that of the more conventional (stage-rating curve) SRC and (Regression) REG approaches. The GEP model was found to be considerably better than the conventional SRC, REG and GP models. GEP was also relatively more successful than GP, especially in estimating large discharge values during flood events. For details of initial GP parameters the original paper may be referred. The paper elaborates the details of the Gene-expression programming, the new variant of GP.

Like applications in Ocean Engineering it can be said that there is a lot of scope for use of GP in the field of Hydrologic Engineering and more and more applications needs to be tried out.

8. Applications in hydraulics

A few applications of GP in Hydraulic Engineering are also reported in reputed journals which are from open channel hydraulics. Various GP models were developed by [36] to predict velocities across a compound channel with vegetated floodplains. The velocity data was collected in a laboratory flume with steady flow and deep channel and relatively shallow vegetated floodplain on either side. The GP model was developed with all 12 variables in dimensional form depicted accurate results though the evolved equation was complex. The GP models were developed with dimensionless variables and separate for main channel and floodplain. Both the velocity prediction on flood plain and main channels showed good correlations with measured values. However the resulting expressions were complex. A dimensionally aware GP was then used to predict the velocity separately in main channel and flood plains. The performance of the symbolic expressions induced by the dimensionless GP for the floodplain and main channel was marginally better than those for the dimensionally aware GP. However, the expressions were more complex and not particularly useful for knowledge induction. The dimensionally aware GP was shown to hold more scientific information, as units of measurement were included, although it was also shown to be open ended in that it does not strictly adhere to the dimensional analysis framework, thereby allowing improved goodness-of-fit whilst yielding on goodness-of-dimension. The paper provides no information about the initial values of GP parameters used in evolving the GP model. GP was applied to the determination of the Chezy's roughness coefficient for corrugated channels in wake-interference flow, i.e. hyper-turbulent flow by [37]. The GP models were calibrated using the experimental data devised by carrying out experiments for 3 plastic corrugated pipes with variations of discharge and slope. GP quite easily and quickly supplied at least two good formulae that fit the experimental data better and are more parsimonious than the monomial formula (mathematical). Moreover, GP has supplied six parsimonious expressions (one or two constants compared to four for the monomial formula) for the Chezy's resistance coefficient, all confirming the dependencies on hydraulic radius, slope and roughness index. It can be said that the two new formulae for the Chezys resistance coefficient, derived from these GP formulae by means of 'mathematical/physical post-refinement', are suitable for explaining the effect of the macro-roughness elements, with respect to the behavior of the rough commercial channels and their traditional expressions for resistance coefficients. The work indicated that this approach, which combines data-mining techniques together with a theoretical understanding, provides very good results. It was also commented that strictly speaking, GP is a data-driven technique, but prior knowledge during the setting up of the evolutionary search and final physical post-refinement of the hypothesis should make it very close to a white box technique, especially when GP is used in scientific discovery problems. The initial model parameters can be found in the original paper. To save space the list is not provided here.

An alternative approach of GP was proposed in the estimation of relative scour depth using field data by [38]. The comparison between the GP model with ANN found that the GP model has good ability of forecasting the scour depth. The discharge intensity and height of fall were used as inputs to estimate scour depth below tail water. The predictive ability of this approach is however clouded by use of very small number of data (total 91 data sets) used for calibration and testing of the model. The values of initial model parameters can be referred from the original paper.

9. Case study I: Soft computing approach for real-time estimation of missing wave heights

The work dealt with application of GP to retrieve the missing/ lost wave data at a particular location using the wave heights at other locations in the region. Six regional networks (with buoys 42001, 42003, 42007, 42036, 42039,42040) were developed in the Gulf Of Mexico (Figure 2) around USA coastline to estimate the wave heights at a location using wave heights at other five locations in the network. The required data from these six buoys was measured by National Data Buoy Center (NDBC, http://www.ndbc.noaa.gov) of National Oceanic and Atmospheric administration of USA (NOAA, http://www.noaa.gov). The common wave data at all the above six locations for the years 2002-2004 was used in the present work. The networks were developed by having one station as target location at a time and remaining five locations as inputs turn by turn. Approximately 70% of the total values were used to calibrate the model and the remaining was kept unseen for testing. While doing this a particular event which occurred during Hurricane Ivan in 2004 at buoy 42040 which involved a Significant Wave Height of 15.96 m was focused for studying the performance of developed models during extreme events. It is to be noted that the exercise was of estimation and not of forecasting for which both the tools did not performed well as noted in the section on applications of GP in Ocean Engineering.

Thus a network was developed with wave buoy 42040 as the target and buoys 42001, 42003, 42007, 42036, 42039 as inputs. Along with 42040 the other locations namely 42003, 42007, 42039 also experienced largest ever wave heights of 11.04, 9.09, 12.05 making the entire event a truly extra ordinary event having a return period of over 5000 years [39]. The initial parameters selected for a GP run were as follows: initial population size 500, mutation frequency 95%, and crossover frequency 50%. The fitness criterion was the mean squared error.

Additionally a three layer Feed Forward Neural Network was also developed for the same buoy network. The results were also compared with a large-scale continuous wave modeling /forecasting systems (NOAA's WAVEWATCH III model) which follows the approach of physics-based model. Though WAVEWATCH III is a continuous running forecasting model it was the only source of information for wave environment at a location and therefore in absence of any reliable observed data, these results were used for comparison. The GP model estimated a wave height of 13.67m as against 15.96 m as compared to 9.05m that of ANN model and 7.82m of WAVEWATCH III, which was an excellent result as far as GP approach is considered. Figure 3 shows the wave plot at 42040 in testing.

From results of all the models developed by both the approaches (ANN & GP), it was observed that all models performed reasonably well in testing as evident by wave height plots, scatter plots along with the correlation coefficient ranging from 0.85 to 0.98, MAE from 0.13 to 0.28, RMSE from 0.20 to 0.45 m and coefficient of efficiency from 0.67 and 0.96. When it was tried to remove 42001 from the network as it is away from the prevailing wind direction by training a separate GP model with 42003, 42007, 42036, and 42039 as 'input buoys' and 42040 as 'target buoy', though the value of correlation coefficient was increased, the peak prediction was not in a fair range of accuracy for extreme event of Hurricane Ivan. Due to better performance of the network with inclusion of buoy 42001 especially for extreme event, buoy 42001 was retained in the network. Also it was found that 42039 was a potential candidate for redeployment in any other suitable position outside the network as

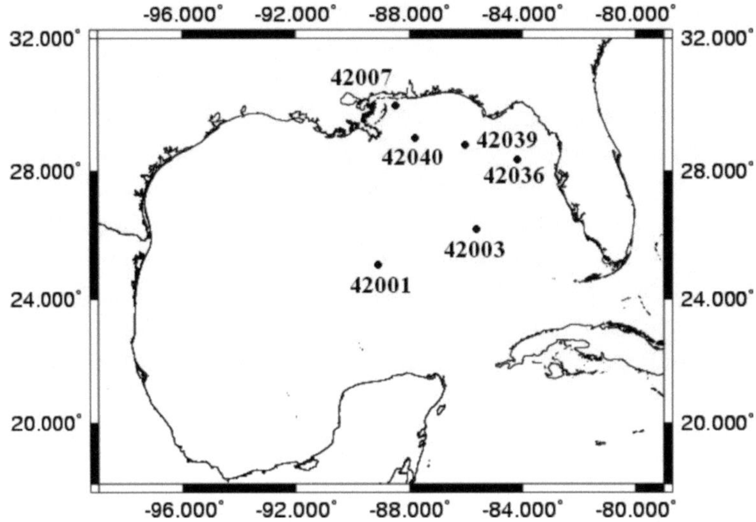

Figure 2. Study area and Buoy Locations (Ref: [6])

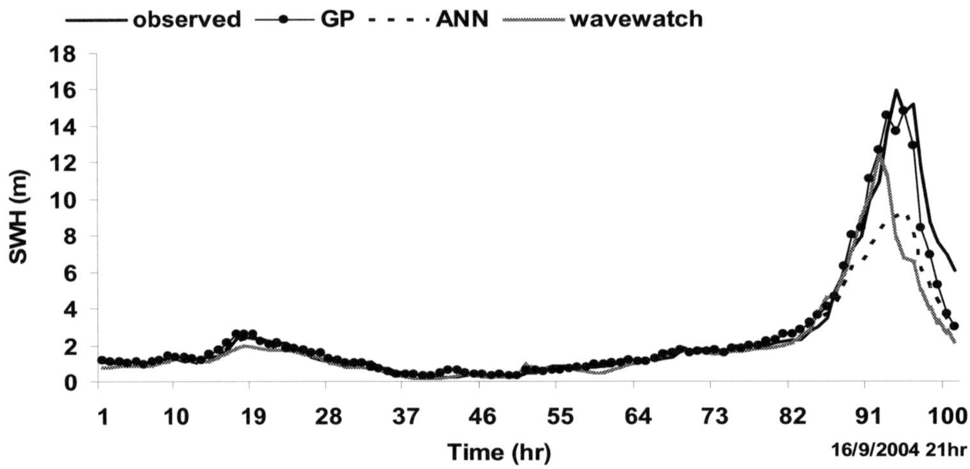

Figure 3. Wave height comparison at 42040 during Hurricane Ivan (Ref: [6])

the buoy network developed for 42039 , provided the wave heights using wave heights at other five locations in the network with the best accuracy achieved between all the networks (r = 0.98). Figure 4(a, b) shows the scatter plots for results of buoy 42039. Table 3 shows results reproduced from [6] giving the details of developed networks along with correlation coefficient between the model estimated and observed values for both GP and ANN models. In general it was shown that GP was superior to other soft tool of ANN and numerical model WAVEWATCH in retrieving the missing wave heights including the extreme events and in redeployment of buoy at other location outside the network.

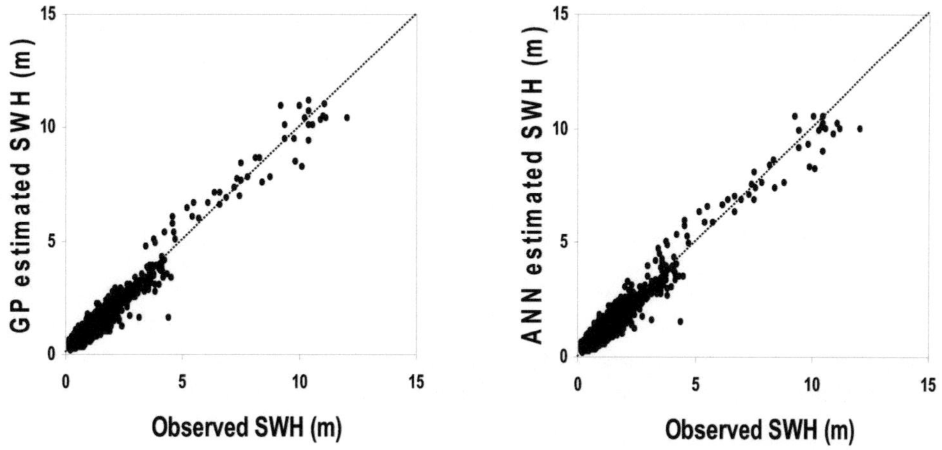

Figure 4. a. Scatter plot for buoy 42039 (GP approach); b. Scatter plot for buoy 42039 (ANN approach) (Ref: [6])

network	Input buoys	Target buoy	r_{ANN}	r_{GP}
BN1	42003, 42007, 42036, 42039, 42040	42001	0.85	0.88
BN2	42001, 42007, 42036, 42039, 42040	42003	0.87	0.91
BN3	42001, 42003, 42036, 42039, 42040	42007	0.90	0.92
BN4	42001, 42003, 42007, 42039, 42040	42036	0.92	0.94
BN5	42001, 42003, 42007, 42036, 42040	42039	0.98	0.98
BN6	42001, 42003, 42007, 42036, 42039	42040	0.94	0.97

Table 3. Results of buoy networks [6]

10. Case study II: Comparison of data-driven modelling techniques for river flow forecasting

In the case study GP was used for prediction of average daily flow values one day in advance at two locations, Rajghat and Mandaleshwar, in the Narmada basin, India using the previous values of measured streamflows at these two locations. The observations of daily average stream flow values at both these stations for the years 1987–1997 were obtained from the Central Water Commission, Narmada Division, Bhopal, India. Considering the variations in daily stream flow values four separate models for the monsoon months of July, August, September and October were prepared along with the one separate but common model for the non monsoon months of November–June. Thus five models were developed in all for each station (total 10 models) to predict discharge at one day in advance. In a view of fair judgment along with GP, ANN and Model trees approach was also employed to develop the models. The number of antecedent discharge values which were used for predicting discharge one day in advance was decided by carrying out the auto-correlation analysis.

The GP models were developed with major fitness function of mean squared error, initial population size of (2048), mutation frequency of (95%) and the cross-over frequency of (53%) with same data division for both ANN and GP models so that their results could be compared. All the developed forecasting models were tested for unseen inputs and their qualitative and quantitative performance was judged by means of correlation coefficient (r) between the observed and forecasted values along with root mean square error (RMSE) and plotting scatter plots between the same. Hydrographs were also plotted to visualize the behavior of the forecasting models particularly for extreme events (peaks).

After examining the results it was observed that for the location of Rajghat in the month of July, ANN model exhibited a reasonable performance in testing with an 'r' value of 0.75 between the observed and forecasted discharges whereas GP model had showed a better 'r' value of 0.78 with better performance for higher values of stream flow, though over-predicted in some instances. The MT model gave a lower 'r' value of 0.7 and prediction of MT model for high stream flows was poor as compared to ANN and GP models. The scatter plot (Fig. 5) between the observed and forecasted discharges confirmed this with a balanced scatter except at the high values of measured stream flows.

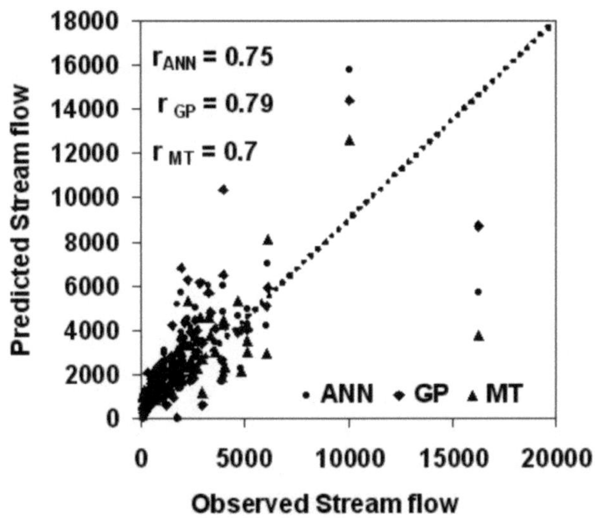

Figure 5. Scatter plot for RajJuly Model

For the months of August and September, models showed similar performance with GP models performing better than their ANN and MT counterparts (r_{GP} = 0.75, r_{ANN} = 0.7, r_{MT} = 0.72 for Raj Aug and r_{GP} = 0.79, r_{ANN} = 0.76, r_{MT} = 0.78 for Raj Sept). For the October model, the predicted discharges in testing were highly in agreement with the observed values for both the models as shown by the discharge hydrograph (Fig. 6). The results were also supported by a high value of correlation coefficient (r = 0.92 for ANN and GP and r = 0.87 for MT) for all the three models in testing.

The Mandaleshwar models behaved in a similar fashion as that of the Rajghat models with correlation coefficients of $r > 0.7$ for all ANN, GP and MT models. For the month of August the performance of all models was reasonable with r values of 0.74, 0.78 and 0.71 for ANN, GP and MT models respectively. The other monthly models of ANN, GP and MT also performed well, with high correlation coefficients in testing ($r > 0.86$). It was again observed that GP models work better while predicting extreme events. The maximum observed discharge of 3790 m^3/s was predicted as 1742 m^3/s by the ANN model, 3342 m^3/s by the GP model and 1718 m^3/s by the MT model. Figure 7 shows discharge hydrographs for the ManNov-June models. The RMSE values also showed a similar trend to that of the correlation coefficients.

Thus it was seen that the GP technique outperforms both ANN and MT in almost all the cases in terms of overall accuracy in prediction. The GP approach based on evolutionary principles has a completely different approach to the ANN technique in that it does not involve any transfer function, and evolves generations of "offspring" based on the "fitness criteria" and genetic operations; this seems to capture the underlying trends better than the ANN technique. Thus it can be said that ANN and MT perform almost equally but GP performed better than both of them where prediction accuracy in both normal and extreme events is concerned.

11. Concluding remarks and future scope

Applications of GP for modeling water flows were discussed in the preceding sections of this chapter. It may be noted that every attempt is made to provide readers the details of GP techniques and their parameters employed in each work. However in view of keeping the length of the chapter in stipulated limits sometimes the readers are referred to the original paper. Details about the data are also provided at appropriate locations. Interested readers may further enquire the authors or download the data whenever possible from the web sites to perform the similar exercise. The applications were from three particular areas of water flows namely Ocean Engineering, Hydrology and Hydraulics. It was shown in all the applications for that modeling of natural random processes of complex underlying phenomenon the Genetic Programming can certainly be employed. The results of this technique were found to be superior than other contemporary soft computing techniques. However it was also seen that the tool is not explored to its full capacity by the research community in any of the above fields. The developed GP models also need to be applied at operational level. For this a partnership between the researchers and practitioners is necessary. The GP models can certainly work as supplementary tool if not as replacement techniques. It can be said that the early days of GP modeling are over and the tool needs to be used more judiciously for the problems worthy of its use. Otherwise a stage will be reached where in GP will be used because data is available. It's use is certainly for the phenomena which are difficult to explain and model. However if the technique is to stay here it needs to be explored further for more challenging problems like modeling of infiltration, high flood events, hurricane path, storm surge, tsunami water levels to name a few.

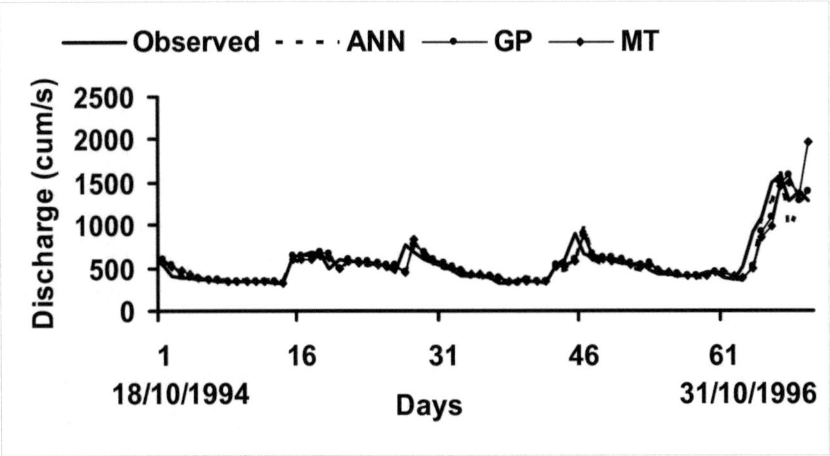

Figure 6. RajOct Model results [13]

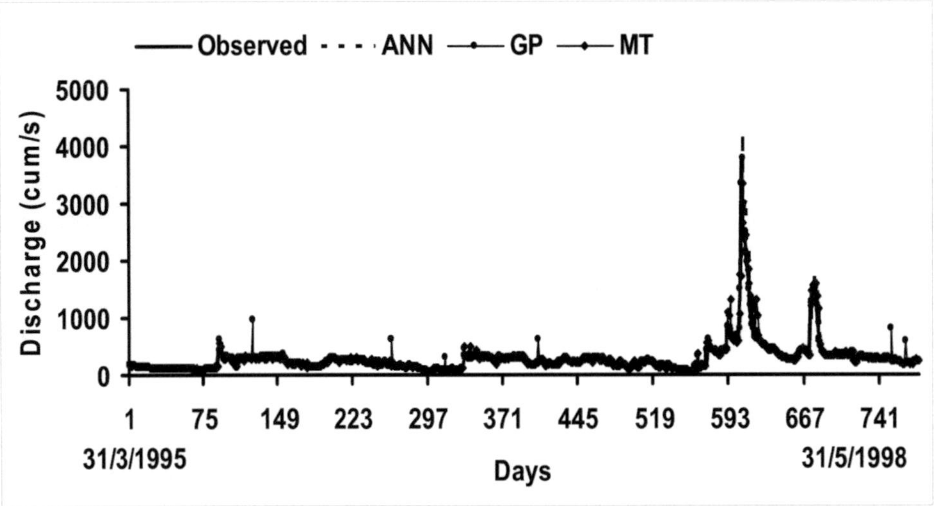

Figure 7. ManNovJune Model results [13]

Author details

Shreenivas N. Londhe and Pradnya R. Dixit
Vishwakarma Institute of Information Technology, Kondhwa (bk), Pune, India
shreel69@yahoo.com, prdxt11@gmail.com

12. References

[1] Zadeh L, (1994) Fuzzy Logic, Neural Networks and Soft Computing. Communications of the ACM 37 (3), 77–84.

[2] The ASCE Task Committee, (2000) Artificial neural networks in hydrology. I: preliminary concepts. J. Hydrol. Engg. ASCE 5(2). 115–123.

[3] Maynard S, (1975) The Theory Of Evolution. Penguin. London.

[4] Babovic V, Keijzer M, (2000) Genetic programming as a model induction engine. Journal of Hydroinformatics. 2(1) pp. 35 – 61

[5] Koza J, (1992) Genetic Programming: On the Programming of Computers by Means of Natural Selection. A Bradford Book. MIT Press.

[6] Londhe S, (2008) Soft computing approach for real-time estimation of missing wave heights. Ocean Engineering. 35. 1080-1089

[7] Brameier M (2004) On linear genetic programming. Ph.D. thesis. University of Dortmund.

[8] Guven A, (2009) Linear genetic programming for time-series modelling of daily flow rate. J. Earth Syst. Sci. 118(2). 137-146

[9] Jain P, Deo M, (2006) Neural networks in ocean engineering. Int. Journal of Ships and Offshore Structures. 1. 25–35.

[10] Maier H, Dandy G, (2000) Neural networks for prediction and forecasting of water resources variables: a review of modelling issues and applications. Environ. Model. Soft. 15. 101–124.

[11] Dawson C, Wilby R, (2001) Hydrological modelling using artificial neural networks. Progr. Phys. Geogr. 25(1). 80–108.

[12] Kambekar A, Deo M, (2012) Wave Prediction Using Genetic Programming And Model Trees. Journal of Coastal Research. Doi: 28(1). 43-50

[13] Londhe S, Charahate S, (2010) Comparison of data-driven modelling techniques for river flow Forecasting. Hydrological Sciences. 55(7). 1163-1173

[14] Kalra R, Deo M, (2007) Genetic Programming to retrieve missing information in wave records along the west coast of India. Applied Ocean Research. 29. 99-111

[15] Ustoorikar K, Deo M, (2008) Filling up Gaps in wave data with Genetic Programming. Marine Structures. 21. 177-195

[16] Charhate S, Deo M, Sanil Kumar V, (2007) Soft and Hard Computing Approaches for Real Time Prediction of Coastal Currents in a Tide Dominated Area. Journal of Engineering for the Maritime Environment. Proceedings of the Institution of Mechanical Engineers, London, M4, 221:147-163

[17] Gaur S, Deo M, (2008) Real time wave forecasting using genetic programming Ocean Engineering. 35. 1166-1175

[18] Jain P, Deo M, (2008) Artificial intelligence tools to forecast ocean waves in real time. The Open Ocean Engineering Journal. 1. 13-21.

[19] Kambekar A, Deo M, (2010) Wave simulation and forecasting using wind time history and data driven Methods. Ships and Offshore Structures. 5(3). 253-266

[20] Ghorbani M, Khatibi R, Aytek A, Makarynskyy O, Shiri J, (2010a) Sea water level forecasting using genetic programming and comparing the performance with Artificial Neural Networks. Computers and Geosciences. 36. 620-627

[21] Ghorbani M, Makarynskyy O, Shiri J, Makarynska D, (2010b) Genetic Programming for Sea Level Predictions in an Island Environment. International Journal of Ocean and Climatic systems. 1(1). pp. 27-35,

[22] Charhate S, Deo M, Londhe S, (2008) Inverse modeling to derive wind parameters from wave measurements. Applied Ocean Research. 30. 120-129
[23] Charhate S, Deo M, Londhe S, (2009) Genetic programming for real time prediction of offshore wind. International Journal of Ships and Offshore Structures. 4(1). 77-88.
[24] Daga, M, Deo M, (2009) Alternative data-driven methods to estimate wind from waves by inverse Modeling. Natural Hazards. 49(2). 293-310
[25] Singh A, Deo M, Sanil Kumar V, (2007) Combined Neural network – genetic programming for sediment transport. Journal of Maritime Engineering, The Institution of Civil Engineers. Issue MAO. 1-7.
[26] Guven A, Azmathulla Md, Zakaria N, (2009) Linear genetic programming for prediction of circular pile scour. Ocean Engineering. 36. 985-991
[27] Savic D, Walters G, Davidson J, (1999) A genetic Programming approach to rainfall-runoff modeling. Water Resources Management. 13. 219-231
[28] Drecourt J, (1999) Application of Neural Networks and Genetic Programming to Rainfall Runoff Modeling. Danish Hydraulic Institute (Hydro-Informatics Techonologies - HIT) June 1999. D2K-0699-1.
[29] Whigham P, Crapper, P, (2001) Modeling rainfall runoff using Genetic Programming. Mathematical and Computer Modelling. 33. 707–721
[30] Khu S, Liong S, Babovic V, Madsen H, Muttil N, (2001) Genetic Programming And Its Application In Real-Time Runoff Forecasting. J of American Water Resources Association. 37(2). 439-450
[31] Babovic V, Keijzer M, (2002) Rainfall runoff modeling Based on Genetic programming. Nordic Hydrology. 33(5). 331-346
[32] Sivapragasam C, Maheswaran R, Venkatesh V, (2007) Genetic programming approach for flood routing in natural channels. Hydrological processes. 22. 623-628
[33] Parasuraman K, Elshorbagy A, Carey K, (2007) Modelling the dynamics of the evapotranspiration process using genetic Programming. Hydrological Sciences. 52(3). 563-578
[34] El Baroudy I, Elshorbagy A, Carey S, Giustolisi O, Savic D, (2010) Comparison of three data-driven techniques in modeling the evapotranspiration process. Journal of Hydroinformatics. 12.4. 365-379
[35] Azmathullah MD, Ghani A, Leow C, Chang C, Zakaria N, (2011) Gene-Expression Programming for the Development of a Stage-Discharge Curve of the Pahang River. Water Resource Management. 25. 2901-2916
[36] Harris E, Babovic V, Falconey R, (2003) Velocity Predictions in Compound Channels with Vegetated Floodplains using Genetic Programming. Int. J. River Basin Management. 1(2). 117-123
[37] Giustolisi O, (2004) Using genetic programming to determine Chezy's resistance coefficient in corrugated channels. Journal of Hydroinformatics. 6.3. 157-173
[38] Azmathullah MD, Ghani A, Zakaria N, Lai S, Chang C, Leow C, (2008) "Genetic Programming to Predict Ski-Jump bucket Spillway Scour. Journal of Hydrodynamics. 20(4), 477-484
[39] Panchang V, Li D, (2006), Large waves in the Gulf of Mexico Caused by Hurricane Ivan. Bulletin of the American Meteorological Society. DOI: 10.1175/BAMS-87-4-481, 481-489.

Chapter 10

Genetic Programming: Efficient Modeling Tool in Hydrology and Groundwater Management

J. Sreekanth and Bithin Datta

Additional information is available at the end of the chapter

http://dx.doi.org/10.5772/52102

1. Introduction

With the advent of computers a wide range of mathematical and numerical models have been developed with the intent of predicting or approximating parts of hydrologic cycle. Prior to the advent of conceptual or process based models, physical hydraulic models, which are reduced scale representations of large hydraulic systems, were used commonly in water resources engineering. Fast development in the computational systems and numerical solutions of complex differential equations enabled development of conceptual models to represent physical systems in almost all arenas of life including hydrological and water resources systems. Thus, in the last two decades large number of mathematical models was developed to represent different processes in the hydrological cycle. Hydrological models can be broadly classified in to three.

1. Physical models
2. Conceptual models
3. Statistical / Black box models

Physical models are reduced scale representations of the actual hydrological system and the responses obtained from these models are up-scaled to estimate the responses of the real system. Conceptual models are based on different individual processes or components of a hydrological process. For example, in modelling the watershed response to a storm event a conceptual model make use of different equations to compute different components like subsurface flow, evapo-transpiration, channel flow, groundwater flow, surface run off etc. The third type of modelling involves using mathematical and statistical techniques to fit a model to a data set which then relates the dependent variable to the independent variables. This type of modelling includes regression models, response matrix, transfer functions, neural networks, support vector machine etc. The most widely used "black box" type modelling approach in hydrology and water resources literature is neural networks. Genetic programming is a potential tool to develop simple and efficient functional relationship between hydrological variables. In spite of the wide range of possible applications in hydrology and water resources, GP has not been widely reported in the hydrology and water resources literature. The focus of this chapter is to discuss the potential applicability of genetic programming to develop simple and computationally efficient hydrological models, in light of a few studies reported in the recent years. The key points discussed are as follows;

1. GP's ability to develop simple models with interpretability to overcome the curse of "black box" nature of data intensive models.
2. Lesser number of parameters used in GP models as compared to parallel neural network architectures.
3. GP's ability to parsimoniously identify the significance of the modelling inputs.

1.1. Genetic programming as a modelling tool

Genetic programming belongs to and is one of the latest members in the family of evolutionary computation. Evolutionary computation refers to the group of computational techniques which are inspired by and emulate the natural process of evolution which resulted in the formation of the entire variety of organisms present on earth. Just as the way evolution and natural selection has resulted in the formation of organisms that are competent and best suitable inhabitants to live in any natural environment, the principle has been applied in computational science to evolve solutions to complex engineering problems which are subject to random and chaotic environments similar to the circumstances in which natural evolution has occurred. Evolutionary computation forms the basic principle behind the evolutionary algorithms like genetic algorithm (GA), genetic programming (GP), Evolutionary programming, evolution strategy, differential evolution. Evolutionary algorithms, widely used in mathematical optimization, are in general based on the application of evolutionary principles like selection, cross-over and mutation to a "population" of candidate solutions over a number of generations to find the optimal solutions to an engineering problem. Genetic algorithm is, for example, a widely used optimization techniques using these principles as the basic "operators" of the algorithm. Genetic programming [1] is similar to genetic algorithm in this aspect that it uses these genetic operators selection, cross-over and mutation in its algorithms. However, the uniqueness of genetic programming is that it performs these operators over symbolic expression or formulae or programs rather than over numbers which represent the candidate solutions. Thus, in genetic programming the candidate solutions are symbolic expressions or formulae. In a modelling framework these symbolic expressions or formulae or programs are candidate models to simulate a physical phenomenon. The parse tree notations of two parent and offspring genetic programs are shown in figure 1. Thus the optimal formula that is evolved by genetic programming can be used as a best fit model for predicting the physical phenomenon under consideration.

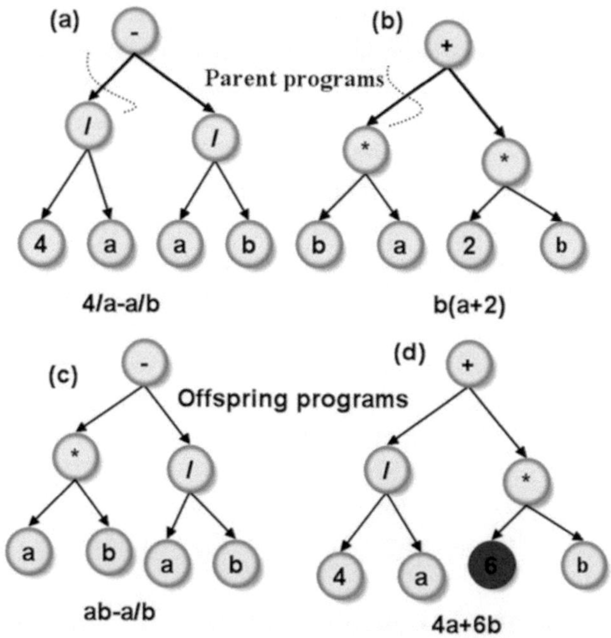

Figure 1. Symbolic representation of parent and offspring genetic programs

In figure 1, two parent programs to model a physical phenomenon are shown. After testing these programs for their modelling performance, they are operated by cross-over operator. That is, parts of the programs are crossed over at the dashed locations to generate the offspring programs. Also, mutation is illustrated by arbitrarily changing the parameter 2 to 6.

In the last decade a few studies in the broad area of hydrology have utilized genetic programming based models for making hydrological predictions. The utility of GP in developing rainfall-runoff models, which are highly non-linear models was addressed in [2] They combined the use of GP based models with other conceptual models in deriving useful hydro-climatic models. It was concluded that GP was able to develop more robust models in that the functional relationships between different model inputs could be easily identified thus resulting in more transparency of the "black box" type of modelling. Another study [3] applied genetic programming and artificial neural networks in hydrology to model the effect of rain on the runoff flow in an urban basin. This study also illustrated the possibility of including the physical basis of the problem in the GP based model. Another research in this direction [4] compared three different artificial intelligence techniques viz, neural networks, adaptive neuro-fuzzy inference system (ANFIS), and genetic programming for discharge routing of a river in Turkey. The study revealed that GP displayed a better edge over the other two modelling approaches in all the statistics compared like the mean absolute error (MAE), mean squared relative error (MSRE) and correlation coefficient. Kisi et al (2010) [5] developed a wavelet gene expression programming (WGEP) for forecasting daily precipitation and compared it with wavelet neuro-fuzzy models (WNF). The results showed that WGEP models are effective in forecasting daily precipitation with better performance over WNF models. Selle [6] utilized genetic programming to systematically develop alternative model structures with different complexity levels for hydrological modelling with the objective of testing whether GP can be used to identify the dominant processes within the hydrological system. Models were developed for predicting the deep percolation responses under surface irrigated pastures to different soil types, water table depths and water ponding times during surface irrigation. The dominant process in the model prediction as determined from the models generated using genetic programming was found to be comparable to those determined using conceptual models. Thus it was concluded that Genetic programming can be used to evaluate the structure of hydrological models. A common aspect of GP based modelling that all these studies reported is the fact that the GP modelling resulted in fairly simpler models which could be easily interpreted for the physical significance of the input variables in making a prediction. Jyothiprakash and Magar (2012) [12] performed a comparative study of reservoir inflow models developed using ANN, ANFIS and linear GP for lumped and distributed data. The study reported superior performance of GP models over ANN and ANFIS models.

2. Simple and interpretable hydrological models using genetic programming

The major drawback of all the data driven modelling approaches is the black box nature of these models, i.e., the user cannot easily identify what is happening in model which computes the outputs corresponding to the inputs supplied to the model. One of the key advantages of genetic programming as a modelling tool is its ability to develop simple hydrological models. The simplicity of the models is close associated with their interpretability. The simpler the models are the better they can be interpreted. This in turn helps in assessing the contributions of different members of the predictor set or inputs in making a particular prediction. Selle and Muttil (2011) utilized this capability of GP to test the structure of hydrological models to predict deep percolation response in surface irrigated pastures. Data obtained using lysimeter experiments were used to develop simple models using genetic programming. The developed models were simple and interpretable which helped in identifying the dominant processes involved in the deep percolation process. Often the developed models could be expressed as simple algebraic equations. The dominant processes identified compared well with the same as used in conceptual models. The study also investigated the recurrence of the models developed using GP in multiple runs and found out that they were consistently coming up with the same model for a given level of complexity of the model. However, the study also reported that as the level of complexity increases recurrence of the generated model were affected and the physical interpretability of the models decreases and hence careful understanding of the complexity of the system is to be considered before a level of complexity is chosen for the GP models.

This however, illustrates that carefully developed GP models remain mathematically simple and are readily interpretable to the extent that the dominant processes which influence the prediction could be readily identified from the model structure. When carefully implemented models can throw light into and identify the key physical processes contributing to the phenomenon predicted and hence the development of the model. This is an important feature lacking from many of the data mining based prediction models resulting from which these modelling approaches are often earmarked as "black-box" models. "Black-box" nature of the prediction models often result in the limited use of such models for practical predictive applications.

2.1. Model complexity of GP and neural networks – Comparative study

The authors had conducted a study [7] to evaluate the complexity of predictive models developed using Genetic programming in comparison with models developed using neural networks. The models based on GP and neural network were developed as potential surrogate models to a complex numerical groundwater flow and transport model. The saltwater intrusion levels at monitoring locations resulting due to the excitation of the aquifer by pumping from a number of groundwater pumping wells were modelled by using GP and neural networks. The pumping rates at these groundwater well locations for three different stress periods were the inputs or independent variables for the model. The resulting salinity levels at the monitoring locations were the dependent variables or outputs.

The GP and ANN based surrogate models were trained based on the training and validation data generated using a three dimensional coupled flow and transport simulation model FEMWATER. The GP models were developed using a software Discipulus, which uses a linear genetic programming algorithm. The ANN surrogate models were developed using a feed forward back propagation algorithm implemented in the software neuroshell. The input data considered were the pumping rates at eleven well locations over three different time periods, constituting 33 input variables. Since pumping at each location can take any real value between the prescribed minimum and maximum these input variables constitute a 33 dimensional continuous space, each dimension representative of a pumping rate at a particular location in a particular stress period. Hence efficient training of the GP and ANN models required carefully chosen input data which is representative of the entire input space. Latin hypercube sampling was performed to choose uniformly distributed input samples from the 33 dimensional input space. An input sample is a vector of 33 values of pumping rate at 11 well locations during three stress periods. The salinity level at each observation location is the dependent variable or output. The values of the outputs required for training the GP and ANN models were generated by running the FEMWATER model. The numerical simulation model was run numerous times to generate the output data set corresponding to each input vector. The input-output data set generated following this procedure was divided into two sets with three quarters of the data in one set and the rest in the other. The larger set was used for training GP and ANN models and the smaller one was used for validating the models. The members of the training and validation sets for both GP and ANN were chosen randomly.

The ANN used in the study was trained in the supervised training mode using a back propagation algorithm. The objective function considered for both the GP and ANN training was minimization of the total root mean square error (RMSE) of the prediction. The prediction error was calculated as the difference between the model (GP or ANN) predicted values and the actual from the numerical model generated data set.

The input-hidden-output layer architecture for the ANN model was optimized by trial and error. Both GP and ANN models had 33 input variables and 3 outputs. The number of hidden neurons in the ANN model was determined by adding 1 hidden neuron during each trial. A sigmoid transfer function and a learning rate of 0.1 were used. In developing the model the back propagation algorithm modifies the connection weights connecting the input-hidden and output neurons by an amount proportional to the prediction error in each iteration and repeats this procedure numerous times till the prediction errors are minimized to a pre-specified level. Thus for any given model architecture (model structure) the neural network model optimizes the connection weights to accomplish satisfactory model predictions. Where as the genetic programming modelling approach is different in that it evolves the optimal model architecture and their respective parameters in achieving satisfactory predictions.

The GP models developed used a population size of 500, mutation and cross over frequencies of respectively 95 and 50 percent. The number of generations were not specified a priory, instead the evolutionary process was stopped when the fitness function was less than a critical value. In order to achieve the simplest models, the mathematical operators where initially kept a minimum and then further operators were added into the functional set. In this manner, initially addition and subtraction were alone added in this set and later the operators multiplication, arithmetic and data transfer were added into the set.

The predictive performance of the GP and ANN models on an independent set of data were found to be satisfactory in terms of the correlation coefficient and minimized RMSE. Figure 2 and 3 respectively shows the ANN and GP predictions of salinity levels at three monitoring locations corresponding to the their corresponding values from the numerical simulation model A dissection of the GP and ANN models were performed to evaluate the model complexity. The modelling framework of the GP models essentially has a functional set and a terminal set. The functional set comprises of the mathematical operations like addition, subtraction, division, multiplication, trigonometric functions etc. The terminal set of GP comprises of the model parameters which are also optimized simultaneously as the model structure is optimized. In our study the developed GP models used a maximum terminal set size of 30. i.e., satisfactory model predictions could be achieved with only 30 parameters for the GP model.

The functional operators essentially develop the structure of the GP models by operating on the input variables. In the GP modelling framework this model structure is not pre-specified unlike the ANN models. Instead, the model structure is evolved in the course of model development by testing numerous different model structures. This approach definitely provides scope for the development of improved model structures as against the ANN method. In the ANN approach where comparatively only a few models are tested in the trial and error approach which does not implement an organized search for better model architectures. The only components that are optimized during the development of the ANN model are the connection weights. Thus the model structure is rigid and is retained as determined by the trial and error procedure. This gives lesser flexibility in adapting the model structure with respect to the process being modelled. In our study it was found that while GP models required only 30 parameters in developing the model the number of connection weights in the ANN models was 1224. This is a metric of the simplicity of the GP models as against the ANN models. From figures 2 and 3 it is observed that despite the simplicity of the model and much lesser number of parameters used GP predictions are very similar to the ANN model predictions. For each hidden neuron added into the ANN architecture the number of connection weights increases by a number equal to the total number of inputs and outputs. Hence there is a geometric increase in the number of connection weights with increase in the number of hidden neurons in ANN architecture.

The comparison of the number of parameters in itself testifies the ability of the genetic programming framework to develop simpler models. The impact of the number of parameters on the model is on the uncertainty of the predictions made using the model. The more the number of parameters, the more uncertainty in them and hence this uncertainty propagates into the predictions made.

3. Parsimonious selection of input variables

Another key feature of the genetic programming based modelling approach is the ability of genetic programming to identify the relative importance of the independent variables chosen as the modelling inputs. Many often in hydrological applications it is uncertain which variables are important to be included as inputs in modelling a physical phenomenon. Similarly time series models are used quite often in predicting or forecasting hydrological variables. For example the river stages measured on a few consecutive days can be used to forecast the river stage for the following days. In doing so the number of past days' flow to be included as inputs into the time series model depends on the size and shape of the catchment and many similar parameters. Most often rigorous statistical tests like auto-correlation studies are conducted to determine whether an independent variable is significant to be included in the model development or not. Once included most often it is not possible to eliminate from most of the modelling frameworks because of the earlier mentioned rigidity of the model structure. For example, in neural networks an insignificant model input should be ideally assigned zero connection weights to the output. However, these connection weights most often don't assume the zero value but converge to very small values near zero. This results in the insignificant variable being influencing the predictions made by a small amount. These results in uncertainties in the predictions made.

The evolutionary process of determining the optimum model structure helps GP to identify and eliminate insignificant variables from the model development. The authors conducted a study dissecting the neural network and GP models developed in the same study described above to evaluate the parsimony in the selection of inputs for model development. GP evolves the best model structure and parameters by testing millions of alternate model structures. The relative importance of the each independent variable in the model development was computed by the recurrence of each independent variable in the best 30 models developed by GP. Thus, if an input appears in all the 30 models its impact factor is 1 and if one independent variable appears in none of the best 30 models its impact factor is 0.

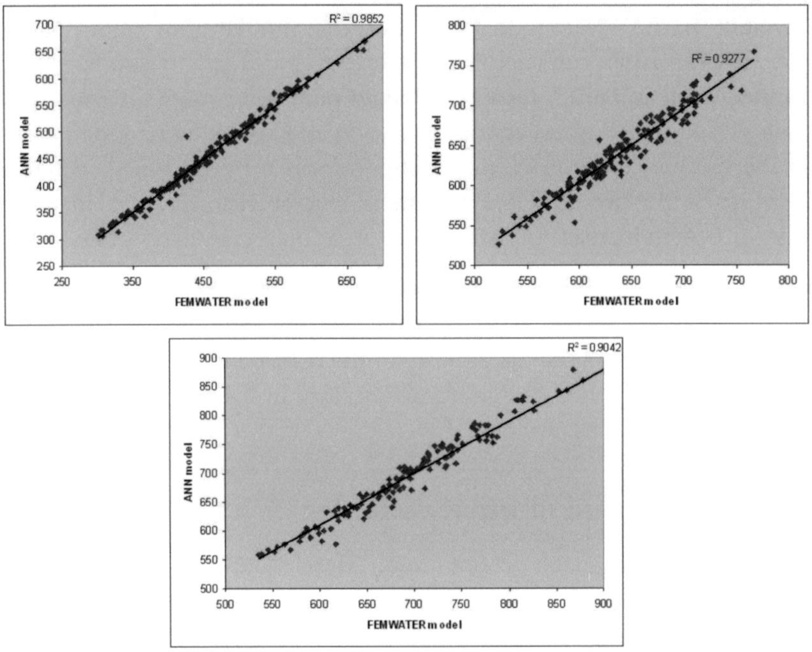

Figure 2. Salinity predictions at three locations by the ANN models

To determine the significance of the inputs in the neural network model a connection weights method was used [7]. In this method the significance of each input is computed as a function of the connection weights which connects it to the output through the hidden layer. The formulae used in [7] were used to compute this;

1. First step in this approach was to compute the product of the input-hidden layer and hidden output layer weights. The, divide this by the sum of products of absolute values of the input-hidden and hidden output layer weights of all input neurons. This is given by Q_{ih} in (2)

$$P_{i,h} = |W_{i,h}| \times |W_{h,o}| \tag{1}$$

$$Q_{ih} = \frac{P_{ih}}{\sum_{i=1}^{ni} P_{ih}} \tag{2}$$

2. Divide the sum of the Q_{ih} for each hidden neuron by the sum for each hidden neuron of the sum for each input neuron of Q_{ih}, for each i. The relative importance of all output weights attributable to the given input variable is then obtained. The relative importance is then mapped to a 0-1 scale with the most important variables assuming a value of 1. A RI value of 0 indicates an insignificant variable.

$$RI = \frac{\sum_{h=1}^{nh} Q_{ih}}{\sum_{h=1}^{nh} \sum_{i=1}^{ni} Q_{ih}} \tag{3}$$

In this manner, the significance of each independent variable (input) to the model was quantified in a 0-1 range as impact factor and relative importance respectively for GP and ANN models. These values for GP and ANN models are plotted in figures 4,5 and 6.

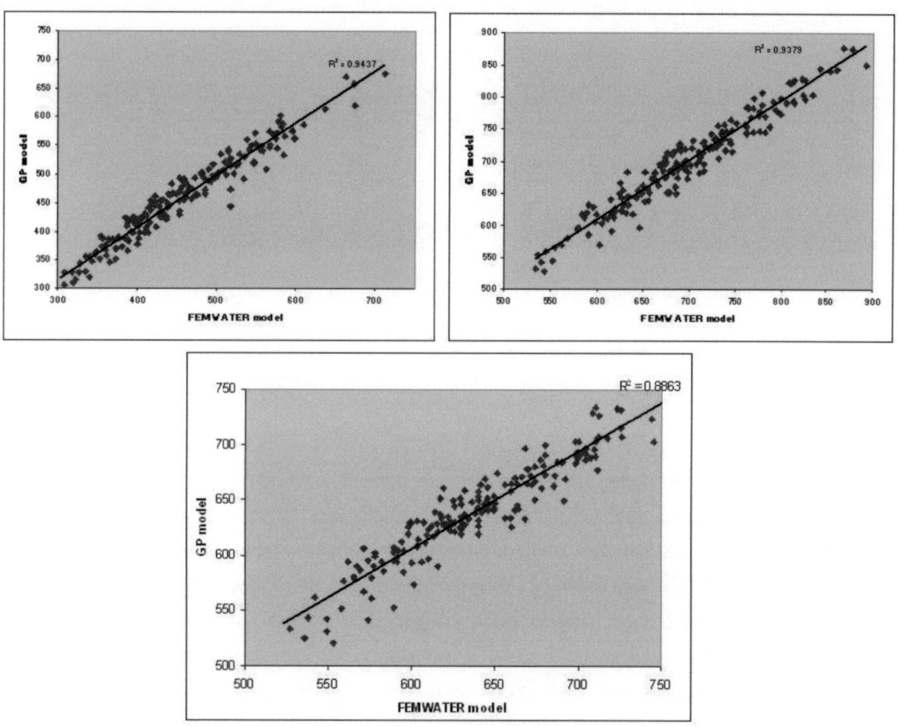

Figure 3. Salinity predictions at three locations by the ANN models

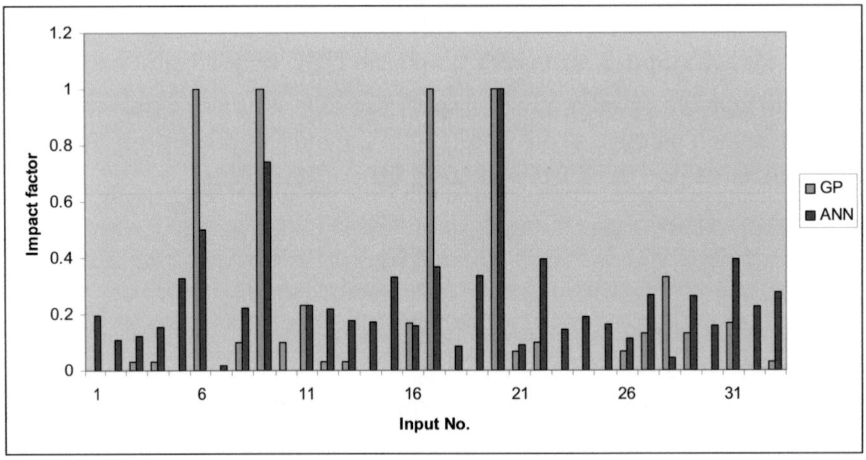

Figure 4. Impact factors of input variables in predicting Salinity at location 1.

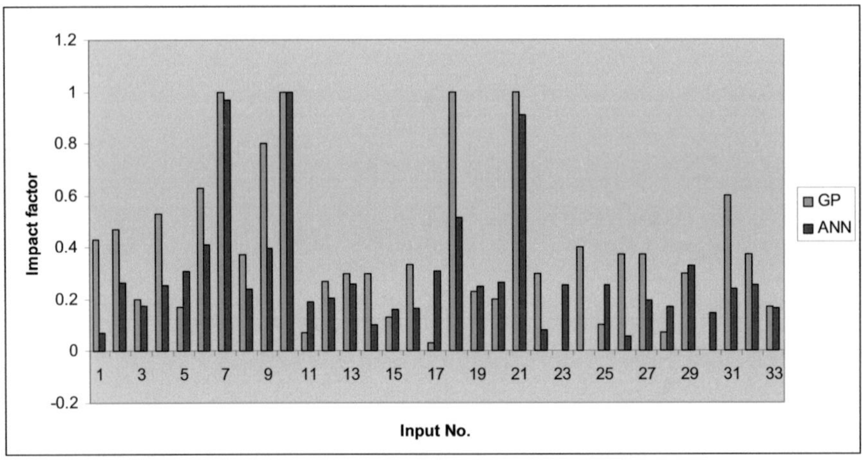

Figure 5. Impact factors of input variables in predicting Salinity at location 2.

From these figures it can be observed that all the variables considered has a non-zero impact in the developed ANN models. Whereas, GP is able to assign zero impact factor to those inputs which are not significant and thus able to eliminate them from the model. This helps in developing simpler models and reducing the predictive uncertainty. In figure 4 it can be seen that GP identified 13 inputs with zero impact factor. This implies that the pumping values corresponding to these inputs have negligible effect on the salinity levels at the observation location. Thus 13 out of the 33 inputs considered are eliminated from the GP models resulting in much simpler models compared to the ANN models where all the 33 inputs take part in predicting the salinity even though some of them are having very less impact on the predictions made. The ability of GP to eliminate insignificant variables is because of the evolutionary nature of model structure optimization. By performing cross-over, mutation and selection of candidate models over a number of generations GP is able to derive the optimum model structure with the most important input variables which are relevant to the model prediction. This inturn help in developing simpler models with fewer uncertainties in the model prediction.

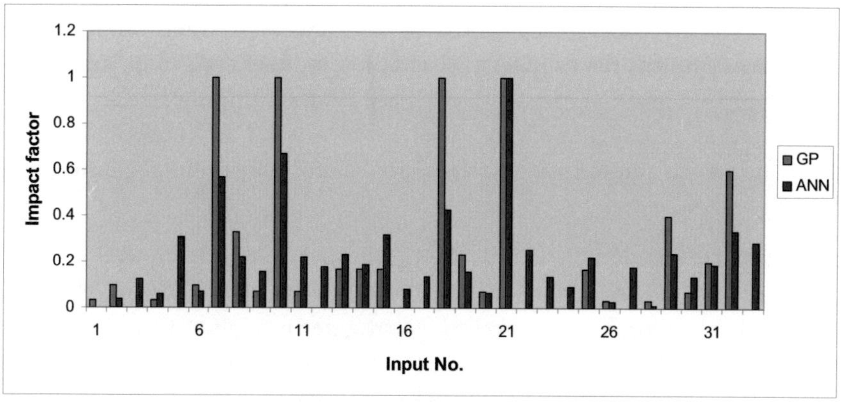

Figure 6. Impact factors of input variables in predicting Salinity at location 3.

4. Multiple predictive model structures using GP

The advent of GP as a modelling tool has paved the way for researches exploring the possibility of multiple optimal models for predicting hydrological processes. Genetic programming, in its evolutionary approach to derive optimal model structures and parameters, tests millions of model structures which can mimic the physical process under consideration. Researches have found that multiple models can be identified using GP which are considerably different in model structures but able to make consistently good predictions. Parasuraman and Elshorbagy [8] developed genetic programming based models for predicting the evapo-transporation. In doing so, multiple optimal GP models were trained and tested and they were applied to quantify the uncertainty in those models. Another study by the authors [9] developed ensemble surrogate models for predicting the aquifer responses to pumping in terms of salinity levels at observation locations. An ensemble of surrogate models based on GP was developed and the ensemble was used to get model predictions with improved reliability levels. The variance of the model predictions were used as the measure of uncertainty in the modelling process.

5. GP as surrogate model for simulation-optimization

A very important application of data intensive modelling approaches is to develop surrogate models to computationally complex numerical simulation models. As detailed elsewhere in this article, the authors have utilized GP in developing potential surrogates to a complex density dependent groundwater flow and transport simulation model. The potential utility of the surrogates is to replace the numerical simulation model in simulation-optimization frameworks. Simulation-optimization models are used to derive optimal management decisions using optimization algorithms in which a numerical simulation models is run to predict the outcome of implementing the alternative management options. For example, the authors developed simulation-optimization models to develop optimal management decisions for coastal aquifers. The optimal pumping from the coastal aquifer can be decided only by considering the impact of any alternative pumping strategy on saltwater intrusion. For this the numerical simulation model needs to be integrated with the optimization algorithm and the impact of each candidate pumping strategy is predicted by using the simulation model iteratively. This involve a lot of computational burden as thousands of numerical model runs are required before an optimal pumping strategy is identified.

GP was used a surrogate model within the optimization algorithm as a substitute of the numerical simulation model in our study (Sreekanth and Datta, 2010). Previous studies have used artificial neural networks as surrogate models to replace groundwater numerical simulation models. Emily et a1 (2005) used genetic programming based surrogate models for groundwater pollution source identification. In our study (Sreekanth and Datta, 2010), it was found that genetic programming could be used as a superior surrogate model in such application with definite advantages. The study intended to develop optimal pumping strategies for coastal aquifers in which the total pumping could be maximized and at the same time limiting the saltwater intrusion at pre-specified limits. In doing so, the effect of pumping on the salinity levels was predicted using trained and tested GP models. The GP models were externally coupled to a genetic algorithm based optimization model to derive the optimal management strategies. The results of the GP based simulation-optimization was then compared to the results obtained using an ANN-based simulation-optimization model. The ability of GP in parsimoniously identifying the model inputs helped in reducing the dimension of the decision space in which modelling and optimization was carried out. The smaller dimension of the modelling space helped in reducing the training and testing required to develop the surrogate models. The study identified that GP has potential applicability in developing surrogate models with potential application in simulation-optimization methodology to solve environmental management problems.

6. Conclusion

The aim of this chapter is to introduce genetic programming as a potential modelling tool for hydrology and water resources applications. Genetic programming belongs to the broad class of evolutionary computational tools developed in recent years. Compared to the vast number of data mining and artificial intelligence applications in hydrology and water resources, the application of GP has been limited in spite of its potential applicability in a wide range of modelling applications. This chapter illustrates a few applications of GP as a modelling tool in the broad area of water resources modelling and management. The studies have found GP to be a useful tool for such applications with some advantages over other artificial intelligence techniques. The major findings reported in this chapter are enumerated as follows;

1. Genetic programming is able to develop simple models for developing the time series forecast models. When compared to the complex architecture of neural networks the GP models are simpler and easy to analyse. This is particularly relevant in developing transparent models for predicting natural phenomena. Complex neural network architectures make ANN model more or less "black-box" in nature, where as simpler GP models makes it easy to analyse the physical significance of each input in the model development.
2. In GP modeling, the optimum model architecture is evolved by GP after testing, most often, millions of alternate model structures and parameters as against the trial and error approach being followed by other artificial intelligence modeling approaches like neural networks. This helps in converging to global optimal solutions in minimizing the error criteria used for model development. Thus GP is able to develop global optimum models for predicting/forecasting hydrological processes and time series.
3. Genetic programming has the capability of parsimoniously selecting the variables for model development from the potential inputs. This helps to prevent redundancy in model development in terms of unnecessary inputs and parameters. In course of the model development GP determines the significance of each input in the model development in an efficient way so that the totally insignificant inputs are eliminated from the model. As shown in the results approaches like neural network models are also able to identify the relative significance of the inputs, they are less efficient in achieving this because of the rigidity of the model structure and connection weights.

These key advantages of GP modeling are illustrated using realistic example in the broad area of hydrology and groundwater management for time series model development and conclusions are drawn which establishes the potential of genetic programming as a modeling and prediction tool for hydrology and water resources application.

Author details

J. Sreekanth[1,2,3] and Bithin Datta[1,2]
[1]*CSIRO Land and Water, Ecosciences Precinct, Australia*
[2]*Discipline of Civil and Environmental Engineering,*
School of Engineering and Physical Sciences, James Cook University, Townsville, Australia
[3]*CRC for Contaminant Assessment and Remediation of the Environment, Mawson Lakes, Australia*

7. References

[1] Koza, J.R., 1994. Genetic programming as a means for programming computers by natural selection. Statistics and Computing, 4(2): 87-112.

[2] Babovic, V., Keijzer, M., 2002. Rainfall runoff modelling based on genetic programming. Nordic Hydrology, 33(5): 331-346.

[3] Rabunal, J. R., Puertas, J., Suarez, J., and Rivero, D. (2006) Determination of the unit hydrograph of a typical urban basin using genetic programming and artificial neural networks Hydrological Processes, vol. 21, Issue 4, pp.476-485

[4] Rahman Khatibi, Mohammad Ali Ghorbani, Mahsa Hasanpour Kashani and Ozgur Kisi (2011) Coparison of three artificial intelligence techniques for discharge routing, Jorunal of Hydrology, 403(3-4), 201-212.

[5] Ozgur Kisi and Jalal Shiri (2010), Precipitation forecasting using wavelet genetic programming and wavelet neuro fuzzy conjunction models, Water Resources Management, 25(13), 3135-3152.

[6] Benne Selle, Nithin Muttil (2010), Testing the structure of a hydrological model using genetic programming, Journal of Hydrology, 397(1-2), 1-9.

[7] Sreekanth, J., and Bithin, Datta., (2011), Comparative evaluation of Genetic Programming and Neural Networks as potential surrogate models for coastal aquifer management, Journal of *Water Resources Management*, 25, 3201 – 3218. (doi: 10.1007/s11269-011-9852-8)

[8] Parasuraman, K., Elshorbagy, A., 2008. Toward improving the reliability of hydrologic prediction: Model structure uncertainty and its quantification using ensemble-based genetic programming framework. Water Resources Research, 44(12).

[9] Sreekanth, J., and Bithin, Datta., (2011), Coupled simulation-optimization model for coastal aquifer management using genetic programming based ensemble surrogate models and multiple realization optimization, *Water Resources Research*, 47, W04516, doi: 10.1029/2010WR009683

[10] Sreekanth, J., and Bithin, Datta., (2010), Multi-objective management of saltwater intrusion in coastal aquifers using genetic programming and modular neural network based surrogate models, *Journal of Hydrology*, 393 (3-4), 245-256

[11] Emily, Zechman, Baha, Mirghani, G, Mahinthakumar and S Ranji Ranjithan (2005) A genetic programming based surrogate model development and its application to a groundwater source identification problem, ASCE conf. Proc. 173, 341.

[12] Jyothiprakash, V. And Magar, R.B., (2012) Multi-step ahead daily and hourly intermittent reservoir inflow prediction using artificial intelligence techiniques using lumped and distributed data, *Journal of Hydrology*, 450, 293-307.

Chapter 11

Comparison Between Equations Obtained by Means of Multiple Linear Regression and Genetic Programming to Approach Measured Climatic Data in a River

M.L. Arganis, R. Val, R. Domínguez, K. Rodríguez, J. Dolz and J.M. Eaton

Additional information is available at the end of the chapter

http://dx.doi.org/10.5772/50556

1. Introduction

The Ebro River is located in north-eastern Spain. After crossing the Catalan coastal mountain system, the Ebro reaches the sea. Along the lower part of the river, about 100 km from the mouth, there is a system of three reservoirs: Mequinenza (1500 hm^3), Ribarroja (210 hm^3) and Flix (11 hm^3). These reservoirs regulate the hydrologic regime of the lower part of the river until it reaches the sea. The Mequinenza and Ribarroja reservoirs were finished in the late 1960s (in 1966 and 1969, respectively), while the Flix reservoir was completed in 1945. About 5 km downstream from the Flix reservoir is the Ascó nuclear power plant, which began its activity in December 1984 [1].

Ascó Nuclear Power Station, located on the Ebro River in Spain (Figure 1), takes river water for cooling purposes. The temperature of discharged water must be less than 13 ºC, however five kilometers downstream a water temperature of nearly 14ºC was estimated and such an anomaly was reported to the nuclear center. A detailed analysis shows the relationship between water temperature variation and the presence of a cascade dam system upstream of the Ascó Nuclear Power Station. Water temperature decreases downstream in the outlets of cascade dam systems [1]. During the winter period there also exists thermal stratification within the river, whereby water temperatures near deep intake areas are considerably less than the ambient temperature. Such a situation impacts water taken for cooling purposes by Ascó Nuclear Power Station.

Throughout the years, the human being has made use of fluvial ecosystems. Some actions have caused changes in the thermal regimes of rivers (eg. [2 ,3]).

Reservoirs and the use of water for cooling are the most important sources of water temperature modifications caused by humans. The use of water for cooling, usually by power plants, causes the water to become warmer [4]. This is often called "thermal pollution".

Reservoirs can cause various effects, depending on various factors such as the climate, the size of the impoundment, the residence time, the stability of the thermal stratification and the depth of the outlet [5]. Due to thermal stratification occurs, the water from deep-release reservoirs is cooler in the summer and warmer in the winter than it would be without the reservoir [6,7]. Water diversions can also alter water temperature regimes because they reduce discharge, which causes water temperature range to increase throughout the year [8]. Irrigation is also known to decrease discharge and increase water temperature [9].

In order to preserve the ecological balance it is very important to have a continuous inspection of water quality in that portion of the river. Freshwater organisms are mostly ectotherms and are therefore largely influenced by water temperature. Some of the expected consequences of a water temperature increase are life-cycle changes [4, 10], and shifts in the distribution of species with the arrival of allochthonous species [11, 12] and the expansion of epidemic diseases [13] as a possible result. Also, aquatic flora and fauna depend on dissolved oxygen to survive and this water quality parameter is a function of water temperature as well.

Water temperature variation analysis, in a river with a cascade dam, involves several hydrological and environmental aspects because of the dams impact on aquatic flora and fauna as shown by [14,15,16,1,17,18,19].

Because temperature is a water quality parameter that affects aquatic flora and fauna, it is important to have mathematical models which allow one to make estimations of water temperature behavior. These models are based on climatic data such as solar radiation, net radiation, relative humidity, air temperature, and wind speed. Accurate water temperature modeling may help diminish the environmental impact of increased water temperature on aquatic flora and fauna within the river.

Genetic programming (GP) algorithms have been used to derive equations which estimate the ten minute average water temperature from known variables such as relative humidity, air temperature, wind speed, solar radiation, and net radiation [20]. Only air temperature and relative humidity were associated with water temperature in some of the resulting equations, even though solar radiation is known to increase water temperature in rivers and ponds.

A correlation analysis could prove the implicit participation of solar radiation as a variable in air temperature, even though an explicit solar radiation term does not appears in the equation. Solar radiation was assumed to be independent with respect to water temperature resulting from neglecting the lag time between a change in the solar radiation value and the corresponding change in water temperature, [1] estimated this lag time to be nearly 160 minutes. By inputting data to both the genetic programming algorithm and multiple linear regression (MLR) in this study, it was possible to identify the relative significance of each climatic variable in estimating water temperature.

Tests were made from data collected at the Ribarroja Station, which is located on the Ebro River in Spain (Figure 1).

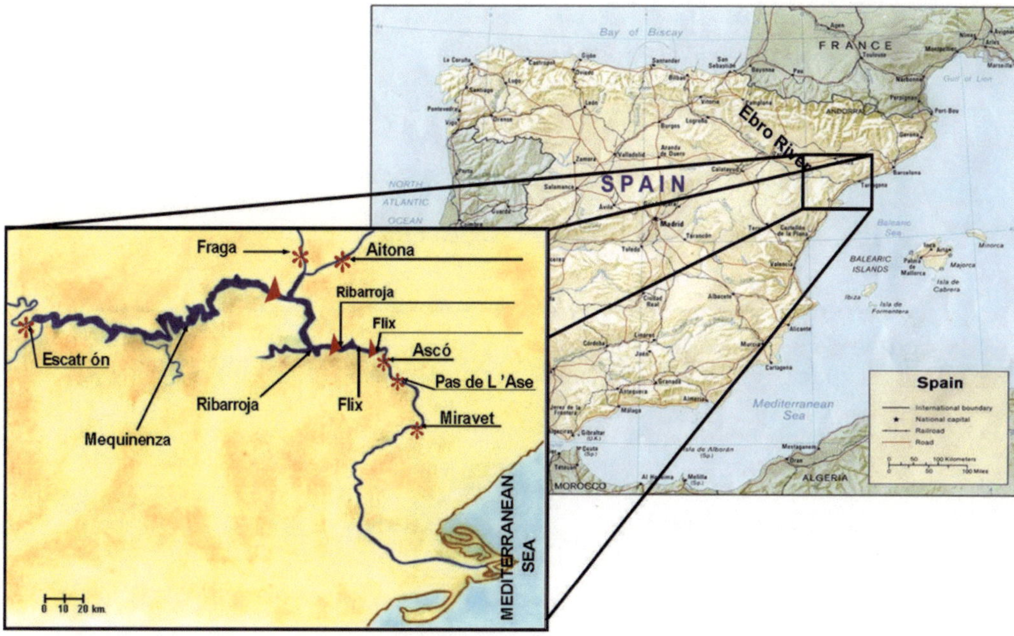

Figure 1. Location of reservoirs and climatic stations on the Ebro River in Spain (Val, 2003 and google.com.mx)

2. Methods

2.1. Genetic programming

Evolutionary Computation (EC) are learning, search and optimization algorithms based on the theories of natural evolution and genetic. The steps of the basic structure of this kind of algorithms are shown in Figure. First, an initial population of potential solutions is randomly created (in the case of a Simple Genetic Algorithm (SGA), the initial population is composed of binary individuals). Then, the individuals of this population are evaluated considering the problem to be solved (environment) where a fitness value is assigned to each individual depending on how close individuals are to the optimum. A new generation is created by selecting the fitter solutions of previous generation and then, genetic operators such as crossover and mutation (Alter P(t) of Figure 2) are applied to selected individuals in order to create a new population (offsprings) which improve their fitness values in comparison to previous generation. This new population is evaluated and selection, crossover and mutation are again applied. This process continues until a termination criterion is reached (this is commonly established as the maximum number of generation).

Genetic Programming (GP) is a class of Evolutionary Algorithm (EA) [21,22,23] where individuals in the population are computer programs, usually expressed as syntax trees or as corresponding expressions in prefix notation (see Figure 3).

```
PROGRAM Evolution-Based Algorithm
        t = 0
        Create Initial Population P(t)
        Evaluate Initial Population P(t)
        While (not termination_criterion) do
                t = t + 1
                Select Individuals for Reproduction P(t) from P(t-1)
                Alter P(t)
                Evaluate New Population P(t)
        end
```

Figure 2. Evolution-based algorithm.

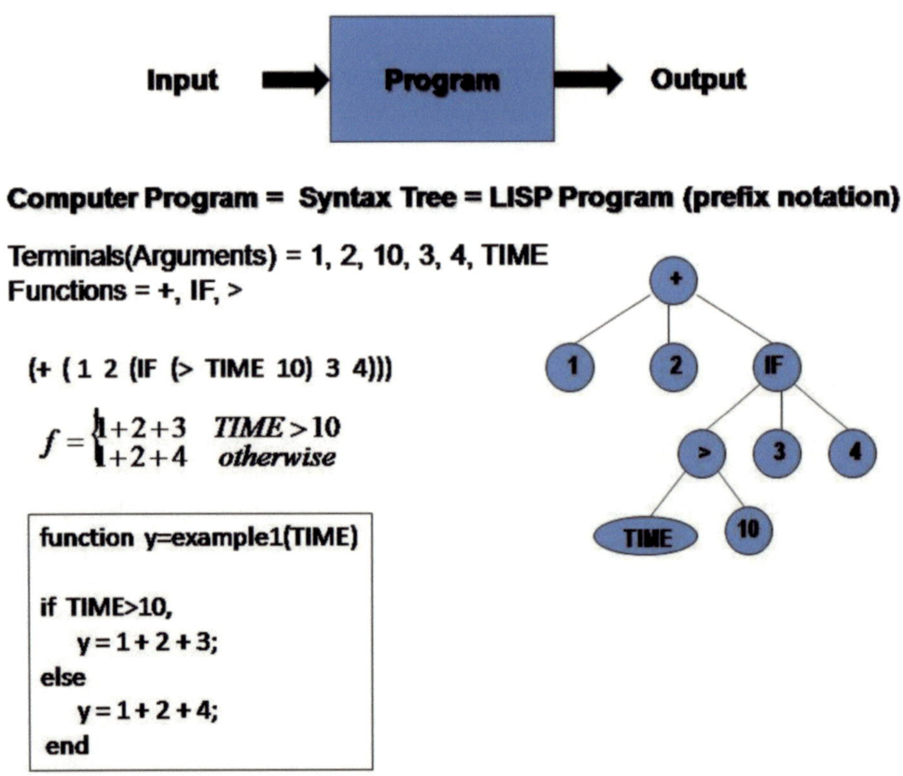

Figure 3. Genetic programming representation: syntax tree, LISP or prefix notation, mathematical function and MATLAB program

As seen from Figure 3, individuals are created based on a function and terminal set according to the problem to be solved. A root node is generally a function selected randomly from the function set. Then, functions and terminals are chosen in order to form the syntax tree that represents an individual. It is important to set a maximum depth or maximum number of nodes, thus the size of the individuals can be control and avoid bloating. Bloat is the rapid growth of programs produced by genetic programming or variable coding heuristics.

The fitness value of the population is usually calculated by running each individual with the problem input data, or testing data, and see how close the output of the program (individual) is to some desired (reference) output specified by the user.

Each generation, fitter individuals are evolved by means of crossover and mutation. Crossover is a sexual genetic operator that takes two parent-individuals, randomly selects a node in each parent and exchanges the associated sub-branch starting from the selected node between the parents producing two new individuals. Due to GP uses variables individuals representation, the selected nodes for crossing over two individuals are different in each parent. Note that if the parents to crossover are identical, the new two offsprings are generally different to the parents because the node selected for crossing over is different in each paren. In contrast to Genetic Algorithms, when two identical parents are crossing over, the offsprings are similar to their parents because the crossing point is the same for both parents and they have the same length.

Mutation is a asexual genetic operator that takes an individual, randomly selects a node and replaces the associated branch for a new branch generated based on the primitive set (functions and terminals sets).

The application of evolutionary computing algorithms has expanded in the last few years to several engineering applications, particularly in regards to hydraulics and hydrological engineering. Examples include: studies of hydroinformatics by [24,25]; studies in rainfall runoff modeling by [26-31] . The unit hydrograph for a typical urban basin was obtained by means of genetic programming in [32].

A study of Chezy's roughness coefficient by [33], who also uses an evolutionary polynomial regression in [34,35].

A deep percolation model using genetic programming was obtained by [36]. Models related to sediments were obtained with genetic programming by [37].

Evapotranspiration phenomena has been predicted by means of genetic programming [38]. The flood routing problem was analyzed by means of genetic programming by [39] and the soil moisture too [40].

In this work, a genetic programming algorithm operating in the MATLAB environment [41] developed at the *Instituto de Investigaciones en Matemáticas Aplicadas y en Sistemas* (IIMAS), *Universidad Nacional Autónoma de México* (UNAM) was applied and compared with a traditional curve adjustment technique, in an attempt to get another useful application of these optimization procedures. Here, a stochastic universal selection method was used [42] (Baker, 1987); crossover operator was used with a probability of 90% (see Table 1). It is important to mention that two different mutation operators were used. The first one with a probability of 5% randomly selects a branch and then it exchanges this selected branch by a new generated one. The second mutation operator works by selecting constant values and with a probability of 5%, these constants are mutated by adding a random value of a defined range.

This climatic data modeling problem is expressed as a symbolic regression, a common application of genetic programming, where function set consists of arithmetic and trigonometric functions and terminals set consists of climatological variables which are described in next section.

2.2. Input data

Water temperature (T_w), solar radiation (r_s), net radiation (r_n), relative humidity (h_r), air temperature (T_a), and wind speed (V_v) data measured at the Ribarroja Station from January to June of 1998 were utilized in this study. The ten minute water temperature average was calculated using all of these variables. Later, the averaged air temperature and relative humidity (in decimals) were filtered to take into account a seven day relay. Data filtering was done with the following equation:

$$Vi_{f_t} = \frac{\sum_{i=t}^{t-k} V_i}{k+1} \tag{1}$$

Where :

V_i is the original independent variable

Vi_{f_t} is the filtered independent variable and

k is the size or widow filter (in this case k=6).

Recorded solar radiation at minute t_i has its influence on water temperature at instant t_{i+160} [1] and such a gap needs to be taken into account for all considered data. For example, the first data point of the dependent variable, ten minute average water temperature at instant t_{i+160}, was coupled with the first data point of the independent variable, such as solar radiation at instant t_i. For the independent variables, net radiation (r_n) and wind speed (v_w) values of t_{i+160} were used, while air temperature and relative humidity values were considered using both seven day filtering and values corresponding to instant t_{i+160}.

2.3. Objective function

The objective function was to minimize the mean square error between the calculated and measured data using the following equation:

$$\min \quad Z = \frac{1}{n}\sum_{n}(Tw - \hat{T}w)^2 \tag{2}$$

Where:

Z is the function to minimize
Tw is the average of measured temperature each ten minute interval in ºC
$\hat{T}w$ is the calculated temperature with the genetic programming algorithm in ºC, and n is the data number.

2.4. Parameter setting

Parameters used in the genetic programming algorithm are shown in Table 1. *MaxNumNodes* corresponds to the maximum number of nodes an individual can have; meanwhile *MaxNodesMut* represents the maximum number of nodes a new created branch can have for mutation. Terminal set represents the independent variables and Tw corresponds to the dependent variable to be modeled.

Parameter	Value	Description
Pcross	0.9	Probability of crossover
Pmut	0.05	Probability of mutation
Pmut_R	0.05	Probability of mutating a node containing a constant
MaxNodesMut	8	Maximum number of nodes for mutation
Nind	200	Number of individuals in the population
MaxNumNodes	30	Maximum number of nodes for each individual
MaxGen	5000	Maximum number of generations (iterations)
Function_Set	+,-,*, /,cos	Function set
Terminal Set	r_s, r_n, h_r, T_a, V_v	Climatological variables

Table 1. Parameter settings

The function *cosine (cos)* was included in the function set due to preliminary tests, where a reduction in mean quadratic error was obtained, included this cosine function. This fact is related to one of the two properties that GP individuals must satisfy: *sufficiency*. This property says that the set of terminals and the set of functions should be defined in order to express a solution to the study problem [23]. The second property, *closure*, specifies that each of the functions in the function set can be able to accept, as its argument, any value and data type that may possibly be returned by any function and any value or data type that can be possibly assumed by any terminal [23]. In this approach, a protected division was implemented in order to avoid a division by zero. In this situation occurs, a high value is returned.

By including the cosine function, associated equation also presented a good reproduction of the periodic behavior of water temperature over time.

2.5. Multiple linear regressions

Multiple linear regressions (MLR) relate a dependent variable, y, with two or more independents variables, $x_1, x_2, x_3,\ldots, x_n$, by means of an equation expressed as:

$$y = a_1x_1 + a_2x_2 + a_3x_3 + \ldots + a_nx_n \tag{3}$$

Coefficients $a_1, a_2, a_3, \ldots a_n$, are weighting factors which allow one to see the relative importance of each variable x_i as y is approached. Indirectly the coefficients can indicate if there is a strong correlation or lack of correlation between x_i and y.

This method is often applied for several hydrology problems such as: forecasting equations for standardized runoff in a region of a country with standardized teleconnection indices, when El Niño or La Niña phenomenon occur [43] (González et al., 2000), or as an auxiliary method in estimating intensity-duration-frequency curves. In this research, regressions were made using the Microsoft Excel data analysis tool.

3. Results and discussion

Measured climatic data of the above variables, corresponding from January to June of 1998, were fed into both the symbolic regression genetic programming model and the multiple linear regression model in order to estimate water temperature. The models were then applied using data from January to June of 1999 in order to approach water temperature averages. Comparisons for the1998 and 1999 results were then made.

The genetic programming algorithm (equation 4) determined the next mathematical model which approaches the water temperature (average of each ten minutes).

$$\begin{aligned} T_w &= (T_a + \cos(\cos((T_a + \cos T_a) * 0.6904149)) + \\ &+ \cos(\cos(1.17748531 * T_a + \cosh_r)) + 1.87808843) * 0.67508628 \end{aligned} \tag{4}$$

Using equation (4), the individual with the best performance reported an objective function value of 0.7922.

Meanwhile, the multiple linear regression model is expressed as follows:

$$\mathrm{T_w} = 0.00022505\mathrm{r_s} + 0.00036289\mathrm{r_n} + 0.66464617\mathrm{T_a} - 0.02807297\mathrm{V_v} - 1.24438982\mathrm{h_r} + 3.87792166 \tag{5}$$

Where:

T_w corresponds to the average water temperature each ten minute interval at instant $t+160$ in ºC

T_a is the average air temperature each ten minute interval, with seven days filtering, corresponding to instant t+160, in ºC

h_r represents the average relative humidity each ten minutes interval, with seven days filtering, corresponding to instant t+160 in decimals

r_s is the average solar radiation each ten minutes interval, at instant t, in W/m^2

r_n corresponds to the average net radiation each ten minutes interval, corresponding to instant t+160, in W/m^2

and finally,

v_v represents the average wind speed each ten minutes interval, corresponding to instant t+160, in m/s.

The objective function value using equation 5 was 0.8724.

Figure 4 represents both measured and calculated water temperature variation versus time using both equations (4) and (5). Measured and calculated water temperature values also appear in Figure 5 with equations (4) and (5) in comparison with the identity function.

Figure 4 indicate similar results for both genetic programming and multiple linear regression models in comparison with measured data.

In Figures 5 the measured data were compared against the identity function and the best correlation between these values was found using genetic programming (r=0.9697).

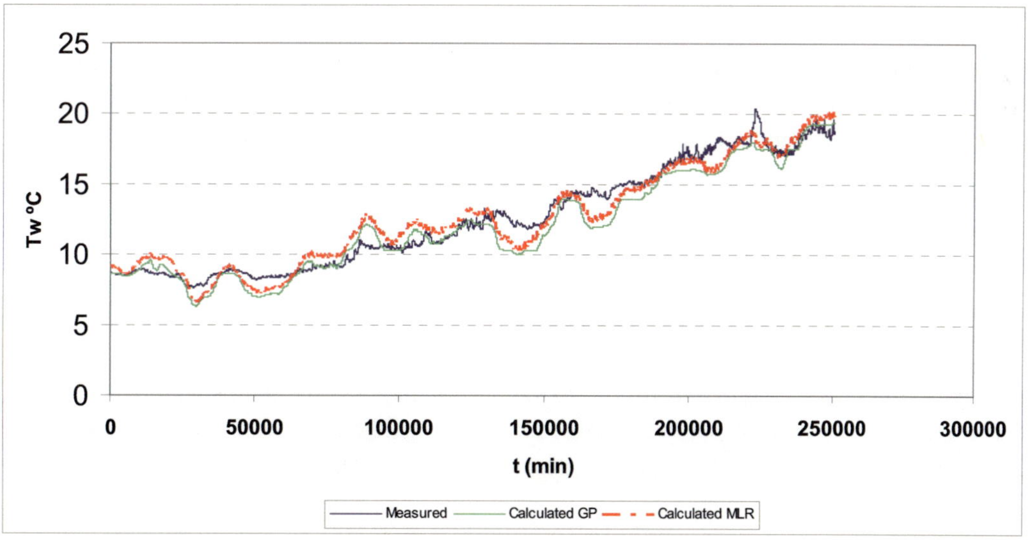

Figure 4. Time variation of measured and calculated water temperature data, Ribarroja Station. January to June, 1998

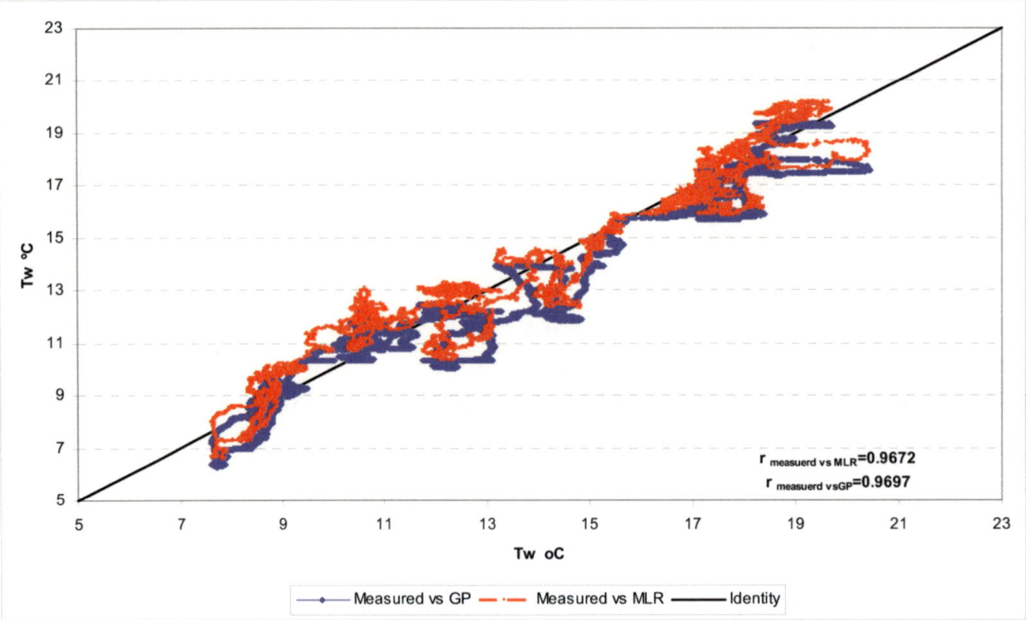

Figure 5. Comparison between genetic programming and multiple linear regression models against measured data and the identity function. Ribarroja Station. January to June, 1998

Water temperature approach with multiple linear regression and genetic programming algorithm from January to June 1999

Equations (4) and (5) were applied to measured data from 1999 at the Ribarroja Station in order to arrive at the average water temperature. Measured water temperature data and the obtained residuals using both models are shown in Figure 6.

According to Figure 6 the differences between measured and calculated water temperature shown were up to 5.5 °C (underestimation) and about 0.5 °C (overestimation) while differences with equation 5 reported an underestimation near to 4.5°C and the overestimation of almost 2°C, so the range of variation in water temperature reported by both equations is almost the same.

In order to get better results in future works must be analyzed the data standardization as a preprocessing to get new mathematical linear and nonlinear models [44], The variables could be standardized by subtracting the mean and dividing by the standard deviation:

$$Z = \frac{T_w - \overline{T}_w}{\sigma_{T_w}} \tag{6}$$

where:

Z standardized variable, dimensionless
T_w variable before standardization, with physical dimensions

$\bar{T}_w$ mean of T_w, with the same units than T_w (the arithmetic average can be used) and

σ_{T_w} standard deviation of T_w, with the same units than T_w

Another possibility to analyze is the splitting of the considered function by taking into account the different times of year that causes a variation in water temperature behavior.

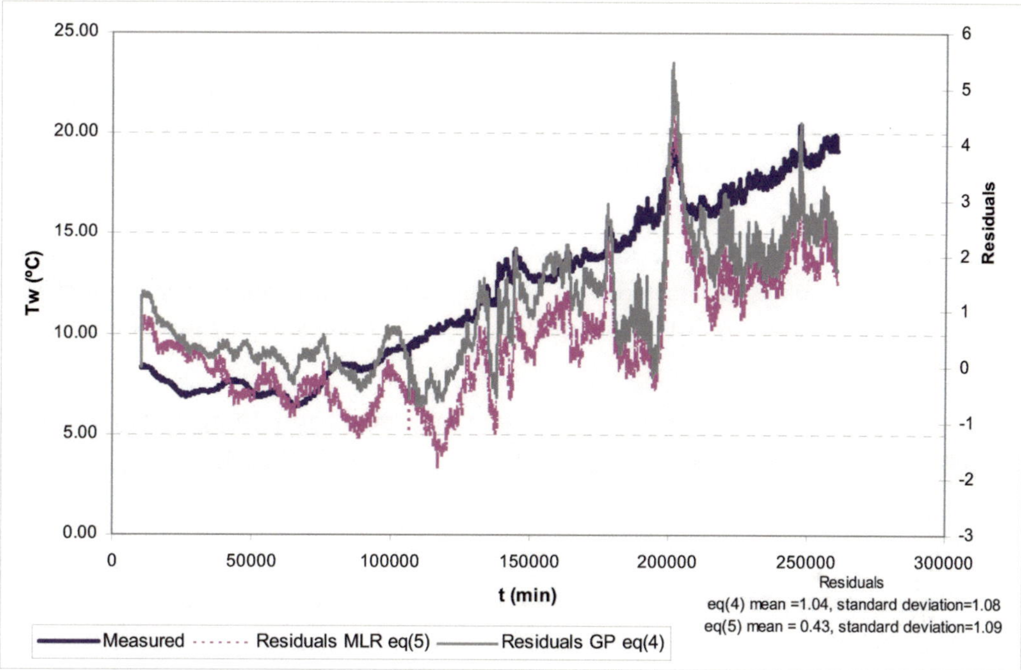

Figure 6. Residuals and measured water temperature data for the year 1999 at the Ribarroja Station in Spain

4. Conclusions

Water temperature adjustment curves, in a gauged station on the Ebro River in Spain, were obtained by means of two procedures: a genetic programming algorithm (equation 4) and a multiple linear regression (equation 5), using data from 1998. The multiple linear regression method yielded a function containing the five considered variables (solar radiation, net radiation, wind speed, air temperature and relative humidity) with each variable weighted. The genetic programming algorithm yielded a function where water temperature was obtained only as a function of air temperature and relative humidity. The others variables were eliminated by the evolution algorithm due to the lack of correlation between water temperature and the remaining variables although solar radiation is implied inside the air temperature term.

Comparing measured data with calculated data, for the year 1998, led to only minor errors in estimating the average water temperature using the genetic programming algorithm. When equations (4) and (5) were applied to another year, 1999, minor mean quadratic error in estimating water temperature was obtained using the multiple linear regression equation (5). The mean quadratic error associated with the multiple linear regression equation (5) for 1999 was 1.375 ºC; whereas with the genetic programming equation (4) was 2.248 ºC. This error can be considered acceptable if one takes in account the average temperature from January to June 1998 was 12.54 ºC, whereas the average temperature in 1999 for the same period was 11.62 ºC. The residuals obtained with equations (4) and (5) using data for the year 1999 had average values of 1.04 ºC and 0.43 ºC, respectively and with this criteria, multiple linear regression model can be considered better than the GP. However, reviewing the standard deviations, both models had almost the same value (1.09 ºC and 1.08 ºC, respectively).

The described procedures are then useful because equations similar to (4) or (5) can estimate important water quality characteristics, such as water temperature, using previously measured climatic data, predicted climatic data, and hydrological parameters for a given time period.

Engineer's criteria and common sense must be considered before to apply any model to simulate physical variables.

Some standardization procedures to the involved data are suggested in order to improve the results from new models that can be obtained.

The methods here applied are undoubtedly useful in several areas of knowledge, and can led us to new approaches to physical phenomena by considering measured field data.

Future work is focuses on the use of NARMAX (Non-linear Autorregressive Moving Average with eXogenous inputs) model combined with genetic programming in order to model the water temperature providing more accurate equations.

Author details

M.L. Arganis and R. Domínguez
PUMAGUA, Universidad Nacional Autónoma de México, México

R. Val and K. Rodríguez
Instituto de Investigaciones en Matemáticas Aplicadas y en Sistemas, Coyoacán, D.F. México

Josep Dolz
Universidad Politécnica de Cataluña, Barcelona, España

J.M. Eaton
Centre for Hydrology, Micrometeorology and Climate Change, Department of Civil and Environmental Engineering, University College Cork, Cork, Republic of Ireland

Acknowledgements

Authors gratefully acknowledge the financial support under the project PAPIIT no. IN109011.

5. References

[1] [1] 23. Val S R (2003) Incidencia de los embalses en el comportamiento térmico del río. Caso del sistema de embalses Mequinenza-Ribarroja-Flix en el Río Ebro. Tesis Doctoral. Universidad Politécnica de Catalunya. Barcelona, España.

[2] Alberto F, Arrúe JL (1986) Anomalías térmicas en algunos tramos de la red hidrográfica del Ebro. Anales de la Estación Experimental Aula Dei 18: 91-113.

[3] Preece RM, Jones HA (2002) The effect of Keepit Dam on the temperature regime of the Namoi River, Australia. River Research and Applications 18: 397-414. DOI: 10.1002/rra.686

[4] Hellawell JM (1986) Biological indicators of freshwater pollution and environment management. Elsevier, London. 546 pp.

[5] Lessard JL, Hayes DB (2003) Effects of elevated water temperature on fish and macroinvertebrate communities below small dams. River Research and Applications 19: 721-732. DOI: 10.1002/rra.713

[6] Ward JV (1985) Thermal characteristics of running waters. Hydrobiologia 125: 31-46.

[7] Webb BW, Walling DE (1993) Temporal variability in the impact of river regulation on thermal regime and some biological implications. Freshwater Biology 29: 167-182.

[8] Meier W, Bonjour C, Wüest A, Reichert P (2003) Modeling the effect of water diversion on the temperature of mountain streams. Journal of Environmental Engineering 129: 755-764. DOI: 10.1061/(ASCE)0733-9372(2003)129:8(755)

[9] Verma RD (1986) Environmental impacts of irrigation projects. Journal of Irrigation and Drainage Engineering 112: 322-330.

[10] Winfield, IJ, Nelson JS (1991) Cyprinid fishes. Systematics, biology and exploitation. Chapman & Hall, London. 667 pp.

[11] Schindler, DW (1997) Widespread effects of climatic warming on freshwater ecosystems in North America. Hydrological Processes, 11: 1043-1067.

[12] [12] Walther, Gr, Post E, Convey P, Menzel A., Parmesan C, Beebee TJC, Fromentin JM, Hoegh-Guldberg O,. Bairlein F (2002) Ecological responses to recent climate change. Nature, 416: 389-395.

[13] Harvell, CD, C. E Mitchell, J. R Ward, S. Altizer, A. P Dobson, R. S. Ostfeld & M. D. Samuel. 2002. Climate warming and disease risks for terrestrial and marine biota. Science, 296: 2158-2162.

[14] Smalley DH, Novak JK (1978). Natural thermal phenomena associated with reservoirs. In Environmental Effect of Large Dams. ASCE.

[15] [15]. Cassidy RA (1989). Water temperature, dissolved oxygen and turbidity control in reservoir releases. In: Alternatives in Regulated River Management.

[16] Mohseni O, Stefan HG (1999). Stream temperature/air temperature relationship: A physical interpretation. Journal of Hydrology 218: 128–141.

[17] Caissie D, El-Jabi N, Satish MG (2001). Modeling of maximum daily water temperature in a small stream using air temperature. Journal of Hydrology 251: 14-28.

[18] Batalla RJ, Gómez CM, Kondolf GM (2004). Reservoir-induced hydrological changes in the Ebro River basin (NE Spain). Journal of Hydrology 290: 117–136.

[19] Morrill JC, Bales RC, Conklin MH (2005). Estimating stream temperature from air temperature: Implications for future water quality. Journal of Environmental Engineering.131: 139-146.

[20] 1. Arganis ML, Val SR, Rodríguez VK, Domínguez MR, Dolz R.J (2005). Comparación de curvas de ajuste a la Temperatura del Agua de un río usando programación genética. Congreso Mexicano de Computación Evolutiva COMCEV.

[21] Cramer NL (1985). A representation for the adaptive generation of simple sequential programs. In Proceedings of International Conference on Genetic Algorithms and the Applications: 183-187.

[22] Koza JR (1989). Hierarchical genetic algorithms operating on populations of computer programs. In Proceeding of the 11th International Joint Conference on Artificial Intelligence. 1: 768-774.

[23] Koza JR (1992) Genetic Programming: On the Programming of Computers by Means of Natural Selection. MIT Press.

[24] Babovic V, Keijzer M (2000). Genetic programming as a model induction engine. Journal of Hydroinformatics 2: 35-60.

[25] [25] Babovic V, Keijzer M, Rodríguez AD, Harrington J (2001). An evolutionary approach to knowledge induction: Genetic programming in Hydraulic Engineering. Proceedings of the World Water & Environmental Resources Congress, May 21-24.

[26] Savic DA, Walters GA, Davidson JW (1999). A Genetic Programming Approach to Rainfall-Runoff Modeling. Water Resources Management 13: 219–231.

[27] Drécourt JP, Madsen H (2001). Role of domain knowledge in data-driven modeling. 4th DHI Software Conference & DHI Software Courses Helsingør, Denmark, June 6-13.

[28] [28]Whigham PA, Crapper PF (2001). Modeling Rainfall-Runoff using Genetic Prograaming. Mathematical and Computer Modeling. 33: 707-721.

[29] Khu ST, Keedwell EC, Pollard O (2004). An evolutionary-based real-time updating technique for an operational rainfall-runoff forecasting model, In: Complexity and Integrated Resources Management, Trans. In Proceedings of the 2nd Biennial Meeting of the International Environmental Modelling and Software Society. 1: 141–146.

[30] Khu ST, Liong SY, Babovic V, Madsen H, Muttil N (2001). Genetic programming and its application in real time runoff forecasting.Journal of the American Water Resources Association. 37: 439-451.

[31] Dorado J, Rabuñal JR, Puertas J, Santos A, Rivero D (2002). Prediction and modeling of the flow of a typical urban basin through genetic programming. Applications of Evolutionary Computing. 190-201

[32] Rabuñal JR, Puertas J, Suárez J, Rivero D (2007). Determination of the unit hydrograph of a typical urban basin using genetic programming and artificial neural networks. Hydrological processes. 21: 476–485.

[33] Giustolisi O (2004). Using genetic programming to determine Chezy resistance coefficient in corrugated channels. Journal of Hydroinformatics. 6: 157-173.

[34] Giustolisi O, Doglioni A, Savic DA, Webb B (2004). A Multimodel Approach to Analysis of Environmental Phenomena. Web site: http://www.iemss.org/iemss2004/pdf /evocomp/giusamul.pdf

[35] Giustolisi O, Doglioni A, Savic DA, Webb B (2007). A multimodel approach to analysis of environmental phenomena, Environmental Modelling and Software. 22: 674-682.

[36] Selle B, Muttil N (2011). Testing the structure of a hydrological model using Genetic Programming. Journal of Hydrology. 397: 1–9.

[37] Aytek A, Kisi O (2008). A genetic programming approach to suspended sediment modelling. Journal of Hydrology. 351: 288– 298.

[38] Izadifar Z, Elshorbagy A (2010). Prediction of hourly actual evapotranspiration using neural networks, genetic programming, and statistical models. Hydrological processes. 24: 3413–3425.

[39] Sivapragasam C, Maheswaran R, Venkatesh V (2008). Genetic programming approach for flood routing in natural channels. Hydrological processes. 22: 623–628.

[40] Makkeasorn A, Chang N-B, Beaman M, Wyatt C, Slater C. (2006). Soil moisture estimation in a semiarid watershed using RADARSAT-1 satellite imagery and genetic programming. Water Resources Research. 42.

[41] The MathWorks (1992). MATLAB Reference Guide.

[42] Baker, J (1987). Reducing Bias And Inefficiency In The Selection Algorithm, Proc. Of The Second International Conference On Genetic Algorithms ICGA. Grefenstette, Ed.: 14-21.

[43] González VRF, Franco V, Fuentes MGE, Arganis JML (2000). Análisis comparativo entre los escurrimientos pronosticados y registrados en 1999 en las Regiones Pacífico Noroeste, Norte, Centro, Pacífico Sur y Golfo de la República Mexicana considerando que estuvo presente el fenómeno "La Niña" y Predicción de escurrimientos en dichas regiones del país en los periodos primavera-verano y otoño-invierno de 2000. Para FIRCO. Informe Final.

[44] Arganis JML, Val SR, Prats RJ, ,Rodríguez VK, Domínguez MR, Dolz RJ (2009). "Genetic programming and standardization in water temperature modelling," Advances in Civil Engineering. Hindawi Publishing Corporation. 2009: 10.

Chapter 12

Inter-Comparison of an Evolutionary Programming Model of Suspended Sediment Time-Series with Other Local Models

M. A. Ghorbani, R. Khatibi, H. Asadi and P. Yousefi

Additional information is available at the end of the chapter

http://dx.doi.org/10.5772/47801

1. Introduction

The experience of applying evolutionary computing to time series describing local physical problems has benefited the modelling culture by showing that many different mathematical formulae can be produced to describe the same problem. This experience brings into the focus the roles of pluralism in the modelling culture as opposed to searching for the best model, where physical problems provide relevance and context to the choice of modelling techniques. Both of these roles are often overlooked and do not directly influence research agenda. Although the focus of this paper is on evolutionary computing, it also promotes a pluralistic modelling culture by studying other modelling techniques, as well as by keeping the role of physical problems in the foreground.

Estimating suspended sediment loads is a problem of practical importance and includes such problems as changing courses in rivers, loss of fertile soil, filling reservoirs and impacts on water quality. The study of these problems in the short-run are referred to as sediment transport and erosion for those in the long-run. Past empirical capabilities remain invaluable but are not sufficient on their own as management and engineering solutions often require an insight into the problem. Empirical knowledge has been incorporated into the body of distributed modelling techniques giving rise to sophisticated modelling software tools but their applications require a great deal of resources. There remains a category of problems, often referred to as time series analysis, which uses the sequences of time variations and predicts the future values. This category of models provides useful information to management of local problems. For instance, such models may be used to schedule dredging requirements or other maintenance activities. Time series analysis is developing into local management tools and it is a focus of this chapter.

The aim of this chapter is to predict suspended sediment load of a river into the future. Besides the traditional empirical Sediment Rating Curve (SRC), there are several strategies for analysing such time series and *evolutionary computing* is one of Artificial Intelligence (AI) approaches, which broadly include capabilities for searching and recognising patterns among others. This chapter also employs Artificial Neural Network (ANN), which is another AI approach. Yet another strategy is to regard time series as outcomes of many random drivers and this assumption is supported by a whole body of probabilistic approaches, where this chapter uses Multi-Linear Regression (MLR) analysis to model the same data. Over the past few decades, research has increasingly focused on the application of deterministic chaos (or chaos theory or dynamic systems) showing that many of apparently randomly varying system behaviours can be explained by deterministic chaos. The concept behind this modelling strategy is that the particular data can largely be explained by deterministic behaviour, where in time the system evolves asymptotically towards an *attractor*. Its random-looking variations are assumed to be an internal feature of the system and depending on its initial conditions, its state under a certain range may become highly erratic but with a predictable behaviour. Evidently, none of these strategies are identical and different models rarely produce identical results. This chapter therefore compares the performance of these modelling strategies for solving an engineering problem.

The study employs 26 years of the Mississippi River data recorded at Tarbert + RR Landings and involve both flows and suspended sediment load. The river discharges about 200 million metric tons of suspended sediment per year to the Gulf of Mexico, where it ranks about sixth in the world today.

2. Literature review

Sediment Rating Curve (SRC) is an empirical approach used by practitioners in the engineering studies of sediment and erosion problems. The log linear rating curve method has been used widely and Sivakumar and Wallender (2005) outline the many flaws associated with this technique, including the lack of fit due to missing variables (e.g. Miller, 1951), retransformation bias (e.g. Ferguson, 1986), and non-normality of the error distribution (e.g. Thomas, 1988). According to Sivakumar and Wallender (2005), the technique has been modified including, among others, use of separate curves for different seasons (Miller, 1951), stratifying the data according to the magnitude of flow and applying a separate curve for each stratum (Glysson, 1987), and use of a single multivariate model instead of multiple rating curves (Cohn *et al.*, 1992). Sivakumar and Wallender (2005) argue that there is not a simple (and universal) 'water discharge-suspended sediment concentration-suspended sediment load' relationship. A brief overview of past studies is as follows.

Kisi, et al (2008) review the application of ANN and neuro-fuzzy techniques to time series analysis of sediment loads at various timescales, uncertainty in the data. Variations of these techniques have also been reported by Jain (2001), Tayfur (2002), Cigizoglu (2004), Kisi (2004), Raghuwanshi *et al.* (2006), Cigizoglu & Kisi (2006). Other studies on the application of ANN to suspended sediment include that by Wang et al (2008), who applied ANN to derive the coefficients of regression analysis for their SRC model.

Aytek and Kishi (2008) used the GP approach to model suspended sediment for two stations on the Tongue River in Montana, USA, and indicate that the GP formulation performs quite well compared to sediment rating curves and multi linear regression models.

Chaotic signals have also been identified in time series of suspended sediment loads by Sivakumar and Jayawardena (2002, 2003), Farmer and Sidorowich, 1987). The outcomes revealed the usefulness of these methods towards an effective prediction capability.

Overall, a general understanding of the analysis of suspended sediment load is yet to emerge and one way to gain an insight into the problem is to carry out inter-comparison studies of the performance of a host of models applied to diversity of rivers of different shapes and sizes.

3. Study area and data

3.1. Understanding the problem

Sediment transport is concerned with entrained soil materials carried in water by erosion on the catchment and within channels. Sediment particles are categorised as follows (i) the saltation load (not discussed here); (ii) bedload (not discussed here) and (iii) suspended load including clay (< $62\mu m$ in particle diameter), silt and sand. Suspended load (both as "fine-grained sediment" and "wash load") is directly a result of the turbulence in water and forms a large proportion of the transported load, where the turbulence is a measure of the energy in the water to carry the load.

Sediment discharge is a measure of the mass rate of sediment transport at any point in space and time and determines whether the load is being transported or deposited. The whole process comprises soil erosion, sediment transport and sediment yield, where the deposited load delivered to a point in the catchment is referred to as sediment yield and is expressed as tons per unit area of the basin per year, measured at a point. Estimation of sediment yield (and soil erosion) is essential for management but these and mathematical models are used to gain an insight into the underlying processes. Sediment yield is estimated by (i) direct measurement, (ii) using local time series models to predict future states; (iii) using mathematical models to study jointly both erosion and sediment processes.

Suspended sediment forms most of the transported load and can be affected by many parameters including rainfall, land use pattern, slope, soil characteristics, e.g. soil moisture content but their considerations lead to distributed models, which are complex. Recorded suspended sediment derives distributed models by serving them as boundary conditions or input sources but their inherent information is not tapped on. There is a case for local models to study the information contained in recorded sediment loads alone in terms of flow and sediment hydrographs. This chapter is concerned with the study of the suspended load of a river, as discussed below.

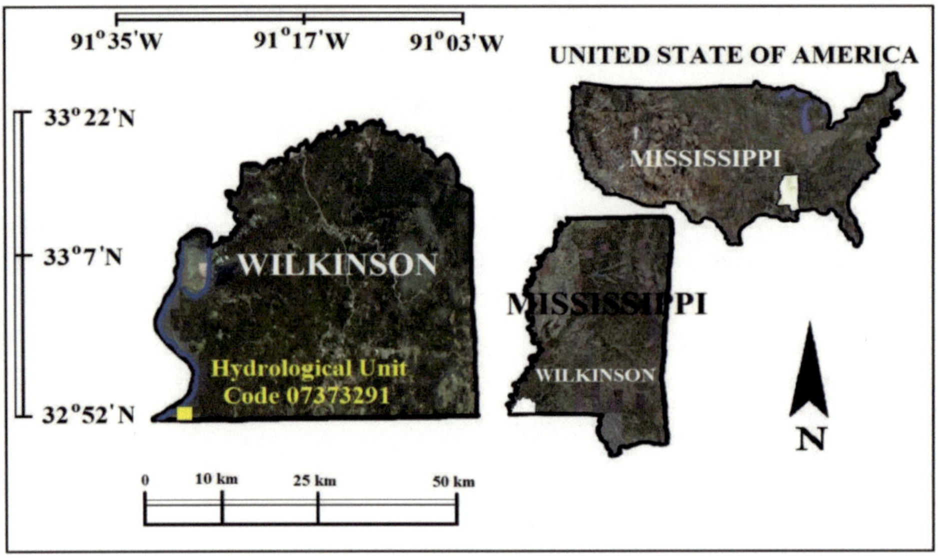

Figure 1. Mississippi River Station at Tarbert + RR Landings (http://pubs.usgs.gov/circ/circ1133/geosetting.html).

3.2. Study area

The flow–sediment time series data of a Mississippi river Station is used in the study, the location of which is shown in Figure 1. The gauge is situated at Tarbert + RR Landings, LA (USGS Station no. 07373291, latitude 30°57′40″, longitude 91°39′52″) and it is operated by the US Geological Survey (USGS) – the location map is shown in Figure 1. The Mississippi River discharges an average of about 200 million metric tons of suspended sediment per year to the Gulf of Mexico and to the ocean.

3.3. Review of data records

Daily suspended sediment measurements for the above station have been made available by the USGS from April 1949. The data used herein span over a period of about 26 years (amounting to 9496 datapoints) starting on October 1, 1949. Figures 2 show the variation of the daily suspended sediment and stream flow series observed at the above station.

Of the 26 water-years of the data sample of daily records of flow and suspended sediment (9496 datapoints), the first 25 water years of data (9131 datapoints) were used to train the models and the remaining 365 datapoints of daily records were used for testing. The statistical parameters of stream flow and sediment concentration data are shown in Table 1. These results show that the overall contribution of the datapoints in the test period is average; its individual characteristics in terms of kurtosis show the annual hydrographs to be less peaked and more flat but at the same time, the suspended sediment load during the year is significantly high. Thus, the minimum values during this year were significantly above the average but persistent and though less dynamic.

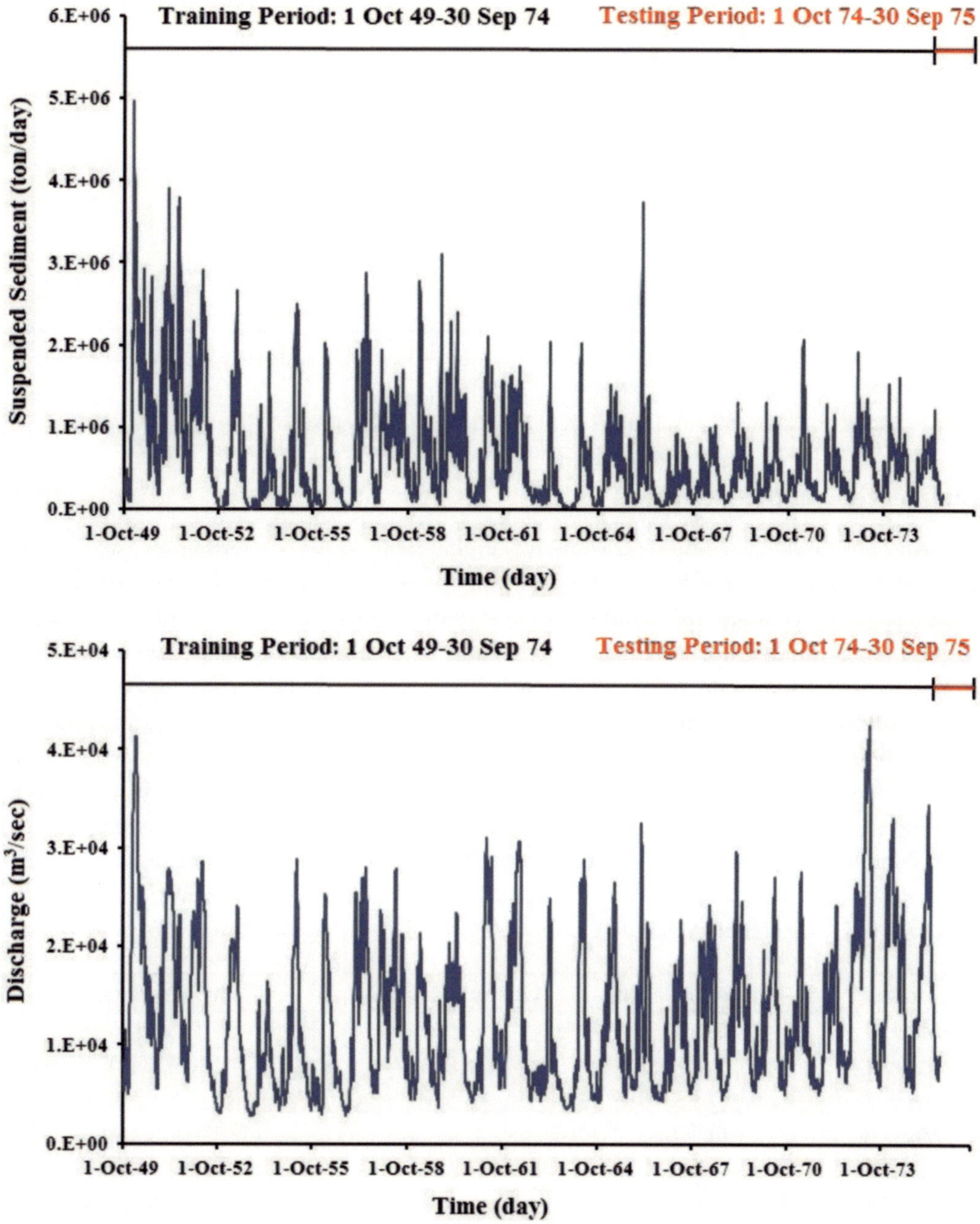

Figure 2. Variation of Daily Suspended Sediment and Flow Data in the Mississippi River Basin

Data Type	Training set		Testing set		All Dataset	
	Suspended Sediment (ton/day)	*Discharge (m^3/sec)*	*Suspended Sediment* (ton/day)	*Discharge (m^3/sec)*	*Suspended Sediment (ton/day)*	*Discharge (m^3/sec)*
Datapoints	9131	9131	365	365	9496	9496
Mean	6.37E5	1.27E4	4.52E5	1.58E4	6.30E5	1.28E4
St dev	6.30E5	7.60E3	2.53E5	7.80E3	6.21E5	7.60E3
Max	4.97E6	4.25E4	1.22E6	3.45E4	4.97E6	4.25E4
Min.	4.00E3	2.80E3	6.70E4	5.40E3	4.00E3	2.80E3
CV	1.0	0.60	0.56	0.49	0.99	0.59
Skew	1.78	0.95	0.10	0.51	1.82	0.93
Kurt	3.98	0.34	-0.98	-0.85	4.20	0.27

*Data = Number of Data; Std = Standard Deviation; Max = Maximum Value; Min = Minimum Value; CV = Coefficient of Variation; Skew = Skewness; Kurt = Kurtosis

Table 1. Statistical Parameters for Dataset from the Mississippi River Basin

3.4. Overview of the models

The sediment rating curve method is the traditional method for converting measured flows to predict suspended sediment load and this paper aims to test the performance of evolutionary computing models but uses a host of other techniques for the inter-comparison purpose. These models are outlined in this section but evolutionary computing is explained in more detail. Their underlying notion is that past values contain a sufficient amount of information to predict the future values and a systematic way of representing this notion is purported in Table 2 in terms of a selection of models. These models, in essence, are reminiscent of regression analysis but GEP, ANN and MLR models approach the problem in their own individual ways to unearth the structure of the information inherent in time series. Notably, the SRC model is expressed by Model 1 and the deterministic chaos model is expressed by Model 0. These models will all be evaluated by using coefficient of Correlation (CC), Relative Absolute Errors (RAE) and Root Mean Square Errors (RMSE).

Model	Input variables	Output variables	The Structure
Model 0	S_{t-1}, S_{t-2}...	S_t	Chaos
Model 1	Q_t	S_t	ANN, SRC
Model 2	Q_t , S_{t-1}	S_t	GEP, ANN, MLR
Model 3	Q_t ,Q_{t-1}	S_t	GEP, ANN, MLR
Model 4	Q_t , Q_{t-1} , S_{t-1}	S_t	GEP, ANN, MLR
Model 5	Q_t,Q_{t-1},Q_{t-2}	S_t	GEP, ANN, MLR
Model 6	Q_t,Q_{t-1},Q_{t-2},S_{t-1}	S_t	GEP, ANN, MLR

Where Q_t and S_t *represent* respectively flow and suspended sediment load at day *t*.

Table 2. Modelling Structures of the Selected Modelling Techniques

3.4.1. Sediment rating curve

Sediment rating-curve is a flux-averaged relationship between suspended sediment, S, and water discharge, Q, expressed as a power law in the form of: $S = aQ^b$, where a and b are coefficients. Values of a and b for a particular stream are determined from data via a linear regression between (log S) and (log Q). The SRC model is represented in terms of Model 1 in Table 2. For more critical views on this model, references may be made Kisi (2005) and Walling (1977), among others.

3.4.2. Evolutionary computing

Evolutionary computing techniques apply optimisation algorithms as a tool to facilitate the mimicking of natural selection. A building block approach to generalised evolution driven by natural selection is yet to be presented, although Khatibi (2011) has outlined a rationale for it. Traditional understanding of natural selection for biological species is well developed, according to which the process takes place at the gene level of all individuals of all species carrying hereditary material for reproduction by inheriting from their parents and by passing on a range of their characteristics to their offspring. The process of reproduction is never a perfect copying process, as mutation may occur from time to time in biological reproductions involving the random process of reshuffling the genes during sexual reproduction. The paper assumes preliminary knowledge on genes, chromosomes, gene pool, DNA and RNA, where the environment also has a role to play. The environment for the production of proteins and sexual reproduction is different than the outer environment for the performance of the individual entities supported by the proteins or produced by sexual reproduction. The outer environment is characterised by (i) being limited in resources, (ii) having no foresight, (iii) organisms tend to produce more offspring than can be supported, a process that is driven by positive feedback loops, and (iv) there is a process of competition and selection. Some of these details are normally overlooked or simplified in evolutionary computing and therefore the paper stresses the point that natural selection takes place at the gene level and this is not directly applicable to that at the social level.

Facts on natural selection are overwhelming but there are myths as well, e.g. the myth of "the survival of the fittest" and this term is widely used in evolutionary computing. Although the fittest has a selective advantage to survive, this is not a guarantee for the survival in the natural world. An overview of the dynamics of natural selection in an environment is that (i) the environment can only support a maximum population of certain size, but there is also a lower size at the critical mass below which a population is at risk of losing its viability; (ii) there is a process of reproduction, during which natural selection operates at the gene level, although there are further processes operating at the individual levels beyond the direct reach of natural selection (e.g. interactions among the individuals catered for by other mechanisms or each individual is under selection pressure by the environment); (iii) the process of reproduction is associated with mutation, which gives rise to the production of gene pools.

A great deal of the above overview has been adopted in evolutionary computing, the history of which goes back to the 1960s when Rechenberg (1973) introduced evolution strategies. The variants of this approach include genetic algorithm (Holland, 1975), evolutionary programming (Fogel et al, 1966), genetic programming (Koza, 1992) and Gene Expression Programming (GEP), Ferreira (2001a). This paper uses the latter approach, which in a simple term is a variation of GP but each of these techniques have differences with one another. These techniques have the capability for deriving a set of mathematical expressions to describe the relationship between the independent and dependent variables using such functions as mutation, recombination (or crossover) and evolution.

This chapter is concerned with GEP and one of the important preliminary decisions in its implementations is to establish the models represented in Table 2 (Models 2-6). There is no prior knowledge of the appropriateness of any of these models and therefore this is normally fixed in a preliminary modelling task through a trial-and-error procedure. Whichever the model choice (Model 2 – Model 6 or similar other ones), each implementation of GEP builds up the model in terms of the values of the coefficients (referred to as terminals) and the operations (functions) through the procedure broadly outlined in Figure 3.

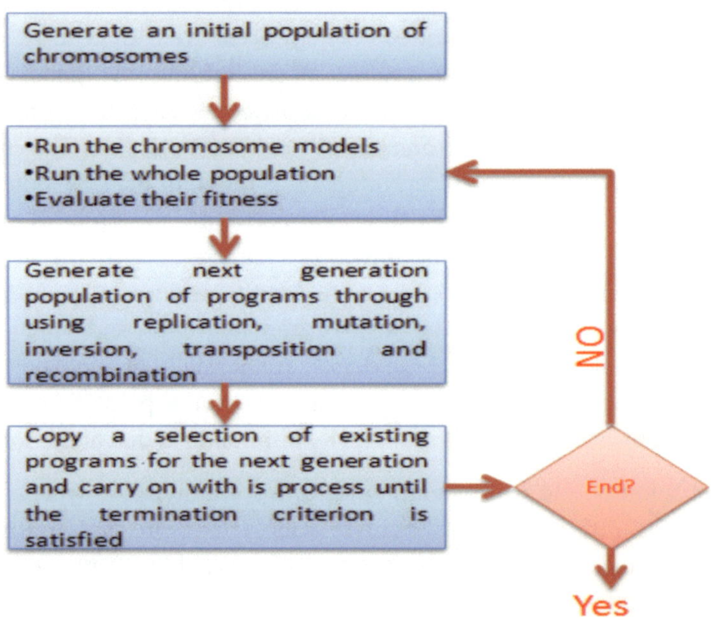

Figure 3. Simplified Outline of Implementation of Evolutionary Programming Models

The working of a gene expression program depicted in Figure 3 is outlined as follows. A chromosome in GEP is composed of genes and each gene is composed of (i) terminals and (ii) functions. The gene structures and chromosomes in GEP are illustrated for the solution that is obtained for the dataset used in this study (see Section 4.2). The terminals as their names suggest are composed of constants and variables and the functions comprise mathematical operations, as shown by (4.a)-(4.f).

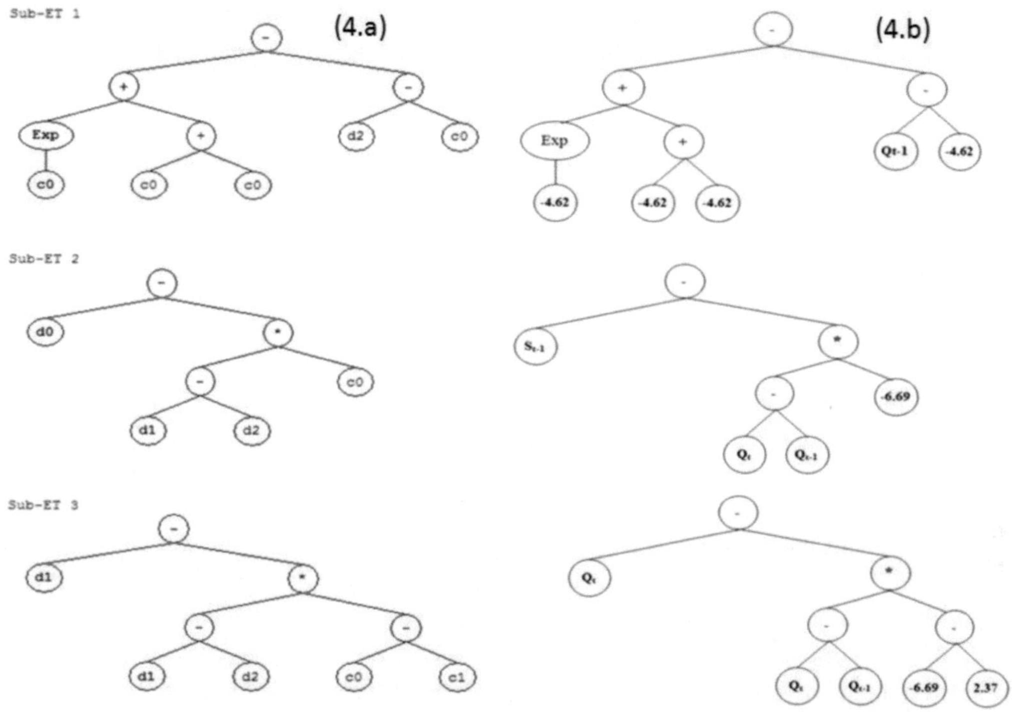

Figure 4. Expression Trees – (a) typical expression tree; (b) the selected GEP model in this study

As the term terminal suggests, it comprises a set of values at the tail-ends of the genes of the chromosomes and these are made meaningful by the functions making up the other component of the genes of the chromosomes. In GEP, these are represented by a bilingual notation called Karva language of (i) genetic codes, which are not deemed necessary for a description here and (ii) expression trees (or parse trees), as illustrated by Figure 4.a and the recommended solution is shown in Figure 4.b, which is transcribed by Equation (4) in Section 4.2. The initial chromosomes of the initial population are no different than the solution shown in Figure 4.b but their difference is that the composition of each of the initial chromosomes is selected often in random and then GEP is expected to improve them through evolution by the strategy of selections, replication and mutation but there are other facilities that not mentioned facilitating a more robust solution and these include inversion, transposition and recombination. The improvements are carried out through selection from one generation to another and this is why this modelling strategy is called evolutionary computation. The main strength of this approach is that it does not set up any system of equation to predict the future but it evaluates the fitness of each chromosome and selects from those a new population with better performance traits.

The GEP employed in this study is based on evolving computer programs of different sizes and shapes encoded in linear chromosomes of fixed lengths, Ferreira, 2001a; Ferreira, (2001b). The chromosomes are composed of multiple genes, each gene encoding a smaller subprogram. Furthermore, the structural and functional organisation of the linear chromosomes allows the unconstrained operation of important genetic functions, such as mutation, transposition and recombination. It has been reported that GEP is 100-10,000 times more efficient than GP systems (Ferreira, 2001a; Ferreira, 2001b) for a number of reasons, including: (i) the chromosomes are simple entities: linear, compact, relatively small, easy to manipulate genetically (replicate, mutate, recombine, etc); (ii) the parse trees or expression trees are exclusively the expression of their respective chromosomes; they are entities upon which selection acts, and according to fitness, they are selected to reproduce with modification.

3.4.3. Artificial Neural Networks (ANNs)

Whilst evolutionary programming emulates the working of Nature, ANNs emulate the workings of neurons in the brain. Both the brain and ANNs are parallel information processing systems consisting of a set of neurons or nodes arranged in layers but this is where the parallel ends. The actual process of information processing in the brain is a topical research issue but the drivers of ANNs are polynomial algebra and there is no evidence that the brains of humans, monkeys or any other animals employ algebraic computations such as optimisation methods. Although there is a great incentive to understand the working of the brain, it is not imperative to be constrained by it and the use of algebra in ANNs is not criticised here but awareness is raised as these two processes are not identical.

The ANN theory has been described in many books, including the text by Rumelhart et al. (1986). The application of ANNs has been the subject of a large number of papers that have appeared in the recent literature. There are various implementations of ANNs but the type used in this study is a Multi-Layer feedforward Perceptron (MLP) trained with the use of back propagation learning algorithm with the following functions: (i) the input layer accepts the data, (ii) intermediate layer processes them, and (iii) the output layer displays the resultant outputs. The number of hidden layers is decided in a preliminary modelling process by finding the most efficient number of layers through a trial-and-error procedure. Each neuron in a layer is connected to all the neurons of the next layer, and the neurons in one layer are not connected among themselves. All the nodes within a layer act synchronously.

This study implements the ANN models in terms of Models 1-6 of Table 2 and Figure 5 shows one of the implementation selected. For each of these models, the data passing through the connections from one neuron to another are multiplied by weights that control the strength of a passing signal. When these weights are modified, the data transferred through the network changes; consequently, the network output also changes. The signal emanating from the output node(s) is the network's solution to the input problem.

In the back-propagation algorithm, a set of inputs and outputs is selected from the training set and the network calculates the output based on the inputs. This output is subtracted from the actual output to find the output-layer error. The error is back propagated through the network, and the weights are suitably adjusted. This process continues for the number of prescribed sweeps or until a prescribed error tolerance is reached. The mean square error over the training samples is the typical objective function to be minimized. After training is complete, the ANN performance is validated. Depending on the outcome, either the ANN has to be retrained or it can be implemented for its intended use.

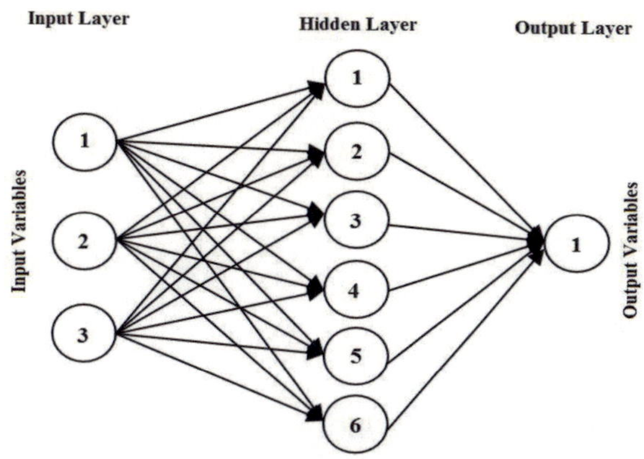

Figure 5. Implementation of the ANN Models and its Various Layers

3.4.4. *Multi Linear Regression (MLR)*

An overview of the data presented in Figure 2 invokes the thought that other than the annual trend within the data, the underlying process is probably random and a more rational way of explaining the data would be through probabilistic approaches. One such method applied to the selected data is the Multi-Linear Regression (MLR) model. It fits a linear combination of the components of a multiple signals x (e.g. recorded flows and suspended sediment timeseries as defined by the Models 2-6 in Table 2) to a single output signal y, as defined by (1.a) (e.g. predicted suspended sediment load) and returns the residual, r, i.e. the difference signal, as defined by (1.b):

~~$y = b + \sum_{i=0}^{N} a_i x_i$~~ $$y = b + \sum_{i=0}^{N} a_i x_i \qquad (1a)$$

~~$r = y - a_1 x_2 - a_2 x_2 - \dots - b$~~ $$r = y - a_1 x_1 - a_2 x_2 - \dots - b \qquad (1b)$$

Where x_i is defined in Table 2 in terms of various models and a_i values are called regression coefficients, which are estimated by using the least square or any other similar method. In this study, the coefficients of the regressions were determined using the least square method.

3.4.5. *Chaos theory*

A cursory view of the suspended sediment record of the Mississippi River in Figure 2 provides no clue to a strategy for its underlying patterns, if any, although annual trend superimposed on random variation may be an immediate reaction of a hydrologist. Another strategy to explore such possible patterns is through the application of chaos theory, more specifically through the "phase-space diagram" as shown in Figure 6 for this river data. A point in the phase-space represents the state of the system at a given time. The narrow dark band in the figure signifies strong determinism but its scattered band signifies the presence of noise and therefore there is a possibility to explain this set of data by chaos theory. The dark band signifies convergence of the trajectories of the phase-space with a fractal dimension towards the attractor of the data, where the dynamics of the system can be reduced to a set of deterministic laws to enable the prediction of its future states.

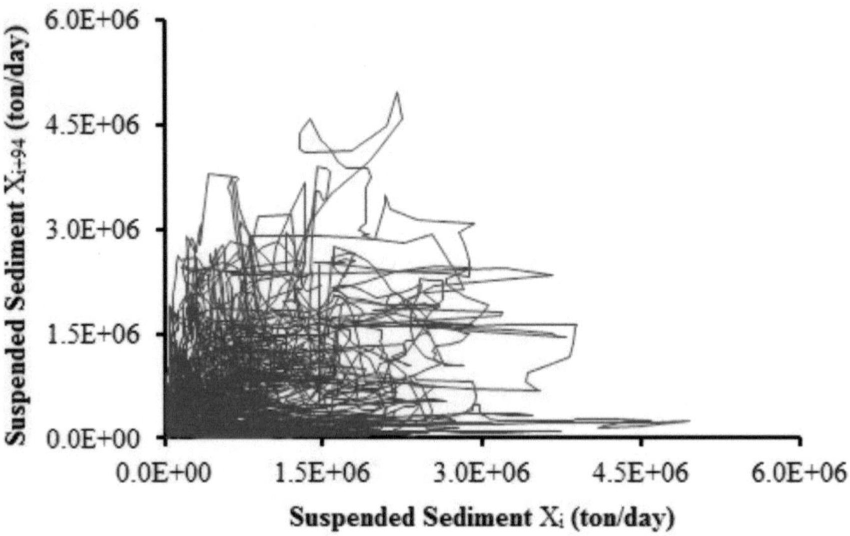

Figure 6. Phase-space Diagram of Daily Suspended Sediment Data in the Mississippi River Basin

Chaos theory is a method of nonlinear time series analysis and involves a host of methods, essentially based on the phase-space reconstruction of a process, from scalar or multivariate measurements of physical observables. This method is implemented in terms of Model 0 of Table 2. It is largely based on the representation of the underlying dynamics through reconstruction of phase-space, originally given by Takens, 1981. It is implemented in terms of two parameters of delay time and embedding dimension, according to which given a set of physical variables and an analytical model describing their interactions, the dynamics of the system can be represented geometrically by a single point moving on a trajectory, where each of its points corresponds to a state of the system. The phase-space diagram is essentially a co-ordinate system, whose coordinates represent the variables necessary to completely describe the state of the system at any moment.

One difficulty in its construction is that in most practical situations, information on every variable influencing the system may not be available. However, a time series of a single variable may be available, which may allow the construction of a (pseudo) phase-space. The idea behind such a reconstruction is that a non-linear system is characterized by self-interaction, and a time series of a single variable can carry the information about the dynamics of the entire multi-variable system. The trajectories of the phase-space diagram describe the evolution of the system from some initial state, and hence represent the history of the system.

This paper applies chaos theory to analyse the suspended sediment load of the Mississippi River data in a similar fashion to the other modelling strategies described above. It uses the local prediction method for training and testing, as outlined below, but it is a traditional practice to apply several methods to build evidence for the existence of chaotic signals in a particular data. These techniques employ the delay-embedding parameters of τ and m, which are unknown a-priori. The following methods are used in this chapter:

1. Average Mutual Information (AMI) is used to estimate τ; and the minimization of the False Nearest Neighbours to do that of the optimal values for the embedding dimension, m.
   AMI (Fraser and Swinney, 1986) defines how the measurements $X(t)$ at time t are related, from an information theoretic point of view, to measurements $X(t+\tau)$ at time $t+\tau$. The average mutual information is defined as:

$$I(\tau) = \sum_{X(i),X(i+\tau)} P(X(i),X(i+\tau))\log[\frac{P(X(i),X(i+\tau))}{P(X(i))P(X(i+\tau))}] \quad (2a)$$

   where i is total number of samples. $P(X(i))$ and $P(X(i+\tau))$ are marginal probabilities for measurements $X(i)$ and $X(i+\tau)$, respectively, whereas $P(X(i))$, $P(X(i+\tau))$ is their joint probability. The optimal delay time τ minimises the function $I(\tau)$ $for\, t=\tau$, $X(i+\tau)$ adds the maximum information on $X(i)$.
   The False Nearest Neighbours procedure (Kennel et al., 1992) is a method to obtain the optimum embedding dimension for phase-space reconstruction. By checking the neighbourhood of points embedded in projection manifolds of increasing dimension, the algorithm eliminates 'false Neighbours': This means that points apparently lying close together due to projection are separated in higher embedding dimensions. when the ratio between the number of false neighbours at the dimension m +1 and m is below a given threshold, generally smaller than 5%, each $m' > m+1$ is an optimal embedding. A poor reconstruction of few embedding states with several components is obtained if m' is too large and the next analyses should not be performed.
2. **Correlation Dimension (CD) method**: is a nonlinear measure of the correlation between pairs lying on the attractor. For time series whose underlying dynamics is chaotic, the correlation dimension gets a finite fractional value, whereas for stochastic systems it is infinite. For an m -dimensional phase-space, the correlation function $C_m(r)$ is defined as the fraction of states closer than r (Grassberger and Procaccia, 1983; Theiler, 1986):

$$C(r) = \lim_{N\to\infty} \frac{2}{N(N-1)} \sum_{i,j=1}^{N} H(r - |Y_i - Y_j|) \quad (2b)$$

where H is the Heaviside step function, $\vec{Y}_i$ is the ith state vector, and N is the number of points on the reconstructed attractor. The number w is called Theiler window and it is the correction needed to avoid spurious results due to temporal correlations instead of dynamical ones. For stochastic time series $C_m(r) \propto r^m$ holds, whereas for chaotic time series the correlation function scales with r as:

$$C_m(r) \propto r^{D_2} \tag{2c}$$

where D_2, correlation exponent, quantifies the degrees of freedom of the process, and defined by:

$$D_2 = \lim_{r \to 0} \frac{\ln C(r)}{\ln r} \tag{2d}$$

and can be reliably estimated as the slope in the $\ln C_m(r)$ vs. $\ln(r)$ plot.

3. **Local Prediction Model**: The author's implementation of the local prediction method for deterministic chaos is details in Khatibi et al (2011) but the overview is that a correct phase-space reconstruction in a dimension m facilitates an interpretation of the underlying dynamics in the form of an m-dimensional map, f_T ,according to

$$Y_{j+T} = f_T(Y_j) \tag{2e}$$

where Y_j and Y_{j+T} are vectors of dimension m, describing the state of the system at times j (i.e. the current state) and $j+T$ (i.e. the future state), respectively. The problem then is to find an appropriate expression for f_T (i.e. F_T). Local approximation entails the subdivision of the f_T domain into many subsets (neighbourhoods), each of which identifies some approximations F_T ,valid only in that same subset. In other words, the dynamics of the system is described step-by-step locally in the phase-space. In this m-dimensional space, prediction is performed by estimating the change of X_i with time, which are observed values of discrete scalar timeseries, with delay coordinates in the m-dimensional phase space. The relation between the points X_t and X_{t+p} (the behaviour at a future time p on the attractor) is approximated by function F as:

$$X_{t+p} \cong F(X_t) \tag{2f}$$

In this prediction method, the change of X_t with time on the attractor is assumed the same as those of nearby points, $(X_{T_h}, h = 1,2,...,n)$. Herein, X_{t+p} is determined by the dth order polynomial $F(X_t)$ as follows (Itoh, 1995):

$$x_{t+p} \cong f_0 + \sum_{k_1=0}^{m-1} f_{1k_1} X_{t-k_1\tau} + \sum_{\substack{k_2=k_1 \\ k_1=0}}^{m-1} f_{2k_1k_2} X_{t-k\tau_1} X_{t-k_2\tau} + \dots + \sum_{\substack{k_d=k_{d-1} \\ \vdots \\ k_2=k_1 \\ k_1=0}}^{m-1} f_{dk_1k_2\dots k_d} X_{t-k_1\tau} X_{t-k_2\tau} \dots X_{t-k_d\tau} \tag{2g}$$

Using n of X_{T_h} and $X_{T_{h+p}}$ for which the values are already known, the coefficients, f, are determined by solution of the following equation:

$$X \cong Af \tag{2h}$$

where

$$X = (X_{T_{1+p}}, X_{T_{2+p}}, \ldots, X_{T_{n+p}}) \tag{2i}$$

and

$$f = (f_0, f_{10}, f_{11}, \ldots, f_{1(m-1)}, f_{200}, \ldots, f_{d(m-1)(m-1)\ldots(m-1)}) \tag{2j}$$

and A is the $n \times (m+d)!/m!d!$ Jacobian matrix which in its explicit form is:

$$A = \begin{bmatrix} 1 & X_{T_1} & X_{T_{1-\tau}} & \cdots & X_{T_{1-(m-1)\tau}} & X_{T_1}^2 & \cdots & X_{T_{1-(m-1)\tau}}^d \\ 1 & X_{T_2} & X_{T_{2-\tau}} & \cdots & X_{T_{2-(m-1)\tau}} & X_{T_2}^2 & \cdots & X_{T_{2-(m-1)\tau}}^d \\ \vdots & & & \vdots & & \vdots & & \vdots \\ 1 & X_{T_n} & X_{T_{n-\tau}} & \cdots & X_{T_{n-(m-1)\tau}} & X_{T_n}^2 & \cdots & X_{T_{n-(m-1)\tau}}^d \end{bmatrix} \tag{2k}$$

In order to obtain a stable solution, the number of rows in the Jacobian matrix A must satisfy:

$$n \geq \frac{(m+d)!}{m!d!} \tag{2l}$$

As stated by Porporato and Ridolfi *(1997)*, even though *F-values* are first degree polynomials, the prediction is nonlinear, because during the prediction procedure every point $x(t)$ belongs to a different neighbourhood and is therefore defined by different expressions for f (Koçak,1997).

4. Setting up models and preliminary results

4.1. Performance of sediment rating curve

The SRC model was implemented by using a simple least squares method leading to

$$S=13.2Q^{1.14} \tag{3}$$

The performance of this model is summarised in Table 3 and shown in Figure 7. Evidently, its performance is poor and the concern raised in the literature on this model is confirmed. This is a sufficient justification to search for reliable models.

Model Input	Training			Testing		
	CC	MAE	RMSE	CC	MAE	RMSE
Model 1: Q_t	0.76	2.62E5	4.11E5	0.82	3.89E5	4.86E5

Table 3. Statistical Performance of the Sediment Rating Curve for the Training and Test Periods

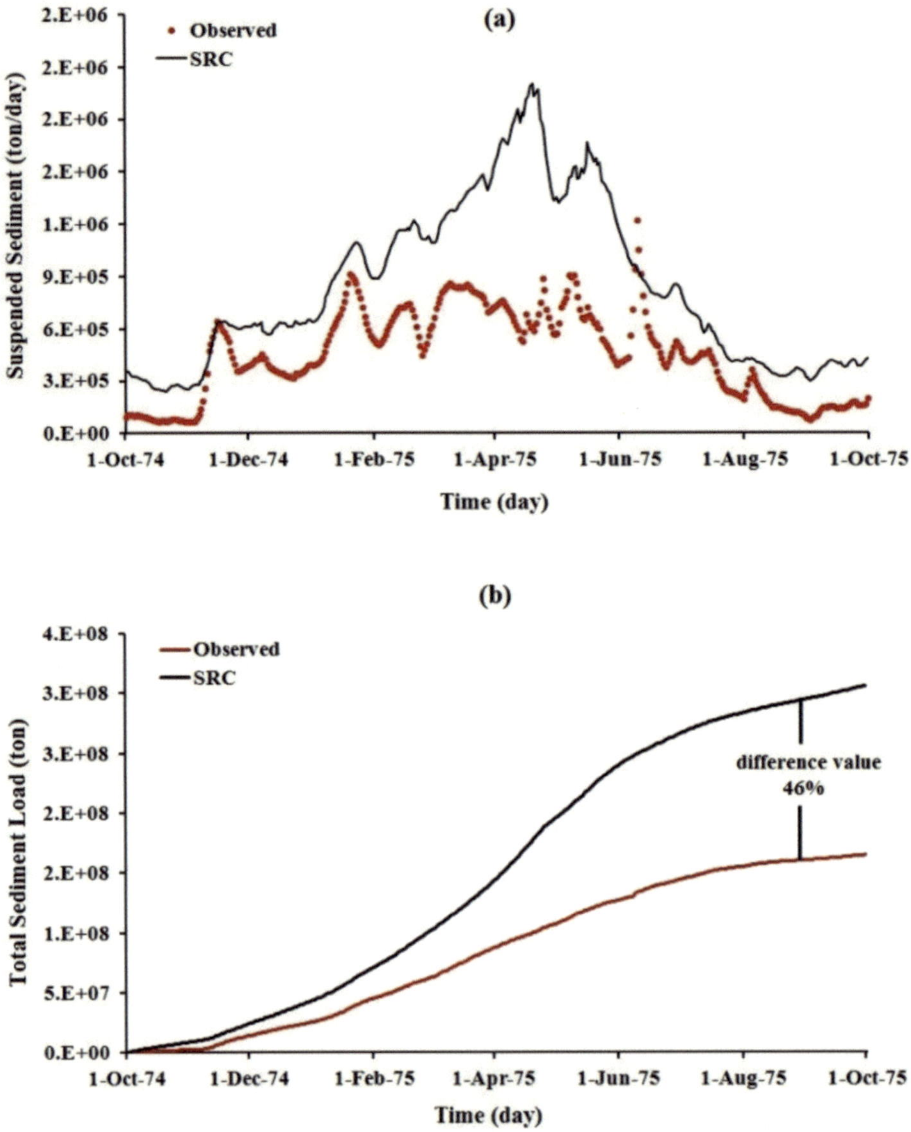

Figure 7. Comparison of Observed Suspended Sediment with that Modelled by SRC; (a) hydrograph, (b) cumulative values

4.2. Implementation of GEP

The preliminary investigation for the construction of a relationship between flows and suspended sediment in GEP requires: (i) the setting of the functions, as discussed below; (ii) the fitness function; and (iii) a range of other parameters, but the default values, given in Table 11, were sufficient in this study. The following functions were investigated:

$$\{+,-,\times\} \quad (4a)$$

$$\{+,-,\times, x\} \quad (4b)$$

$$\{+,-,\times, x^2\} \quad (4c)$$

$$\{+,-,\times, x^3\} \quad (4d)$$

$$\{+,-,\times, e^x\} \quad (4e)$$

$$\{+,-,\times, \ln(x)\} \quad (4f)$$

The performance of each function was investigated in terms of CC, MAE, and RMSE and the results are shown in Table 4.a for the training periods. The results show that (i) the model performances are more sensitive to the choice of independent variables than the function choices; (ii) the models not including suspended sediment time series perform poorly; and (iii) the model performance is not overly sensitive to the choice of the function. Appendix I, Table 11 specifies the fitness function to be Root Relative Squared Errors (RRSE).

Model		Q_t	Q_t , S_{t-1}	Q_t ,Q_{t-1}	Q_t , Q_{t-1} , S_{t-1}	Q_t,Q_{t-1},Q_{t-2}	Q_t,Q_{t-1},Q_{t-2},S_{t-1}
4.a): $\{+,-,\times\}$	CC	0.77	0.99	0.78	0.99	0.78	0.99
	MAE	2.79E5	3.88E4	2.78E5	3.25E4	2.79E5	3.37E4
	RMSE	4.13E5	8.43E4	4.07E5	7.74E4	4.05E5	7.98E4
(4.b): $\{+,-,\times, x\}$	CC	0.77	0.99	0.77	0.99	0.77	0.99
	MAE	2.82E05	3.87E04	2.81E05	3.80E04	2.78E05	3.27E04
	RMSE	4.15E05	8.42E04	4.14E05	8.36E04	4.10E05	7.75E04
(4.c): $\{+,-,\times, x^2\}$	CC	0.77	0.99	0.78	0.99	0.78	0.99
	MAE	2.82E05	3.89E04	2.78E05	3.25E04	2.76E05	3.45E04
	RMSE	4.15E05	8.43E04	4.08E05	7.74E04	4.05E05	8.02E04
(4.d): $\{+,-,\times,x^3\}$	CC	0.77	0.99	0.77	0.99	0.77	0.99
	MAE	2.43E5	3.89E4	2.76E5	3.21E4	2.76E5	3.41E4
	RMSE	4.05E5	8.43E4	4.12E5	7.76E4	4.13E5	8.03E4
(4.e): $\{+,-,\times,e^x\}$	CC	0.77	0.99	0.77	0.99	0.77	0.99
	MAE	2.81E5	3.88E4	2.81E5	3.56E4	2.42E5	3.64E4
	RMSE	4.15E5	8.43E4	4.14E5	8.16E4	4.00E5	8.23E4
(4.f): $\{+,-,\times,\ln(x)\}$	CC	0.76	0.99	0.76	0.99	0.78	0.99
	MAE	2.56E5	3.89E4	2.64E5	3.25E4	2.60E5	3.21E4
	RMSE	4.09E5	8.42E4	4.10E5	7.72E4	4.02E5	7.72E4

Table 4. a. Statistical Performance of a Selection of Functions for the Training Period

The performance of the GEP model is presented in Table 4.b, according to which there is not much to differences between performances of a number of the alternative models but (4.e) is selected in this study for the prediction purposes (its expression tree is given in Figure 4) and given below.

$$S_t = S_{t-1} + 16.77Q_t - 16.77Q_{t-1} - 13.87 \quad (5)$$

Model		Q_t	Q_t, S_{t-1}	Q_t, Q_{t-1}	Q_t, Q_{t-1}, S_{t-1}	Q_t,Q_{t-1},Q_{t-2}	Q_t,Q_{t-1},Q_{t-2},S_{t-1}
(4.a): {+,-,×}	**CC**	0.83	0.99	0.84	0.99	0.84	0.99
	MAE	3.99E5	2.34E4	4.01E5	2.32E4	4.08E5	2.08E4
	RMSE	4.72E5	3.87E4	4.73E5	4.06E4	4.79E5	3.75E4
(4.b) {+,-,×,x}	**CC**	0.83	0.99	0.84	0.99	0.84	0.99
	MAE	3.99E05	2.33E04	4.01E05	2.28E04	3.96E05	2.34E04
	RMSE	4.69E05	3.87E04	4.70E05	3.08E04	4.65E05	4.04E04
(4.c) {+,-,×,x^2}	**CC**	0.83	0.99	0.84	0.99	0.84	0.99
	MAE	4.00E05	2.35E04	4.01E05	2.32E04	3.79E05	2.31E04
	RMSE	4.69E05	3.86E04	4.71E05	4.06E04	4.67E05	3.96E04
(4.d): {+,-,×,x^3}	**CC**	0.83	0.99	0.83	0.99	0.83	0.99
	MAE	3.87E5	2.35E4	4.00E5	2.10E4	3.96E5	2.06E4
	RMSE	4.94E5	3.87E4	4.75E5	3.81E4	4.69E5	3.69E4
(4.e): {+,-,×,e^x}	**CC**	0.83	0.99	0.84	0.99	0.84	0.99
	MAE	3.98E5	2.35E4	3.97E5	2.06E4	3.80E5	2.17E4
	RMSE	4.67E5	3.86E4	4.66E5	3.64E4	4.84E5	3.73E4
(4.e): {+,-,×,ln(x)}	**CC**	0.83	0.99	0.83	0.99	0.83	0.99
	MAE	3.90E5	2.35E4	3.90E5	2.40E4	3.81E5	2.29E4
	RMSE	4.93E5	3.86E4	4.81E5	4.18E4	4.69E5	4.05E4

Table 4 b. Statistical analysis of the estimated values for the test period

Figure 8 compares modelled suspended sediment against their observed values, according to which the improvement by GEP is remarkable compared with SRC. Overall, the GEP modelling results follow observed values rather faithfully both in values and patterns, although there are still discrepancies in predicted values.

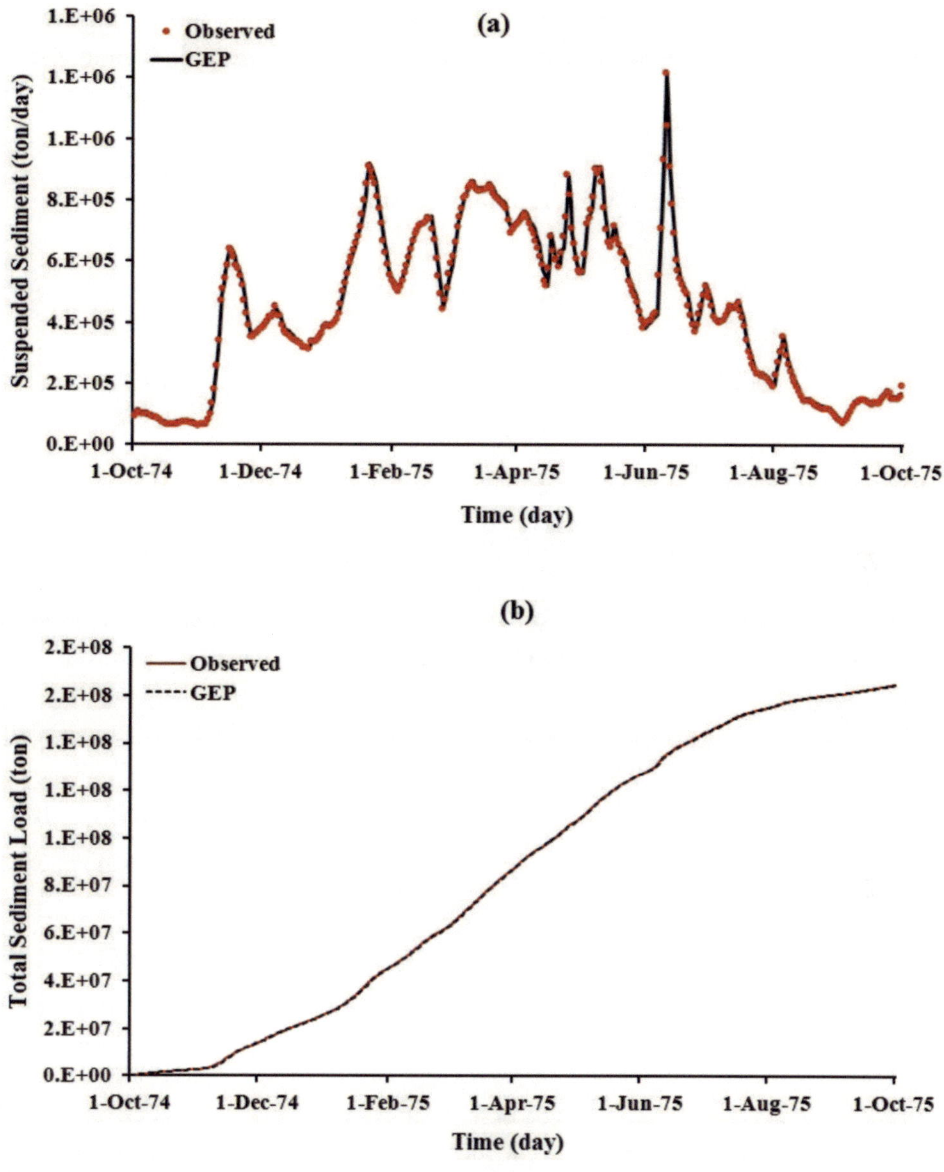

Figure 8. Comparison of Observed Suspended Sediment with that Modelled by GEP; (a) hydrograph, (b) cumulative values

4.3. Implementation of ANN

ANN implements another AI approach to the data represented in Figure 2 by another strategy, as described in Section 3.4.3. A preliminary investigation was carried out to make decisions on the choice of the models given in Table 2 (Models 1-6) and the ANN structure in terms of the neuron structure of the various layers. Table 5 presents model structures investigated. The preliminary modelling task also included a normalisation function for the data. In this study, MATLAB was employed to develop the ANN model and its *mapstd* function was selected for the normalisation (further defaults values are given in Table 11). The investigated ANN model structures are defined in Table 5 and their results for both the training and testing periods are presented in Table 6.

Model Identifier	Model Inputs	Training	Testing
Model 1	Q_t	2-5-1	2-5-1
Model 2	Q_t , S_{t-1}	3-5-1	3-5-1
Model 3	Q_t ,Q_{t-1}	3-7-1	3-7-1
Model 4	Q_t , Q_{t-1} , S_{t-1}	4-6-1	4-6-1
Model 5	Q_t,Q_{t-1},Q_{t-2}	4-9-1	4-9-1
Model6	Q_t,Q_{t-1},Q_{t-2},S_{t-1}	5-12-1	5-12-1

Table 5. ANN Structure (number of nodes in layers)

The performances of Models 1-6 are shown in Table 6 in terms of the values of three statistical indices of CC, MAE and RMSE. The performance of different models in terms of CC is remarkably high but Model 4 (Q_t , Q_{t-1} , S_{t-1}) produce less deviations, which is selected for the final run.

	Model Training			Model Testing		
Model Inputs	CC	MAE	RMSE	CC	MAE	RMSE
Q_t	0.999	2.32E4	2.70E4	0.999	2.16E4	2.30E4
Q_t , S_{t-1}	0.999	2.59E4	3.12E4	0.996	2.17E4	2.64E4
Q_t ,Q_{t-1}	0.999	2.00E4	2.79E4	0.981	4.19E4	4.84E4
Q_t , Q_{t-1} , S_{t-1}	**0.999**	**2.01E4**	**2.51E4**	**0.998**	**1.18E4**	**1.37E4**
Q_t,Q_{t-1},Q_{t-2}	0.991	7.57E4	8.42E4	0.942	8.47E4	8.41E4
Q_t,Q_{t-1},Q_{t-2},S_{t-1}	0.995	5.66E4	6.42E4	0.976	4.63E4	5.47E4

Table 6. Statistical Performance of the Selected Model Structure for the Training and Testing periods

4.4. Implementation of the MLR model

The MLR modelling strategy was implemented using Mathematica to derive regression coefficients for both periods of model fitting (training in the AI terminology) and testing using different statistical indices (CC, MAE and RMSE) given in Table 7, which shows that Model 2 (Q_t , S_{t-1}) performs relatively better than the others. The regression equation suggested by this technique is given by:

$$\boldsymbol{S_t} = 0.24\boldsymbol{Q_t} + \mathbf{30.99}\boldsymbol{S_{t-1}} \tag{6}$$

	Model Training			Model Testing		
Model Inputs	CC	MAE	RMSE	CC	MAE	RMSE
Q_t	0.77	2.41E5	4.05E5	0.833	3.85E5	4.96E5
Q_t , S_{t-1}	**0.994**	**3.90E4**	**8.40E4**	**0.988**	**2.40E4**	**3.90E4**
Q_t ,Q_{t-1}	0.78	2.40E5	3.97E5	0.837	3.85E5	4.98E5
Q_t , Q_{t-1} , S_{t-1}	0.993	3.30E4	7.60E4	0.987	2.50E4	4.10E4
Q_t,Q_{t-1},Q_{t-2}	0.779	2.40E5	3.95E5	0.840	3.84E5	4.96E5
Q_t,Q_{t-1},Q_{t-2},S_{t-1}	0.993	3.30E4	7.70E4	0.987	2.50E4	4.10E4

Table 7. Statistical analysis of the estimated values for the train and test period

4.5. Implementation of the deterministic chaos model

A visual assessment for the existence of chaotic behaviour in the suspended sediment time series was presented in Figure 9, although it was not conclusive evidence but just invoked the possibility of the existence of a low-dimensional chaos. Traditionally, several techniques are employed to show the existence of low-dimensional chaos and below the results of the determination of the dimensions of the phase-state diagram are given:

1. Using the AMI method, the delay time, is estimated for the data as the intercept with the x-axis of the curves by plotting the values of the AMI evaluated by the TISEAN package (Hegger *et al.*, 1999) against delay times progressively increased from 1 to 100. The value of delay time is calculated as the first (local) minimum in the variation of AMI against varying delay time from 1 to 100 day. The results are shown in Figure (9.a), signifying a well-defined first minimum at delay time of 94 day. The delay time is then used in the determination of the sufficient embedding dimension using the percentage of false nearest neighbours for the time series. Figure (9.b) shows the results of the false nearest neighbours method for embedding dimension *m*, by allowing it to vary from 1 to 40 and hence its value is 28.
2. The presence of chaotic signals in the data is further confirmed by the correlation dimension method. Figure (10.a) shows the relationship between correlation function $C(r)$ and radius r (i.e. $\ln C(r)$ versus $\ln(r)$) for increasing m, whereas Figure (10.b) shows the relationship between the correlation dimension values $D_2(m)$ and the embedding dimension values m. It can be seen from Figure (10.b) that the value of correlation exponent increases with the embedding dimension up to a certain value and then saturates beyond it. The saturation of the correlation exponent is an indication of the existence of deterministic dynamics. The saturated correlation dimension is 3.5, (D_2=3.5). The value of correlation dimension also suggests the possible presence of chaotic behaviour in the dataset. The nearest integer above the correlation dimension value (D_2=4) is taken as the minimum dimension of the phase space.

3. Local prediction algorithm is used to predict suspended sediment time series. The procedure involves varying the value of the embedding dimension in a range, say 3-8, and estimating the CC and RMSE. The embedding function with the highest coefficient of correlation is selected as the solution. These are given in Table 8 for Mississippi River basin for the dataset with daily time interval, as well as a selection of other time steps. It shows that the best predictions are achieved when the embedding dimension is m=3 produce the best results.

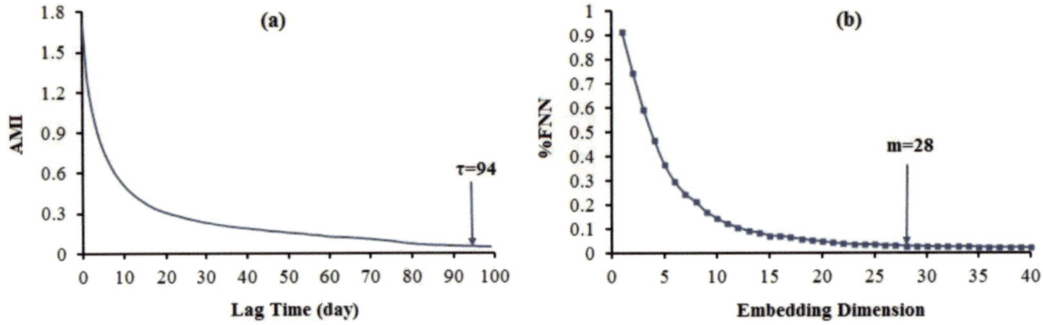

Figure 9. Analysis of the Phase-Space Diagram of Suspended Sediment Data in the Mississippi River basin; (9.a): Average Mutual Information; (9.b) Percentage of false nearest neighbours

m	CC	RMSE
3	**0.988**	**4.00E4**
4	0.988	4.10E4
5	0.986	4.30E4
6	0.985	4.60E4
7	0.986	4.40E4
8	0.987	4.20E4

Table 8. Local Prediction Using Different Embedding Dimension for the Mississippi River Dataset

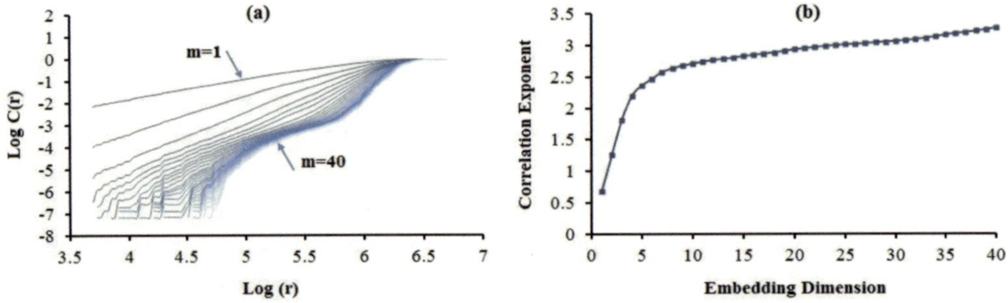

Figure 10. Correlation Dimension Method to Identify the Presence of Chaos Signal in the Dataset; (10.a): Convergence of log$C(r)$ versus log(r); (10.b): saturation of correlation dimension $D_2(m)$ with embedding dimension m – this signifies chaotic signals in the Dataset

5. Inter-comparison of the models and discussion of results

Table 9 summarises the performance and main features of each and all of the modelling strategies. The results presented so far confirms the experience that the traditional SRC model performs poorly and may only be used for rough-and-ready assessments. However, the results by the GEP model show that considerable improvements are likely by using it. This section also analyses the relative performance of the various modelling strategies. An overall visual comparison of all the results is presented in Figure 11, according to which GEP, ANN, MLR and local prediction models perform remarkably well and similar to one another.

Model	Performance	Model Structure	Outcome	Comments
SRC	Poor	Model 1	Eq. (3)	For rough-and-ready estimates
GEP	Good	Model 4	Eq. (4.e)	
ANN	Good	Model 4	→	The model is bounded to software
MLR	Good	Model 2	Eq. (6)	
Chaos	Good	Model 0	→	Needs expertise to implement

Table 9. Qualitative Overview of the Performances of Various Modelling Strategies

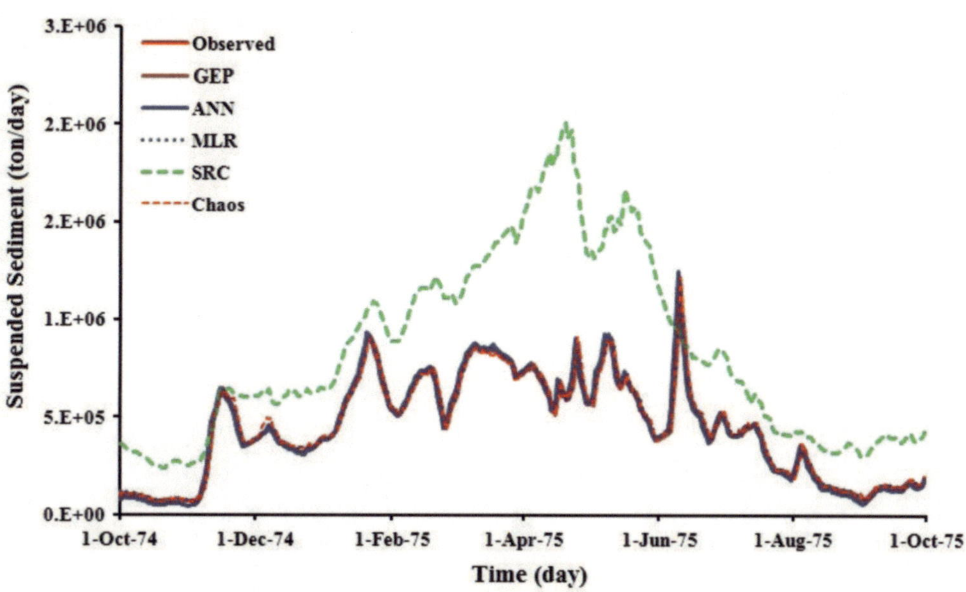

Figure 11. Model Predictions for Suspended Sediment – Performances of GP, ANN, MLR, Chaos (closest to observed), and SRC (poor)

Scatter diagrams are also a measure of performance. These are presented in Figures 12, which provides a quantitative basis that (i) SRC performs poorly and (ii) there is little to choose between the other models, although the performance of ANN stands out.

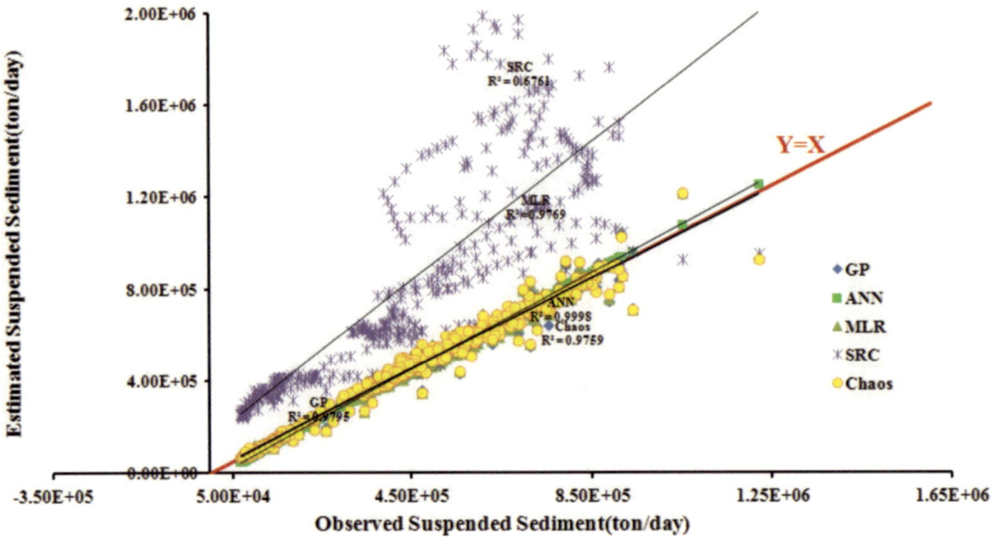

Figure 12. Scatter between Modelled and Observed Suspended Sediment Load

The relative performances of GEP, ANN, MLR and local prediction models are not still visible from Figure 12 and therefore attention is focused on the differences between the GEP and ANN models with respect to their corresponding observed values. Figures 13 shows the respective results for both the GEP and ANN models and that of ANN is remarkable, as the differences are nearly zero. It may be reported that those of local prediction model and MLR are very close to that of GEP.

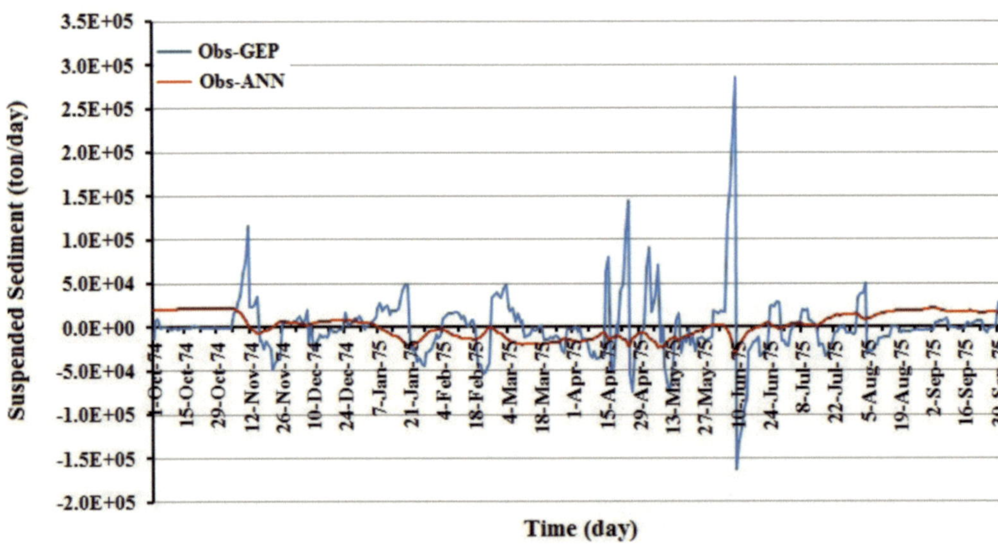

Figure 13. Performances of the ANN and GEP Models – y-ordinates: observed – modelled values

Due to the importance of the volume of transported sediment, the total predicted values are also compared with that of the observed values for the testing period and the results are presented in Table 10. The table show that the traditional SRC model is in error by as much as nearly 50% but the other models perform well, among which the error in the performance of ANN is the lowest. It is also noted that, despite the good performance of ANN models, it is not transferrable, like the GEP models. The implementation of both ANN and deterministic chaos models require considerable expertise.

Model	Actual Val. (ton/year)	Estimation Val. (ton/year)	Dif. Val. (%)
SRC	1.65E8	3.06E8	+46 %
GEP	1.65E8	1.65E8	- 0.4 %
ANN	1.65E8	1.64E8	- 0.3 %
MLR	1.65E8	1.66E8	+0.6 %
Chaos	1.65E8	1.66E8	+0.7 %

Table 10. Total Volume of Suspended Sediment Predicted by each of the Models at Gauging Station for the Mississippi River basin

The chapter presents the performance of the GEP model, as a variation of evolutionary programming, to forecast suspended sediment load of the Mississippi River, the USA. GEP is just a modelling strategy, where any other relevant strategy is just as valid if its performance is satisfactory. The overall results show that the information contained in the observed data can be treated by the following modelling strategies:

1. **Evolutionary computing**: this produced a formula to forecast the future values in terms of recorded values of flows and suspended sediment. The results show that the strategy can be successful in identifying a number of different formulae.
2. **Emulation of the working of the brain**: this successfully fitted an inbuilt polynomial to the data. It performs better than the other tested models but is not readily transferrable as it resides in particular software applications.
3. **Regression analysis**: this produced a regression equation, according to which the future values would regress towards average recorded values, in spite of the presence of noise.
4. **Deterministic chaos**: this produced future values of suspended sediment load by identifying an attractor towards which the system performance would converge even when the internal system behaves erratically.

The only common feature in the above modelling strategies is their use of optimisation techniques. Otherwise, they are greatly different from one another but remarkably, they produce models fit for purpose and can explain the data. Undoubtedly, the data can be explained by many more sets of equations or by other possible strategies. This emphasises that models are just tools and the modelling task is to test the performance of the various models to add confidence to the results. Yet the poor performance of the traditional SRC underlines the fact that a good performance cannot be taken for granted.

A review of the data (in Section 3) shows that the overall contribution of the datapoints in the test period is average; its individual characteristics in terms of kurtosis shows that the annual hydrographs are less peaked and more flat but at the same time the suspended sediment load during the year was significantly high. Thus, the minimum values during this year were significantly above the average but persistent and though less dynamic. However, all the four modelling strategies coped well with these data peculiarities. If the data during the test period have a more pronounced feature not very common during the training period, the various local modelling strategies are likely to perform poorly in their own unique way and one of the greatest tasks of research in modelling should be investigations to understand these unique features and not to sweep them under the carpet.

A general view projected by the investigation in this chapter is that the performance of modelling techniques must not be the only basis of practical applications. Equal attention must also be paid to the quality of the data used. If the data suffers from inherent uncertainties, no good model will compensate for the inherent shortfalls.

6. Conclusion

This chapter presents an investigation of the performance of the Gene Expression Programming (GEP) models of suspended sediment load of the Mississippi River, the USA. The study employs the Mississippi River data spanning 26 years involving both flows and suspended sediment load, of which the first 25 years of the data is used for training and the remaining for the prediction of one year into the future. This investigation concurs with the past findings that the performance of sediment rating curve, an empirical technique used widely in practice, can lead to gross errors. This alone underlines the value of other modelling techniques capable of producing reliable results with less than 1% of errors.

The chapter promotes a pluralist culture of modelling and although presents the GEP model as the focus, it also presents the application of other techniques to model the same data. The other models comprise: artificial neural networks, multi-linear regression analysis and deterministic chaos. The chapter outlines the modelling strategy underlying each of these techniques and the results show in spite of their differences they produce similar results inflicting less 1% of errors. The lowest errors are associated with the artificial neural networks for this set of data but each of these techniques should be considered as reliable. The volume of sediment load is an important management parameter and the error associated with each model was estimated for each model. The results show that the traditional SRC model suffers from gross errors by as much as 50% but the other tested models perform well, among which the error in the performance of ANN is the lowest. ANN is noted for its good performance but with some drawback that these models are not transferrable, like the GEP models. It is noted that the implementation of ANN requires an ANN-platform for further modelling and deterministic chaos models require considerable expertise.

Author details

M. A. Ghorbani, H. Asadi and P. Yousefi
University of Tabriz, East Azerbaijan, Iran

R. Khatibi
Consultant Mathematical Modeller, Swindon, Wilts., UK

7. Appendix

Symbols

SRC	**Sediment Rating Curve**	
MLR	Multi Linear Regression	
Q_t	Discharge Series	
S_t	Sediment Series	
MLR	X_i	Term of Various Model
	a_i	Values Called Regression
Chaos	T	Delay Time
	$C_m(r)$	Fraction of states
	H	Heaviside Step
	N	Number of Points
	D_2	Correlation Exponent
	Y_j	Vectors of Dimension
	M	Dimensional phase Step
	A	Jacobean Matrix
	$x(t)$	different neighbors
	R	Radius Spherical
	$C(r)$	Correlation Function

Appendix I

Table 11 Defaults Values Employed in Implementing GEP and ANN Models

GP		ANN	
Training parameters	**Values**	**Training parameters**	**Values**
Crossover rate	0.1	Goal	Mean Square Error
Mutation rate	0.044	Epochs	10 - 100
Inversion	0.1	Training algorithm	Trainlm
IS Transposition	0.1		
RIS Transposition	0.1		
1-point Recombination	0.3		
2-point Recombination	0.3		
Gene Recombination	0.1		
Gene Transposition	0.1		
Population (Chromosome) size	30		
Head Size	7		
Number of Genes	3		
Linking Function	Addition		
Random Numerical Constants	Yes		
Number of generation	1000		
Arithmetic functions	(4.a)-(4.f)		
Fitness Function	RRSE: RRSE: Root Relative Squared Errors		

Table 11. Default Parameter Values Used by the Model

8. References

Aytek, A., and Kisi, O. (2008). A genetic programming approach to suspended sediment modeling, J. Hydrol., 351, 288-298

Cigizoglu, H.K. & Kisi, O. (2006) Methods to improve the neural network performance in suspended sediment estimation, *J. of Hydrology*, 317, 221-238.

Cigizoglu, H.K., (2004) Estimation and forecasting of daily suspended sediment data by multi layer perceptrons. *Advances in Water Resources* 27, 185–195.

Cohn TA, Caulder DL, Gilroy EJ, Zynjuk LD, Summers RM. (1992). The validity of a simple statistical model for estimating fluvial constituent loads: An empirical study involving nutrient loads entering Chesapeake Bay. *Water Resources Research* 28(9): 2353–2363.

Farmer, D.J., Sidorowich, J.J., (1987a). Predicting chaotic time series. Phys. Rev. Lett. 59, 845–848.

Farmer, J.D., Sidorowich, J.J., (1987b). Exploiting chaos to predict the future and reduce noise. In: Lee, Y.C. (Ed.), Evolution, Learning and Cognition. World Scientific, River Edge, NJ, pp. 277–330.

Ferguson RI. (1986). River loads underestimated by rating curves. *Water Resources Research* 22(1): 74–76.

Ferreira C. (2001a). Gene expression programming in problem solving. In: 6th Online World Conference on Soft computing in Industrial Applications (invited tutorial)

Ferreira C. (2001b). Gene expression programming: a new adaptive algorithm for solving problems. Complex Syst 13(2):87–129

Fraser, A.M., Swinney, H.L., (1986). Independent coordinates for strange attractors from mutual information. Physical Review A. 33(2), 1134-1140.

Ghorbani MA, Khatibi R, Aytek A, Makarynskyy O, Shiri J (2010) Sea water level forecasting using genetic programming and comparing the performance with artificial neural networks. J Comput Geosci 36(5):620–627

Glysson GD. (1987). *Sediment transport curves.* US Geological Survey Open File Report 87–218.

Grassberger, P. and Procaccia, I., (1983). Characterization of strange attractors. Physical review letters, Vol. 50, No. 5, 346-349.

Hegger, R., Kantz, H., Schreiber, T., (1999). Practical implementation of nonlinear time series methods: The TISEAN package. Chaos. 9, 413-435.

Itoh, K., (1995). A method for predicting chaotic time-series with outliers. Electron. Commun. Jpn. 78 (5), 44–53.

Jain, S.K. (2001) Development of integrated sediment rating curves using ANNs. *J. Hydraul. Eng* ASCE 127(1), 30–37.

Kennel, M., Brown, R., Abarbanel, H.D.I., (1992). Determining embedding dimension for phase- space reconstruction using a geometrical construction. Phys Rev A .45, 3403–11.

Khatibi, R., (2011), "Evolutionary Systemic Modelling for Flood Risk Management Practices," Journal of Hydrology Vol. 401 Issue 1-2, Pp 36–52 (http://dx.doi.org/10.1016/j.jhydrol.2011.02.006)

Kisi, O. (2004b) Multi-layer perceptrons with Levenberg-Marquardt optimization algorithm for suspended sediment concentration prediction and estimation. *Hydrol. Sci. J.* 49(6), 1025–1040.

Kisi, O. (2005). "Daily river flow forecasting using artificial neural networks and auto regressive models", Turkish J. Eng. Env. Sci. vol 29, 9-20.

Kisi, O., (2005b) "Suspended sediment estimation using neuro-fuzzy and neural network approaches", *Hydrol. Sci. J.*, 50(4), 683-696.

Koza JR (1992) Genetic programming: on the programming of computers by means of natural selection. MIT, Cambridge

Miller CR. (1951). *Analysis of flow-duration, sediment-rating curve method of computing sediment yield.* US Bureau of Reclamation Report: Denver, Colorado.

Porporato, A, Ridolfi, L., (1997). Nonlinear analysis of river flow time sequences, Water Resources Research.33(6), 1353-1367.

Rumelhart, D.E. and McClelland, J.L. (Eds.), (1986)."Parallel Distributed Processing". Explorations in the Microstructure of Cognition, 1. MIT Press, Cambridge

Sivakumar, B., (2002). A phase-space reconstruction approach to prediction of suspended sediment concentration in rivers, *Journal of Hydrology*, 258(1-4), 149-162,

Sivakumar, B., and A.W. Jayawardena, (2002). An investigation of the presence of lowdimensional chaotic behavior in the sediment transport phenomenon, *Hydrological Sciences Journal*, 47(3), 405- 416.

Sivakumar, B., and A.W. Jayawardena, (2003). Sediment transport phenomenon in rivers: An alternative perspective, *Environmental Modeling and Software*, in press.

Sivakumar, B., Wallender, W.,(2005). Predictability of river flow and suspended sediment transport in the Mississippi River basin: a non-linear deterministic approach. J. Earth Surf. Process. Landforms 30, 665–677

Takens, F.,(1981). Detecting strange attractors in turbulence, in *Dynamical Systems and Turbulence, Lecture Notes in Mathematics 898*, D. A. Rand and L. S. Young (eds.), 366-381, Springer-Verlag, Berlin.

Tayfur, G. & Guldal, V. (2006) Artificial neural networks for estimating daily total suspended sediment in natural streams, *Nordic Hydrology*, 37, 69-79.

Tayfur, G. (2002) Artificial neural networks for sheet sediment transport. *Hydrol. Sci. J.* 47(6), 879–892.

Theiler, J., (1986). Spurious dimension from correlation algorithms applied to limited time series data.Phys Rev A. 34. 2427-2432.

Thomas RB. (1988). Monitoring baseline suspended sediment in forested basins: The effects of sampling of suspended sediment rating curves. *Hydrological Sciences Journal* 33(5): 499–514.

Ustoorikar K, Deo MC (2008) Filling up gaps in wave data with genetic programming. Marine Structures 21:177–195

Wilks DS. (1991). Representing serial correlation of meteorological events and forecasts in dynamic decision-analytic models. Monthly Weather Rev 119:1640–1662

Yu-Min Wang, Seydou Traore and Tienfuan Kerh (2008), "Monitoring Event-Based Suspended Sediment Concentration by Artificial Neural Network Models" WSEAS TRANSACTIONS on COMPUTERS, Issue 5, Volume 7, May 2008

Walling, D. E., 1977: Limitations of the rating curve technique for estimating suspended sediment loads, with particular reference to British rivers. In: Erosion and solid matter transport in inland waters (Proceedings of the Paris symposium, (July, 1977), IAHS Publ., 122, 34-38.